BEYOND ALTERITY

SPEKTRUM: *Publications of the German Studies Association*

Series editor: David M. Luebke, University of Oregon

Published under the auspices of the German Studies Association, *Spektrum* offers current perspectives on culture, society, and political life in the German-speaking lands of central Europe—Austria, Switzerland, and the Federal Republic—from the late Middle Ages to the present day. Its titles and themes reflect the composition of the GSA and the work of its members within and across the disciplines to which they belong—literary criticism, history, cultural studies, political science, and anthropology.

Beyond Alterity

German Encounters with Modern East Asia

Edited by

QINNA SHEN and MARTIN ROSENSTOCK

berghahn
NEW YORK · OXFORD
www.berghahnbooks.com

Published in 2014 by

Berghahn Books

www.berghahnbooks.com

© 2014 Qinna Shen and Martin Rosenstock

Library of Congress Cataloging-in-Publication Data

Beyond alterity : German encounters with modern East Asia / edited by Qinna Shen and
Martin Rosenstock.
   p. cm. — (Spektrum ; volume 7)
   Includes bibliographical references and index.
   ISBN 978-1-78238-360-4 (hardback) — ISBN 978-1-78238-361-1 (ebook)
   1. Germany—Relations—Japan. 2. Japan—Relations—Germany. 3. Germany—
Relations—China. 4. China—Relations—Germany. 5. Germany—Intellectual
life—20th century. 6. Japan—Intellectual life—20th century. 7. China—Intellectual
life—20th century. I. Shen, Qinna, author, editor of compilation. II. Rosenstock,
Martin, author, editor of compilation.
   DD120.J3B48 2014
   303.48'24305—dc23

                                                                            2013041899

British Library Cataloguing in Publication Data

A catalogue record for this book is available from the British Library

Printed on acid-free paper

ISBN: 978-1-78238-360-4 hardback
ISBN: 978-1-78238-361-1 ebook

❧ CONTENTS ❧

∾: ILLUSTRATIONS :∾

❧ ACKNOWLEDGMENTS ❧

This volume would not have been possible without the dedication and support of David Luebke and the members of *Spektrum*'s editorial board. Their vision of a line of volumes that assemble scholarly essays bound together by thematic coherence, originality, and interdisciplinarity has guided our endeavors. We are immensely grateful to Berghahn Books for their support of Asian German Studies. There are many individuals to thank: Sara Lennox and Young-sun Hong for introducing Asian German Studies into the American academy in 2009 and thus initiating much exciting new scholarship; the external and internal peer reviewers for sharing their time and expertise with our authors and us; the three anonymous reviewers of the manuscript for their constructive criticism and thoughtful suggestions that helped us restructure and revise the volume. The following individuals helped us significantly during the editorial process: Tobias Boes, Petra Fachinger, Mila Ganeva, Todd Heidt, David D. Kim, Mary Rhiel, and Valerie Weinstein. A special thank you goes to Cynthia Walk for contributing financially to the production of high-quality images and to Marion Wielgosz for her technical expertise in solving formal issues we encountered while compiling the volume. We would also like to thank Loyola University Maryland and Gulf University for Science and Technology for their unfailing support over the years. Last but not least, it is the commitment of our authors that has carried this project to fruition. The collaboration with so many great scholars has made the editing of this volume both a pleasure and a rewarding learning experience for us.

INTRODUCTION

Re-investigating a Transnational Connection
Asian German Studies in the New Millennium

MARTIN ROSENSTOCK and QINNA SHEN

The present volume on Asian German Studies is a multidisciplinary effort to explore the German sociohistorical and aesthetic representations of China and Japan from the imperialist era to contemporary times. The term "Asian German Studies" was coined in 2006 by Mita Banerjee, an American Studies professor of Indian-German descent at the University of Mainz in Germany. She believes that this transnational connection constitutes a neglected aspect of the multicultural discourses in present-day Germany, and she called for an "alternative framework" to lay bare "national structures of racialisation" and show up "transnational possibilities of resistance."[1] Her proposition met with a tepid response in the German academy. In an essay of the following year, she describes her endeavors as a quixotic fight against windmills.[2] Germanists in the United States, however, embraced further research into the relationship between the German-speaking countries and Asia, though their approaches in most cases proved less focused on political activism than Banerjee envisioned.[3] We have borrowed Banerjee's term because of its evocative brevity, but our volume also pursues lines of inquiry that point beyond the field she originally staked out.

Banerjee's idea of Asian German Studies owes much to Asian American Studies, as she herself states.[4] It is also part of a larger academic trend to view and analyze (contemporary) culture as fluid and beholden to exchange. Scholars of this phenomenon generally emphasize plurality and hybridity, while sometimes also critiquing neoliberal capitalism and its effects.[5] Within this new transnational paradigm, the Asian German connection deserves more scrutiny. "We create the locations we study," writes Paul Jay in *Global Matters: The Transnational Turn in Literary Studies*, "and this recognition ought to encourage us to continue to remap the geographies of literary and cultural forms."[6] Stuart Taberner points to "the significant subgroup of fictional texts that attempt to reimagine Germany transnationally" as an area of study that demands attention.[7] Due to the spatiotemporal attributes of Asian German Studies, research in this field can also further discussions in areas as diverse as postcoloniality, nation and state, race and gender, cultural comparability, transculturation, and global modernity. In the current volume, we have chosen to focus on two East Asian countries, China and Japan. This allows for more specificity, as the relationship between these countries and the German-speaking countries is marked by themes that remain absent from the relationship between the German-speaking countries and other Asian countries, such as India. These themes include, among others, a history of economic rivalry, integration, and uneasy codependence, the notorious metaphor of the "Yellow Peril," as well as the manifest effects of Communist and fascist ideology. We would like to emphasize that this collection engages with the transnational connection between the German-speaking countries—not of the, or a, German nation-state—and modern East Asia. While a majority of the contributions focuses on German history and culture narrowly defined, the volume also contains works that address the (imperial) Austrian and the Swiss-German relationships to East Asia. The "German" in Asian German Studies is therefore to be understood as a cultural space defined by the German language, a framing we believe is justified by the strong continuities that exist within the cultures of the German-speaking countries vis-à-vis China and Japan.

The history of the political, economic, and academic relations of the German-speaking countries with East Asia has received significant scholarly attention in recent years.[8] George Steinmetz's *The Devil's Handwriting* (2007), for example, contains two long chapters on the German colonial endeavors in China. Suzanne L. Marchand's *German Orientalism in the Age of Empire* (2009) focuses mostly on relations with the Near and Middle East, but also considers the growing interest in the German and Austrian academy in East Asia from the late nineteenth century onward to the 1930s. Steinmetz shows that the study of colonial politics and culture requires attention to the particular locale and to the ethnographic portrayal of its inhabitants in the metropole during, but also before, the colonial period. There was no uniform German colonial policy and thus the outcomes in the Wilhelmine Reich's respective colonies were vastly different. While, for instance, Germany's colonial regime in Southwest Africa, today Namibia, produced segregation and genocide, in Qingdao, after an initial period of aggressive suppression of the Chinese, a spirit of cooperation developed that even allowed for a modicum of political participation by the colonized.[9]

Japan entered the cultural imaginary of the German-speaking countries in a sustained manner later than China, which had been a strong presence therein already during early modern times. The reforms during the Meiji period, beginning in the late 1860s and lasting until the years preceding World War I, brought Western experts in a wide range of disciplines, from medicine and science to engineering and military technology, to the Empire of the Rising Sun. This led to a sudden increase in the attention paid to the country. However, while the perception, in particular in Germany, of Japan throughout much of these years was extraordinarily positive, the sense of technological superiority contributed to an image of the country as a romantic place that time forgot. Though political events were to disabuse Europeans and Americans of such notions in relatively short order, these views of Japan lingered on, and—as this volume shows—may continue to resonate even to this day. The European self-perception of being the teacher to the student Japan may also account for the fact that the first German university chair in Japanology was only established in 1914. Sinology, however, hardly fared much better, with the first chair established in 1908.[10]

Marchand portrays the difficulties scholars from Germany and Austria had throughout the nineteenth century in understanding the East on its own terms, instead of projecting Western notions onto this space and thus by one remove indulging in Western self-exploration. In many cases, even within the academy a true appreciation of East Asian cultures was not forthcoming, and both condescension and self-absorption prevailed. In extreme cases the two civilizations were portrayed, in Hegelian fashion, as polar opposites, with East Asia figuring as the unassimilable Other to the ideal of "the classical or Christian self."[11] Contrary to diagnoses of "oriental stasis" though,[12] the political events around the turn of the twentieth century, especially the Sino-Japanese War of 1894–95, the so-called Boxer Rebellion in 1900, and the Russo-Japanese War of 1905, rendered China and Japan suddenly and unmistakably "world-historical."[13] In addition, European *fin-de-siècle* malaise suggested "engagements with new kinds of 'otherness' for those … sick of bourgeois culture at home"[14] and thus also raised the stock of East Asian cultures. After World War I, these factors contributed to a neoromantic orientalism in the Weimar period that manifested itself in the translation of many Chinese classics, most prominently by Richard Wilhelm, and also left traces in the literary works of such writers as Alfred Döblin and Bertolt Brecht.[15] These productive years ended in 1933, after which German oriental studies became thoroughly racialized and restricted its inquiries to the paradigms sanctioned by Nazi ideology. Following the *Machtergreifung*, the academic community also experienced a significant decline in numbers, as many scholars were compelled to go into exile.[16]

The postwar era then brought the break-up of European colonial empires, expedited by national liberation movements, in the so-called Third World. Immanuel Wallerstein, writing in the late 1990s, addressed the pressures on Eurocentrism in this new historical period:

[I]n the period since 1945, the decolonization of Asia and Africa, plus the sharply accentuated political consciousness of the non-European world everywhere, has affected the world of knowledge just as much as it has affected the politics of the world-system. One major such difference, today and indeed for some thirty years now at least, is that the "Euro-centrism" of social sciences [and the humanities] has been under attack, severe attack. The attack is of course fundamentally justified, and there is no question that [we] must overcome the Eurocentric heritage which has distorted [our] analyses and [our] capacity to deal with the problems of the contemporary world.[17]

Western self-evaluation features strongly in the current era of accelerated globalization and of Europe's decentering in much of the political and economic discourse. The term "accelerated globalization" emphasizes the speed of the transformations that have occurred since the late twentieth century.[18] Globalization itself then appears as a much longer historical process, reaching back to the early modern period, not as a postmodern and postnational phenomenon of the world becoming a global village.[19] The time frame of our volume, overlapping partly with those of Steinmetz's and Marchand's studies, extends the scholarly investigation to this age of accelerated globalization, in particular through the analysis of literature and film. The choice of the imperialist era as the earlier chronological boundary of the volume appeared obvious. Eric Hobsbawm has coined the phrase of "the short twentieth century" to designate the continuum of events and developments that occurred within the time period from the collapse of the post-Napoleonic European order during World War I to the fall of the Iron Curtain and the disintegration of the Soviet Union in 1991.[20] In the area of international politics that is certainly a very plausible proposition. A case might be made, however, that there also exists a larger arc, one we still inhabit today. This arc has its point of origin in the latter decades of the nineteenth century, when European powers divided up the world among themselves, and is in the process of finding its resting place, as the formerly subjugated peoples become world players in their own right. This long twentieth century of sorts, one spanning three centuries, is the period our volume addresses.

The transformations attendant upon accelerated globalization are, as Arjun Appadurai has argued, also cultural and symbolic.[21] To attempt explications of such transformations constitutes the very raison d'être of cultural studies. But why today the strong interest in East Asia, its present as well as past? One need not be a Marxist to acknowledge that critical projects can rest partly on economic reality. Since the rise of Japan as an economic superpower, arguably one of the opening moves of accelerated globalization, the West has become ever more preoccupied with, perhaps at times uncomfortably so, all aspects of East Asia, from food to sports, from management styles to production mechanisms, and from spirituality to brainteasers. The appearance of the Asian Tigers throughout the 1980s and of the People's Republic of China as an economic colossus in the 1990s have only served to bolster this trend and to absorb ever more attention of the West's commentators, academic or popular.

Yet despite the fact that European nations (as well as the United States) have been viewing Japan as an economic competitor since the country's victory in the First Sino-Japanese War and today may consider China's rise both an economic and an ideological challenge, the voices in support of cooperation and engagement appear stronger than those in favor of boycott or antagonism. This may, for one, be due to the fact that contemporary Europe is in no position to coerce East Asian nations, least of all those of at least equal technological prowess and economic might. (The situation was notably different around the turn of the twentieth century when European powers were quick to send out their armies to contain the "Yellow Peril."[22]) In addition, the Asian communities in Europe, particularly in Germany, Austria, and Switzerland, are small, and their presence has not provoked nearly as much friction and debate as for instance that of immigrant communities from North Africa or the Near East. The many issues connected with religion and its practice, symbols, and ethical as well as legal principles that beset the relationship between the Islamic world and the West today remain largely absent from the relationship between the German-speaking countries and East Asia, and by comparison the areas of disagreement carry less of a visceral charge.

We have chosen not to arrange the essays in this volume along a time line. Rather, we organized them into four sections centered around themes that have governed much of the recent academic debates on the intellectual and cultural relationship between East Asia and the German-speaking countries. The first section, under the title "Japan and Germany in the Shadow of National Socialism," considers aspects of the interaction between the two Axis powers during the 1930s and 1940s; the second, "From 1920s Leftist Collaboration to Global Capitalism," investigates a wide range of cultural, political, and economic features that characterize the Chinese-German relationship from the early decades of the twentieth century to the present; the third, "Negotiating Identity in Multicultural Germany," makes a case for the fact that, from Weimar Germany to the Berlin Republic, hybrid Asian-German identities have been present in the cultural makeup of the German-speaking countries; and finally, the fourth section, "Trade, Travel, and Ethnographical Narratives," looks broadly at how economic and cultural engagement has shaped Western perceptions of East Asia. For reasons of clarity, however, we did not forgo the time line entirely and retained a roughly chronological order within each section. We hope that we have succeeded in assembling works that, as one likes to say, speak to each other, that one essay further illuminates a topic or continues an investigation where another has left off.

* * * * *

The National Socialists not only subjected the study of East Asia to their program of *Gleichschaltung* but also made a crucial decision related to the region in terms of Germany's international politics. In the 1920s and 1930s, Germany had befriended China, mostly to gain access to the large Chinese market. Weimar had gone so far as to send a semiofficial group of military advisers to assist Chiang Kai-shek in modernizing his military. The Nazi regime then, however, gradually redirected the country's East Asian alliance from China to Japan, which shared Germany's fascist ideology. In 1936, Japan officially became the partner of choice when the two countries signed the Anti-Comintern Pact against the Soviets. When in 1937 the simmering Chinese-Japanese conflict erupted into all-out war, Germany sided with its new ally. In 1938, Germany withdrew its advisers to China along with its ambassador, bringing to an end diplomatic relations between the two countries.[23] Our volume's first part, "Japan and Germany in the Shadow of National Socialism," uses filmic and literary texts to gauge the Japanese-German relationship. The section opens with Ricky Law's essay on how the political situation colored the representation of Japan in German newsreels of the interwar period. He charts a trajectory from an orientalist and stereotyped image of Japan in the mid 1920s to the depiction of Japan as a "beast" in the early 1930s, the latter a response to Japanese aggression toward China, at that time still Germany's ally. As the coalition between Nazi Germany and Japan became imminent in the mid 1930s, the country's on-screen image changed again. German media began portraying expansionist Japan as an exemplar of martial prowess, making the country appear again—in a disturbing manner—"beautiful" as in the 1920s.

Arnold Fanck's transnational *Bergfilm* or mountain film, *The Samurai's Daughter* (1936–37), the topic of Valerie Weinstein's essay, was designed to promote the German-Japanese alliance. However, the political subtext is not the primary focus of Weinstein's essay. Instead, she examines how *The Samurai's Daughter* inverts genre conventions, depicting Japan "as both Germany's double and as its perfect opposite," and investigates how this film works through notions of conflict inherent in such a relationship. The image of the West, as in many works from German-speaking countries analyzed in this collection, is not all positive. On the contrary, Fanck's film sympathizes with a putatively ambivalent view of the Japanese toward Westernization. Ultimately, the Japanese protagonist embodies a new Japan that synthesizes native traditions and modernity through his choice of a Japanese over a German bride. The couple's decision to farm and reproduce in Manchuria foregrounds this new Japan's expansionist might.

The question of what bound Nazi Germany and Japan together is also the theme of a little known essay contest Sarah Panzer brings to public knowledge. The *Deutsch-Japanische Gesellschaft* sponsored this contest in the spring of 1944 with the aim of bolstering the alliance between the two nations. One of the points most frequently made by the essayists is the shared martial tradition as illustrated by the heavily idealized concept of the *Soldatenvolk*. Panzer argues that this specific way of connecting the two peoples is neither orientalist nor exoticist, but rather represents a form of transcultural romanticism constructed around idealized images of masculine heroism. What emerges from the entries, submitted by a remarkably diverse subsection of the German populace, is an undeniable appreciation for those aspects of Japanese culture and ethics that could be placed in parallel with popular tropes from German romantic nationalism.

The Nazi rise to power and the German-Japanese alliance put an end to the Weimar-era collaboration between Chinese and German left-wing political activists. In both China and Germany, leftists had been hoping for successful Socialist revolutions. In the event, only one did in fact succeed, though a part of Germany began its own Socialist experiment after the war. Our second section, "From 1920s Leftist Collaboration to Global Capitalism," investigates aspects of the Chinese-German relationship from the early decades of the twentieth century to the present. The first essay, Weijia Li's contribution, explains why Chinese students chose Weimar Germany as their destination and why the German Communist Party, the KPD, believed that it could profit from the experiences left-leaning Chinese had made in their home country, though in social and economic terms China at the time differed vastly from Germany. Li contends that, in addition to political contacts, cultural collaboration was crucial to the depiction of China in the leftist press such as *Die Rote Fahne* and contemporary German literature. German leftist reports on the anti-imperialist protests in China and its civil wars (1927–1936) showcased Communist internationalism, anticipating a similar bond between East Germany and China.

Qinna Shen looks closely at East German Cold War documentaries about China, produced by the GDR with an eye toward lending ideological support to East Asia's Socialist nation-building projects and reassuring East Germans of the correctness of their own Socialist path. By way of examining the films' narrative and visual codes, the essay explores the relationship between ideology and realpolitik in the GDR, the latter dominated by pragmatic concerns regarding political relations with West Germany and the Soviet Union. From the late 1950s to the early 1980s, the Sino-Soviet Split undermined the commitment based on ideological affinity between the GDR and China. As a result, the 1980s films display only a weakened revolutionary romanticism and an increase in bland discussions of technology and commercial exchange. Thus these films form a narrative of disillusionment, connecting the two poles of colonialism and accelerated globalization.

Martin Rosenstock's essay concludes this section by investigating how a contemporary German historical novel articulates notions of a European identity in the context of present-day Western anxieties regarding the advent of China as a major player in global politics. The novel in question, Gerhard Seyfried's *Yellow Wind* (2008), has the Boxer Rebellion of 1900 as its theme. Given that the genre of the modern historical novel from the time of its invention in the early nineteenth century has been bound up with the rise of nationalism, the question poses itself how an example of the genre reflects this issue today. Rosenstock argues that *Yellow Wind* is concerned not so much with national as with civilizational identity and constructs the image of a West unified defensively against an East Asian country, thus modifying generic paradigms.

* * * * *

Banerjee criticized her homeland's Germanist establishment for being slow to embrace minority studies or to expand the canon so as to reflect the cultural production of the communities that have settled there since the end of World War II. According to her, mainstream German-language culture rarely appears to regard the presence of these communities as a matter of course.[24] North American Germanists have been more open to the study of these minority cultures or to the project of globalizing literary studies in general. They share this interest with a large number of their colleagues in literary studies, as can been seen from a host of journal issues dedicated to these subjects.[25] With an eye to cultural studies as a whole, Edward Said in 1999 spoke optimistically of "scholars of the new generation [who] are much more attuned to the non-European, genderized, decolonized, and decentered energies and currents of our time."[26] In no small degree the American academy's interest in works written from "the margin" is due to the lived reality of American life, characterized by increasing diversity and a decline of the near-hegemonic status the country's Anglo-Saxon heritage enjoyed for much of its history. With so much attention paid to creative and social endeavors of Americans with hyphenated identities, it comes as no surprise that American Germanists are focusing some of their attention on the Asian-German connection, which partly explains the large number of essays by authors working in the American academy in this collection.

The question arises as to the boundaries of the field. Deniz Göktürk has argued that "minority studies" are "primarily concerned with the politics of recognition and dynamics of inclusion or exclusion within the nation state."[27] Petra Fachinger focuses on the affective and political investments in these processes of in- and exclusion, identifying counter-discursive strategies in works by second-generation "marginal" writers in Germany who "all endeavour to resist marginalization while simultaneously experiencing or celebrating the margin as a site of empowerment."[28] Minority studies certainly also inspires Asian German Studies, though the field extends the discussion in new directions. In line with recent efforts to highlight interculturality, our volume conceives of

Asian German Studies not as limited to examining works of Asian-German fiction writers and essayists like Yōko Tawada, Kien Nghi Ha, Anant Kumar, and Lingyuan Luo. Rather, we view scholarship dealing with the relationship, either cultural or historical, between German-speaking and Asian countries as belonging to the field. The artist's ethnicity is not of major importance, and in fact most of the works analyzed here are those of native Germans. Our volume's philosophy is in this respect consistent with Stuart Taberner's "broader conceptualization of transnationalism in contemporary German-language literature [which includes] not only minority authors but also those described— not entirely unproblematically—as nonminority writers."[29]

Cultural production by artists from the Asian minorities of course remains a crucial part of Asian German Studies, and two of the essays in our volume's third section, "Negotiating Identity in Multicultural Germany," highlight their work. Cynthia Walk's essay opens this part by exploring an intriguing aspect of Weimar cinema, namely, the films Anna May Wong made in Europe with German directors after putting her Hollywood career on hold. Recent scholarship suggests that the actress's performances abroad constituted a deliberate effort to break free from orientalist constraints she had been subjected to in the American film industry. Walk elucidates the cultural and political circumstances of Wong's films in Germany in the context of the country's loss of its colonies after World War I and asks to what extent these films really allowed Wong to engage in a performative display of race and gender that redefined her screen persona. The implications of this question are far-reaching in terms of the ability of Weimar culture to open up a space for negotiated ethnic identities.

Markus Hallensleben addresses a central text by Yōko Tawada, which is likewise concerned with negotiating various identities and cultural subscriptions. Her novella *The Bath* blends different themes and genres, from metamorphosis to translation and from Japanese ghost stories to German fairy tales. The result is a collage- and palimpsest-like text that aims to give voice to the diverse elements of its literary ancestry, while also foregrounding the materiality of language and media-technological aspects of image creation. Hallensleben's reading moves through the different layers that make up Tawada's narrative. He pays close attention to processes of inscription, should they occur in relation to seminal moments in a character's life, reference analog photography or spaces of collective cultural memory, or chart the various metaphorical dimensions ascribed to the female body. The cross-mapping of avant-garde literature and bio art suggests that Tawada's writings deconstruct the biopolitical territorialization of gender images and can thus be seen in analogy to current body art performances.

Encountering an alien culture enriches self-understanding and promotes the realization of one's own inadequacies, a proposition borne out by Erika

Nelson's analysis of Doris Dörrie's 2008 film *Cherry Blossoms*. The film shows the graceful manner in which Japanese culture deals with bereavement, something German culture accomplishes far less elegantly. *Cherry Blossoms* follows a German widower to Japan where he hopes to honor his late wife's memory and atone for how his own shortcomings limited the range of her creative and emotional expression. Nelson explores the various intertextual reference points of Dörrie's film, such as Yasujiro Ozu's seminal film *Tokyo Story*, and shows how initial disorientation in the unfamiliar surroundings develops into a successful quest for self-knowledge and redemption. Of special importance in this process is the Zen concept of MA as a space in between and the Japanese dance form of Butoh, which allow for the negotiation of loss and open up for the Westerner the possibility of accepting the transitory nature of existence.

Many critiques of Western readings of the Orient focus on "symbolic geography" and "ideological constructions."[30] While this is certainly a rewarding approach, we have chosen to conclude the volume with a more "hands on" section that highlights real-life cross-cultural encounter, misunderstandings and instances of disorientation included. "Trade, Travel, and Ethnographical Narratives" considers how a wide array of economic and cultural engagements has shaped Western perceptions of East Asia. Trade and travel, emblematized perhaps most compellingly by the continent-spanning Silk Road, together formed the basis of the earliest instances of contact between the two regions. Exchange was beneficial to both sides, the West receiving first technical knowledge from Asia, for instance how to manufacture paper, and later cultural inspiration, in areas such as design and architecture. China and Japan ultimately adopted many Western innovations in medicine, education, law, administration, and military science, though these advances frequently came at the price of exploitative unequal treaties. Our final section opens with Chinyun Lee and Lucie Olivová's case study of an instance of turn-of-the-twentieth-century globalization. The piece, an example of "everyday history," describes how the manufacture of a simple consumer item like the hairnet between 1890 and 1939 linked China's Shandong province and Vysočina, an area that belonged to the Austro-Hungarian Empire at the time and became part of Czechoslovakia after World War I. Lee and Olivová's thorough research is grounded in archival materials discovered in museums in Chefoo, Austrian government records, and in consular and commerce reports about the Austrian hairnet industries. The authors illustrate the affinity between two impoverished and originally agrarian regions by considering the impact of economic transformation on individuals and families.

Taking us to Japan, Gabriele Eichmanns investigates three short texts by contemporary German and Austrian authors Thomas Brussig, Sabine Scholl, and Marcel Beyer. In these texts, the writers attempt to negotiate their encounters with alterity as they write about their experiences of various aspects of contemporary Japan. Japanese culture appears as a semiotic system that proves impervious to Western efforts at explication and in fact throws into doubt the entire project of Western culture to derive meaning from one's surroundings through careful analysis. The writers attempt to come to grips with the inadequacy of their analytic capacities by rendering difference through various rhetorical devices, for instance, ironic self-stylization. Ultimately, it appears that while Japanese culture itself may prove untranslatable, the encounter with it allows for a more comprehensive understanding of one's own perspective on the world.

Jeroen Dewulf's contribution on the Swiss writer Hugo Loetscher concludes both this section and our volume by revisiting many of the themes that have surfaced throughout the essays. Loetscher's work is characterized by "a fascination for commonalities" between different cultures. His interest in hybridity and globalism in the postcolonial world led him to East Asia not in search of the radically unfamiliar, but rather to experience places where European and Asian cultures mingle. Dewulf analyzes the tensions between Loetscher's non-exoticizing way of writing and his failure to escape completely a Eurocentric perspective. His advocacy of viewing East and West not as opposites but as complementary elements of a global culture harmonizes well with the politics implied in various works examined in this volume.

* * * * *

Asian German Studies differs from fields defined by subject, such as gender, diaspora, or globalization. Asian German Studies is delineated by geography. A subject can become relevant to the field if this subject bears on a trajectory between a German-speaking country and Asia. The field is interdisciplinary and not beholden to chronological periodization, and we believe that this collection allows for an appreciation of the reach of questions that fall within the purview of Asian German Studies. Seen together, these essays show that the moments of contact, be they political, economic, or cultural in nature, between the German-speaking countries and China and Japan since about 1890 have been richly productive. This is not to downplay racism and chauvinism, which existed and exists on both sides. As can be seen from the contributions, however, in many cases the cultures of the German-speaking countries have responded with genuine interest and creativity to notions and concepts of Chinese and Japanese origin. And even when the responses have been tinged with antagonism, those that go beyond kneejerk reactions or the mobilization of clichés arguably always do involve meaningful engagement. These processes are likely to continue. A degree of cultural convergence as a result of globalization is inevitable, but East Asia and Europe will certainly remain distinct and thus sites of productive cross-cultural encounters.

We are aware of this volume's noncomprehensive nature. We also realize that owing to the (academic) backgrounds of the majority of the authors, the essays collected here mostly have a Western German Studies point of view. We hope that this collection will inspire similar works that address the Asian-German relationship from the Asian perspective. First and foremost, our volume represents an effort to take stock of various lines of inquiry scholars are currently pursuing; obviously there are many more. What we are confident in is that this collection illustrates the richness of Asian German Studies and the multiform ways in which it can enlarge, impact, and contribute to various other areas of study. The moment when a field becomes aware of its own existence suggests that a certain tipping point has been reached in the accumulation of knowledge, that related scholarly pursuits must now be located within a context of likeminded efforts, and that the field ought to position itself vis-à-vis larger cultural and theoretical debates. Labels such as "Asian German Studies" matter. Labels promote recognition and public awareness. They also systematize, confer legitimacy, and stimulate research. For all these reasons we believe that the present volume on Asian German Studies is a timely product and a useful contribution to the further establishment of this subfield within German Studies.

Notes

1. Mita Banerjee, "Bollywood Meets the Beatles: Towards an Asian German Studies of German Popular Culture," *South East Asian Popular Culture* 4, no. 1 (April 2006): 20.
2. "ein Kampf gegen Windmühlen." Mita Banerjee, "Ethnizität als Buhfrau der Nation: Über disziplinäre Umwege und die (Un)Möglichkeit ethnischer (Selbst)Artikulation," in *Re/Visionen: Postkoloniale Perspektiven von People of Color auf Rassismus, Kulturpolitik und Widerstand in Deutschland*, ed. Kien Nghi Ha, Nicola Lauré al-Samarai, and Sheila Mysorekar (Münster, 2007), 297. See also Sara Lennox's review of the book in *Wasafiri*, ed. Mark Stein, special issue: *African Europeans* 56 (2008): 79–81.
3. Banerjee, "Ethnizität als Buhfrau der Nation," 297.
4. Banerjee, "Bollywood Meets the Beatles," 20.
5. See, e.g., Michael Hardt and Antonio Negri, *Empire* (Cambridge, M.A., 2000).
6. Paul Jay, *Global Matters: The Transnational Turn in Literary Studies* (Ithaca, 2010), 4.
7. Stuart Taberner, "Transnationalism in Contemporary German-Language Fiction by Nonminority Writers," *Seminar: A Journal of Germanic Studies* 47, no. 5 (Nov. 2011): 628.
8. Just to mention a few recent English publications: Christian W. Spang and Rolf-Harald Wippich, eds., *Japanese-German Relations, 1895–1945: War, Diplomacy and Public Opinion* (London, 2006); George Steinmetz, *The Devil's Handwriting: Precoloniality and the German Colonial State in Qingdao, Samoa, and Southwest Africa* (Chicago, 2007); Suzanne L. Marchand, *German Orientalism in the Age of Empire: Religion, Race, and Scholarship* (Cambridge, U.K., 2009); Lee M. Roberts, *Germany and the Imagined East* (Newcastle, 2009); Veronika Fuechtner and Mary Rhiel, eds., *Imagining Ger-*

many *Imagining Asia: Essays in Asian-German Studies* (Rochester, N.Y., 2013); Joanne Miyang Cho and David Crowe, *Germany and China: Transcultural, Historical and Political Encounters from the Enlightenment to the Twentieth Century* (New York, 2014; forthcoming).

9. Steinmetz, *The Devil's Handwriting,* 470ff.
10. For a more comprehensive depiction of the Japanese-German relationship, see, e.g., Spang and Wippich, *Japanese-German Relations, 1895–1945;* Josef Kreiner, ed. *Deutschland—Japan: Historische Kontakte* (Bonn, 1984); Walter Gebhard, ed., *Ostasienrezeption im Schatten der Weltkriege: Universalismus und Nationalismus* (Munich, 2003); and Thomas Pekar, *Der Japan-Diskurs im westlichen Kulturkontext (1860–1920): Reiseberichte—Literatur—Kunst* (Munich, 2003).
11. Marchand, *German Orientalism,* 372.
12. Marchand, *German Orientalism,* 375.
13. Marchand, *German Orientalism,* 373.
14. Marchand, *German Orientalism,* 373.
15. Marchand, *German Orientalism,* 482.
16. Marchand, *German Orientalism,* 488.
17. Immanuel Wallerstein, "Eurocentrism and Its Avatars: The Dilemmas of Social Science," *New Left Review* 226 (1997): 93–94. Cited from Edward Said, "Globalizing Literary Study," *PMLA* 116, no. 1 (January 2001): 65.
18. The term "accelerated globalization" can be found, e.g., in Jan Aart Scholte's *Globalization: A Critical Introduction* (London, 2000).
19. Jay, *Global Matters.*
20. Eric Hobsbawm, *The Age of Extremes: The Short Twentieth Century, 1914–1991* (London, 1994).
21. See, e.g., Giles Gunn, "Introduction: Globalizing Literary Studies," *PMLA* 116, no. 1 (January 2001): 21.
22. Iikura Akira, "The 'Yellow Peril' and Its Influence on Japanese-German Relations," in *Japanese-German Relations,* ed. Spang and Wippich, 80–97.
23. Bernd Martin, ed. *The German Advisory Group in China: Military, Economic, and Political Issues in Sino-German Relations, 1927–1938* (Düsseldorf, 1981). See also Spang and Wippich, "Introduction—from 'German Measles' to 'Honorary Aryans': An Overview of Japanese-German relations until 1945," in *Japanese-German Relations,* 1–18.
24. See Banerjee, "Ethnizität als Buhfrau der Nation."
25. See, e.g., *New German Critique,* special issue *Minorities in German Culture* (1989); *New German Critique,* no. 92, *Multicultural Germany: Art, Performance and Media* (Spring–Summer 2004); *PMLA* 116, no. 1 (January 2001).
26. Said, "Globalizing Literary Study," 65. Rey Chow might serve as an example of this new generation, when she provides an iconoclastic critique of Derrida's reading of the Chinese writing system, demonstrating to what extent he is beholden to an orientalist fantasy of the East as difference. See Rey Chow, "How (the) Inscrutable Chinese Led to Globalized Theory," *PMLA* 116, no. 1 (Jan. 2001): 71.
27. Deniz Göktürk and Barbara Wolbert, "Introduction," *New German Critique,* no. 92, *Multicultural Germany,* 3–4.
28. Petra Fachinger, *Rewriting Germany from the Margins: "Other" German Literature of the 1980s and 1990s* (Montreal, Q.C., 2001), 18.
29. Taberner, "Transnationalism in Contemporary German-Language Fiction," 641.
30. Todd Kontje, *German Orientalisms* (Ann Arbor, M.I., 2004), 1, 12.

PART I

Japan and Germany
in the Shadow
of National Socialism

CHAPTER 1

.

Beauty and the Beast
Japan in Interwar German Newsreels

RICKY W. LAW

Introduction

Until the early twentieth century, German descriptions and imagination of East Asia could be articulated only through verbal or pictorial means. After World War I, as Germany rebuilt its severed links to the outside world, it also had at its disposal a new tool—films—to depict its encounters with foreign civilizations. By 1919, cinema had matured as a key element in German popular media, so that the three main forms of motion pictures, namely newsreels, documentaries, and feature films, were already present and familiar to spectators. Then, in the 1920s and 1930s, film underwent another phase of expansion and transformation that enabled it to rival newspapers, magazines, and radio as a conduit for amusement and information in society. Especially in disseminating knowledge about distant lands and peoples, the silver screen with its combination of graphics, animation, and gradually audio would present itself as an alluring substitute for the masses of Germans with no opportunity ever to travel abroad. After all, if a picture is indeed worth a thousand words, then a motion picture with its thousands of frames can speak a million.

Accordingly, this article traces and analyzes the influence newsreels exercised in molding public perceptions of Japan in interwar Germany and the implications of these depictions for the relations between Berlin and Tokyo in the mid 1930s. Newsreels are chosen as the subject of exploration because they appeared more frequently and regularly before cinemagoers than the other two forms of film, and yet have received far less scholarly attention. This essay presents the case that the medium depicted Japan first as a quaint, mysterious beauty that subsequently morphed into a violent, unpredictable brute. Yet, as Germany fell under the spell of National Socialism it also came to perceive a militant Japan on screen under a different, favorable light, so that Japan's onscreen transformation in Germany coincided with and corresponded to the diplomatic rapprochement between the two regimes.

Newsreels as Interwar Medium and Historical Source

Well before the Nazi movement gained the authority to dictate what and how much the population was entitled to know, newsreels had been informing the German public of events around the nation and the world. Shortly after the outbreak of World War I, the pioneering cinematographer Oskar Messter introduced newsreels to the populace so as to display battlefield footage in theaters in Germany, and by 1920 newsreels already made up an integral part of most cinematic experiences. In fact, since newsreels usually headed a film program, they also initiated most first-time cinemagoers to the world of motion pictures. Likewise, when films came equipped with audio beginning in the early 1930s, the first sound to greet many audience members was frequently the announcement, "Achtung! Achtung! Sie sehen und hören die Deulig-Tonwoche" (Attention! Attention! You are watching and hearing the Deulig Audio Newsreel).

In the interwar era, the studios of Deulig (Deutsche Lichtbild-Gesellschaft), Ufa (Universum Film-AG), and Emelka/Bavaria (Münchener Lichtspielkunst) produced most of the newsreels, each typically lasting ten to twenty minutes. Known literally as the "weekly show" (*Wochenschau*), a fresh newsreel was released every week, almost invariably on Thursdays, to summarize the happenings of the previous seven days. Normally, no overarching theme governed a show's content; instead it consisted of vignettes a few minutes in length on some noteworthy events, curious tales, or trivialities. The tardiness of the weekly show as a medium—days or even weeks could pass before footage of an incident made its way on to a screen—meant that newsreels actually brought little news because breaking stories would long since have been announced in newspaper extras or on the radio. Rather, newsreels animated recent events that spectators had already read or heard about elsewhere. Partly as a result, and particularly in the comparatively calm mid 1920s, newsreels mostly concentrated on happenings in sports, the arts and sciences, celebrity culture, foreign affairs, and the lighter side of politics. By the late 1930s, motion pictures were considered to wield such influence in society and present such powerful tools for the management of the public mood that both Hitler and Goebbels took a keen interest in the production of newsreels, often previewing the reels before approving their distribution to theaters nationwide.[1] Still later, during World War II, the regime even resorted to ordering cinemas to lock their doors after the newsreel began so that no one could enter afterward to watch the feature film without first ingesting the propaganda.[2]

Quite an impressive number of newsreels from the interwar years remain today in various states of preservation and are offered for use by the Federal Film Archives in Berlin-Wilmersdorf.[3] Broadly speaking, far fewer specimens from the 1920s than the 1930s have survived; many from the 1920s are fragmentary and the events depicted therein are so out of context that precise dating is all but impossible. The collection of newsreels from the 1930s, in particular the Ufa and the Deulig shows with sound, is much fuller but still nowhere near complete, and individual shows sometimes suffer from missing segments or lack of the audio track. For the purposes of this essay one should therefore keep in mind the constraints that obtain when trying to reconstruct history through film and the probability that Japan appeared in newsreels that are now irretrievably lost.

Japan the Beautiful

Japan debuted in German newsreels in the atmosphere of relative stability and relaxation during the middle Weimar years. Among extant newsreels from the 1920s, Japan and East Asia together appeared as subjects only sporadically. In keeping with the peaceful time and playful tone of the medium, newsreels frequently painted East Asia as an exotic environment of enigma and excitement. For instance, in 1925 viewers saw in a segment called "Blue Jackets Touring Famous Chinese Temples" German sailors traveling in China.[4] The uniformed sightseers were shown watching demonstrations of martial arts, hiking in the Chinese countryside, and posing for photographs in front of a pagoda. Of course, in and of itself the excursion hardly amounted to a newsworthy item, but the alien quality of the scenery and the adventurous nature of the activities sufficed to catapult it onto the big screen.

In the same vein, a number of shows from the late 1920s depicted scenes of ordinary Japanese religious ceremonies. In early 1927, an Emelka newsreel introduced moviegoers to the visual spectacle of a Shinto festival.[5] It featured participants dressed for the occasion—women in kimonos, men with straw hats—chanting and parading a portable shrine through a town. The revelers also beat a gigantic drum, though the silent reel could do justice neither to the singing nor to the instrument. Then in mid 1928, a Deulig newsreel brought to screens what it labeled a "Japanese Parish Fair."[6] In fact the film captured a Bon festival, a Buddhist celebration recalling the spirits of ancestors. Again spectators saw Japanese in pretty, festive costumes, stepping and flailing rhythmically to perform the Bon dance. Later in the year, a newsreel reported that the city of Beppu had erected a 25-meter-tall statue of Buddha.[7] Footage highlighting the size of the structure would not only have awed spectators but also elicited laughs by juxtaposing a few diminutive monks struggling to clean the statue with the outsized cupped palms in which they all fit comfortably.

Although the opening of the Beppu Buddha qualified as news for the purposes of German newsreels, there already existed so many giant effigies of dei-
ties in Japan that the completion of another one should not have raised many
eyebrows. Also, observance of some Shinto or Buddhist holiday took place so
frequently in the country that it usually would not warrant extraordinary attention. Yet portrayals of these mundane occurrences in Japan somehow found
their way as current affairs to cinemas across Germany, so much so that Japan made news simply for being Japan and doing what Japan did normally. Or
rather, Japan made news simply for being what Japan was *thought* to be and
doing what Japan was *thought* to do normally. Certainly, far more happened in
Japan than the construction of sacred idols or celebration of festivals, but these
activities conformed to the widespread, preexisting German image of Japan as a
land of ageless traditions and arcane beliefs. The consumers of these newsreels
expected to see a certain version of Japan, and the producers furnished corre-
sponding scenes to fulfill the vision, thereby reinforcing and perpetuating stereotypes of Japan. Even when in 1929 an Emelka newsreel supposedly revealed
an unfamiliar side of Japan by playing a segment on the "Modern Woman in
Japan," it still could not help but choose scenes of Japanese women attempting awkwardly in their kimonos to master the imported game of billiards.[8]
Similarly, a Deulig program in 1934 showed Japanese women belatedly leaving
their kimonos behind to try on revealing Western bathing suits. The narrator
commented that "different times bring different customs. What was impossible
twenty years ago is now a common sight—demonstrations of swimwear mod-
eled on European fashion on a Japanese beach."[9] For German spectators these
reels would help reaffirm their dismissal of Japan as merely a clumsy imitator
trying to ape or catch up with the civilized West, a stereotype prevalent among
some Europeans since the late nineteenth century.[10]

Where Japan managed to match or even supersede Western accomplishments, newsreels greeted such instances not with encouragement or even self-
congratulation but with unease. For example, in 1925 a Deulig show depicted
Japanese warships on a tour arriving in San Francisco Bay.[11] The visiting and
home sailors hail and salute each other across the water, and the Japanese ships
fire shots in honor of the host. An admiral of the U.S. Navy boards the flagship
Asama, where he is welcomed by smartly uniformed Japanese seamen. This
particular segment lasted longer than usual, and the camera lingered over the
sleek Japanese ship and its still-smoking guns. The film's pairing of the Japanese
and American ships created the impression that the fleets shared a parity of
sorts and that Japan had achieved the status of a great power alongside Western nations. Yet for the Germans who remembered the glory of the High Seas
Fleet as well as the shame of its post–World War I liquidation, from which Japan benefited by acquiring a few ships and U-boats, Japan's brandishing of the
very sea power that helped it conquer Germany's Pacific colonies would arouse
far less admiration than resentment.

In another newsreel, released by Ufa in 1936, the narrator announced "Roar of Guns in New York" to lead a story on a Japanese squadron visiting New York Harbor.[12] The sequence of events paralleled that in the 1925 show: guest and host hail each other, Japanese sailors salute the boarding party, and the shore battery and Japanese warships exchange honorary gunfire. The addition of audio, however, drastically enhanced the overall impact of the footage. Thus cinemagoers no longer had to wonder what sounds accompanied the scene but could hear for themselves—as much as equipment permitted—an officer's command in Japanese to the shipmen to stand at attention and the cannons roaring deafeningly. If beforehand film projectors displayed to spectators only moving frames silently demonstrating Japanese military might and threat, then loudspeakers made that danger more visceral by ringing audiences' ears with blasts of naval gunfire.

As a matter of fact, the depiction in German newsreels in the 1920s of a Japan amusing for its curious blend of East and West such as playing billiards in kimonos gave way in the next decade to one that raised alarm for its oriental inscrutability armed with occidental firepower. To be sure, special occasions such as a Shinto festival reenacting a whale hunt, the passing of notable individuals, or the commemoration of Commodore Perry's "opening" of Japan still occupied screen time.[13] Even in some of these seemingly innocuous events, however, the specter of a relentlessly rising Japan still reared its head. For example, an Ufa newsreel in 1934 chose as its subject the funeral of Tōgō Heihachirō, the admiral who almost single-handedly propelled Japan into the ranks of great powers by trouncing a Western state in the Russo-Japanese War.[14] Also in 1934, in explaining Perry's legacy, a Deulig narrator pointedly commented that "eighty years ago Japan was still an island country cut off from the world and untouched by European and American civilization. In 1854, American ships led by Admiral [sic] Perry arrived in Shimoda. Japan became acquainted with modern civilization and from this point onward the Japanese nation developed at an anomalously rash pace into today's world power."[15] Japan's contemporaneous encroachments on China likely tainted the coverage so that Japan appeared militaristic and expansionistic even in reports on unrelated events, especially since at this time Germany was helping China with weapons and advisers in its struggle against Japan. Indeed, Japan would increasingly become a byword for violence and bloodshed in newsreels in the mid 1930s.

Japan the Bestial

Already in the relatively tranquil mid 1920s, newsreels frequently carried stories on various nations' armed forces, though mostly focusing on peacetime maneuvers involving awe-inspiring pieces of military hardware.[16] East Asia, however, stood out as the only region that threatened to turn chatters of war into reality. For a few weeks in 1927 viewers saw scenes of skirmishes in China as parts of its ongoing civil war.[17] Then in 1929 in a segment titled "Danger of War in the East" they watched footage of Chinese troops preparing for an imminent clash with their Russian counterparts.[18] Thus, the possibility of a military confrontation in East Asia seemed to simmer just beneath the surface of peaceful coexistence.

Ultimately, Japan, not the Soviet Union, brought war to Asia, and newsreels allowed German audiences glimpses of the events unfolding far away. By the time fighting between Japan and China broke out on 28 January 1932 in what became known as the Shanghai Incident, all three major studios stood ready and equipped to relay the spectacular images and sounds of the conflict.[19] For most viewers the battle not only meant their first exposure to real combat on screen, but also it would come to define the presentation of Japan in newsreels for the rest of the decade.[20]

For the duration of the battle from 28 January to 3 March, sights and sounds of war came to monopolize the portrayals of Japan. On 10 February, just two weeks after the outbreak of fighting, *Deulig Audio Newsreel No. 6* was already playing footage of combat in cinemas across Germany. The narrator launched the segment by announcing, "Shanghai stands at the center of the world's interest today: Japan marching on East Asia's great commercial city of 2.7 million inhabitants."[21] As viewers gawked at footage of the city shot from the air, the narrator explained that the dense Chinese district of Chapei was set ablaze by Japanese aerial bombs and artillery shells.[22] That is, three years before Riefenstahl exploited the same camera technique for the propaganda film *Triumph of the Will* and five years before the *Luftwaffe* experimented with the same offensive tactic in Guernica, German cinemagoers had already experienced through newsreels of the destruction of Shanghai the horror of a modern military's attacks on civilians, perpetrated in this case by Japan. In contrast to the 1920s silent films that could not let footage "speak" for itself, in the 1930s audio newsreels on war came chock-full of noises of exploding bombs, buzzing warplanes, thudding machine guns, and wailing victims, shaking the walls of the cinema and perhaps even spectators in their seats. In other words, the contemporaneousness of the advances in audio technology and of the outbreak of violence made possible the "fully scored" projection of the Sino-Japanese conflict onto German screens, and thus rendered more real and immediate the menace Japan posed to world peace.[23]

Moreover, sights and sounds of war—in today's media parlance—sucked the oxygen out of the room regarding coverage on Japan. Since a newsreel was made up of segments on different topics, it could not devote an entire program to a single subject, and so the Japanese campaign in Shanghai in essence displaced all other stories on Japan. Only under this circumstance could the Deulig newsreel relegate the continuing Japanese incursion into Manchuria to "other news" after the headline assault on Shanghai. This segment featured Japanese soldiers in combat as they storm the city of Harbin after heavy fighting. Interestingly, the filmmakers exercised an editorial touch by inserting into the footage generic audio effects not captured on site but added afterward in a studio. For example, the audience heard rhythmic drumbeats (as in a ceremonial parade) as Japanese combat troops marched past burning buildings, and in the background unintelligible human voices that presumably stood for Japanese. The artificial sounds, though incongruous in hindsight, would have helped lead cinemagoers' imaginations closer to the battlefield by enlivening the scene and would thus also have contributed to the emotional impact that these depictions of Japanese violence made.

The rest of the month witnessed the daily Japanese bombardment of Shanghai and the newsreels' weekly bombardment of German moviegoers with footage of Japanese brutality. *Deulig Audio Newsreel No. 9* opened the segment on the war with sounds of gunfire and explosions, and closed it with images of Japanese armored cars zipping past urban ruins and burning buildings collapsing.[24] The following week, *Deulig No. 10* exhibited and elicited sympathy for the victims by contrasting Chinese helplessness with Japanese aggression.[25] The film showed a Japanese convoy rumbling through streets lined with rubble, while soldiers ruthlessly disperse a crowd of refugees. The next scene ratcheted up the tension further by focusing on a woman carrying her infant in a deserted street and trudging wearily before heavily armed Japanese troops who seem on the verge of triggering unspeakable violence on the mother and child. Just as cinemagoers clutched their armrests with sweaty palms in dreadful anticipation, the camera zoomed in on a wounded Chinese man bemoaning his suffering. Interspersed with the man's sighs and screams and breaking from the genre's normally staid tone, the narrator lamented that "the shelling of the city has visited the inhabitants with immense misery." As the camera panned from a throng of fleeing civilians and on to children in rags nibbling on morsels in the street, he continued, "Thousands upon thousands of refugees. Everyone is starving and has to rely on the public dole."[26]

That same week, *Emelka Audio Newsreel No. 77* also devoted screen time to the war and thereby guaranteed that most Germans who went to the cinema that week would see Japanese atrocities and lawlessness.[27] To open the segment "The Conflict in the East: The Latest Images from Shanghai," the announcer declared, "Chapei is burning."[28] The footage showed the harbor engulfed in smoke and flame after burning for three days and nights. He added that in spite of intervention by the European powers, the aggressors press on deeper into the city and its environs, while the screen displayed streets littered with corpses—victims caught in the crossfire or killed by naval bombardments or air raids. In this way, the newsreel bore witness to the dawn of modern warfare and the first application of terror bombing in populated areas.[29]

Moral condemnations aside, pragmatic spectators might well rationalize that Germany had more to gain by cozying up to powerful Japan than hapless China, but they could not have maintained that argument for long in face of the other evidence in the newsreels. True, the Emelka announcer did point out, "Although the Chinese regiments are resisting desperately, they must still retreat steadily before the incomparably more modern war machines of the Japanese."[30] Yet viewers who entertained a favorable impression of Japan's military prowess would have been disabused of that notion even before the intermission. Later in the same program a segment showcased a special maneuver of the combined U.S. Pacific and Atlantic Fleets near Hawai'i.[31] The armada of ships and aircraft dwarfed anything shown on screen hitherto, and was meant to remind Japan of America's ability to project its power overseas and protect its interests in East Asia. China itself too seemed determined not to fall easy prey to Japanese expansionism. *Deulig No. 10* concluded its coverage with the observation, "But China is hanging in there," and footage of a great demonstration in Nanking venting popular anger.[32] The last newsreel story on the conflict also boded ill for further Japanese adventurism. In a rare feat for the newsreel as a medium for capturing breaking news, *Deulig Audio Newsreel No. 23* played original footage of the bomb blast that killed the Japanese commander in Shanghai and injured other Japanese dignitaries prematurely celebrating their victory in China.[33] Though some cinemagoers might come to admire Japanese strength, they could also not miss the damaging consequences of such exploits for Japan.

Judging from the newsreels' presentation of Japan after Shanghai, successes in China not only pushed Japan into a looming showdown with America, but within the home country they also fed militarism and undermined civilian rule. Moreover, the war's intermittent but never-ending nature also hinted at its becoming a quagmire; newsreel after newsreel depicted Japan winning battle after battle but never the war. For example, in early 1933, not yet a year after the Shanghai Incident, Japanese forces reprise their role of weary victors in *Deulig Audio Newsreel No. 60.*[34] The announcer explained that viewers were watching the first footage of the Japanese-occupied city of Shan Hai Kuan on the Great Wall, and that conquering the city, "the invasion gateway into the province of Jehol, is for Japan worth the withdrawal from the League of Nations."[35] As the segment ended dramatically with the demolition of the ancient fortress and city, cinemagoers would have wondered why Japan would foolishly risk international condemnation and American disapproval in return for minor gains against a vast enemy.

Newsreels answered this question by shifting to domestic changes in Japan. The Great Wall, however fragile a barrier before modern arms, did provide a boundary marker between Japanese-dominated Manchukuo and China proper, resulting in a de facto ceasefire from 1933 to 1937 and thus removing combat as a theme for portraying Japan on screen. Rather than returning to the more innocent themes prior to Shanghai, newsreels zoomed in instead on Japan's descent into militaristic irrational exuberance, if not downright collective madness. "War Fever in Japan," proclaimed the narrator in *Deulig Audio Newsreel No. 57*, as footage showed enthusiastic children, youngsters, and women in traditional clothes seeing off a division headed for Manchuria.[36] Throngs of flag-waving well-wishers congest the streets and line the marching route of the soldiers and even the railroad for the troop transports. The scene repeats itself at the harbor, where the crowd nearly pushes into the water in its excessive enthusiasm to bid the warriors farewell. Conspicuously missing are the normal expressions of sadness and grief when loved ones depart for foreign battlefields; the people even appear jubilant to see the soldiers go. In fact, viewers saw more tear-soaked handkerchiefs in a 1934 segment on Berliner children leaving for a field trip to the Baltic coast than in the footage of the Japanese sending their sons, brothers, and friends to a possible death faraway.[37] Even though no major military action took place at the time, the newsreel still depicted a martial Japan—one with symptoms of victory disease.

For the next few years, until the outbreak of full-scale confrontation between Japan and China in 1937, the newsreels' diagnoses of Japan's condition deteriorated. All Japan seemed obsessed with war, or at least German viewers could only come to that conclusion since newsreels depicted little else of Japan. For example, *Fox Audio Newsreel Nr. 38* from September 1933 showcased airraid drills in Tokyo. Footage showed thick clouds of smoke rising from the city, warplanes buzzing buildings and civilians, and flak firing into the air. People playacting dead and wounded victims and a real burning tram complete the pandemonium. The narrator commented that, "The whole world is guarding against attack from the air. Even a country as amply armed with aircraft as Japan runs air-raid drills."[38] Then in October 1934, *Deulig Audio Newsreel No. 148* asked, "What does a Japanese schoolgirl do in her free time?" As cinemagoers, amused or alarmed, watched young Japanese women marching in file with rifles to a firing range and shooting at targets, the film continued, "They learn to shoot, not just a Tesching [handgun] or pistol…. Maybe one day she will stand by her man for real."[39] To complete this portrayal of a Japan crazed with regimentation and indoctrination, *Deulig Audio Newsreel No. 157* showed a clip of Japanese boys mimicking soldiers and engaging as units in mock combat against each other. Some man wooden sticks standing in for machine guns, others crawl under and cut imaginary barbed wire, while a few wriggle in painted boxes to simulate tanks moving. The narrator observed, not without a little irony, "These tiny Japanese do not mess around with tin soldiers any more. Only the war-game battlefield with machine guns and 'Jump up, march, march!' make the eight-year old heart pound harder."[40] From the newsreels, Japan appeared drunk with militarism and expansionism, so much so that even its youngest members knew not the gravity of violence and treated combat as a diversion.

Alarmingly, the children's older brothers and fathers also played war, but with real weapons. In *Ufa Audio Newsreel No. 277* in 1935 cinemagoers saw footage of a maneuver in Manchukuo attended by the Japanese-backed emperor Pu-Yi.[41] Although the soldiers supposedly sport Manchurian colors, their uniforms look indistinguishable from those of the Japanese troops in previous newsreels; not to mention that most Germans who read newspapers would know that Manchukuo amounted to little more than a puppet state. Later in the year, *Deulig Audio Newsreel No. 174* reported Pu-Yi traveling to Japan to pay homage to his patron Hirohito.[42] The monarchs, in costumes richly bedecked with medals they never earned, are surrounded by other uniformed dignitaries as they salute soldiers and sailors lining the street. Again Japan emerged as a land dominated by men specialized in waging war. Finally, in late 1935 *Deulig Audio Newsreel No. 207* depicted Hirohito, "on the white steed of the Mikado" and in full military garb, presiding over an exercise of his armed forces involving masses of men, tanks, and warplanes.[43] Thus, since 1932 newsreels had been chronicling for German audiences Japan's degeneration into a mobilization society in which everyone from eight-year-olds all the way up to the emperor—precisely those with no immediate risk of actually dying in combat—indulged in hallucinations of battlefield heroics and glory.

Beauty and Beast Became One

It should have surprised no attentive spectators, then, when Japan at last unleashed a full-scale war against China. In fact, in 1936 an Ufa program had already revealed a Japanese troop buildup in "Turbulent Asia"; a lone old lady's sobbing as she sees the soldiers off is drowned out by the crowd cheering and waving flags.[44] By July 1937, however, German-Japanese relations had undergone a fundamental realignment with the Anti-Comintern Pact, and the newsreels' portrayal of Japan reflected the new diplomatic reality. Beginning in August, newsreel after newsreel relayed stories of the war, but with a perspective different from that of 1932. An Ufa narrator declared that "the situation in the Far East is again tense" and excused Japanese overreaction by faulting the Chinese for allegedly shooting a Japanese soldier, an unverified claim that the newsreels treated as factual.[45] As footage of Japanese troops entering Beijing rolled, a Bavaria-newsreel announcer proclaimed, "The Japanese in Peking, to the rejoicing of their countrymen," yet viewers did not see jubilant Japanese expatriates but instead poor, resigned Chinese sitting in the dirt indifferently eyeing their conquerors.[46] In case anyone still doubted where the regime's sympathies lay, *Ufa Audio Newsreel No. 368* coupled a story on Japanese troops puncturing a Chinese defense line in Shanghai with a segment on Japanese officers in Berlin observing an air-raid drill.[47] In addition, while in 1932 the newsreels highlighted concrete Chinese suffering, in 1937 they switched to trumpet strategic Japanese success. Not only did Japan conquer more territories, it also gained more exposure on screen at China's expense. Thus an Ufa story titled "War Theater Northern China" focused only on Japanese soldiers in armored trains rolling into Beijing and not on their impact on the Chinese populace.[48] Likewise, in November, *Ufa Audio Newsreel No. 374* displayed under the segment "China" mostly footage of Japanese offensive actions. Spectators saw the Japanese field headquarters, Japanese soldiers using dogs as messengers, and Japanese firing on camouflaged enemy positions—that is, anything but "China."[49] Even the camera angle betrayed a bias toward Japan. In contrast to the newsreels in 1932 that zoomed in on individual suffering wrought by aerial bombing, in 1937 the camera literally sided with the attacker by shooting from the bombardier's point of view as the airplane dropped bombs on faceless masses in the city below.[50]

From early 1938 onward, just when the last German advisers to China were recalled home, the newsreels also unambiguously conveyed the Nazi regime's preference for militaristic Japan over helpless China. For example, in February, *Ufa Audio Newsreel No. 388* showed footage of Japanese units in their "unstoppable advance" in China across the Yellow River.[51] The narrator added admiringly that although Chinese troops had detonated a bridge in an attempt to hinder the invaders, the Japanese overcame the obstacle by quickly erecting a pontoon bridge. The newsreel also stigmatized the Chinese government's training of female volunteer fighters as "following the Bolshevist model," but, as we have seen, no such accusation was raised when cinemagoers watched Japanese girls being taught how to shoot. Most poignantly in demonstrating the filmic fusion of power and aesthetics, the sequence of Japanese cavalry charging toward the camera and thus on the silver screen toward the audience would have left spectators with a deep impression of Japan's martial prowess. In all likelihood the scene was not captured impromptu as part of actual combat but carefully staged and choreographed, with the camera strategically placed and angled on the ground to dramatize the cavalrymen's speed and size. To wit, the artistic treatment of Japanese violence on film achieved a veritable union of force and beauty.

For the rest of the Sino-Japanese War, until the Japanese attack on Pearl Harbor, the presentation in newsreels of the conflict diverged from the war itself. While the war spread wider, destroyed more properties, and took more lives, reports in the newsreels became more repetitive, more formulaic, and farther from the truth. Viewers saw scene after scene of city after city in China conquered by the Japanese, so much so that the stories became indistinguishable from one another. At times the newsreels even sank to the level of mere propaganda for Japan, as when an Ufa program from late 1938 showcased Japanese soldiers playing with Chinese children and having a jolly time, accompanied by lighthearted music to enhance the fantasized visual effect. Still, neither the staged episode nor the claim that "normal life has returned to the city" could hide the piles of rubble in the background.[52] By that point, of course, the newsreels had ceased to convey news and lost much of their credibility.

In the Eye of the Beholder

Although Japanese aggression in Shanghai in 1937 mirrored that in 1932 (if anything Japan far outdid itself the second time around), German newsreels handled the two instances differently. In 1932, they channeled to cinemas images of destruction of Chinese properties and lives, but five years later they captured only a triumphant Japan with little regard for the concomitant human casualties. Indeed, as far as can be established, no German audience saw any clip of the orgy of rapine and killing that came to be known as the Nanking Massacre.[53] It can no longer be ascertained whether such footage, if any existed, was censored, but it seems likely that external interference played a role in ensuring that not a single scene from the six-week-long string of atrocities reached the silver screen.[54] The changes in the portrayals of Japan were caused not by its actions, for both in 1932 and 1937 the country used a pretext to invade China by besieging and bombarding Shanghai, but rather shifts in domestic German politics and attitude. During those years Germany radically changed from an internationally oriented republic to a unilaterally acting dictatorship. What the filmmakers and narrators of the Weimar Republic found inhumane and dangerous in Japan in turn became decisive and admirable under the Nazi regime.

In other words, as seen in the newsreels, fundamental transformations took place in the mid 1930s concurrently in both countries that allowed the increasingly authoritarian Germany to perceive the increasingly aggressive Japan in a positive light. As Japan escalated its campaign against China, reports on the war also came to dominate the overall presentation of Japan on screens, displacing the previous portrayal of a quaint land of superstition and tradition. That is, the prevailing perception in the 1920s of Japan as a beauty, mysterious and dainty, became replaced in the early 1930s by one of Japan as a beast, unpredictable and brutal. Then, in the mid 1930s, changes in aesthetical tastes in Germany, dictated by National Socialist politics, led to more abstract and artistic depictions of the same Japanese violence. So, to be precise, Japan was never beauty *and* the beast in the interwar newsreels; rather it was beauty, then the beast, and then Nazism found beauty in the beast. The crowd of religious revelers in the 1920s morphed in the 1930s into the warmongering mob wishing troops good hunting. The traditional garments villagers wore in the 1920s became military uniforms in the 1930s. The energy that went into honoring the peaceful Buddha in the 1920s was diverted in the 1930s into churning out war machines. Under normal circumstances, Japanese aggression would have evoked opprobrium, as it did in much of the West, but circumstances in Germany were anything but normal. Japan's descent into militarism coincided with Nazism's rise in Germany, and the two rogue regimes worked hand in hand to overturn the existing world order. What struck others as bestial in fact appeared quite beautiful to the Nazis, so much so that newsreels' depictions of Japan throughout the Nazi period remained remarkably free of derogatory comments on race. Beauty, it seemed, was indeed in the eye of the beholder.

Notes

1. During the war Goebbels received a draft edition of the newsreel on Saturdays before forwarding it to Hitler, who reviewed and critiqued it on Monday, so that the final version could be released later in the week. See Jeremy Noakes, ed., *Nazism 1919–1945 Volume 4: The German Home Front in World War II* (Exeter, 1998), 504.
2. On the locking of cinemas during World War II, see Sabine Hake, *German National Cinema* (New York, 2002), 64.
3. For more on using newsreels and documentaries in the Federal Archives, see the guidebook, Bundesarchiv-Filmarchiv, *Wochenschauen und Dokumentarfilme 1895–1950*, ed. Peter Bucher, Findbücher zu Beständen des Bundesarchivs 8 (Koblenz: Bundesarchiv, 2000).
4. "Blaujacken beim Besuch berühmter chinesischer Tempelbauten," *Emelka-Deulig-Wochenschau-Sujets*, 1925, Findbuch-Signatur 538. Unfortunately the state of preservation and organization of early or fragmentary newsreels does not render them convenient for research or documentation. Therefore I try to provide as much information as possible on any film cited, including the original or archival title, release date and call number in the guidebook of the Federal Archives (Findbuch-Signatur).
5. *Emelka-Wochenschau-Aufnahmen*, 1927, Findbuch-Signatur 1375.
6. "Japanische Kirchweih," *Deulig-Wochenschausugets Nr. 17*, 1928.
7. "Zu Ehren Buddhas," *Ufa-Deulig-Opel-Wochenschau Sujets Nr. 2*, 1928.
8. "Die moderne Frau in Japan," *Emelka-Woche Nr. 48*, 19 November 1929, Findbuch-Signatur 502.
9. "Andere Zeiten, andere Sitten. Was vor 20 Jahren noch unmöglich war, heute ist es ein gewohntes Bild. Vorführungen von Bademoden nach europäischem Vorbild in einem japanischen Seebad," in *Deulig-Tonwoche Nr. 137*, 15 August 1934, Findbuch-Signatur DTW137/1934.
10. One might think of cartoons from the late 1800s, especially those by the French caricaturist Georges Bigot, depicting Japanese in ill-fitting Western clothes as monkeys.
11. "Japanische und amerikanische Kriegsschiffe begrüßen einander in der Bay von San Francisco," *Deulig-Woche*, 1925, Findbuch-Signatur 513.
12. "Kanonen-Donner in New York," *Ufa-Tonwoche Nr. 314*, 9 September 1936, Findbuch-Signatur UTW 314/1936.
13. *Ufa-Tonwoche Nr. 277*, 25 December 1935. Audio missing.

14. *Ufa-Tonwoche Nr. 200*, 4 July 1934, Findbuch-Signatur UTW 200/1934. Throughout this essay the names of Japanese persons are rendered in the last name–first name format.

15. "Vor 80 Jahren war Japan noch ein weltabgeschiedenes Inselreich, unberührt von der Zivilisation Europas und Amerikas. Im Jahre 1854 landeten amerikanische Schiffe unter dem Kommando Admiral Perrys in Schimoda. Japan lernte die moderne Zivilisation kennen und von diesem Zeitpunkt an entwickelte sich die japanische Nation in ungewöhnlich raschem Tempo zur jetzigen Weltmacht," in *Deulig-Tonwoche Nr. 125*, 23 May 1934, Findbuch-Signatur DTW125/1934.

16. Examples include an American naval exercise that appeared in *Emelka-Woche Nr. 44*, 26 October 1927, Findbuch-Signatur 490; a Reichswehr autumn drill in *Emelka-Woche Nr. 38*, 14 September 1927, Findbuch-Signatur 487; and a Royal Air Force maneuver in the mid 1920s in *Emelka-Wochenschau-Sujets*, ca. 1924–26, Findbuch-Signatur 1296. Incidentally, naval exercises seemed an especially popular subject for newsreels.

17. See *Emelka-Woche Nr. 32*, 3 August 1927, Findbuch-Signatur 483; *Emelka-Woche Nr. 35*, 24 August 1927, Findbuch-Signatur 484.

18. "Kriegsgefahr im Osten! China rüstet sich auf den Krieg mit Rußland," *Emelka-Woche Nr. 28*, 3 July 1929, Findbuch-Signatur 500.

19. The Shanghai Incident refers to the war in and around Shanghai from January to March of 1932. The Manchurian Incident in September 1931 had reignited anti-Japanese passions among the Chinese, eventually leading to confrontations between Chinese and Japanese civilians in Shanghai. Japan used the pretext of protecting its interests from disturbance to amass a force outside the city, and proceeded to attack both the city and Chinese units nearby from land, sea, and air. Both sides poured men and resources into the battle; Chiang Kai-shek sent some of the German-trained and -equipped troops to help resist the Japanese. By 3 March, Japan had gained the upper hand and the defenders withdrew from their positions. The Western powers used the lull to broker a ceasefire which ultimately led to the end the military action. For more, see Donald A. Jordan, *China's Trial by Fire: The Shanghai War of 1932* (Ann Arbor, M.I., 2001). Ufa inaugurated its newsreel program with sound on 10 September 1930; Fox, on 11 September. Emelka followed suit later on 24 September. Deulig caught up by releasing its first sound newsreel on 6 January 1932.

20. Of course, the World War I veterans among audience members had not only seen but lived actual combat. Their exposure to war, however, remained limited to their individual perspectives, since no one person could experience fighting on land, at sea, and in the air, which all featured prominently in footage of the Sino-Japanese conflict. They also showed heavy urban fighting in densely populated areas, something not seen in World War I. In addition, between 1918 and 1932 an entire new generation of Germans had grown up knowing war only indirectly and after the fact.

    Hypothetically, the fighting during the Manchurian Incident would have provided the first footage of actual war seen in cinema. Yet it is no longer possible to know for certain, as no newsreel from September 1931 to February 1932 seems to have survived. The earliest programs showing combat between China and Japan were filmed in Shanghai in early 1932.

21. "Schanghai steht heute im Mittelpunkt des Weltinteresses. Japan in große Handelsstadt Ostasiens, welche 2.7 Millionen Einwohner hat, eingedrungen," in *Deulig-Tonwoche Nr. 6*, 10 February 1932, Findbuch-Signatur DTW 6/1932.

22. The newsreel's footage from the air scooped by several months those in the Nazi propaganda film *Hitler über Deutschland* (*Hitler's Flight over Germany*).

23. The enhancement of combat scenes on film through the addition of sound has been noted. See Anton Kaes, *Shell Shock Cinema: Weimar Culture and the Wounds of War* (Princeton, 2009), 212; Julia Encke, *Augenblicke der Gefahr: Der Krieg und die Sinne. 1914–1934* (Munich, 2006), 111–193.

24. *Deulig-Tonwoche Nr. 9*, 2 March 1932, Findbuch-Signatur DTW 9/1932.

25. *Deulig-Tonwoche Nr. 10*, 9 March 1932, Findbuch-Signatur DTW 10/1932.

26. "Ungeheures Elend hat die Beschießung der Stadt unter den Bewohnern hervorgerufen…. Tausende und abertausende Flüchtlinge. Alle haben Hunger und müssen öffentlich gespeist werden," *Deulig-Tonwoche Nr. 10*.

27. No Ufa show from this period appears to have survived, but it seems highly likely that the program of that week would have mentioned the war in some fashion.

28. "Chapei brennt," in "Der Konflikt im Osten. Die letzten Bilder aus Shanghai," *Emelka-Tonwoche Nr. 77*, 10 March 1932, Findbuch-Signatur 1266.

29. Technically, footage of the French destruction of parts of Damascus in 1925 should qualify as the first film of a deliberate aerial attack on a city. Yet unlike the coverage of the bombing of Shanghai, viewers only saw the aftermath of the raid and not the raid itself. See *Emelka-Deulig-Wochenschau-Sujets*, 1925.

30. "Zwar wehren sich die chinesischen Regimente verzweifelt, doch müssen sie vor den ungleich moderneren Kriegsmitteln der Japaner Schritt für Schritt zurückweichen," in *Emelka-Tonwoche Nr. 77*.

31. The same naval exercise was also shown in *Deulig-Tonwoche Nr. 8*, 24 February 1932, Findbuch-Signatur DTW 8/1932.

32. "Aber China läßt sich nicht unterkriegen," in *Deulig-Tonwoche Nr. 10*.

33. *Deulig-Tonwoche Nr. 23*, 9 June 1932, Findbuch-Signatur DTW 23/1932. The assassination took place on 29 April but the newsreel did not show footage of it until 9 June. Thus, though the camera managed to record the event as it unfolded, the time needed for transporting and editing the actual reels delayed its appearance on screen by more than a month.

    The Japanese commander in Shanghai, General Shirakawa Yoshinori, died from his wounds, and Admiral Nomura Kichisaburō and Ambassador Shigemitsu Mamoru were gravely injured. Despite their serious injuries—Nomura lost the use of his right eye, Shigemitsu had to have his right leg amputated—both went on to play critical roles in Japanese foreign policy in the coming years. Nomura worked as ambassador to the United States and tried to come to an understanding with Washington until the attack on Pearl Harbor in December 1941. Shigemitsu, often seen as a moderate, served as foreign minister during the war once the tide turned against Japan in 1943. Ultimately he would sign for Japan the Instrument of Surrender in 1945.

34. *Deulig-Tonwoche Nr. 60*, 22 February 1933, Findbuch-Signatur DTW 60/1933.

35. "Shan Hai Kuan ist das Einfallstor in die Provinz Jehol, deren Besitz Japan den Austritt aus dem Völkerbund wert ist," *Deulig-Tonwoche Nr. 60*.

36. "Kriegsbegeisterung in Japan," *Deulig-Tonwoche Nr. 57*, 1 February 1933, Findbuch-Signatur DTW 57/1933.

37. In *Deulig-Tonwoche Nr. 137* in 1934 there was a very touching scene of Berlin mothers reluctantly parting with their children off to an excursion to the Baltic. Cries of "Auf Wiedersehen" could be heard throughout the segment, and some mothers and children are weeping before the prospect of a brief separation.

38. "Die ganze Welt schützt sich gegen Luftangriffe. Selbst ein mit Flugzeugen reichlich versehenes Land wie Japan organisiert Luftschutzübungen," in *Fox Tönende Wochenschau Jahrg. VII Nr. 38*, ca. September 1933.

39. "Was tut die japanische Studentin in ihrer Freizeit? Sie lernt Schießen. Nicht mit Tesching oder Pistole…. Und vielleicht wird sie einmal im Ernst bei ihrem Mann stehen," in *Deulig-Tonwoche Nr. 148*, 31 October 1934, Findbuch-Signatur DTW 148/1934.

40. "Diese kleinen Japaner geben sich nicht mehr mit Zinnsoldat ab. Nur das Kriegspielgelände mit Maschinengewehr und, Sprung auf, marsch, marsch!' läßt das achtjährige Herz höher schlagen," in *Deulig-Tonwoche Nr. 157*, 2 January 1935, Findbuch-Signatur DTW 157/1935.

41. *Ufa-Tonwoche Nr. 277*, 9 January 1935, Findbuch-Signatur UTW 227/1935.

42. *Deulig-Tonwoche Nr. 174*, 1 May 1935. Audio missing.

43. "Auf dem Schimmel des Mikado," in *Deulig-Tonwoche Nr. 207*, 18 December 1935, Findbuch-Signatur DTW 207/1935.

44. "Unruhiges Asien," *Ufa-Tonwoche Nr. 302*, 17 June 1936, Findbuch-Signatur UTW 302/1936.

45. "Die Lage im Fernen Osten ist wieder gespannt," in "Kampf um Peiping," *Ufa-Tonwoche Nr. 362*, 11 August 1937, Findbuch-Signatur UTW 362/1937. The Marco Polo Bridge Incident, which triggered the wider war, took place on 7 July. This Ufa program is the earliest still extant newsreel covering the outbreak of war. The missing Japanese soldier in question was probably not attacked by Chinese troops.

46. "Die Japaner in Peking, umjubelt von ihren Landsleuten," in *Bavaria-Tonwoche Nr. 37*, 8 September 1937, Findbuch-Signatur 389.

47. *Ufa-Tonwoche Nr. 368*, 22–26 September 1937, Findbuch-Signatur UTW 368/1937.

48. "Kriegsschauplatz Nordchina," *Ufa-Tonwoche Nr. 364*, 25 August 1937, Findbuch-Signatur UTW 364/1937.

49. "China," *Ufa-Tonwoche Nr. 374*, 5 November 1937, Findbuch-Signatur UTW 374/1937.

50. "China," *Ufa-Tonwoche Nr. 372*, 10 October 1937, Findbuch-Signatur UTW 372/1937.

51. "In unaufhaltsamem Vormarsch setzten japanische Abteilung bei China über den Gelben Fluss…. Auch Frauen an die Front, mit Stahlhelm und Gewehr, nach bolschewistischem Vorbild," in *Ufa-Tonwoche Nr. 388*, 9 February 1938, Findbuch-Signatur UTW 388/1938.

52. "Die kleinen Chinesen haben sich, wie man sieht, mit den japanischen Soldaten gut angefreundet. Auch sonst zeigt die Stadt wieder ein friedliches Bild und das normale Leben geht wieder seinen täglichen Gang," in *Ufa-Tonwoche Nr. 431*, 7 December 1938.

53. The sole surviving filmic evidence of the massacre appears to be the reels shot by the American Episcopalian missionary John Magee. Magee had copies of the film made and sent to the U.S. and German governments. Georg Rosen of the German embassy in Nanking recommended that Hitler himself watch the footage. Rosen, in a document reproduced in John Rabe, *John Rabe: Der gute Deutsche von Nanking*, ed. Erwin Wickert (Stuttgart, 1997), 256–257, advised his superiors in the Foreign Ministry:

> Während der—übrigens noch immer bis zu einem nicht unerheblichen Grade andauernden—Schreckensherrschaft der Japaner in Nanking hat der Reverend John

Magee, Mitglied der amerikanischen *Episcopal Church Mission*, der seit etwa einem Vierteljahrhundert hier ansässig ist, Filmaufnahmen gemacht, die ein beredtes Zeugnis über die von den Japanern verübten Greueltaten ablegen…. Charakteristisch für seine selbstlose Absicht und sein reines Wollen ist die Tatsache, daß ihm eine handelsmäßige Verwertung seiner Filmaufnahmen fernliegt, und daß er der Botschaft von sich aus eine Kopie zu den an die Shanghaier Kodak-Vertretung zu zahlenden Kopierkosten, die dem Auswärtigen Amt auf sicherem Wege vorgelegt werden wird, angeboten hat. Eine Beschreibung der den einzelnen Bildschnitten zugrunde liegenden Vorgänge in englischer Sprache liegt bei. Sie stellt, ebenso wie der Film selbst, ein darart erschütterndes Zeitdokument dar, daß der Film mit einer wörtlichen Übersetzung dieser Beschreibung dem Führer und Reichskanzler vorgeführt werden möge.

54. Another account of the massacre, namely, the presentations and lectures by John Rabe in Berlin upon his return to Germany, was censored by the Nazi authorities. Remarkably, Rabe was not only a respected German merchant in Shanghai, but also a member of the Nazi Party. Whereas the censorship of feature films, which allowed a long period for editing and refilming, usually left a paper trail for historians, the government's meddling in the production of time-sensitive newsreels was far less well documented.

CHAPTER 2

Reflecting Chiral Modernities
The Function of Genre in Arnold Fanck's
Transnational *Bergfilm, The Samurai's Daughter*
(1936–37)

VALERIE WEINSTEIN

In 1935, Nagasama Kawakita, the successful Japanese film producer and importer, invited Arnold Fanck to Japan to direct a Japanese film that would appeal to the international export market.[1] Fanck had an international reputation and is remembered by fans, critics, and film historians as the creative genius behind the German *Bergfilm*, or mountain film, an oeuvre with which Kawakita and his target audiences were familiar when he invited Fanck to Japan.[2] According to Fanck's memoirs, Kawakita issued this invitation to him, as opposed to a Hollywood director, because "the Germans had greater empathy with foreign peoples,"[3] an unlikely story given the Japanese discomfort with Nazi racial ideology.[4] More likely than not, Kawakita's choice of Fanck as director had to do with the developing alliance between Japan and Germany, which would soon become the two dominant axis powers of World War II. Germany had strong involvements in China and initially did not recognize Japanese-occupied Manchukuo. With the rise of the Nazi regime, however, Germany looked more and more like a potential ally and the two empires initiated informal talks in 1935 with an eye to improving political relations.[5] At this same time, German foreign policy was turning away from China (for whom Germany was a preferred trade partner and arms supplier) toward the goal of making Japan Germany's main ally in Asia.[6] The first German-Japanese co-production (and not a successful trendsetter in this regard),[7] *Die Tochter des Samurai* (The Samurai's Daughter) was filmed during the negotiation of the German-Japanese Anti-Comintern Pact, in which one of Fanck's producers was involved.[8] Given Fanck's right-wing political sympathies, Nazi control over the distribution of films in Germany, and the Japanese funding, infrastructure, and political support behind the film, *The Samurai's Daughter* explicitly promoted German-Japanese alliances, purported affinities between the Germans and the Japanese, and Japanese expansionism in Manchuria. The film also was saturated with other Nazi ideals such as racial purity, blood and soil patriotism, and return to the homeland.[9]

While spending a year and a half in Japan, sampling the culture, and only partially heeding the advice of his Japanese producers, dramaturges, cast, and crew, Fanck did his best to obey the directive of the Japanese minister of culture, which was "to write a film that could be understood also in Europe and America, because … Japanese film themes are incomprehensible abroad. But the film must nevertheless in all respects be authentically Japanese."[10] Personality conflicts and disagreements about the accuracy of Fanck's representations of Japanese culture led to a split between him and codirector Mansaku Itami, resulting in the production of two separate films using the same cast, locations, and basic treatment.[11] Itami's film *Atarashiki Tsuchi* (The New Earth) opened in Japan to poor reviews and the accusation of being "un-Japanese," if Fanck is to be believed;[12] Fanck's version, by contrast, broke box-office records. Critical reception, however, was mixed. According to Fanck, the film met with glowing reviews as "a true Japanese film,"[13] yet Japanese sources cited by Michael Baskett express disapproval of Fanck's infusion of German aesthetics and Nazi politics into a Japanese film.[14] Janine Hansen's detailed analysis of the Japanese reception suggests that critics were not impressed with the cinematic value or the cultural subtlety of either film, but they praised Fanck more for cinematic reasons especially because of his landscape shots; they also to some extent forgave his cultural inaccuracies because he was a foreigner and could not be expected to know any better.[15] By all accounts, however, "the Fanck version was a sensational hit with Japanese audiences."[16] *The Samurai's Daughter* launched the career of Setsuko Hara, one of Japanese cinema's great female stars, and Fanck claims in his memoir to have been invited to the imperial palace for an audience with Prince Takamatsu, who praised his understanding of the Japanese "soul."[17] As per Propaganda Ministry directives, *The Samurai's Daughter* opened to great fanfare and reasonably positive reception in Berlin.[18]

In this essay, I am not interested in determining whether or not Fanck succeeded, as he claims, in making an "authentic" Japanese film. Nor is the film's function as overt political propaganda my primary concern. More salient to my inquiry is the remarkable fact that Fanck fulfilled the Japanese minister of culture's directive and found a way to make a more or less acceptably "Japanese" film that was comprehensible to German audiences and spoke to audiences both in Japan and in Germany. Not only was the film a transnational production, but also it had transnational thematic, aesthetic, and ideological appeal. Made for export but successful at home, the film fit into German paradigms and viewing habits without fully alienating Japanese consumers. In other words, despite the film's overt political agenda, and despite its cultural inaccuracies, it resonated with the experiences, fantasies, and desires of Japanese and German viewers in the mid 1930s. Additionally striking is the strong resemblance between *The Samurai's Daughter* and Fanck's earlier films. The thematic and aesthetic continuities between *The Samurai's Daughter* and Fanck's earlier work provide a useful analytical framework for understanding the experiences and fantasies represented in *The Samurai's Daughter*. By invoking major features of the *Bergfilm* genre and inverting its basic structure, Fanck was able in this film to address both German and Japanese audiences and to construe their experiences of modernity as discrete yet complementary, seemingly alike yet subtly different, positing a relationship—as between one's two hands—that can be described as chiral.

Pioneered by Fanck and developed further by his protégés Luis Trenker and Leni Riefenstahl, the *Bergfilm* is a genre commonly understood as glorifying Alpine landscapes and extreme winter sports and helping define German national identity. It frequently is associated with the Weimar Republic, the fragile German democracy that lasted from 1918 to 1933. Insofar as the production and content of *Bergfilme* straddled boundaries between Germany, Austria, Switzerland, and Italy, and the films reached an international audience, we can more accurately describe the *Bergfilm* as a transnational genre—albeit a Eurocentric one. Fanck's two final feature films, *The Samurai's Daughter* and *Ein Robinson: das Tagebuch eines Matrosen* (A Robinson: The Diary of a Sailor, 1939–40), filmed on location in Japan and Patagonia, respectively, strongly bear his signature as an auteur and share significant features with his earlier Alpine films. Closer scrutiny of these later films suggests that the *Bergfilm* was neither exclusively a Weimar genre nor one that focused solely on the German nation. Identifying the generic conventions of the *Bergfilm* in *The Samurai's Daughter* can help us understand the filmic process of meaning-making, as well as the sources of the film's transnational appeal. By inserting Japanese characters, images of Japan, and cultural concerns shared by Japanese and German viewers into an internationally recognized generic framework, Fanck's transnational production spoke to both Japanese and German film markets.

The *Bergfilm* was a commercially successful genre whose popularity peaked in the early 1930s.[19] It can be recognized by a handful of distinct features, the most obvious of which is the films' spectacular alpine footage and the athletic and cinematic challenges they showcase. The visual style of the *Bergfilm* has been described by Eric Rentschler as an "overwhelming mix of aura and abstraction" that modifies Romantic representations of sublime nature with modern filmic styles and techniques.[20] According to Christian Rapp, the "Freiburg School" of cinematography developed by Fanck's cameramen was characterized by a long list of features: movement; personal, physical, and artistic adventurousness; large teams; outdoor filming; and technical experimentation.[21] The sublime visions of the *Bergfilm* communicated the experience of mountain climbing with overwhelming, frame-crowding images, spatial abstraction, clouds, fog, at times unclear focus, and contrast of light and shadow.[22]

According to Rentschler, the "appeal" of the mountain film for its contemporaries resided in its use of modern technologies to address "pre-modern yearning,"[23] animating previously inaccessible landscapes and bringing them closer to viewers in what was perceived as an unmediated way.[24] Rapp describes Fanck's alpine landscapes as mystified central players in his dramas.[25] Hansen refers to "nature" as Fanck's "leading lady" and calls the conquest of her the genre's main theme.[26] The *Bergfilm*'s seeming mysticism and escapism, and its promotion of heroism and self-sacrifice, have earned it frequent criticism for being "anti-modern," "reactionary," or "proto-fascist."[27]

Also characteristic of the *Bergfilm*, after Leni Riefenstahl's filmic debut in 1926, are melodramatic narratives organized around love triangles, whose logic, direction, and pace take a back seat to the films' spectacular visuals. Rentschler describes the genre in its mature form as "a precarious balance between the expressive shapes of nature and the romantic triangles of melodrama."[28] Men's competition over a woman features as prominently as does their struggle against the mountain. Rentschler argues that this disruptive female presence is central to the genre. Like the mountain, "woman" is a seductive force; she is both allied with and pitted against nature and technology and needs to be subdued visually and in narrative.[29]

Due no doubt to its Japanese setting and cast and lack of Alpine athleticism, *The Samurai's Daughter* never has been treated as a *Bergfilm*, and thus, as a seeming anomaly among Fanck's better known work, has received little scholarly attention. Yet, as will be shown, it shares significant features with Fanck's earlier films. Some plot synopsis is helpful in this regard. *The Samurai's Daughter* begins with a young man named Teruo returning home to Japan after university study in Germany. He is accompanied by an attractive blonde journalist named Gerda. Mitsuko, Teruo's adoptive sister, to whom he long has been engaged to be married, is devastated by Gerda's arrival with her betrothed, and Teruo's biological and adoptive families both are upset by his rejection of their plans and traditions. Although it is unclear whether Teruo and Gerda truly have a romantic or sexual relationship, as his families fear, his desire and admiration for Gerda are evident. Teruo struggles between his loyalties and desires, between filial obligation and the individualism and personal freedom he has grown to value in the West. Even as Gerda decides to return to Germany, Mitsuko, wearing her wedding kimono, begins an arduous climb, ultimately intending to jump into an active volcano. Teruo pursues and stops her, burning his feet severely. As Mitsuko nurses his injuries, Teruo realizes that his family has chosen well for him. He and Mitsuko marry and move to Japanese-occupied Manchuria to colonize, farm, and bear children.

While not set in the Alps, *The Samurai's Daughter* deploys strategies characteristic of the *Bergfilm*, mirroring some and inverting others. In doing so, the film reproduces some of the earlier films' appeal while creating new meanings. Spectacular shots of Japanese landscapes predominate, hearkening back, as in Fanck's earlier films, to German Romantic painting (see Figure 2.1).

Such shots and sequences, made possible through the latest filmic technologies—including the first telephoto movie lens, invented specifically for this picture[30]—showcase Japanese landscapes and cultural practices and bring *The Samurai's Daughter's* exotic, distant locale closer to the European spectator. At the same time montages of modern, urban Japan, similar to those of Berlin in German films of the 1920s and 30s, and typical of the New Objectivity, construe modernity in Japan as parallel to that in Germany.[31] As in the earlier *Bergfilme*, the intersection between modernity and tradition is prominent both visually and narratologically and the narrative is organized not-so-subtly around a love triangle. This film's reflections and reversals of earlier models depict Japan as both Germany's double and as its perfect opposite, making Fanck's use of genre consistent with the discursive tradition of "Japan as mirror image of Europe"[32] and contemporary discussions of Germany and Japan's "similarity and hence their appropriateness as allies."[33] Whereas in earlier *Bergfilme* like *Der heilige Berg* (The Holy Mountain, Arnold Fanck, 1925–26) or *Die weiße Hölle vom Piz Palü* (The White Hell of Piz Palü, Arnold Fanck and G.W.

Figure 2.1. *The Samurai's Daughter* screenshot, 1:22:09. The holy volcano.

Pabst, 1929), men compete over a woman and scale frigid Alpine heights, in *The Samurai's Daughter* the gender constellation of the love triangle is reversed and the dangerous mountain is hot, not cold. A man must choose between two women, a choice made only after a strenuous climb up scorching, rocky terrain to stop one of them from flinging herself into a holy volcano. I would argue that *The Samurai's Daughter*'s manipulations and inversions of the mountain film genre were central both to its negotiation of transnational relations and to its transnational appeal.

When the ocean liner bearing Teruo and Gerda approaches harbor, a caption reads "Westwind," indicating the typhoon of modernity breaking on Japan, a typhoon embodied by the symbolically named Gerda Storm,[34] a German woman whose presence threatens to undermine traditional Japanese family dynamics.[35] The narrative featuring Gerda follows the mode of the *Bergfilm*, addressing tensions between tradition and modernity, reexamining gender within such a context, introducing a woman as the prime irritant, and resolving the love triangle and the surrounding tensions through a treacherous mountain climb. The love triangle between Teruo, Mitsuko, and Gerda acts out some of the difficulties caused by the rapid modernization and Westernization of Japan launched by the Meiji Restoration in 1867 and accelerated after World War I, a process wherein German institutions, leaders, and intellectuals provided influential models.[36] More generally, *The Samurai's Daughter* explores the problem of where and how to find the correct balance between the seductions of modernization and valued traditions, an issue that no doubt resonated with many spectators, both Japanese and German.

That the love triangle between Teruo, Gerda, and Mitsuko embodies the dramatic encounter between Japan and the West and the resulting clash between tradition and modernity is established early in the film, during a scene on the ship's deck in which Gerda interviews Teruo about his life story (see Figure 2.2). As encapsulated in this single shot, the interview scene on the ship stages a close encounter between Germany and Japan that is both harmonious and conflicted. In the setting we see a mix of traditional and modern, Japanese and German imagery. The ship's deck is decorated with paper lanterns and branches of cherry blossoms connoting traditional Japan, while the rafters are hung with strings of international flags, dominated by the flags of the Nazi Party and the Imperial Japanese Army, referencing contemporary politics. The protagonists are of a piece with this setting and the encounter it symbolizes. For the most part, they seem at ease with one another and in their mixed milieu. Gerda lounges in a flowered, kimono-like gown, blending in with the cherry blossoms, and balancing the image. Embracing Japanese culture is easy for her, perhaps because of that inherent German "empathy with foreign peoples" posited by Fanck. Teruo likewise seems comfortable with modernity and Westernness. His slacks, shirt, and tie conform to European

Figure 2.2. *The Samurai's Daughter* screenshot, 0:09:13. Gerda and Teruo on deck.

fashion standards and his relaxed posture and pleasure in smoking a cigarette suggest that he has become accustomed to the luxuries of European life. Such images suggest that contact and transculturation between Germany and Japan are simple and painless.

The harmony of this shot and of the interaction between Gerda and Teruo, however, are disrupted by the dialogue. Gerda asks Teruo why he was adopted by an old, wealthy family. He hesitates to answer and eventually admits that he is supposed to carry on the Yamato name and bloodline. A close-up on Gerda's face and the change in the tone and pace of her voice as she puzzles out that he therefore must be engaged to the daughter of his adoptive family makes her disappointment evident. Teruo likewise answers slowly with a serious look on his face, and refers to his long betrothal as a "misfortune" (*Unglück*).

As does the mountain in Fanck's alpine films, in *The Samurai's Daughter*, the Japanese landscape plays a central role. It constitutes the spectacle, motivates the action, and functions symbolically. After a brief title sequence of what Western audiences would have construed as typical Japanese images and music, Fanck introduces stunning shots of the Japanese archipelago, its harsh landscape battered by waves, typhoons, and earthquakes, crowned by craggy steaming and snowcapped volcanoes. To anyone familiar with Fanck's work, his signature is unmistakable. We repeatedly see the "mix of aura and abstraction" described by Rentschler.

The dialogue emphasizes that the harsh environment has shaped the Japanese character. On the ship, Teruo tells Gerda that storms, earthquakes, and volcanic eruptions make the Japanese people brave; as an island chain, the nation has enjoyed times of tranquil isolation and has been battered by storms from abroad, typically from the West. The Japanese people, Mitsuko's German tutor tells Gerda, are volcanic as well, and the women seemingly dormant until they erupt; images and rumbles of the erupting volcano, thunder, and lightning foreshadow Mitsuko's suicide attempt.

This harsh Japanese landscape also drives the action, a dominant theme in this film that calls both on the *Bergfilm* tradition and on contemporary political and scientific discourses.[37] As reported in *Licht-Bild-Bühne*'s announcement of Fanck's contract with Kawakita, Fanck conceived this film from the beginning as a "Volk ohne Raum" (people without space) picture, a film promoting expansionism in the National Socialist sense of a racially superior people limited by political boundaries conquering lands held by the racially inferior in order to fulfill its destiny.[38] The craggy coastlines and volcanoes favored by Fanck's cinematographers leave little space for the rice paddies of Teruo's family's farm and seem to push him to till the Manchurian soil in the final scene. The shots of Manchurian farmland, by contrast, picture vast, fertile space, awaiting the Japanese farmers' diligence and agricultural technology. What the film does not thematize, at least not directly, is the fact that Manchuria was by no means an empty country awaiting the Japanese, but rather that the Japanese military conquered Manchuria. A few shots of Japanese soldiers guarding farms and colonists hint at this reality.

Encouraging expansionism is not the only function of the depictions of Japan's imposing landscape. As is typical of Fanck's *Bergfilme*, in *The Samurai's Daughter* Japan's landscape and environment also are symbolically charged. In one of the opening scenes, an earthquake shakes Teruo's family home when the news arrives that he will be returning from Europe. Many of the objects shaken in this scene, shown in close up, are traditional ones such as dolls, religious statuettes, and samurai swords. In a vatic moment, we see traditional culture and the Japanese family, built on unstable ground, shaken by Teruo's arrival from the West. Superimposed titles and dialogue equate modernity with a stormy west wind and Teruo's return to more traditional practices and attitudes as driven by an east wind. Mitsuko's father announces to Gerda, as the two overlook the sea, that a storm is coming for his people from the West and hers from the East.[39] He speaks of the family as the foundation of Japanese culture, as a home assailed by storms, even as Fanck shows us waves breaking against rocky cliffs.

Even as the natural imagery deployed highlights cultural conflict and difference, Fanck's symbolic use of nature underscores artistic sympathies and affinities between Germans and Japanese. In *The Samurai's Daughter*, Fanck construes heavy-handed artistic and symbolic use of nature, such as his own, as characteristic of Japanese culture. Both Mitsuko and her father write poetry using natural imagery to represent the conflict caused by Teruo. Instead of a suicide note, Mitsuko leaves behind a poem that reads: "The tender cherry blossoms fall, floating, to the ground, in order to make space for the surging fruit."[40] In this poem, Mitsuko describes herself and her death as beautiful, delicate, and ephemeral falling cherry blossoms, and Gerda as robust, ripe, and sensual—and her taking Mitsuko's place as the expected outcome of a natural process. Mitsuko's poem also evokes clichés and stereotypes familiar to Western viewers, of Asian women being fragile, passive, resigned to their fate, and inevitably defeated in competition with Western women, as in Puccini's *Madame Butterfly*. Mitsuko's father likewise turns to symbolic uses of nature in his poetry, employing a natural disaster as a metaphor for Europe's catastrophic influence on Japanese families, relationships, and traditions: "A flood is coming from the West—it dissolves familial bonds. And sons no longer bow before their fathers."[41] The natural imagery here places blame not on Gerda and Teruo as individuals, but rather on the sea of Western values such as sexual freedom, individuality, and personal liberty that drown traditional values and practices.

Japanese perceptions of modernity and modernization find a filmic echo in the problems and eventual solutions articulated in *The Samurai's Daughter*. Modernity in Japan has been characterized by Harry Harootunian as "co-eval" with modernity in Europe and the United States; that is to say, the Japanese version of modernity was "an inflection of a larger global process," contemporaneous yet also different.[42] According to Harootunian, Japanese philosophical, political, and cultural thinkers understood modernity to be an uneven process characterized by speed, shock, consumerism, desire, and alienation, and expressed dislocations that they attempted to overcome with visions of unity rooted in cultural traditions. While acknowledging difference, Harootunian's textual and historical analyses also highlight connections between Japanese and European thought and often evoke German philosophy, as in his introductory account of the "unevenness" he posits as central to Japanese experiences and discourses of modernity:

> Thinkers and writers responded to Japan's modernity by describing it as a *doubling* that imprinted a difference between the new demands of capitalism and the market and the force of received forms of history and cultural patterns. Although this conception of doubling was frequently seen as a unique emblem of Japan's modern experience, its logic showed that modernity everywhere would always result in what the philosopher Watsuji Tetsurō, and others who figure promi-

nently in this book, called a "double life" (*nijū seikatsu*), and what Ernst Bloch, commenting on German life in the early 1930s, described as the "synchronicity of the non-synchronous, the simultaneity of the non-contemporaneous." Both writers point to the jarring coexistence of several pasts and the present in the now of everydayness.[43]

The Samurai's Daughter thematizes exactly this "jarring coexistence" of pasts and present, described by both Japanese and German philosophers, on visual, aural, and narrative levels. It resolves the conflict with a satisfying vision of unity and wholeness (marriage, childbearing, and colonial expansion), akin to those cited by Hartoonian, and which he links to fascism explicitly throughout his argument.

Mapping the conventions and concerns of the mountain film onto the Japanese landscape, as *The Samurai's Daughter* does, spoke not only to Japanese spectators' experiences of modernity but also to German audiences' concerns. It is by now commonplace to state that Nazi ideology and numerous German texts and films from the Weimar and Nazi periods were marked by ambivalence toward modernity and nostalgia for an idealized past. Images of Japan merged into such discourses, layering onto them concepts of "East" and "West." Bill Maltarich discusses the early twentieth-century German notion of "the corrupting influence of the West on Japan" and the concurrent idealization of traditional Japan: "First, Germans saw the Japanese culture as a potential source of renewal for a Europe in cultural crisis, and second, in the face of a modernized and threatening Japan, Germans turned toward views of the old Japan for comfort and to understand the Japanese psyche and the (negative) western influence on it."[44] As Maltarich shows, such views of the Japanese were integrated easily into National Socialism's version of "Reactionary Modernism," as described by Jeffrey Herf, the merging of modernity with German national traditions.[45] *The Samurai's Daughter* can be seen as part of these discourses as well. Its advocacy of a Japan parallel to Germany, which integrates influences from the modern West with traditional culture and values, underlies a call for a strong foundation of military and colonial power, emphasized by the film's closing shot of a Japanese soldier guarding Japanese farmers in Manchuria. As envisioned in *The Samurai's Daughter*, Japan's successful negotiation of East and West, modernity and tradition, ultimately makes the Japanese powerful, a threat that the film defuses by promoting German-Japanese alliance and showcasing the beauty of traditional Japan.

A number of scenes foreground the apparent kinship between Japan and Nazi Germany. When Gerda first sees Tokyo, she remarks on how much it looks like Berlin. When Teruo goes to consult a priest about his situation, the priest is shown standing in front of a swastika, an integral part of his temple's architecture (see Figure 2.3).

Figure 2.3. *The Samurai's Daughter* screenshot, 0:47:09. Buddhist priest in his temple.

While this shot emphasizes a kind of cultural *Wahlverwandschaft* between Japan and Nazi Germany, the priest elaborates on the relationship between East and West as one of kinship *and* difference: he advises Teruo both to adopt Western notions of progress and to remember that he is only one link in the chain of his ancestors and is responsible to all of them. Such a position would have been recognized by German audiences as similar to Nazi concepts of the individual vis-à-vis the *Volk*. In another realm, however, *The Samurai's Daughter* construes too close an alliance between Japan and Germany as problematic. While values may be similar, and cultural contact and cooperation desirable, too much interaction threatens to undermine precisely those values and traditions that Germans and Japanese, according to Fanck's vision, ought to respect. Thus the love triangle in this film speaks not only to the tensions between modernity and tradition but also to the political situation between Japan and Germany in a way consistent with the latter's obsession with racial and cultural purity.

Gerda, played by Ruth Eweler, a beauty queen who was featured in advertisements for "Robert's Only Blond"[46] shampoo as "the ideal German type,"[47] represents the West in a seductive and stereotypically German form. The German press frequently cited Eweler's blondness, beauty, and "aryanness" in discussions of this film.[48] Tall, striking, and impeccably dressed, she is able to compete visually with the exotic spectacle Fanck makes of the Japanese. She also offers a point of identification for German spectators—the primary target audience for this film. As a journalist, Gerda positions herself explicitly as an observer. Her interviews provide an excuse for excursive, explanatory dialogue.[49] She also calls attention to cultural difference in such scenes as the obligatory clumsy first encounter with chopsticks. Gerda's style of femininity also signifies Western modernity, particularly when juxtaposed to Mitsuko's kimonos, traditional charms and skills, and demure comportment. Confident and assertive, Gerda has a profession, behaves as an equal with men, and makes her own free choices regarding her romantic relationship. Unlike Mitsuko, she does not yield to decisions made by her father, family, or lover. Gerda eats alongside Mitsuko's father as an equal or honored guest while Mitsuko, kneeling and bowing, serves them. Gerda debates Teruo about the comparative value of individual freedom and familial obligation, telling him that the former, which he learned in Europe, was a false lesson, yet telling his adoptive father that the dominance of the family over the individual in Japan is too harsh. Ultimately, Gerda uses her personal freedom to do what she feels is right for Teruo and Mitsuko and to promote familial obligation, removing herself from the picture and returning to Germany.

While Gerda Storm represents the "Westwind" battering Japan, Teruo and Mitsuko represent two elements in modern Japan that must reconcile to achieve (expansionist) colonial and military success. Michael Baskett refers to the product as "a new breed of imperial subject—an ideal hybridization of rural and urban—epitomized by Teruo."[50] Teruo struggles between the temptations and freedoms offered by the West and established notions of duty and filial piety. His struggles are encapsulated in a scene in a bar, in which the blending of East and West, traditional and modern, and Teruo's inability to choose between the two are depicted as confounding and overwhelming.[51] Clash, confusion, and indecision are staged here in the action, mise-en-scène, sound, editing, and visual effects (see Figure 2.4).

In the bar scene, Teruo is unable to choose between the beauty and the alcoholic beverages offered him by a Japanese woman on his right, and a Caucasian woman who joins him on his left. When he tries the sake, he seems surprised by his own enjoyment of it, and a close up on the face of the woman offering it, the romantic swing tune played in the background by the band, and Teruo's expression indicate that he appreciates her beauty as well. Blurred by liquor and his indecision, Teruo's attention is torn between the jazz band and dancers and a third woman in a kimono playing traditional music on a shamisen. The bar becomes a flurry of Western and Eastern fashions, dancing, and music, with flashing lights and loud noises, layers of images and sounds superimposed upon one another by edits and dissolves. This scene and the sensory overload it stages also depict the fantasy of the uneven and "jarring coexistence of several pasts and the present" that Harootunian locates in Japanese and German inter-

Figure 2.4. *The Samurai's Daughter* screenshot, 0:35:38. Teruo in a bar.

war thought.[52] Teruo's difficulty negotiating this unevenness—in reconciling modernity and tradition, Eastern and Western desires and pleasures—creates an intolerably chaotic state.

Teruo must resolve his indecision and confusion in order for the film to conclude happily. We witness his ongoing reacculturation to Japan and growing realization of his own correct destiny as the film progresses. His biological sister, a textile factory worker able to balance modern urban life and traditional roles and customs, helps Teruo learn to feel at home again in Japan. For example, she accompanies him to theatrical and musical performances and sumo wrestling matches. When he visits his former teacher and priest, he is told that he must learn to look not only forward to Western modernity but also back at Eastern traditions. Initially appearing in Western garb and with eyes only for Gerda, Teruo dons traditional Japanese dress more frequently as the film proceeds, at first when visiting his family home, where he is reminded of his love for his family and the mud of the rice paddies. By the time Gerda leaves and Mitsuko attempts suicide, Teruo finally has been primed to acknowledge his duty to his family and to marry Mitsuko.

Mitsuko, the "Samurai's Daughter" of the film's title, not only was central to its marketing[53] but also remains key to its plot and political message. Like Teruo, she needs to find a balance between tradition and modernity and despite her initial submissive appearance should not be seen as a static or one-dimensional character. As Mitsuko's actions dislodge Teruo's and the audience's assumptions, she seems to change into a character fit to join him on the road to modernity. Initially introduced to us demurely feeding park animals, and shot at times through gates and bars, Mitsuko appears to be confined by her upbringing. She almost is destroyed by her dependence on her father and on the betrothed who rejects her. In the course of the film, however, we witness her rich education in traditional and modern subjects. We find out that she has been learning German and see her wear not only traditional garments but Western dress as well. Ultimately, Mitsuko's strength and other virtues are revealed[54] and she helps Teruo learn to blend modernity and tradition (see Figure 2.5).

As in Fanck's other *Bergfilme*, here too the climax and the key to resolution take place on a mountain. The painfully long yet spectacularly beautiful scene on the volcano paints it as a sublime site of personal and national rebirth. Mitsuko's climbing the jagged, sulfurous slopes and Teruo's pursuit across diverse treacherous landscapes result, after great suspense, in marriage rather than death. Mitsuko's suicide attempt, which first seems to signal submission and resignation, becomes a demonstration of strength. She attracts the husband she desires by scaling a mountain in kimono and geta; Teruo must win *her* by braving hazardous terrain and coaxing her back from death at the crater's

Figure 2.5. *The Samurai's Daughter* screenshot, 0:25:59. Mitsuko awaiting Teruo in the hotel.

rim. Several minutes of spectacular volcanic eruption and destruction follow, leading the spectator to believe that the two have died together. Yet, eventual intermittent dissolves show Teruo carrying Mitsuko out of the smoke, and they emerge from near death to a new life together. During Teruo's convalescence (for he burned his feet after having removed his shoes to swim through a swamp) Mitsuko's und Teruo's individual well-being and relationship are renewed, which, in turn, will lead to familial and national growth. Teruo's joy when Mitsuko reveals to him that she speaks German cements their love and represents the harmony between East and West, tradition and modernity that they will find in their relationship. Mitsuko summarizes this harmony with her awkward oral conjugation of the German verb *gefallen* (to please): "I will please you; you will please me..."[55] to which Teruo responds "and you will be a good wife to me."[56] This strange and stilted dialogue in German reminds the spectator of Germany's role in Teruo's and Mitsuko's education, and its role in their rejuvenation, partnership, and in the success of the nation to which they belong. Specifically, Teruo's and Mitsuko's union and their reconciliation of modernity and tradition prepare them to colonize Manchuria, to cultivate the earth and bear children there. The political ramifications of the romantic happy ending are emphasized by the addition of two final scenes: one at Teruo's father's farm, where, overlooking the rice terraces, he speaks of Japan's long history and tradition and that now the Japanese are too many for the limited soil of their islands; the second showing Teruo farming land in Manchuria, with Mitsuko and their new infant, watched over by a soldier.

Despite its ham-handed ideological messages and torturously slow pace, remarked upon by a number of critics, including Joseph Goebbels,[57] *The Samurai's Daughter* had broad audience appeal in both Japan and Germany. In large part, elements that made Fanck's earlier *Bergfilme* internationally popular contributed to the film's success. New filmic technologies brought the landscape closer to spectators with violence and sublime beauty. For European viewers, the zoom in on Japanese culture and daily life was an exotic adventure as well. The melodramatic love triangle, so despised by Fanck's critics, personalized an earthquake that shook both Japan and Germany in the late nineteenth and early twentieth centuries, the shock of rapid modernization and its perceived challenge to cultural traditions. The personalization of that shock and Fanck's bringing of the sublime, exotic, and traditional back within the public's reach, I would argue, must have constituted a large portion of this transnational production's appeal.

Notes

1. Janine Hansen reveals details that question Fanck's assertion on who invited whom. See Janine Hansen, *Arnold Fancks* Die Tochter des Samurai: *Nationalsozialistische*

Filmpropaganda und Japanische Filmpolitik (Wiesbaden, 1997), 46–48. Hansen's study also illustrates, however, how important it was to Kawakita and to Japanese critics to open up the export market for Japanese films. See Hansen, *Fancks Tochter*, 62–78. Peter High also suggests that Fanck instigated the project. See Peter B. High, *The Imperial Screen: Japanese Film Culture in the Fifteen Years' War, 1931–1945* (Madison, 2003), 159.

2. Several of Fanck's *Bergfilme* had been very successful in Japan. See Hansen, *Fancks Tochter*, 7, fn. 16 Hansen, "Celluloid Competition: German-Japanese Film Relations, 1929–1945," in *Cinema and the Swastika: The International Expansion of Third Reich Cinema*, ed. Roel Vande Winkel and David Welch (New York, 2007), 189. The German trade press reported on the Japanese releases and reception of *The Holy Mountain* (1926), *The White Hell of Piz Palü* (1929), *Storms over Mont Blanc* (1930), and *S.O.S. Iceberg* (1933). See *Filme aus Japan: Retrospektive des japanischen Films 12. September—12. December 1993* (Berlin, 1993), 44, 45, 50, 58. In his memoirs Kawakita describes Fanck as having been known for *Bergfilme* such as *The Eternal Dream* (1934). See *Filme aus Japan*, 89.

3. "die Deutschen ein größeres Einfühlungsvermögen für fremde Völker hätten." Quoted from Arnold Fanck, *Er führte Regie mit Gletschern, Sturmen und Lawinen. Ein Filmpionier erzählt* (Munich, 1973), 328. The translation, like all others in this essay, is mine.

4. Bill Maltarich, *Samurai and Supermen: National Socialist Views of Japan* (Oxford, U.K.; Bern, 2005), 30, 66–67, 193–194; Arthur Stam, *The Diplomacy of the "New Order." The Foreign Policy of Japan, Germany and Italy: 1931–1945* (Sosterberg, 2003), 16–17; Hansen, *Fancks Tochter*, 5.

5. Ian Nish, *Japanese Foreign Policy in the Interwar Period* (Westport, C.T., 2002), 106–107.

6. Maltarich, *Samurai and Supermen*, 59–65.

7. Only one other Japanese-German coproduction was made in this period, *The Holy Goal* (1939), "a semi-documentary on the Olympic preparation two Japanese ski jump athletes undergo with their German coach." See Hansen, "Celluloid Competition," 190. "[N]either Ufa nor any other German film company [nor Joseph Goebbels] regarded the Japanese market as a field of expansion worth pursuing." See Hansen, "Celluloid Competition," 187–188. While Nazi film policy, as well as individual war films, music films, and newsreels, did influence subsequent Japanese film production, *The Samurai's Daughter* apparently did not leave much of a mark. See Hansen, "Celluloid Competition," 189–196; Hansen, *Fancks Tochter*, 107–122.

8. Hansen, *Fancks Tochter*, 5.

9. For a detailed analysis of the film as political propaganda, see Hansen, *Fancks Tochter*.

10. "einen Film zu schreiben, der auch in Europa und Amerika verstanden werden könne, denn … die japanischen Filmthemen [seien] im Ausland unverständlich. Aber der Film müsse dennoch in allem echt Japanisch sein." Fanck, *Er führte Regie*, 332. According to Hansen, Kawakita also saw this as the main point of the project. See Hansen, *Fancks Tochter*, 49.

11. For details about the split and the differences in the films, see Hansen, *Fancks Tochter*, 53–55; High, *The Imperial Screen*, 159–163; Michael Baskett, *The Attractive Empire: Transnational Film Culture in Imperial Japan* (Honolulu, 2008), 128.

12. Fanck, *Er führte Regie*, 353.

13. "unjapanisch," "einen echt japanischen Film." Fanck, *Er führte Regie*, 353.

14. Baskett, *The Attractive Empire*, 129–130.

15. Hansen, *Fancks Tochter*, 62–78.

16. High, *The Imperial Screen*, 162.

17. Fanck, *Er führte Regie*, 354. Similar wording about Fanck and the Japanese "soul" can be found in the Reichspropaganda Ministry's directive to the press about discussions of the film. See Hansen, *Fancks Tochter*, 57. Praise for the film's authenticity was prominent in the German press, but not the Japanese press. See Hansen, *Fancks Tochter*, 82.

18. Fanck, *Er führte Regie*, 361–363. Hansen, *Fancks Tochter*, 57–59.

19. Christian Rapp, *Höhenrausch: Der deutsche Bergfilm* (Vienna, 1997), 9–11.

20. Eric Rentschler, "Mountains and Modernity: Relocating the *Bergfilm*," *New German Critique* 51 (1 September 1990): 147–148. See also Rapp, *Höhenrausch*, 25–26.

21. Rapp, *Höhenrausch*, 95–104.

22. Rapp, *Höhenrausch*, 80.

23. Rentschler, "Mountains and Modernity," 150, 160.

24. Rentschler, "Mountains and Modernity," 145–147. See also Rapp, *Höhenrausch*, 71–83.

25. Rapp, *Höhenrausch*, 15–16.

26. "Hauptdarstellerin." Hansen, *Fancks Tochter*, 7.

27. Rentschler, "Mountains and Modernity," 138–140.

28. Rentschler, "Mountains and Modernity," 142. See also Rapp, *Höhenrausch*, 9.

29. Rentschler, "Mountains and Modernity," 153–161.

30. Matthias Fanck, *Weisse Hölle—Weisser Rausch. Arnold Fanck: Bergfilme und Bergbilder 1909–1939* (Zurich, 2009), 157.

31. Maltarich studies National Socialist discussions of "historical parallelism" between Japan and Germany. See Maltarich, *Samurai and Supermen*, 224–243.

32. Maltarich, *Samurai and Supermen*, 96.

33. Maltarich, *Samurai and Supermen*, 146.

34. Hansen, *Fancks Tochter*, 37.

35. The association of Gerda and Germany with the West is inconsistent with the dominant National Socialist view, as described by Bill Maltarich, of Germany being, like Japan, against the West and the modernity and capitalism embodied by the United States and Great Britain. See Maltarich, *Samurai and Supermen*, 18.

36. Maltarich, *Samurai and Supermen*, 38–42.

37. See Maltarich on "Blut und Boden." Maltarich, *Samurai and Supermen*, 131–140.

38. Hansen, *Fancks Tochter*, 47. *The Samurai's Daughter* bears an obvious kinship to "Heim ins Reich" (return to the Reich) films like *The Prodigal Son* (Der verlorene Sohn, Luis Trenker, 1933–34) as well.

39. Whereas throughout the film modernity is construed as a storm striking Japan from the West, few clues are given as to what the storm striking Germany from the East might be. Interpreted in its political context, this puzzling comment could refer to the perceived threat of Bolshevism from the Soviet Union, located east of Germany and west of Japan, which the contemporaneous German-Japanese Anti-Comintern Pact was intended to combat.

40. "Es fallen die zarten Blüten/ der Kirsche schwebend zu Boden,/ Um Raum zu geben/ der drängenden Frucht."

41. "Es naht eine Flut/ von Westen –/ Die löst die Bande/ der Familie./ Und die Söhne verneigen/ Sich nicht mehr –/ Vor ihren Vätern."

42. Harry Harootunian, *Overcome by Modernity: History, Culture, and Community in Interwar Japan* (Princeton, 2000), xvi–xvii.

43. Harootunian, *Overcome by Modernity*, xvii.
44. Maltarich, *Samurai and Supermen*, 114.
45. Maltarich, *Samurai and Supermen*, 141–148.
46. "Roberts nur Blond."
47. Irene Guenther, *Nazi Chic? Fashioning Women in the Third Reich* (Oxford, U.K., 2004), 106.
48. Hansen, *Fancks Tochter*, 84.
49. Hansen, *Fancks Tochter*, 39.
50. Baskett, *The Attractive Empire*, 127.
51. Baskett reads this scene as symbolic of Teruo's indecision between "traditional" and "modern" and "a general desire for urban, modern life itself." Baskett, *The Attractive Empire*, 127.
52. Harootunian, *Overcome by Modernity*, xvii.
53. The German title drew on exotic, sexualized stereotypes of Japanese women. Such pandering became even more direct when the film was re-released in the early 1940s with the title "Die Liebe der Mitsu" (Mitsu's Love). Although the Japanese title, *The New Earth*, puts Japan's colonial ambitions at the fore, Japanese audiences and critics gravitated to Mitsuko, and the film served as a star vehicle for Setsuko Hara.
54. Hansen, *Fancks Tochter*, 37.
55. "Ich werde dir gefallen. Du wirst mir gefallen."
56. "Und du wirst mir eine gute Frau sein."
57. Hansen, *Fancks Tochter*, 58.

CHAPTER 3

Prussians of the East
The 1944 Deutsch-Japanische Gesellschaft's
Essay Contest and the Transcultural Romantic

SARAH PANZER

In the emerging field of Asian German Studies, the shadow of the German-Japanese relationship looms large, even if it is still only partially understood. The alliance between Japan and Germany during World War II has been a subject of ongoing debate among historians—was it really just a marriage of geopolitical convenience, a "hollow alliance" in the words of one author, or did it reflect a deeper commonality politically or culturally?[1] During the spring of 1944, the *Deutsch-Japanische Gesellschaft*, an organization devoted to expanding and enriching social and cultural contacts between the two nations, gave the German people an opportunity to define the purpose and utility of the alliance for themselves. A short notice in the 16 March issue of the *Völkischer Beobachter*, the newspaper of the German National Socialist Party (NSDAP), announced an essay contest sponsored by the DJG with the theme: "What binds Germany and Japan together in the fight against the United States of America a.) Politically b.) Economically and c.) Culturally?" The essays, in order to be eligible for a prize, were required to be between eight and fifteen typed pages in length. In each of the three categories, cash prizes were to be awarded for first, second, third, and fourth place; first place, in addition to being published, was to receive 3,000 RM, second place was allotted 1,000 RM, and third and fourth place were worth 500 RM each.[2] These generous prizes, which were highlighted in several of the contest's other advertisements, point to the significance accorded this exercise in public participation by the DJG as well as by its silent partner, the Foreign Office.[3]

The *Deutsch-Japanische Gesellschaft* was formed in November 1929 as a public society dedicated to deepening the German-Japanese relationship and to improving German knowledge about Japan and Japanese culture.[4] The group was reorganized in 1933 after the expulsion of several high-profile Jewish members, and throughout the 1930s and 40s an increasingly cooperative relationship with both the Ministry of Propaganda and the Foreign Office, prompted as much by generous funding as by ideology, meant that events and activities sponsored by the DJG often emphasized propagandistic utility over accurate information. What the participants in the 1944 essay contest could not know was that the initiative for the competition did not originate with the DJG, but rather the Foreign Office. In a 24 February circular marked confidential, the Berlin headquarters of the DJG informed its regional branches of the motivation behind the upcoming essay contest: "By request of the Foreign Office, the *Deutsch-Japanische Gesellschaft* will soon announce an essay competition, which will help in collecting effective opportunities for propaganda in the collaboration between Germany and Japan. The fact that we are organizing this competition at the request of the Foreign Office is to be strictly kept from public knowledge."[5] The question arises why this involvement by the Foreign Office, although not surprising given its relationship with the DJG, was to be kept secret. The circular specifically mentions propaganda as one of the main purposes of the contest; in all likelihood the Foreign Office wanted to use the submitted essays in order to gauge the effectiveness of propaganda about Japan and the German-Japanese alliance. This information could then be used to inform and direct new propaganda campaigns for officials and media outlets.

If the purpose of the contest was to assess the German public's reception of government-sponsored propaganda, the results suggest that the state's propaganda was not always entirely persuasive. Although many of the essayists, consciously or not, echoed tropes and themes from published monographs and periodicals, their feelings about the effectiveness of such materials in conveying information was decidedly ambivalent. Unteroffizier Arthur Schulze explains in a letter accompanying his essay that, in his opinion, although it should be the duty of every German soldier to understand the *Weltanschauung* of his nation and why it is fighting the current war, the official state propaganda is unfortunately often written by the educated in language too complicated for the common man.[6] Anni Haderer, a war widow from Ennstal, refers to a similar sense of disconnect between the propaganda generated by politicians and scholars and the thoughts and sympathies of the common German: "When I read about your competition, my first thought was that only scholars, politicians, and individuals with advanced knowledge and skill were capable of handling this topic. Yet the longer I thought about it—and I could not let it go—the more I came to the realization that the voices of ordinary people should make themselves heard here too, in order to show the leading figures of the allied nations that their alliance, their common goals, and their common fight was supported by the will and the understanding of the *Volk*."[7] If the Foreign Office intended the essay contest to act as a source of feedback for the propaganda created and disseminated from above, comments like this from the essayists suggest that they saw their essays as an alternative model of "civic propaganda," created by the people for the people.

Because of this reinterpretation, the tone of the essays is often polemical rather than reflective, with clear and inviolable distinctions drawn between cultured and honorable Germans and Japanese and their American enemies, depicted as little better than gangsters. The atrocities and war crimes committed by both the German and Japanese militaries obviously give the lie to this rhetoric, but the essayists remain mostly silent about the culpability of their own troops, preferring instead to focus on a romanticized and heroic past. The contrast between the valorization of German and Japanese martial ethics by average Germans and the actual behavior of German and Japanese officers and servicemen, whether toward civilians in China and Eastern Europe or allied POWs, is striking to the present-day reader. We can and will certainly identify telling silences in how the essayists write about the conflict, but it is difficult to gauge just how much they actually knew, or to what extent they believed their own rhetoric. Therefore, this piece constitutes primarily an attempt to reconstruct how they understood the German-Japanese alliance, its significance and purpose.

This civic propaganda can tell us a great deal about the existing German image of Japan and Japanese culture during the Third Reich. Even a brief perusal reveals recurring tropes and themes. The statements made about the United States, its culture and history, are intriguing and deserve further scrutiny. Yet the parallels drawn between Germany and Japan demonstrate a much more active engagement between the essayists and state-generated propaganda. Of the various links identified between German and Japanese culture, one of the most pervasive can be summarized by the concept of *Soldatenvölker*. Although not the only way in which the essayists construct a link between the Germans and the Japanese, the idea of two peoples singularly identifiable by their martial spirit is by far the most popular argument for cultural affinity.[8] A participant from Osnabrück chose to answer all three categories in the most direct way possible: "For 1, 2, and 3: soldierly spirit [*Soldatengeist*]."[9] Leo Feichtenschlager is a bit more forthcoming in his articulation of this idea: "Germany and Japan may rightly call themselves *Soldatenvölker*. They are both *Soldatenvölker* just as much from a thousand-year old tradition as from an always self-propagating upbringing. A *Volk* cannot be raised as true soldiers if they do not carry the avocation within themselves."[10] The essayists, by linking German and Japanese culture and history in this specific way, are voicing a distinct variant of discourse about the non-Western world that is neither orientalist nor exoticist; rather, it represents a form of transcultural romanticism constructed around idealized images of masculine heroism.

Whereas national romanticism was often deployed in the nineteenth century in order to define nations as distinct and unique, the relationship between Germany and Japan during the first half of the twentieth century gave rise to a particular rhetoric of commonality. Unlike orientalism or exoticism, both predicated on obvious boundaries of cultural difference, the language and tropes deployed in Germany by both German and Japanese intellectuals, thinkers, and scholars explicitly sought to make Japanese history and culture more immediately recognizable and familiar to a German audience. Yet the symbols deployed were largely drawn not from the modern world, but from a romanticized medieval past. This romantic vision of Japanese culture was over-whelmingly coded as masculine, martial, and heroic; if the French *Japonisme* of the eighteenth and nineteenth centuries was constructed around images of the geisha and teahouses, the German *Japonismus* of the twentieth century was built on the samurai and bushido, martial arts and *seppuku*. This creative re-construction of Japanese history and culture served as the foundation to the transcultural romanticism that defined a dominant German image of Japan during the first half of the twentieth century, an image that predated the Third Reich and was not necessarily predicated on the regime's political or racial ideology. The essayists drew upon a repository of existing cultural tropes and associations in order to suggest a relationship of kindred spirits between Ger-man and Japanese culture; for the surprisingly diverse community of Germans interested in Japanese culture at least, the alliance between Germany and Japan during World War II was not strategic but rather an expression of common values and goals.

The Essays

The results of the essay contest were, by all accounts, better than expected. Of the 420 essays submitted that met the eligibility criteria, 122 addressed the political question, 42 the economic question, 57 the cultural question, and the remaining 199 attempted to cover all three categories in some fashion.[11] What impressed the DJG officials even more was the high proportion of essays submitted by servicemen (205 essays); in looking through the essays it is not at all uncommon to read designations of the essayist's current locations such as "On the Front," "In the East," or "Onboard." The contest's judges were also impressed by the overall quality; Herbert von Dirksen, a former German am-bassador to Tokyo and the president of the DJG's branch in Breslau (present-day Wrocław), was struck that so many military men had submitted excellent work, considering the difficulties of life on the front. He also commented on the uniformly good standard of analysis among the essays submitted by civil-ians, although he noted that many of them suffered from "the tendency of the German to write too much and his love of detail."[12] The demographic compo-sition of the essayists was also much more diverse than would be otherwise suspected, with essays submitted by contributors from all over the Reich as well as from allied nations in a few cases, by multiple female essayists, and by individuals with markedly different levels of education and training. Most of the essays survived the war and are kept at the Bundesarchiv in Berlin-Lichterfelde; the prizewinning essays, however, seem to have been lost during the attempt to have them published.[13]

One of the most immediately apparent ways in which the conceptualization of the Germans and the Japanese as *Soldatenvölker* finds support is through the use of symbolic language and imagery. The samurai and the ethical system of bushido function as the Japanese equivalents to the Germanic/Teutonic knight and his code of chivalry. Rudolf Haake from Kauen makes the comparison explicit: "What we Germans understand by gallantry and chivalry is expressed for the Japanese in 'bushido.' It is almost even more honorable for the Japanese to die a hero's death for the *Vaterland* than it is for us Germans."[14] Similar comparisons between the samurai and the German knights appear in many of the essays; Major G. Neicke's essay on culture in particular makes repeated use of this symbolic bridge between the German and the Japanese martial spirit.[15] Another example appears in the essay submitted by Oberleutnant Rolf Seeber from Jüterborg, in which he states that "[i]t is to be found foremost in both *Völker*, this specific soldierly tradition, which was expressed in Japan in the samurai and in Germany in the medieval knight."[16] In these essays and many others, the root of the comparison between Japanese and German culture is specifically located in martial traditions, which are inscribed with specific moral qualities and forms of behavior. Indeed, in most of the essays the role of the samurai as an ethical role model, with bushido as the code of behavior, provides the dominant theme.

The historical understanding of samurai and bushido was repeatedly modified and re-inscribed by various Japanese nationalist groups during the nineteenth and twentieth centuries; rather than the complex and evolving institutions that they were, their public image became symbolically reified by the legacies of tragic romantic figures like Saigô Takamori and General Nogi Maresuke.[17] The German essayists' understanding of bushido is ultimately a mirror image of this romanticized re-imagining of bushido as a historically static code of martial ethics, an image created in part through the active intervention of nationalist Japanese professors and intellectuals living and working in Germany. The virtues of bushido, taken together, are placed in parallel with German chivalry (*Ritterlichkeit*) in the same way that the samurai are compared to the medieval knight. The virtues invoked appear fairly consistently throughout the essays, with their value clearly understood as self-evident. A good example of this rhetorical maneuver can be found in the essay of Wilhelm Arp, an *Arbeitsführer* from Gablonz, who explains that the alliance between Germany and Japan was inevitable as "[b]oth here and there loyalty and obedience, camaraderie and sacrifice, disregard of the self, bravery and courage in the face of death, severity and resoluteness can all be found together, purity and clarity the likes of which is only still to be found among the peoples that have already found their way to us."[18] Most of these virtues figure repeatedly in the essays, along with "preparation and readiness for anything, strict self-discipline and composure, a high feeling of honor and duty, tough yet respectful conduct during war, chivalry toward the defeated foe,"[19] "loyalty unto death, bravery, courage, willingness to sacrifice for the *Vaterland* combined with a modest lifestyle,"[20] or "soldierly discipline, this vigil for duty, sacrifice, order, right, and cleanliness."[21] In every case, these virtues are worthy not just in and of themselves, but because they are common to both the Germans and the Japanese. In identifying and listing these traits and attributes, the essayists are reifying a presupposed spiritual affinity between the German and Japanese peoples that is specifically oriented toward what one may call romanticized martiality.

According to the essayists, the shared *Ritterlichkeit* of the Japanese and the Germans not only brings them closer together but also distinguishes them from other peoples and nations. Several of the essays use the original three-way relationship (Germany/Japan versus the United States) in the essay prompt in order to draw a clear distinction between the imagined soldierly spirit of the Japanese and German armed forces and their American counterparts. Hans-Georg Bennecke, a conscript at the Ministry of the Reich's Air Force in Wilhelmshorst, mentions that in American propaganda the martial virtues upon which the Germans and Japanese pride themselves are radically reconfigured as "a lust for war, bloodthirstiness, or dissoluteness," which he dismisses as slander so ridiculous as to be laughable.[22] Dr. Hans Thierbach from Breslau also addresses the differences between the average German or Japanese soldier and his American counterpart: "The American has no idea that the true warrior avoids that kind of fanatical hate, that he is chivalrous toward defeated foes and gracious to the weak, because his land never had an aristocracy of the sword (*Schwertadel*). He can imagine a true warrior only as a mercenary, who suppresses with brutal violence peaceful people. Yet precisely in this area of martial ethics are the deep connections between Germany and Japan."[23] As he clearly states, it is the shared tradition of chivalry that brings the Germans and Japanese together, yet it is also this adherence to a higher form of soldierly responsibility that makes them appear so threatening to other peoples, who lack the historical education to distinguish between a principled warrior and an amoral thug. This shared history of a martial aristocracy, enlightened practitioners of a noble and heroic code of behavior in war and in peace, allowed each nation to flourish culturally and then to find the other in the wasteland of modern civilization. Although it may seem questionable to deploy class-based institutions as evidence of a national ethos, this is precisely what many essayists do, the most common assumption being that the samurai/knights functioned as aspirational figures for the rest of the nation. Oberfähnrich Hempel embeds this basic idea into the historical narrative of Japan's modernization to great effect:

> When the Shogunate was abolished and the many daimyos, partly voluntarily and partly through force, relinquished their autonomy in favor of the imperial concept, hundreds of thousands of samurai became superfluous overnight. They literally became homeless with their families…. Thus Japan's noblest estate, its ruling stratum, fell into horrible external destitution. They used every means that could be reconciled with honor, and they succeeded…. The scion of old samurai families became an officer, a bureaucrat, a diplomat, a businessman, an academic, a teacher, and an entrepreneur; in short, he pushed into all professions and brought thereby the composure and the spirit of the Japanese elite in its very essence to the *Volk*. The rulers [Herren] did not descend into the *Volk*, rather they raised the entire *Volk* up into rulers.[24]

This is the key to the repeated references to the samurai and bushido in the essays: an aristocratic ideal which becomes broadened into a national ethos only comprehensible from within or by similarly inclined *Soldatenvölker*. Arthur Schulze, the essayist mentioned above who criticized much of the state's propaganda as too complicated for the average man, summarizes this argument of a popularized aristocracy quite nicely: "Because the Japanese *Volk*, like us, … had a knighthood, which was called the samurai, and because those samurai gave the Japanese *Volk* a code to live by just as our knights gave to us, the Japanese are a working *Volk* and a martial *Volk* that loves and honors its heroes—in short, it is a *Soldatenvolk* like us."[25] A martial and heroic spirit, transmitted from above and willingly emulated by the broader population, is ultimately what makes both Germans and Japanese *Soldatenvölker* and binds them together culturally.

A variation of this idea can also be found in the repeated reference to the Japanese as the "Prussians of the East." This slogan, which was popular in contemporary German writings about Japan, functioned in much the same way as the comparisons between the samurai/bushido and the Germanic knights and the extrapolation that an aristocratic system of moral behavior, heavily coded as martial and masculine, was transmitted to the nation and became the basis for a shared spirit of honor and heroism. Johannes Barth is one of the many essayists to employ the slogan: "It is well known that the same soldierly spirit prevails in Japan as in Germany and the Japanese are not called the Prussians of East Asia for nothing. On both sides can be found the same regard for the rank of soldier; here and there it is an honor to wear the 'bunten Rock.'"[26] In much the same way as the alignment of the romanticized images of knight and samurai, the reading of "Prussian-ness" in this context is highly idealized and revolves around several key symbolic reference points: Frederick the Great, Otto von Bismarck, the Prussian officers corps. A Gefreiter Küppers complicates this association somewhat by identifying a form of visceral animosity that confronts all "Prussians":

> The people like to speak of the Japanese as the "Prussians of the East," and as is common for such popular slogans, it happily simplifies for the informed a complicated reality. The slogan *Prussians of the East* indicates to us a fixed point, from which we can take a position on the question posed: the world's hate burns against the potent *Preußentum* in the German Empire and the enemy's propaganda launches their agitation campaigns against us to good effect with the known French saying: "La Prusse, c'est le crime de l'Europe," (Prussia is the crime of Europe). And the *Preußentum* of the East in the form of heroic Japan is quite similarly, especially for the USA, the great bone of contention. Japan's political self-reliance and the methods it has been forced to use in order to preserve this freedom, so similar to those used by Germany, are for the Americans "the crime of East Asia."[27]

Within both constellations of martial symbolic imagery, whether medieval knight/samurai or the more modern Prussian empire and its Japanese equivalent, the tendency is to deemphasize any historical or cultural differences between Germany and Japan in order to idealize both traditions as heroic and worthy of shaping their respective nation's spirit. At the same time, Germany and Japan are clearly separated out from other *Kulturvölker*, both in Asia and in Europe.

A slightly different strategy in arguing for a unique relationship between German and Japanese culture is the recitation of well-known mytho-historical events or stories.[28] Like the symbolic language discussed above, the historical events most popular are overwhelmingly martial. By far the two most frequent reference points are *Chûshingura*, or *The Tale of the 47 Ronin*, and the Mongol invasions of the thirteenth century. *Chûshingura* is one of the most famous and enduring pieces of the Japanese dramatic canon; based loosely on historical events it tells the story of forty-seven ronin (masterless samurai) attempting to redeem their dead master's honor by murdering the man responsible for his disgrace and forced *seppuku*, that is, ritual suicide. Due both to its continuing popularity in Japan and its dramatic content, *Chûshingura* became the Japanese theatrical piece most often adapted for the German stage during the first half of the twentieth century.[29] It is therefore not surprising that many of the essayists were aware of *Chûshingura*'s basic plot, characters, and themes; what is more interesting is the way in which the essayists integrated the kabuki piece into their larger argument about German and Japanese cultural affinity. *Chûshingura* becomes the "Japanese *Nibelungenlied*," with a series of direct comparisons between plots, characters, and themes drawn in order to support, again, the contention that the Germans and the Japanese are both *Soldatenvölker*.

The connection between *Chûshingura* and the *Nibelungenlied* is presented by many of the essayists as immediately obvious; both stories deal with the problem of reconciling tensions between honor and duty, between loyalty to a leader and adherence to the law.[30] Gefreiter Karl Buttgereit from Vienna gives one of the simpler formulations of the issue (and makes an error regarding the number of ronin): "In Japan the story of the 49 ronin speaks of loyalty and honor just as the Nibelungen- and Gudrunlied does in Germany."[31] Similarly, an unnamed essayist from Wiesbaden draws a connection between Hagen von Tronje's sacrifice of his personal honor by killing Siegfried and Yuranosuke's role as the leader of the forty-seven ronin, which forces him to publicly dishonor himself in order to evade suspicion.[32] Ultimately, however, both figures prove themselves as honorable. Obergefreiter Wilhelm Kobsa, an engineer writing from the Russian front, creates one of the more elaborate series of correlations between the two stories:

> In Japan, as in Germany, the heroic exists in numbers among the oldest creations. The Nibelungenlied of the Japanese, the drama "The Treasury House of the Loyal 47," shows such related motifs that it substantiates a similar intellectual attitude in the Japanese and the German past. A document of the *Samuraigeist* here, heroism in the Nibelungen epic there. Unwavering, all-suffering fealty, the resolution to avenge the honor of the prince, whether called Asano or Gunther, whether it is the ronin Dischi [Yuranosuke] or the liegeman Hagen who emerges as avenger, in Etzel's castle the Nibelungen fought and in Kari's palace the Ronin fulfilled their oath.[33]

The concept of fealty unto death in the service of a higher calling is ultimately what most of the essayists who refer to *Chûshingura* find most appealing. Like the *Nibelungenlied*, the Japanese play is a tragedy that requires the death of its protagonists in order to reconcile the tension between honor and loyalty.

The question of a heroic death is therefore at the forefront of these references to *Chûshingura* and the *Nibelungenlied*. Obergefreiter Joseph Gassen from Breslau chooses to focus on death as an abstract principle. He writes, "We found it difficult as children that Siegfried had to be slain, despite being more sympathetic to us, and yet the principle lay somewhere else entirely. The hero Siegfried had to fall in order to satisfy the basic idea of absolute fealty by Hagen toward his king."[34] In much the same way, the deaths of Yuranosuke and his fellow ronin appear necessary in order to uphold the principle of loyalty. Major Albert Kropp focuses specifically on the ideal of a heroic death: "The story of the 47 ronin or of the 47 loyalists is to the Japanese *Volk* a national property like the Lay of the Nibelungen is to the German nation. Loyalty to the death!… seppuku! The upbringing to self-discipline and *Todesverachtung* reached its height in the cult of self-disembowelment."[35] His invocation of *seppuku* as the ultimate expression of an honorable death reflects an interest shared by many essayists in the Japanese attitude toward death and dying and what this revealed about the ideology and morals of Japanese culture. The practice of *seppuku*, ritual self-disembowelment, also popularly known as *harakiri*, was a source of endless fascination. Gefreiter Hasso Härlen's essay contains one of the longest and most descriptive discussions of *seppuku* as a particularly Japanese martial institution:

> With this perspective we must seek to understand the readiness for death of the Japanese; as Europeans we will perhaps not fully succeed. Above all we must be on guard against the common opinions about harakiri: it is not an expression of complacency toward death and pain, which would ease the resolution to commit suicide. Its nature lies much more in that suicide by harakiri has found a completely authoritative form, a strict ritual, which is much more adapted toward making the decision to commit suicide more difficult rather than easier. Harakiri is not easy, and whoever makes a mistake in any way invites shame upon himself and his clan. On the other hand, however, the correctly completed harakiri is suited to redeem shame.[36]

Härlen here is clearly speaking about *seppuku* with admiration, yet unlike samurai/bushido, *seppuku* has no clear German equivalent. Major Neicke compares *seppuku* to the German duel, but this is a strained comparison, to say the least.[37] Coupled with the interest in *seppuku* as a ritual for restoring an individual's honor is a German curiosity about the apparent willingness of the Japanese to sacrifice themselves without fear or doubt. This *Todesverachtung*, or disregard for death, is invoked many times, often in a tone of envy or awe. Paul Lehmann from Jena notes that "[i]n terms of the surrender of life in wartime the sober matter-of-factness of the Japanese readiness for death seems to exceed even the German willingness to sacrifice."[38] Japanese fortitude in the face of death appears as something to be admired and emulated. Interestingly enough, the consolation prize awarded by the DJG was a copy of Erwin Bälz's *Über die Todesverachtung der Japaner*; clearly, this was an attitude encouraged by the Nazi state.[39]

This attitude toward death also shapes some of the comparatively rare references to the current conflict, which is often noticeable only by its absence. The essayists castigate American war conduct, like the bombing of German cities, yet rarely offer a contemporary counter-example of German or Japanese *Ritterlichkeit*; whether this is due to a growing public awareness of the two militaries' complicity in atrocities is hard to verify, although it seems a possibility. The points at which the essayists do choose to discuss German or Japanese actions in the wars of the twentieth century tend to focus on the manners of dying rather than on specific military achievements. Dr. Peter Wolter from Düsseldorf invokes images from both world wars to present military systems that are equally recognizable for their supreme dedication to the nation: "That the young Germans storm into death with the song of their *Volk* on their lips, that the Japanese soldiers allow the ashes of their fallen comrades to participate in the conquest of the enemy fortress … is in each case a distinguishing expression of the ethos of these *Völker*."[40] In effect then, the Germans and Japanese are just as unique in death as they are in life, although the possibility for individual survival seems increasingly incompatible with national victory.

The most common reference point from World War II are the Japanese suicide pilots, which the essayists describe admiringly without offering a clear German parallel.[41] Friedrich Baser uses the example of these pilots as evidence of the loyalty of the Japanese to their nation, juxtaposed against the counter-example of American "mercenary" pilots.[42] Alfred Wäsche, a German infantry-man, understands them as a model of military might: "When the German *Volk* hear of a successful sinking by the Japanese air force, which occurs when one or more pilots plunge with their machines onto the enemy's ship, without thinking of their own rescue, they admire the bravery and the heroic courage of the Japa-nese *Volk*, which is expressed in this deportment."[43] For both of these essayists, the decision by Japanese pilots to sacrifice their lives to advance their nation's military objectives, a practice we now know was more often than not socially coerced, is an instructive example for the German *Volk* regarding the dedica-tion necessary to secure victory at any cost, a sentiment increasingly shared by many of the high-ranking officials in the Nazi state. Given the quickly deterio-rating situation on both the Western and Eastern front, this rhetoric about a glorious death in battle provides a dark undertone conspicuous in several of the essays—the individual must die so that the *Volk* may live.

The Mongol invasions of the thirteenth century, in contrast to *Chûshingura*, served as a more complex subject. Not simply providing the East Asian coun-terpart to Germany, several essayists conceive of Japan as significantly more successful in terms of its national development than their own country. Rather than being defeated and politically fractured by the Mongols, the essayists ar-gue, the Japanese repelled the invasions through a combination of good luck and national fortitude—a demonstration of common purpose that the essay-ists contemplate with wistful envy. Major Kropp, already cited above, men-tions the Mongol invasions as a point of historical commonality between the Germans and the Japanese: "Genghis Khan's Mongol horde!—That was in the 13th century—The knights stood watch for the West, rent by inner disputes, in the Silesian Ostmark and stemmed the barbaric flood from the Asiatic steppes. The empire of Japan had it easier—the gods helped to defend them against the Mongols' assault—terrible storms destroyed the enemy fleets and the rest of the invaders were slain."[44] This establishes the basic narrative that many essayists use to describe the Mongol invasions; whereas Europe barely escaped complete subjugation, the Japanese decisively repulsed both invasions. Kropp attributes the Japanese success here solely to the so-called *kamikaze*, the

typhoon winds that destroyed the fleets. Ulrich Schäfer from Graz acknowledges that even with the fortunate turn of events it was ultimately "the fierce
and heroic steadfastness of the Japanese … which allowed the Japanese to completely destroy the foe."[45] He uses the two critical battles of Liegnitz (1241)
and Tsushima (1281) to illustrate the different outcomes of the Mongol military campaigns in the West and the East, noting that it was only because of
internal political problems that the Mongols did not drive deeper into Europe.
Although the Battle of Liegnitz, also known as the Battle of Liegnica or the
Battle of Wahlstatt, was long considered a victory, albeit an exceedingly narrow
one, it was neither as absolute nor as dramatic as the clashes between Japan's
forces and the Mongols—indeed modern historical interpretations have come
to consider Liegnitz a defeat for the allied European army.

Yet as with so many other symbols deployed in the service of propaganda,
the actual events are secondary to the meaning ascribed to them. These battles were deemed important by the essayists not necessarily because of what
happened, but because they could be made to fit a grander narrative about
the diverging developmental tracks of the German and Japanese nations. This
narrative maintained that although both the Germans and the Japanese are
intrinsically *Soldatenvölker*, the Mongol invasions of Central Europe and the
Japanese islands revealed, respectively, the political and social fragmentation
of the German *Volk* and the unity of the Japanese, which the Tokugawa Sho-
gunate was later able to harness in pursuance of its own strategic goals. Dr.
Erich Schneider from Dresden alludes to this view in his description of the
Mongol invasions: "Because the Japanese were already a martial *Volk* before
the Prussian state even existed. In 1281 they repelled the attack of the Mongol
Khan Kublai with a strengthened naval force, and in 1596 the Japanese regent
Hideyoshi raised an army of around a half-million men, which he sent off on
a giant fleet in order to invade Korea."[46] Whereas it took Prussian leadership
to unite Germany in the nineteenth century, Japan had successfully carried out
national military operations on a grand scale during the late sixteenth century.
Hugo Filipschek is more explicit. He explains that, "[t]he external pressure
welded the Japanese together into a *Volk* and they became favored. All the fleets
that Kublai Khan sent for the invasion of Japan were destroyed by massive
storms. From then on Japan was a *Kriegerstaat*. On the estates of the liege lords,
the 'daimyo,' the samurai, the warrior caste, grew and their rules became the
dominant moral outlook. It demanded heroism and endurance, sympathy and
the protection of the weak, as well as sacrifice for social justice."[47] Pressure from
the Asian mainland united the Japanese people as a *Soldatenvolk*, whereas the
political splintering of the Germans prevented them from reaching their true
heroic potential until much later. This key difference in the historical development of German and Japanese culture suggests reasons as to why it was Japan
in particular that appealed to frustrated German romantics—if their own past

was irredeemably marred by humiliations like the Mongol invasions or the social and economic tragedy of the Thirty Years' War, the Japanese martial past provided an unbroken legacy of national cohesiveness and purpose.

Through the deployment of symbolic signposts like samurai/bushido and references to historical events the essays suggest Japan and Germany's common destiny as *Soldatenvölker*. The narratives in the essays focus on the restoration of a heroic past as the driving impulse behind the current struggle. The alliance of Japan and Germany is judged essential because only these two countries can truly understand and sympathize with each other. Several essayists allude to the "yellow peril" rhetoric that strained relations between Japan and many Western nations during the early twentieth century so as to castigate this rhetoric as a destructive fantasy propagated specifically in order to keep Germany and Japan apart. Obergefreiter Gerhard Walleiser, for instance, writes: "The bloodcurdling fairy-tale of the Yellow Peril was invented. The most fantastic suppositions and combinations were put into the world, in order to ascribe to Japan aggressive intentions against the white race and thereby to isolate it within world politics and international business. We can now speak about it calmly; even in Germany there were many authoritative personalities that believed in this phantom. They did not see the ones pulling the strings, who went about eliminating an inconvenient nation, one just as unloved as the Germans."[48] We see here a reference to the assertion, voiced also by Gefreiter Küppers above as well as several other essayists, that Japan and Germany were two singularly unpopular countries, regarded by others as dangerous; hence the plot to keep them apart. Although Walleiser is circumspect in his description of this international conspiracy, of the Germans duped by it—note his allusion to Wilhelm II's fervent support of the "yellow peril" rhetoric—as well as of the agents behind it, other essayists are not so coy. Max Hinder from Bad Schandau makes much the same argument more bluntly. In his telling, the Anglo-American nations and European Jews not only recognized the affinity between Germany and Japan early on but also the danger in any future alliance. In response, they created and spread the myth of the "yellow peril" and of the Japanese being incomprehensible to the Western mind. The Germans, unfortunately, in their weakness, did not possess the qualities or resources to discover the truth for themselves.[49] The key to these statements is the belief that the Germans were deceived, and that any cultural misunderstandings between Japan and Germany most likely resulted from German internal weakness rather than from Japanese "exoticness" because, prior to the NSDAP's ascension to power, the Germans were detached from their true nature and spirit.

In a spirit similar to the discussions of the Mongol invasions, these arguments suggest a distinct sense of unease about German cultural stability, especially when compared to that of the Japanese. Otto Knigge relates Japan's efforts during the latter half of the nineteenth century to achieve parity with the Western Great Powers: "It was unshakeable during its seclusion because it remained true to its own soul, despite the eternal attacks on the spirit of its people. The remarkable appearance of its expansion of power came into effect during the war against China 1894/95 and against Russia 1904/5. All *Kulturstaaten* watched closely, yet none were *völkisch* enough to stand with Japan. Before World War I, Japan hoped to ally itself with Germany. It was a shame that at the time, caught in Jewish thought and distant from our race, instead of a *Volk* striving toward freedom only the 'Yellow Peril' was seen."[50] The Germans, as a fellow *Soldatenvolk*, should have been the nation to recognize Japan for what it was, yet Germany was too weak culturally and socially. Implicit in all of this is of course the notion that it was the Nazi *Machtergreifung* that returned Germany to itself and ultimately facilitated mutual recognition between the two nations. Although Japan may not have been a role model for Germany politically, there is the distinct sense in many of the essays that Japan, whether by luck or by design, had managed to enter the modern world with its culture and native spirit intact to a degree that had largely eluded Germany.

Yet despite the somewhat ambivalent judgments on Germany's past, the narratives constructed by the essayists invariably, and unsurprisingly, point toward a glorious and redemptive future. Konsul E. Timm, an employee of the Association of Dutch-Indian Firms (Arbeitsgemeinschaft Niederländisch-Indischer Firmen) in Amsterdam, comes up with one of the more elaborate narratives of German and Japanese parallel history. He relates how they were both subjected to a foreign political system and a proselytizing religion during the sixth and seventh centuries—in Japan's case the Chinese court culture and Buddhism, in Germany's case the Holy Roman Empire and Christianity—and how there was a subsequent backlash against the foreign culture and a return to cultural authenticity spurred by colonization to the northwest and northeast, respectively. Following this period of renewal both nations withdrew from the world, he argues, until they reemerged to ascent and triumph.[51] Josef Pascher, an *Oberlokomotivführer* from Vienna, remarks that "[h]ere and there a re-orientation is increasingly fostering masculine virtues."[52] Finally, Dr. Fred Fritsch ends his essay on culture with a note struck, in one form or another, by many in declaring that "[a]fter the victory two lights, the light of the north in us and the light of the east, will become one single light, two helmets will be fastened tighter and two hands will grip each other more firmly."[53] Although such platitudes are to be expected in an exercise like this, it is interesting how they fit into the larger argument of the essays. Japan is accorded the status of equal partner, not just of strategic ally: the bond between Germany and Japan is founded on a shared martial spirit forged in a medieval tradition of chivalry and dedicated to the cultural integrity of the *Volk*.

Conclusion

Even in the final months of World War II, many German social and cultural organizations were still actively promoting their various agendas. The DJG's essay contest was only one of its many events during 1944–45, yet it provides a unique perspective on how the German population interacted with, responded to, and reframed news and propaganda about the war and their East Asian ally. In examining the essays, one finds that the writers predominantly viewed Japan as a kindred martial culture; they deployed symbolic imagery, myths, and other narratives to argue for a shared identity as a *Soldatenvolk*. Moral and heroic virtues rather than race formed the basis of perceiving the Japanese. This rhetoric creates a relationship between Germany and Japan that defies the categories typically used when speaking about Western/non-Western interaction. We should therefore think of the Japanese-German dynamic as a form of transcultural romanticism, idealizing the attributes of two cultures in order to posit an intrinsic similarity. Ultimately, Japanese culture was well-suited for this variant of *Kulturtransfer* because it offered a narrative of uninterrupted cultural development and integrity that resonated with longstanding anxieties about the ruptures in German history. Given the German romantic fascination with reconstructing a lost past, whether the *Germanentum* of Tacitus or medieval chivalry, the image of Japan as having maintained its cultural coherence into the modern period was understandably attractive. The essayists built upon these associations in order to argue that Germany and Japan possessed a unique cultural understanding of each other that transcended strategic political or military planning.

Notes

1. Karl Drechsler, *Deutschland-China-Japan 1933–1939: Das Dilemma der deutschen Fernostpolitik* (East Berlin, 1964); Cornelia Freidank and Günther Krause, *Die Japaner und die Deutschen. Geschichte einer Wahlverwandtschaft* (Tokyo, 1994); Hayashima Akira, *Die Illusion des Sonderfriedens: deutsche Verständigungspolitik mit Japan im Ersten Weltkrieg* (Munich, 1982); Gerhard Krebs, ed., *Japan und Preussen* (Munich, 2002); Gerhard Krebs and Bernd Martin, eds., *Formierung und Fall der Achse Berlin-Tokio* (Munich, 1994); Josef Kreiner, ed., *Japan und die Mittelmächte im Ersten Weltkrieg und in den zwanziger Jahren* (Bonn, 1986); Johanna Meskill, *Hitler & Japan: The Hollow Alliance* (New York, 1966); Holmer Stahncke, *Die diplomatischen Beziehungen zwischen Deutschland und Japan 1854–1868* (Stuttgart, 1987); Werner Stingl, *Der Ferne Osten in der deutschen Politik vor dem Ersten Weltkrieg 1902–1914* (Frankfurt, 1978); Rolf-Harald Wippich, *Japan und die deutsche Fernostpolitik 1894–1898* (Stuttgart, 1987).
2. "Preisausschreiben der Deutsch-Japanischen Gesellschaft," *Völkischer Beobachter*. 16 March (1944): 2. Similar notices appeared in several other major German periodicals during April–May 1944, including those meant for active German servicemen, such as *Panzerfaust* and *Wacht im Südosten*.

3. By comparison, the average weekly wage in 1944 for a German male industrial worker was 42.85 marks. Gerhard Bry, *Wages in Germany 1871–1945* (Princeton, 1960), 251.
4. The earliest incarnation of the Deutsch-Japanische Gesellschaft was formed in 1888 by the philosopher Inoue Tetsujirô, who was a visiting lecturer at the Friedrich-Wilhelms-Universität in Berlin; this society, also known as the Wa-Doku-Kai, had little influence in actively shaping popular views about Japan and was ultimately dissolved in 1912 or 1913.
5. Rundschreiben an die DJG-Zweigstellen, signed by Trömel, 2.24.1944. BArch R 64IV/180, p. 91.
6. BArch R 64IV/51, p. 42.
7. BArch R 64IV/46, p. 132.
8. Despite being such a rich and complete set of source material, these essays have received relatively little attention up until now. Günther Haasch has a brief description of them and their content in his edited volume about the Deutsch-Japanische Gesellschaften. Bill Maltarich places them alongside other contemporary written sources about Japanese culture in his work *Samurai and Supermen*. Along with the heavy emphasis on German/Japanese martial culture, as discussed above, the essays also contain rich material for an analysis of the portrayal of American culture. Günther Haasch, ed., *Die Deutsch-Japanischen Gesellschaften von 1888 bis 1996* (Berlin, 1996); Bill Maltarich, *Samurai and Supermen. National Socialist Views of Japan* (Oxford, U.K., 2005).
9. BArch R 64IV/41, p. 142.
10. BArch R 64IV/44, p. 191.
11. Niederschrift über die sechste Vollsitzung des Deutsch-Japanischen Kulturauschusses, 7.20.44. BArch R 64IV/39, p. 5.
12. Letter from von Dirksen to the DJG, 6.21.44. BArch, N 2049/64, p. 14.
13. In the *Deutsch-Japanische Nachrichten* from 6 June 1944, the names of the contest's winners were announced, with a short note that there would be no first place prize for the political category because no essay had achieved a satisfactory standard of excellence. BArch R 64IV/41, p. 24.

    However this information is false; the top prize in the political category was initially awarded to Dr. Konrad Praxmarer but was later rescinded when it was discovered that Dr. Praxmarer was, at that time, being held in Dachau for sending a letter critical of the political climate in Germany to Hitler. The situation was resolved, owing to Dr. Praxmarer's chronic mental issues, which were most likely the result of five years spent in captivity in the Soviet Union. His name was suppressed in the official documentation of the contest's results, but available documentation suggests that officials in the DJG purposefully did not name a replacement winner so that they could still covertly send the first-place prize money to Praxmarer's wife and children. BArch R64IV/55, pp. 232–270.
14. BArch R 64IV/44, p. 216.
15. BArch R 64IV/53, p. 186.
16. BArch R 64IV/54, p. 117.
17. Saigô Takamori (1828–1877) was an influential samurai during the Meiji Restoration who, after leaving governmental service over a disagreement about a planned invasion of Korea, was enlisted in the Satsuma Rebellion (1877). He was killed during the Battle of Shiroyama, according to popular legend, by committing *seppuku* after being injured. Despite his role in an open rebellion against the government, he is a revered

figure in Japanese history and has often been dubbed the "last samurai." Nogi Maresuke (1849–1912) was the commanding general at the Japanese siege of Port Arthur during the Russo-Japanese War; despite the horrific casualties, including Nogi's two sons, the eventual victory made Nogi a hero in Japan. He and his wife committed *seppuku* in 1912, immediately following the death of the Meiji emperor, which posthumously made Nogi into a modern model of samurai devotion and loyalty.

18. BArch R 64IV/44, p. 108.
19. BArch R 64IV/47; p. 228.
20. BArch R 64IV/55, p. 117.
21. BArch R 64IV/52, p. 23.
22. BArch R 64IV/47; p. 112.
23. BArch R 64IV/50, p. 175.
24. BArch R 64IV/52, pp. 271–272.
25. BArch R 64IV/51, pp. 45–46.
26. BArch R 64IV/44, p. 69. The 'colored frock' is a reference to the soldier's uniform, particularly in the period of the eighteenth and nineteenth century.
27. BArch R 64IV/52, p. 21.
28. I use the phrase "mytho-historical" here to denote that, although some of the events in question did take place in one form or another, the way in which they were related had been shaped and smoothed to fit into a more conveniently romantic narrative, often, although not always, in order to suit a particular political purpose.
29. In December 1938, Erwin Toku Bälz staged a two-act excerpt from *Chûshingura* titled "Kaya no Sampei" (The Sacrificial Death of Sampei) in cooperation with the training academy for actors of the Deutsche Theater in Berlin; the piece was staged as a rhapsody in German, but with the actors performing in the traditional style of kabuki, with theatrically accurate costume and makeup. The success of this initial experiment seems to have encouraged a series of new adaptations of *Chûshingura* by German novelists and playwrights, many of whom were quite well known and successful in their own right. From 1938 to 1945 German audiences would have had access to four dramatic adaptations (Mirko Jelusich's *Samurai*, Curt Langenbeck's *Treue*, Ernst Reinacher's *Die Siebenundvierzig Ronin*, and Alfred Schneider's *Bushido*) and two novels (Arthur Ernst Grix's *Tschikara* and Hanns Maria Lux's *Die Verschwörung der 47 Samurai*) based on *Chûshingura*.
30. The *Nibelungenlied* is an epic poem from Germany's medieval past, although the content is largely based on Germanic pre-Christian myths and motifs. The story, which focuses on the death of Siegfried at the Burgundian court and the revenge of Kriemhild, was subsequently reworked during the nineteenth and twentieth centuries by artists like Richard Wagner and Fritz Lang and became a repository of popular images and associations that many Germans in 1944 would have recognized and understood.
31. BArch R 64IV/46, p. 184.
32. BArch R 64IV/46, p. 53.
33. BArch R 64IV/55, p. 99.
34. BArch R 64IV/55, p. 61.
35. BArch R 64IV/47, p. 95.
36. BArch R 64IV/52, p. 8.
37. BArch R 64IV/52, p. 187.
38. BArch R 64IV/46, p. 229.

39. Erwin Bälz was the father of Erwin Toku Bälz, whose importance in popularizing *Chûshingura* in Germany was mentioned earlier. See note 29. Bälz worked in Japan as a medical doctor for many years, served as personal physician to the Meiji and Taisho emperors, and was an instrumental figure in the founding and early years of Tokyo Imperial University's medical school. BArch R 64IV/49, p. 247.
40. BArch R 64IV/47, p. 147.
41. The kamikaze program had not yet been organized at the time of the DJG's essay contest, and so the essayists were actually referring to the so-called *jibaku* pilots, who independently and spontaneously chose to dive-bomb their aircraft into enemy ships, often due to serious damage that made the safe return of the pilots impossible.
42. BArch R 64IV/49, p. 173.
43. BArch R 64IV/52, p. 122.
44. BArch R 64IV/ 47, p. 69.
45. BArch R 64IV/47, p. 134.
46. BArch R 64IV/47, p. 196
47. BArch R 64IV/45, p. 105.
48. BArch R 64IV/52, p. 238.
49. BArch R 64IV/49, p. 190.
50. BArch R 64IV/44, p. 138.
51. BArch R 64IV/45, p. 58.
52. BArch R 64IV/47, p. 16.
53. BArch R 64IV/50, p. 169.

PART II

From 1920s Leftist Collaboration to Global Capitalism

CHAPTER 4

Otherness in Solidarity
Collaboration between Chinese and German Left-Wing Activists in the Weimar Republic

WEIJIA LI

Chinese left-wing activists living in Germany were not only observers of political developments in the Weimar Republic but in many cases also initiators of a collaboration with German left-wing activists, especially those in the German Communist Party (KPD). The interaction between Chinese and German left-wing activists was complex and went far beyond attendance at each other's political events. Occurring on both a personal and a cultural level, this interaction inspired a China-wave in German left-wing literature that is an essential and unique aspect of the China-reception in twentieth-century German culture. This encounter stimulated by the political collaboration is a noteworthy example of the flow of ideas, people, and culture across national boundaries. Thus, the collaboration between Chinese and German activists and the cultural exchange between these two groups are important research topics from the perspectives of both Chinese Studies and German Studies. Yet, despite the topic's great merit, scholars from the two fields have seldom collaborated or exchanged information on the subject.

Since the 1980s, several German scholars in Chinese Studies have attempted to examine the Chinese-German political collaboration within the context of political history. In 1988, Roland Felber and Ralf Hübner presented one of the most comprehensive studies on the political engagements of Chinese left-wing activists living in Germany. This study, entitled "Chinesische Demokraten und Revolutionäre in Berlin," revealed the institutional cooperation between the KPD and the Chinese Communist Party (CCP) by pointing out the existence of a Chinese party cell in the KPD—the so-called "Circle for Chinese Language in the Communist Party of Germany" (CCLG).[1] The study by Felber and Hübner draws upon what was then the newly published memoir of Hu Lanqi,[2] a former CCLG member who lived as a college student in Berlin from

1929 to 1933.[3] This book, published in China in 1986, became one of the most frequently cited sources in Chinese Studies on the collaboration between Chinese and German left-wing activists. However, it was not until 1996 that Frank Wagner, professor of German literature at Humboldt University, discovered Hu Lanqi's friendship with the German writer Anna Seghers, as evidenced by several photos taken in Berlin between 1929 and 1932, showing Hu together with Seghers and her children.[4] This finding was essential because it provided an indisputable example of the contact between Chinese and German left-wing intellectuals in the Weimar Republic.

More recently, another interesting and important aspect of the collaboration has been provided by Dagmar Yü-Dembski, a German scholar in Chinese Studies whose research focuses on the life experiences of Chinese immigrants in Berlin from the 1920s to the early 1930s. She profiles Chinese political activists in Berlin, highlighting their personal lives as immigrants in the German capital and their interactions with native left-wing activists. As her main sources, Yü-Dembski uses memoirs written by such eyewitnesses as Han Sen, a German-born son of CCLG member Xie Weijin, and a biography of Zhu De, a Communist student in Berlin in the early 1920s who later became commander-in-chief of the Communist army in China.[5] Recent research by Sinologist Thomas Kampen reveals similar activities of other important Chinese left-wing activists, such as Liao Huanxing,[6] a central figure in the collaboration between the KPD and the CCP.[7] Another German scholar in Chinese Studies, Joachim Krüger, emphasizes Liao Huanxing's role as a translator and writer for the German left-wing press.[8] In addition, my recent research on China-related works by Anna Seghers also indicates a personal connection between Liao Huanxing and Seghers.[9] Seghers even built into several of her literary works Liao's actual name and his personal experiences.

Despite these valuable findings, there has been little dialogue between scholars of German Studies and Chinese Studies who share an interest in German-Chinese left-wing political collaboration. This is particularly regrettable since such a conversation would have a substantial impact on scholarly inquiries anchored in transnational political history, cultural studies, and literary studies. Furthermore, due to ideological and historical reasons, along with the Eurocentric defense of the traditional German literary canon, China-related works by German-speaking left-wing writers have been overlooked and underappreciated. This lack in critical attention has not allowed for an appreciation of the remarkable differences in the representations of China and the Chinese between the works of left-wing writers and those of their contemporaries with different political backgrounds. Hence, an investigation of the German-Chinese left-wing political collaboration and its transcultural impact remains a significantly understudied topic with the potential not only to cross national borders but also disciplinary boundaries.

This essay attempts to build a bridge between Chinese Studies and German Studies in the investigation of the German-Chinese left-wing political collaboration and the transnational and transcultural flow of ideas that resulted from political activism. The subject is examined from a perspective informed by the approaches of Asian German Studies, whose investigative tools provide new transnational and interdisciplinary frameworks and narratives and thereby enrich inquiries in German Studies and Chinese Studies alike. To establish the boundaries of the discussion, I first examine the historical context of this collaboration and explore the specific motivations of both the Chinese and German collaborators in the context of political history. Drawing upon my readings of German and Chinese leftist publications, the essay then illustrates the leftist collaboration in the areas of press and education that have not been touched on by previous research in Chinese Studies. Focusing on the transcultural encounter resulting from the collaboration between German and Chinese left-wing intellectuals, the final part of the essay illuminates the genesis of what we can refer to as the China-wave in left-wing German literature during the Weimar Republic.

To illustrate the distinctive features of the China-reception in German left-wing literature, I especially discuss works by Seghers, who serves as the most persuasive example of a new trend in the China-reception of German intellectual culture at the time. I provide brief plot summaries of the works discussed, but this essay does not deliver a close textual analysis of each literary work and should not be read in the context of literary studies alone. Rather, my aim is to promote more transnational and interdisciplinary discussions on the Chinese-German relationship during the Weimar period and to shed light on the dynamics of the interplay between a political movement and a culture.

Political Collaboration between the KPD and the CCP

From 1925 to 1927, the KPD organized many demonstrations and rallies in Germany to support anti-imperialist movements in China. This time period constitutes the high point of the coordinated efforts of German and Chinese left-wing activists. The national anti-imperialist movement in China began with protests against a bloody crackdown on demonstrators by the Shanghai Municipal Police, mainly composed of Europeans and Japanese, in the city's foreign-controlled International Settlement on 30 May 1925. German and Chinese activists quickly organized a response. In June and July of 1925 alone, demonstrations took place in fourteen German cities: Berlin, Hamburg, Saarbrücken, Mannheim, Frankfurt am Main, Bremen, Leipzig, Düsseldorf, Jena, Essen, Magdeburg, Chemnitz, Dresden, and Halle.[10] All of these demonstrations, with speeches by both German and Chinese activists, were organized by the KPD and the Germany-based section of the Chinese nationalist Kuomintang Party (KMT), which had a Berlin office controlled by left-wing nationalists and Communists. As time went on, coordination between the KPD and the Chinese left-wing activists improved to a point where they succeeded in launching demonstrations in direct response to the latest developments in China.[11] Chinese sources recounting these events provide more detail on the planning of such demonstrations: first, the Association of Chinese Students in Germany, led by left-wing nationalists and Communists, would organize meetings to motivate Chinese immigrants and would distribute pamphlets on the anti-imperialist movements in China to German citizens and newspaper publishers. Some of these pamphlets also expressed sympathy for the Germans "suffering under the Versailles Treaty" as a strategy to gain their support.[12] In most cases, the Chinese left-wing nationalists and Communists then called for an initial meeting regarding the demonstrations. The KPD was responsible for most of the organizing and advertising, while Chinese activists were divided into different groups to deliver speeches at the rallies taking place in various cities. In addition to the KPD's organizations (including the Internationale Arbeiterhilfe), left-wing activists from Korea, India, Turkey, and other nations were also invited to organizational meetings and routinely asked to organize their members for participation in the rallies.[13] Throughout the late 1920s, the CCLG gradually came under the KPD umbrella, a process that deepened and extended the collaboration. As proof of this collaboration, previous research has often mentioned a photo taken during a rally organized by the KPD on 5 April 1927 in the Berliner Sportpalast, the largest meeting hall in the German capital at that time. The photo shows the CCLG member Xie Weijin presenting KPD leader Ernst Thälmann and Wilhelm Pieck, a founding member of the International Red Aid and later the GDR's first president, with two flags, one from the Chinese Workers' Union and one from the Chinese United Peasants.[14]

The integration of the CCP's section in Germany (i.e., the CCLG) into the KPD in July 1927 marked the beginning of the institutional collaboration between the two Communist parties. After the Chinese civil war started in early 1927, many CCP members living abroad returned to China to join the battle. The European sections of the CCP had to reorganize their remaining members into smaller party cells and then integrate them into the Communist parties in their host countries.[15] The CCLG kept its relatively independent status while reporting both to the Chinese representative in the Comintern and the Central Committee of the KPD.[16] Members of the CCLG were strictly Chinese Communist students.[17] According to Hu Lanqi's memoir, the CCLG had nine members by the end of 1932.[18] Besides attending meetings and rallies organized by local party cells and the KPD's Central Committee, the CCLG was also involved in other political activities under KPD leadership.

The "China-Driven" Motivations of the Collaboration

Besides shared ideological values, there were some "China-driven" motives that brought the left-wing activists from Germany and China together. Major incentives lay in the political struggles both Communist parties faced during the late 1920s and early 1930s in the two countries. The KPD had to confront the National Socialist German Workers' Party (NSDAP), whose emergence and growth posed a threat to the KPD's very existence. According to the Comintern's "ultra-left" policy, the KPD was required to work with Communist parties from other countries rather than with the Social Democratic Party of Germany (SPD) and Socialists in Germany, whom it attacked as "social fascists."[19] In addition to offering the possibility of a cohesive working relationship, the Chinese Communists possessed valuable knowledge in regard to confronting opposing parties in critical situations. Unlike the KPD, which focused its energy mainly on the German parliamentary front, its Chinese counterpart had been organizing military struggle. In 1927, the nationalist Field Marshal Chiang Kai-shek had purged Communists from the United Front against warlords in China. In response, the CCP organized several uprisings against Chiang Kai-shek and his army, which initiated a civil war between the KMT and the CCP (1927–37). For the Comintern, China's revolution was of crucial importance for the worldwide Communist movement. Coordinated by the Comintern, the KPD expected to gain solidarity from the CCP and, more importantly, to learn from the experiences of its Chinese counterpart for future battles against the NSDAP. An article in which former Berlin CCLG member Wang Bingnan reports on one of his meetings with Ernst Thälmann between August and September of 1932 proves the existence of this policy.[20] According to Wang, Thälmann was closely following the latest developments of the civil war in China, and he asked Chinese Communists in Berlin to take part in meetings of the KPD's local party cells in order to report on the "experiences and the lessons" learned by the CCP in the civil war.[21] Thälmann also asked the CCLG to assign a member who should regularly write reports on the Chinese civil war for the newspaper *Die Rote Fahne* (The Red Flag), the central publication of the KPD. Thälmann pointed out that the KPD should learn from the war experiences of the CCP in preparation for an underground battle that would ensue once the KPD lost its legal status.[22] However, the CCP's potential as a role model for the KPD was not its only draw.

Beyond the immediate political situation in China, the country's history and culture had constituted a source of genuine fascination to Western intellectuals since the early modern age. At least since the Enlightenment era, however, the European image of the country frequently also comprised strong elements of self-projection. From the interest in Confucius's teachings in the eighteenth century to the condemnation of China as a "police state" at the beginning of the nineteenth century, or from the chauvinistic depiction of China as the "Gelbe Gefahr" (Yellow Peril) to the centuries-long enthusiasm for Chinese arts and philosophy, China consistently provided material to Europeans engaged in fashioning their own identity. German left-wing activists, in line with this pattern, found it particularly intriguing that China had experienced two revolutions within less than twenty years (1911 to 1927). When Chinese nationalists overthrew the Qing Dynasty, and with it four thousand years of Chinese monarchy, in the Xinhai-Revolution of 1911–12, politically progressive activists across Europe were riveted by the speed and significance of the transformation. For them, China had finally established a connection with the Western-centered, modern world. Europeans began to take notice of this country for something besides its classical philosophy and fine arts.

Before the young Republic of China was able to recover from political turmoil, social disorder had already given rise to various ideological and political movements whose growth drew the attention of both the left and right in Europe. With the intervention of the Soviet Union from the early 1920s onward, the Communist influence in China noticeably expanded. The political unrest occurred partly in the context of economic transformation. In the 1930s, China's industry began to develop, particularly on the eastern coast, with Shanghai as the nation's industrial center. Deteriorating working conditions in factories triggered the emergence of labor unions and workers' movements that electrified their European counterparts. When the CCP, with its army, grew into the strongest Communist power in the East during the late 1920s, China became the center of attention among German left-wing activists seeking a foreign alliance.[23] The military uprising led by the CCP as well as the subsequent civil war gained China even more attention among European Communists and left-wing intellectuals. What impressed them most was the remarkable contrast between the image of China as a static nation defined by thousands of years of ancient culture and its now constantly changing political landscape. These developments made cooperation with Chinese left-wing activists an even more compelling proposition. In addition to that, most of these Chinese activists were students at German universities, often in their early twenties, which made them an intriguing group for German left-wing activists, especially the intellectuals.

Chinese Students in Germany as Attractive Collaborators

For many Chinese students in 1920s and 1930s, studying at European universities provided not only an opportunity to learn from the West's superior science and technology, but also, and more importantly, to gain a firsthand look at the social-political models of those democratic nations that had repeatedly defeated China militarily in the nineteenth century and had discriminated against the country ever since.[24] To the extent that the decision to study in the Western world was politically driven, the active participation of Chinese students in local political movements in Germany and their overall political engagement seem logical. These activities also established the basis of cooperation between the Chinese and German left-wing activists, who both adhered to the concept of internationalism promoted by the Comintern in Moscow.

For young Chinese students seeking opportunities to study in Europe, Germany became an attractive destination after World War I. As a reward for joining the allies, China had been promised the return of the German colonies of Qingdao and Jiaozhou Bay. However, the Treaty of Versailles assigned both Qingdao and Jiaozhou Bay to Japan. The allies' betrayal sparked a Chinese nationalist and anti-imperialist reaction known as the May Fourth Movement. As Germany was no longer the target of this protest movement, the political and emotional barriers to Sino-German cultural and economic exchange disappeared, at least partially. Worldwide recognition of German universities and the relatively low cost of living in Germany after the period of hyperinflation (1921–24) also made the country attractive to Chinese students.[25] In addition, German industry and cultural institutions actively promoted the admission of Chinese students. Inspired by their French and British competitors, German companies and interest groups, such as AEG, Siemens & Halske, and the Reichsverband der deutschen Industrie (Imperial Federation of German Industry), sponsored many Chinese students.[26] During the summer semester of 1924, ninety-six Chinese students registered at the Friedrich-Wilhelms-Universität in Berlin.[27] In 1927, the Club of Chinese Students in Germany (founded in 1902) counted more than five hundred members.[28] In Berlin alone, there were more than three hundred registered Chinese students in 1931.[29] Many Germans had favorable impressions of the Chinese students because of their politeness and Confucian ethics that were believed to coincide with European humanist traditions.[30] Unlike their fellow citizens who worked in small businesses, such as Chinese restaurants, and usually lived in an exclusively Chinese community in the Friedrichshain area, the majority of Chinese students came from bourgeois families and enjoyed close contact with Germans. They preferred the Charlottenburg area and lived near Kurfürstendamm.[31]

The political environment in postwar Germany, especially in Berlin, provided an unstable yet compelling platform for Chinese left-wing activists seeking opportunities for collaboration. From the earliest days of the Weimar Republic, left-wing parties had played important roles. The KPD was the biggest legal Communist party outside of the Soviet Union and the workers' movement was becoming both the focus and the tool of left- and right-wing political parties. This intrigued left-wing activists from China, where the workers' movement was inspired by its Western counterparts, and political battles between different parties were influenced both by the West and the Soviet Union. Mirroring the political situation in China at that time, among the Chinese students in Germany there were nationalists, Socialists, Communists, and anarchists, and they often competed with and debated each other. According to a report sent by the Central Committee of the CCP to the Comintern on 13 June 1922, there were eight Chinese Communists living in Germany.[32] No later than 1923, the CCP organized a party cell in Germany consisting of the three groups of Chinese Communists in Berlin, Göttingen, and Frankfurt.[33] It is important to note that, besides the Communists, there were other Chinese left-wing activists living in Germany. For example, Cheng Qiying,[34] a well-known Socialist activist among Chinese students in Berlin, worked closely with the Internationale Sozialistische Kampfbund (International Socialist Militant League) founded by Leonard Nelson, though she was married to Xie Weijin, a Communist and an important leading member of the CCLG.[35] To gain the support and loyalty of Chinese students abroad, the KMT opened information offices in many large cities across Europe in the early 1920s. These were also intended to function as information channels between China's KMT government and the foreign media. Most of these foreign offices were run by Chinese nationalist students.[36] In Berlin, the left-wing nationalists competed against their right-wing counterparts to gain control of the office.[37] In response to the development of the United Front of the KMT and the CCP in China, Chinese Communists living in Europe joined—as individuals—the KMT's European sections in June 1923.[38] Some of them became leading members of the KMT section in Germany, for example Zhu De and Liao Huanxing, who used the KMT office in Berlin to foster collaboration between German and Chinese Communists.[39] Many of the student activists could converse fluently and even publish in German, which enabled them to play an active role in collaborating with the German left-wing activists in the areas of press and education.

Collaboration in Leftist Press and Education

In the left-wing press at the time, the political collaboration between the KPD and the CCLG received a lot of coverage, as it was perceived to foster the exchange of vital information between Chinese activists and their German counterparts. The political situation in China itself, primarily with regard to the Chinese Civil War in the early 1930s, was also one of the most prominent topics in papers like the KPD's *Die Rote Fahne* and the *Arbeiter Illustrierte Zeitung* (Workers' Illustrated Newspaper or AIZ), as well as *Linkskurve* (Left-Hand Curve), the journal of the Association of Proletarian-Revolutionary Writers.[40] All of these left-wing publications reported on the KMT's and CCP's joint formation of the United Front and their military campaign against warlords in northern China from 1922 to 1927 (the so-called Northern Expedition). In July of 1929 alone, *Die Rote Fahne* published seventeen reports on the civil war in China. During Chiang Kai-shek's so-called Encirclement Campaigns between 1929 and 1931 that aimed at controlling the CCP's territories in southern China, *Die Rote Fahne* published at least one article per week on the development of the battles.[41] These reports often tried to present CCP military successes in defending its territory. Sample headlines include "Rote Armee operiert erfolgreich" (The Red Army Operates Successfully)[42] and "Weitere Siege der Roten Truppen in China" (Further Victories of the Red Troops in China).[43] Other reports portrayed the Chinese revolution since 1927 as promising a worldwide Communist movement, thus aiming to foster hope among German leftists. Such reports include "Von Sowjet-Kanton zu Sowjet-China" (From Soviet Canton to Soviet China)[44] and "Der Kommunismus in China unüberwindlich" (Communism in China Invincible).[45] In most cases, the events reported occurred just one or two days before the date of publication. There were also reports on economic developments in the CCP's Soviet zones (e.g., "Die erste Sowjet-Banknote in China" [The First Soviet Banknote in China]).[46] Notably, several reports were based on translations of Chinese texts that were either accounts of personal experiences in the revolution or official letters and telegrams to the KPD from various organizations led by the CCP. On 20 July 1929, *Die Rote Fahne* published the German translation of an article entitled "Genossin Hsü Yen, Frauenleiterin in Kwangtung schreibt der 'Roten Fahne' über die chinesischen Sowjets" (Comrade Hsü Yen, Women's Leader in Canton Writes to "Die Rote Fahne" on the Chinese Soviets). A German translation of a letter of greetings sent from the Central Committee of the First Congress of the Chinese Soviets to the KPD was published in *Die Rote Fahne* with the title "Die chinesischen Sowjets grüßen das kommende Sowjetdeutschland" (The Chinese Soviets Greet the Future Soviet Germany), along with a photocopy of the original letter in Chinese.[47] The CCP's newspaper *Hong Qi Bao* (Red Flag Daily), which circulated underground in Shanghai, sent an official letter of congratulations to *Die Rote Fahne* on its twelfth anniversary in 1930. *Die Rote Fahne* published a German version of the letter along with the original Chinese text.[48] On 24 February 1931, *Die Rote Fahne* published an article entitled "Ein chinesischer Soldat über die Rote Armee" (A Chinese Soldier on the Red Army) that is believed to have been written by a Chinese government soldier who defected to the Red Army during Chiang Kai-shek's invasion of the Soviet zones. The Chinese Communists in Berlin (i.e., the CCLG members) played an essential role in the translation and publication of these Chinese texts in *Die Rote Fahne*. They also authored several articles in the left-wing press.

Prominent figures from various left-wing groups contributed to the dissemination of information concerning left-wing interests. On 28 May 1932, *Die Rote Fahne* published an article entitled "Den Schi Chua, ein chinesischer

Student erzählt sein Leben" (Den Schi Chua, A Chinese Student Recounts His Life) that presented the political turmoil in China from a personal perspective. The author of this article is Sergei Tretyakov, whose play *Roar China!* premiered in Germany in 1930 and was one of the earliest European plays depicting China's anti-imperialist struggle at the beginning of the 1920s. Tretyakov based his article on an interview he conducted during his time as a lecturer in Russian literature at a Chinese university with an actual Chinese student, Den Schi Chua. Chinese Communist leaders also contributed to the China-focus of the German left-wing press. Between 17 December 1932 and 2 January 1933, *Die Rote Fahne* delivered a series of articles, entitled "The Red Haifeng," that detailed the establishment and development of the first rural Soviet county in China, Haifeng County. The author was the founder of the rural Soviet zone, Peng Pai, one of the CCP leaders at the time, and a peasants' rights activist. The texts in *Die Rote Fahne* were German translations of selected chapters from his book, *Haifeng Nongmin Yundong* (Report on the Peasants' Movement in Haifeng), originally published in China in 1926. Apparently CCLG members did the translation for *Die Rote Fahne*.

A central figure in the political collaboration between the German and Chinese left-wing press was Liao Huanxing. From 1923 to 1927, Liao worked undercover as the official representative of the KMT and was responsible for its information office in Berlin. At the same time, he was one of the founders of the first CCP party cell in Germany, established in 1922, and leader of the Chinese Communists in Berlin until 1928. Both Liao's activities as a Communist writer and the work of his KMT office were vital to the network of left-wing activists in Berlin. Beginning in 1925, Liao worked closely with Willi Münzenberg and the Internationale Arbeiterhilfe (IAH).[49] He helped Münzenberg organize the first international conference of the League against Imperialism in Brussels in 1927.[50] Translating and writing for the left-wing press were Liao's secondary activities. He contributed to Münzenberg's *Arbeiter Illustrierte Zeitung* and wrote regularly for the Comintern's publication, *Internationale Presse-Korrespondenz* (Inprekorr).[51] The famous American left-wing journalist Agnes Smedley worked closely with Liao's information office in Berlin, and she used this contact to obtain a substantial amount of information for her China-related reports. This collaboration also was one of the motivating forces behind Smedley's decision in 1927 to go to China, from where she reported for eleven years.[52]

The CCLG also played a unique role in the KPD's ideological education programs. As an important institution serving the KPD's propaganda strategy, Marxistische Arbeiterschulen (Marxist Workers Schools), also known as MASCH, were founded in many cities, offering workers evening courses in the sciences, foreign languages, and other practical skills, as well as in Marxist and Communist doctrine. While Laszlo Radvanyi (alias Johann Lorenz Schmidt) was the leader of MASCH for the greater Berlin area from 1927 to 1932. CCLG members were not only taking evening courses regularly but also contributing to the course offerings.[53] During the 1932–33 school year, MASCH responded to the great interest German left-wing activists had in China by offering Chinese language courses, which, not surprisingly, were taught by CCLG members.[54] Laszlo Radvanyi's family, especially his wife Anna Seghers, maintained close contact with the CCLG's only female member, Hu Lanqi.

Collaboration among left-wing activists was not confined to national or party politics. It also had a profound influence on cultural encounters between Chinese and German left-wing intellectuals. In addition to Taoism, which had fascinated many European intellectuals from the turn of the twentieth century onward, the political turmoil in China and its unpredictable outcome also drew significant attention among left-wing German sinologists in the 1920s and early 1930s. In 1922, Philipp Schaeffer, a Communist sinologist and Buddhist scholar and also a classmate of Anna Seghers in Chinese courses at the University of Heidelberg, published his essay "Der Bolschewismus in Asien" (Bolshevism in Asia) in the monograph *Washington: Verlauf und Ergebnisse der Konferenz* (Washington: The Progress and Results of the Conference), edited by his Sinology professor F. E. A. Krause.[55] Schaeffer's article was one of the earliest German publications on the development of communism in East Asian countries. In the Third Reich, Philipp Schaeffer actively participated in anti-Nazi resistance activities and was beheaded in 1943. Karl August Wittfogel was a Communist Sinologist and had studied since 1914 with prominent German Sinologists, such as August Conrady at the University of Leipzig, Otto Frank in Berlin, and Richard Wilhelm in Frankfurt am Main.[56] In 1926, Wittfogel investigated China's recent development in his monograph *Das erwachende China: Ein Abriss der Geschichte der gegenwärtigen Probleme Chinas* (The Awakening China: A Survey of the History of China's Contemporary Problems), in which he in fact went beyond a mere recounting of history to describe China's battle against Western colonial oppression as promising a brighter future for mankind. In 1927–28, Wittfogel published *Sun Yat Sen: Aufzeichnungen eines chinesischen Revolutionärs* (Sun Yat-sen: Notes of a Chinese Revolutionary), which aimed to correct some of the misinterpretations of Sun's political philosophy, as they had arisen based on an early German translation of a Russian brochure. Wittfogel's corrections and especially his comprehensive foreword make the book the first systematic German-language introduction to Sun Yat-sen, who led the Xinhai-Revolution and overthrew the Qing Dynasty. In this new edition, the translation of Sun's articles and their citations were proofread by a Chinese native, Dr. Lo Liang-Chü, at the China Institute, founded by Richard Wilhelm in Frankfurt am Main. Wittfogel further explored China's current situation from socioeconomic and historical perspectives in his comprehensive study *Wirtschaft und Gesellschaft Chinas* (China's Economy and Society), published in 1931. This seven hundred–page study represents the first volume of a more ambitious project which, however, he was not able to complete. Due to his political affiliation and anti-fascist activities, Wittfogel was sent to a concentration camp in the Emsland in 1933. He managed to escape and emigrated to the United States in 1934. After breaking with communism, he was allowed to continue his research in KMT-controlled China between 1935 and 1937.[57]

The exchange, however, of ideas across the national boundaries and the transcultural encounter between German and Chinese left-wing intellectuals not only left a mark in the areas of press and education, but also inspired a new wave of China-reception in German literature during the 1920s and 1930s.

The China-Wave of Left-Wing German Literature

As a result of the left-wing German-Chinese political collaboration, German culture experienced a new wave of China-reception. The China-reception in German culture and literature in the early twentieth century can be illustrated as follows: first, the translation and adaptation of ancient Chinese literature, notably poetry from the Tang Dynasty (618–907), by Wilhelm Grube, Martin Buber, Hans Bethge, and Klabund, etc.; second, the search for otherness in the social-historical discussion on China's past as revealed in Max Weber's *Konfuzianismus und Taoismus* (Confucianism and Taoism, 1915) and Oswald Spengler's *Der Untergang des Abendlandes* (The Decline of the West, 1917); and third, the Taoism-reception promoted by the German translation of *Dao De Jing* (Tao Te King, 1921) and other Taoist classics by Richard Wilhelm and reflected in works such as Alfred Döblin's novel *Die drei Sprünge des Wang-lun* (The Three Leaps of Wang Lun, 1916). In contrast to all these three features of China-reception, which focused on ancient Chinese culture and philosophy, the new wave of China-reception during the Weimar Republic, initiated by the left-leaning writers, was intended to redirect the attention of German readers to contemporary China. On the one hand, China's political turmoil and the escalating battles among different factions and ideologies provided German left-wing writers with rich material for their literary work; on the other hand, their personal contact with Chinese student activists ensured a more accurate portrayal of the people and the country. The writers' genuine interest in depicting people's lives and struggles in contemporary China enabled them to abandon the conventional image of China and the Chinese in the German literary tradition, which had often been created through a racist, imperialist, and orientalist engagement with the country. The focus on current political issues, the collaboration with Chinese counterparts, and the effort to create a new image of China and the Chinese are the three distinctive characteristics of the China-wave of German left-wing literature in the Weimar Republic.

Current political events like the Chinese workers' movement in the late 1920s, the Chinese civil war, and the Japanese invasions of China beginning in 1931 became the most significant topics in left-wing German literature.[58] One of the earliest literary depictions of the revolution was F.C. Weiskopf's long poem *Kantoner Kommune* (Canton Commune), written in 1927 after he had heard news on the radio of the failure of the Cantonese Soviet zone due to its military disadvantage when facing Chinese government troops.[59] Bertolt Brecht's *Die Maßnahme* (The Measures Taken, also known as The Decision, 1930), one of his most famous *Lehrstücke*, is a pertinent example of the literary reception of China's political situation among German left-wing intellectuals. This play is based on historical events. Between January and May 1929, trade unionists and even diplomats from the Soviet Union were agitating in the Chinese cities along the Chinese Eastern Railway, the northern route of which began in Mukden (today's Shenyang) and connected China and the Soviet Union. Some of these Russians were arrested on suspicion of espionage.[60] In Brecht's play, four Russian Communist agitators, who stand in front of a "control chorus" symbolizing the Communist Party, have to justify their decision to eliminate their young Chinese comrade. The Chinese comrade was assigned by the party to help the Russian Communists with secret agitation among the poor people in Mukden. However, he refused to behave in a tactical way in various dangerous situations. His premature compassion and hasty, rigid political opinions threatened to expose the identity of the agitators and thus jeopardized the cause. To ensure the uprising of local workers, the Russians had to kill their Chinese fellow agitator. However, they did so with his own agreement, so none of them would be arrested by the Chinese authorities. For several weeks during his work on the play, Brecht discussed it with Hanns Eisler, who composed songs and music for the choruses, and his brother Gerhart Eisler, who had been sent by Moscow on a secret mission to China in November 1929 where he participated in reorganizing local CCP cells in Mukden and Shanghai along the lines of classical Marxism-Leninism.[61]

A production by Erwin Piscator, based on Friedrich Wolf's play *Tai Yang erwacht* (Tai Yang Awakens, 1930) that depicted the Chinese workers' movement in Shanghai in the late 1920s, became a sensation on the Berlin stage, reported on twice by *Die Rote Fahne*.[62] In the play, Tai Yang, a young female worker in a Shanghai textile manufacturing plant, who dreams of a better life, becomes the mistress of the company owner. However, she later falls in love with a worker named Wang who is organizing a workers' uprising against the greedy company owner and his brutal rule. Wang awakens her class-consciousness and sense of dignity and helps her understand the relationship between collective interest and personal happiness. Tai Yang then becomes one of the organizers of the uprising. Wolf's intention was "to show, with the example of China, how a nation courageously and forcefully began to defend itself against capitalist exploitation."[63] In *Tai Yang Awakens*, the name of the CCP leader, Mao Tse-tung, appeared for the first time in a German literary work.

At the end of 1932, writer Egon Erwin Kisch published *China geheim* (China Secret), chronicling a journey he had made to China that year.[64] Under an alias, Kisch visited several major cities, including Qingdao, Shanghai, Nanjing, and Beijing.[65] *China geheim* presents a social-political panorama of contemporary China, describing exploitative practices by foreign capitalists as well as the civil war between the CCP and the KMT. Kisch was shocked by the poor living conditions, both in the cities and urban areas, but was also intrigued by the richness of Chinese culture and traditions. In this, he was typical of his generation of German left-wing intellectuals.

Seghers, a Sinology student at Heidelberg University from 1920 to 1924, published several essays and short stories as well as two novels between the 1920s and the 1950s depicting political, social, and economic developments in China. The short story "1. Mai Yanschuhpou" (May 1st in Yanschuhpou) was published on 1 May, International Workers' Day, 1932 in *Die Rote Fahne*. The story describes the preparation and development of a workers' uprising in Shanghai, at the time China's largest industrial district. Seghers's descriptions of the political situation of the unions and the workers' everyday lives are surprisingly accurate. Some details of the uprising are identical with those of a historical event, an uprising organized by the CCP among Shanghai workers in March 1927.[66]

In 1932, Seghers published the short story "Die Stoppuhr" (The Stopwatch), set in the context of battles between CCP and KMT forces during the civil war in the early 1930s. In this story, German military advisors in Chiang Kai-shek's army use stopwatches to train Chinese government soldiers in strict discipline and precise tactics. Ironically, when the third military campaign against the CCP's Soviet zones in the southern provinces begins, the soldiers turn their guns—precisely at the same moment, as if guided by a stopwatch—on their officers, initiating a soldiers' uprising and defection to the Red Army. The dramatic ending of this story is based on historical events, namely, several soldiers' revolts that occurred during military campaigns launched by Chiang Kai-shek's army between 1930 and 1931. Some regiments defected to the Red Army, weakening Chiang's offensives. *Die Rote Fahne* reported on 29 March 1931 that initiating soldiers' uprisings had long been a strategic policy objective of the CCP. *Die Rote Fahne* also published a German translation of a CCP-authored defection appeal aimed at Chiang's troops.[67] On 23 June 1931, the paper reported on the success of such appeals with extensive details, such as location, names of the divisions, the number of soldiers that had deserted, etc.

Seghers's next short story, "Der Führerschein" (The Driver's License), illustrates Chinese resistance against the Japanese invasion of Shanghai. On 28 February 1932, the Chinese newspaper *Shen Bao*, one of the most influential left-wing publications in Shanghai, had reported a heroic act of a Chinese man named Hu A'mao, chauffeur of a former vice-minister. When forced to serve as a driver for the Japanese, Hu A'mao plunged a military truck loaded with four Japanese soldiers and ammunition into the Yangtze River. Four months later, in June 1932, "Der Führerschein" was published in *Die Linkskurve*, with a note after the text: "Nach einer chinesischen Korrespondenz" (based on a Chinese correspondence). The protagonist is a chauffeur who experiences the brutality of the Japanese military during the First Battle of Shanghai in the spring of 1932. The Japanese soldiers capture and kill many Chinese civilians, yet they spare the chauffeur's life because his professional skills are useful. Pointing guns at the chauffeur's head, Japanese officers force him to drive a military vehicle to another place in the city. During the transport, the chauffeur witnesses how lives are destroyed and the city is shattered by Japanese occupation troops. Driving across a bridge above the Yangtze River, the chauffeur suddenly turns the wheel and the vehicle crashes at a high speed into the water. In this story, published barely one month after the Battle of Shanghai, Seghers intended to show the willingness of the Chinese to sacrifice themselves in resistance to the Japanese invasion and also to demonstrate that their motivation was not necessarily nationalism or patriotism but rather "pure conscience."[68]

Seghers's 1932 novel, *Die Gefährten* (The Fellows), presents a panorama of European and Chinese revolutionary activities in the 1920s and 1930s. The main Chinese figures of this novel are the brothers Liau Yen-kai, a seasoned revolutionary living in London and Moscow, and his younger sibling, Liau Han-tschi, a student observing the workers movement in Berlin. Both of them return to China to participate in the revolution when Chiang Kai-shek launches his military campaign against the CCP and its Soviet zones. At the end, the younger brother is captured due to a treasonous act committed by a comrade, while Liau Yen-kai, after a precarious journey, finally reaches his destination in a Soviet zone that has survived the latest attack of Chiang's troops. In this novel, Seghers vividly depicts the Limehouse Chinatown in London, the lives of Chinese students in Germany and their encounters with their German host families, activists organizing campaigns among Chinese sailors at the port of Hamburg, and the political struggles between left-wing and right-wing Chinese students in Berlin. Seghers's personal contacts with Chinese student activists in Berlin played an essential role in the creation of the Chinese themes in the novel, which to this day remains the only piece of German literature portraying Chinese political activists living in exile in Europe.

The new wave of literary works invested in a response to China's current political events emerged from collaborations between German and Chinese left-wing intellectuals. German left-wing writers like Friedrich Wolf, Egon Erwin Kisch, and Anna Seghers maintained close contact with Chinese political activists in Berlin. A member of the Association of Proletarian-Revolutionary Writers, Wolf stated that the play *Tai Yang Awakens* was based on a story a Chinese student in Berlin told him.[69] Egon Erwin Kisch's secret journey to China was arranged by CCLG member Xie Weijin in Berlin.[70] Many of Seghers's literary works are inconceivable in the absence of her relationships with Chinese left-wing intellectuals. During the Second International Conference of Proletarian and Revolutionary Writers in Charkow in November 1930, she met the Chinese delegate Emi Hsiao (Xiao San), who himself was one of the four leaders of the workers' uprising in Shanghai portrayed in her short story "1. Mai Yanschuhpou."[71]

In her essay, "Verwirklichung" (Realization, 1953), Seghers confirmed her contacts with Chinese students in Berlin in the 1920s and that they had informed her about Chiang's military campaigns against the CCP.[72] According to a report by *Die Rote Fahne* on 13 January 1933, Seghers was planning to work together with a Chinese woman, apparently Hu, on a novel depicting the development of women's rights in China.[73] At one point, Hu even lived in Seghers's Berlin home.[74] In another essay, "Kleiner Bericht aus meiner Werkstatt" (A Sketch from My Workshop), published in 1932 in *Die Linkskurve*, Seghers created a dialogue between a German writer, "S," and her Chinese colleague, "L," as they work together on the opening paragraph of a short story about a workers' uprising in Shanghai. Their conversation focuses on the purposes and methods of description in a literary text. Seghers encourages writers to participate in changing the world by carefully describing their current environment. This essay portraying the collaboration between a German and a Chinese writer is one of Seghers's most important statements of her aesthetic and political values.

My research also reveals the friendship between Seghers and Liao Huanxing.[75] In addition to the brothers Liau in *The Fellows*, Chinese protagonists in Seghers's works often carry the surname Liau. The novel *Die Toten bleiben jung* (The Dead Stay Young, 1949), which depicts the rise of the Nazis in Germany and the resistance to them, includes a Chinese figure named Han-sin Liau. The fictional name corresponds exactly to the historical Liau Han-sin. In the novel, Liau is an undercover Communist in the KMT army, trained by German military advisors in China. Liau manages to steal military secrets from one of the German officers, Wenzlow, who is the son of a Prussian officer and fascinated by the rise of National Socialism. The fictional Liau's double identity mirrors that of the historical Liao Huanxing, who was both the KMT representative and a Communist leader in Berlin.[76] Would this suggest that Seghers was familiar with Liao's functions and political engagements in Berlin? My archival research brought to light five letters that were exchanged between

Liao's German wife Dora Liao and Seghers.[77] Although these letters were written between January and April 1955, they reveal a firm friendship between Liao Huanxing's and Seghers's families going back to the 1920s. In her letter to Dora Liao, Seghers mentions that she and her husband still remember what Liao's apartment in Berlin looked like at the time, and she recalls seeing Liao's infant son in the late 1920s. Dora Liao asks in one of her letters if Seghers's husband was with her all the time during her exile in Mexico and whether her Jewish mother had survived the concentration camps.[78] This friendship explains why Seghers often named the protagonists in her China-related works Liau. Such instances of close personal contact among German and Chinese left-wing intellectuals undeniably influenced their perception of each other's culture and contributed to the keen interest some German left-wing writers developed in China and the Chinese people during that period. Seghers was so impressed by the Chinese students and intellectuals she had known in Berlin that, throughout her life, she included a China-theme in many of her works.

The political collaboration decisively influenced the perception of China and Chinese culture among German left-wing intellectuals. They abandoned the conventional image of China and the Chinese people in German literature since the Enlightenment. The country no longer appeared as Herder's "embalmed mummy."[79] Works by Friedrich Wolf, Egon Erwin Kisch, and especially Anna Seghers describe China as dynamic, trying to break free from tradition. In their works, China serves neither as a satirical miniature for a critique of Europe nor as a spiritual escape from European reality. China and its people are no longer consigned to an exotic or fairy tale-like realm, but rather exist as concrete, realistic elements of contemporary reality, firmly connected with world political movements. For more than two hundred years, from the Enlightenment era to the early twentieth century, the Chinese characters in the majority of German literary works with Chinese themes were almost exclusively, and stereotypically, Chinese emperors, monks, and philosophers. Promoted by the German-Chinese left-wing political collaboration, Chinese students, workers, soldiers, and peasants, with their hopes and fears, desires and defeats, finally appear in German left-wing literature during the Weimar years. It is important to note that it was mainly the left-wing German intellectuals who shifted their focus from classical Chinese philosophy and culture to the contemporary social and political dynamics of the country. In doing so, Seghers and other left-wing German writers purposefully confronted the Eurocentric, racist, imperialist, and colonialist perception of East Asian cultures, which dominated the German literary tradition.

The German-Chinese left-wing collaboration was significantly curtailed after the KPD lost its legal status and became systematically persecuted by the Nazis from early 1933 onward. Chinese left-wing activists either left Germany or—like their German counterparts—went underground. Contrary to what one might expect, so far no documents have surfaced confirming that there were CCP members among the approximately one hundred Chinese in Nazi concentration camps.[80] Hu Lanqi was the only CCLG member captured by the Nazis. Sentenced to three months in jail in April 1933, she was released in June and left Germany soon after.[81] The Socialist Cheng Qiying was arrested and then deported in February 1933.[82] Her husband, CCLG member Xie Weijin, went into exile with their son in Switzerland in 1933. In 1936, he joined the International Brigades and fought in the Spanish Civil War. While most of the CCLG members left Germany between 1933 and 1936, a small CCP cell remained in the country until 1937.[83] Current scholarship, however, knows very little about the possible post-1933 collaboration between the underground KPD and the remaining Chinese Communists in Nazi Germany. In the field of literature, the auspicious new trend of China-reception was interrupted by the rise of Nazi Germany and thus had only a transitory impact on the representation of China and the Chinese in German culture. Current ideological and cultural political environments are not particularly favorable to further inquiries on this subject. For example, Liao Huanxing's activities in Berlin and his role as a key figure in the German-Chinese collaboration have been purposely minimized in the CCP's official party history because he worked as the secretary of Wang Ming, Mao's rival, in Moscow after leaving Germany in 1928.[84] Therefore, Liao is rarely mentioned in studies conducted by Chinese scholars in the field of political history. On a similar note, many literary scholars often ignore the important role the China-wave of German left-wing literature had in fighting the nationalist, racist prejudice against other nations. Sadly, the left-wing political collaboration, rooted in a campaign against political oppression and economic inequality, is frequently and purposely disremembered.

Notes

1. Roland Felber and Ralf Hübner, "Chinesische Demokraten und Revolutionäre," in *Wissenschaftliche Zeitschrift der Humboldt-Universität zu Berlin, Reihe Gesellschaftswissenschaft*, 37.2 (1988), 167. The German term, "Der Zirkel für chinesische Sprache in der Kommunistischen Partei Deutschlands," is a literal translation based on Hu Lanqi's memoir.
2. This essay uses the Pinyin system for Chinese names. However, Wade-Giles equivalents are provided in the footnotes for names that appear predominantly in Wade-Giles romanization in printed publications. Chinese names appearing in newspaper articles and literary works are kept in their original form when cited in this essay.
3. Hu Lanqi, *Hu Lanqi hui yi lu (1901–1936)* [Hu Lanqi's Memoir (1901–1936)] (Chengdu, 1985).
4. Two of these photos are published in Frank Wagner et al., eds., *Anna Seghers: Eine Biographie in Bildern*, 2nd ed. (Berlin, 2000), 66f. In October 1951, Seghers visited China as a member of a GDR delegation to celebrate the second anniversary of the foundation of the People's Republic of China. Hu Lanqi and Cheng Qiying visited Seghers in her hotel room without permission from Chinese officials, which led to

political retaliation afterward. Both Hu and Cheng suffered political persecution during the Cultural Revolution (1967–77). Hu was expelled from the CCP and labeled a rightist. Cheng Qiying committed suicide. In a kind of self-censorship, neither Seghers nor Hu Lanqi ever mentioned their friendship in public. See Weijia Li, *China und China-Erfahrung in Leben und Werk von Anna Seghers* (Oxford, U.K., 2010), 162f.

5. Zhu De's biography was written by the famous American journalist Agnes Smedley in the 1950s. See Agnes Smedley, *The Great Road. The Life and Times of Chu The* (New York, 1956). Han Sen's memoir delivers a more detailed description of the life experiences of his father, Xie Weijin. See Han Sen, *Ein Chinese mit dem Kontrabass* (Munich, 2001).
6. Or Liau Han-sin, according to the Wade-Giles spelling system.
7. Thomas Kampen, "Liao Huanxing oder Tang Xingqi. Für KP und Kuomintang in Berlin," *Das Neue China* 6 (2001): 29–31.
8. The collaboration between Chinese and German Communists in the Weimar Republic is rarely mentioned in the official history of the Chinese Communist Party (CCP) due to historical and ideological reasons, as well as the political discourse in Germany since the fall of the Berlin Wall. Without the participation of Chinese scholars, research so far has been conducted mainly by German scholars in Chinese Studies.
9. Li, *China und China-Erfahrung,* 199 fn. 89.
10. Felber and Hübner, "Chinesische Demokraten und Revolutionäre," 159f.
11. Felber and Hübner, "Chinesische Demokraten und Revolutionäre," 159–160.
12. Yongxiang Wang, et al., *Zhongguo Gongchandang Lü Ou Zhibu Shihua* [The European Sections of the Chinese Communist Party] (Beijing, 1985), 232–233.
13. Wang, *European Sections of the CCP,* 232–233.
14. Dagmar Yü-Dembski, *Chinesen in Berlin* (Berlin, 2007), 51. See also Felber and Hübner, "Chinesische Demokraten und Revolutionäre," 161.
15. Wang, *European Sections of the CCP,* 267. According to Wang, these CCP party cells were often called "Zhong Guo Yu Yan Zu" (Chinese-speaking group). Felber and Hüber translate this as "the Circle for Chinese Language," (e.g., the Circle for Chinese Language in the French Communist Party (CCLF) and the Circle for Chinese Language in the German Communist Party (CCLG)). See note 1.
16. Bingnan Wang, "Yi ci nan wang de hui jian: Ji nian en si te tai er man dan chen yi bai zhou nian [An Unforgettable Meeting: As A Tribute to the 100th Birthday of Ernst Thälmann]," *Ren min ri bao* (17 April 1986): 8.
17. For detailed information on the members of the CCL from 1929 to 1932, see Li, *China und China-Erfahrung,* 201–202.
18. Lanqi Hu, *Hu Lanqi hui yi lu* [Hu Lanqi's Memoir], 2 vols. (Chengdu, 1985), vol. 2, 255.
19. James J. Ward, "'Smash the Fascists...' German Communist Efforts to Counter the Nazis, 1930–31," *Central European History* 14 (1981): 34.
20. Li, *China und China-Erfahrung,* 82.
21. Wang, "An Unforgettable Meeting," 8.
22. Wang, "An Unforgettable Meeting," 8.
23. Heng-yü Kuo and Mechthild Leutner, eds., *Komintern und die Sowjetbewegung in China,* vol. 1 (Münster, 2000), 53.
24. Li, *China und China-Erfahrung,* 61.
25. Li, *China und China-Erfahrung,* 59.
26. Felber and Hübner, "Chinesische Demokraten und Revolutionäre," 167.
27. Felber and Hübner, "Chinesische Demokraten und Revolutionäre," 167.

28. Yü-Dembski, *Chinesen in Berlin*, 67.
29. Felber and Hübner, "Chinesische Demokraten und Revolutionäre," 167.
30. Yü-Dembski, *Chinesen in Berlin*, 28.
31. Yü-Dembski, *Chinesen in Berlin*, 26.
32. Xin Li and Tiejian Chen, eds., *Zhong guo xin min zhu ge ming tong shi* [History of China's New Democratic Revolution] (Shanghai, 2001), 419.
33. Li and Chen, *New Democratic Revolution*, 420.
34. Chen Chi-yin, according to the Wade-Giles spelling system.
35. Han Sen, *Ein Chinese mit dem Kontrabass*,10.
36. Felber and Hübner, "Chinesische Demokraten und Revolutionäre," 148.
37. Dagmar Yü-Dembski, "'China in Berlin', 1918–1933: Von chinesischem Alltag und deutscher Chinabegeisterung," in *Berlin und China: Dreihundert Jahre wechselvolle Beziehungen*, ed. Heng-yü Kuo (Berlin, 1987), 124.
38. Wang, *European Sections of the CCP*, 162ff.
39. Wang, *European Sections of the CCP*, 244.
40. Li, *China und China-Erfahrung*, 54.
41. Li, *China und China-Erfahrung*, 54.
42. *Die Rote Fahne*, 28 August 1930.
43. *Die Rote Fahne*, 16 January 1931.
44. *Die Rote Fahne*, 11 December 1930.
45. *Die Rote Fahne*, 30 January 1931.
46. *Die Rote Fahne*, 19 February 1931.
47. *Die Rote Fahne*, 14 September 1930.
48. *Die Rote Fahne*, 30 November 1930.
49. Wang, *European Sections of the CCP*, 232.
50. Wang, *European Sections of the CCP*, 244.
51. The archive in the Russian Center for the Conservation and Study of Modern History Documents holds about one thousand pages of reports written in German by Liao Huanxing. See Joachim Krüger, "A Regular Chinese Voice from Berlin to Moscow. The China-information of Liau Huanxing 1924–1927," *The Chinese Revolution in the 1920s*, ed. Mechthild Leutner and Roland Felber (London, 2002), 177.
52. Li, *China und China-Erfahrung*, 121.
53. Li, *China und China-Erfahrung*, 82. In their article, Felber and Hübner mistakenly call MASCH "a workers' college" ("eine marxistische Arbeiterhochschule"). This error could be attributed to an inadequate translation from the Chinese text in Hu Lanqi's memoir.
54. Gabriele Gerhard-Sonnenberg, *Marxistische Arbeiterbildung in der Weimarer Zeit (MASCH)* (Cologne, 1976), 100.
55. The Washington Naval Conference was a military conference organized by the United States and held in Washington D.C., from 12 November 1921 to 6 February 1922. The United States, Japan, and seven other Western nations with interests in the Pacific Ocean and East Asia attended. Treaties signed among the nations forced China to give up its ambition to regain control in Tsingtao and Manchuria. The Washington Conference also enabled the rise of Japan as one of the dominant powers in the Pacific.
56. Li, *China und China-Erfahrung*, 51.
57. Matthias Messmer, *China: Schauplätze west-östlicher Begegnung* (Vienna, 2007), 374.
58. Focusing on the Chinese revolution was not a cultural phenomenon among only German left-wing intellectuals at that time. French novelist André Malraux published *Les*

Conquérants (The Conquerors, 1928), dealing with the attempts of Chinese national-ists and their Communist advisors to defeat the political influence and economic domi-nation of Western imperialists. In 1933, Malraux published his masterpiece, *La Condi-tion Humaine* (Man's Fate), depicting the workers' uprising against Chiang Kai-shek in Shanghai.

59. Eva Müller, "Kunst und Politik. Deutsch-chinesische Literaturbeziehungen seit den 20er und 30er Jahren," in *Deutschland und China. Beiträge des Zweiten Internationalen Symposiums zur Geschichte der deutsch-chinesischen Beziehungen Berlin 1991* (Munich, 1994), 256.

60. Richard Thornton, *The Comintern and the Chinese Communists, 1928–1931* (Seattle, 1969), 93.

61. Jost Hermand, "Unvorhersehbare Folgen: Die drei Eislers und Brechts 'Maßnahme'," *Brecht Jahrbuch* 30 (2005), 365.

62. *Die Rote Fahne*, 16 January and 23 January 1931.

63. Friedrich Wolf, *Gesammelte Werke* XVI, ed. Else Wolf and Walther Pollatschek (Ber-lin, 1960–68), 330.

64. There are two other travel accounts depicting China's political situation and especially the revolution of the late 1920s: Arthur Holitscher's *Das unruhige Asien. Reise durch Indien, China, Japan* (The Unsettled Asia. Travel to India, China, and Japan) was pub-lished in Berlin in 1926. In 1930, Manabendra Nath Roy published his *Revolution und Konterrevolution in China* (Revolution and Counterrevolution in China) after his journey to China in 1927.

65. Wang Liying, *Erfahrungen im Reich der Mitte. Deutsche Reiseberichte über China in der ersten Hälfte des 20. Jahrhunderts* (Münster, 2002), 140.

66. Li, *China und China-Erfahrung*, 93f.

67. Li, *China und China-Erfahrung*, 103.

68. Li, *China und China-Erfahrung*, 97.

69. Friedrich Wolf, *Aufsätze über Theater*, ed. Else Wolf and Walther Pollatschek (Berlin, 1957), 240.

70. Thomas Kampen, "Xie Wenjin und die Gebrüder Kisch," *Das Neue China* 6 (2001): 27–28.

71. Li, *China und China-Erfahrung*, 70, 92f.

72. Li, *China und China-Erfahrung*, 58.

73. Li, *China und China-Erfahrung*, 69, 198 fn. 85.

74. Frank Wagner, "Eine Frau und ihr Name," *Argonautenschiff* 5 (1996): 275. See also Li, *China und China-Erfahrung*, 67–69.

75. Li, *China und China-Erfahrung*, 199 fn. 89.

76. Li, *China und China-Erfahrung*, 128.

77. Li, *China und China-Erfahrung*, 199 fn. 89.

78. Li, *China und China-Erfahrung*, 199 fn. 89.

79. Johann Gottfried Herder, *Ideen zur Philosophie der Geschichte der Menschheit* (Darm-stadt, 1966), 284.

80. Yü-Dembski, "Chinesenverfolgung im Nationalsozialismus," *Bürgerrecht & Polizei/ CILIP* 58 (3/1997): 75.

81. Lanqi Hu, *Memoir*, 277ff.

82. Yü-Dembski, "Chinesenverfolgung im Nationalsozialismus," 73.

83. Felber and Hübner, "Chinesische Demokraten und Revolutionäre," 172.

84. Li, *China und China-Erfahrung*, 71.

CHAPTER 5

A Question of Ideology and Realpolitik
DEFA's Cold War Documentaries on China

QINNA SHEN

During the Cold War, the ideological concepts of anti-colonialism, anti-imperialism, and anti-capitalism were paradigmatic to Communist internationalism and the solidarity movement among Socialist countries.[1] Socialism presented itself as the vanguard of peace in the world and capitalism as historically connected with colonialism and, after World War II, with the further economic exploitation of the Third World by various means. The postwar era witnessed civil wars, national divisions, and anti-colonial struggles in Latin America, Africa, and Asia. These continents also became the sites where Cold War rivals demonstrated their political, ideological, economic, and cultural prowess.[2] As a Soviet satellite state, the German Democratic Republic (GDR) not only nurtured its ties with the Soviet bloc countries in Eastern Europe, but also with Socialist regimes in the Third World.[3] This essay concentrates on the bilateral relationship between the GDR and the People's Republic of China (PRC) and how the GDR's state-sponsored film company, DEFA (Deutsche Film-Aktiengesellschaft), represented China so as to assist the Central European country's foreign policy toward the Socialist brother country in East Asia. Instead of fictional films, DEFA primarily used documentaries to introduce domestic audiences to other Socialist countries, in this case China, while locating the GDR within the world arena.

Ideological common ground shared by states belonging to the Socialist camp obviously provided the basis for bringing the geographically and culturally distant countries of the GDR and China together. China was one of the eleven countries, all of them Communist, that recognized the GDR upon its founding in 1949 by establishing diplomatic relations as early as 25 October 1949. Although the PRC also faced diplomatic "containment" campaigns led by the United States, Western countries as well as the nonaligned world were generally readier to accept Mao's China than the island regime of Taiwan. The United Kingdom, for example, recognized the PRC on 5 January 1950 out of economic considerations. The GDR, by contrast, had a fierce, unrelenting, and also stronger rival. Capitalizing on its economic superiority, the Federal Republic of Germany (FRG) engaged in a rigorous isolation campaign against East Germany from 1949 until the early 1970s. In December 1955, the FRG announced publicly that it would break diplomatic relations with any country that established similar relations with the GDR. This controversial but very effective foreign policy was dubbed the Hallstein Doctrine in 1958 after the hawkish foreign secretary, Walter Hallstein. Facing this diplomatic blockade, any official or de facto recognition was strategically important for the fledgling Socialist GDR in its competition for international legitimacy. Thus the GDR persistently, though with limited success, pursued recognition from the nonaligned world.[4] Drawing the short stick in terms of realpolitik, the GDR played up the ideological card by both aligning its own struggles with the anti-imperialist cause in Third World countries and by expressing solidarity with indigenous leftist forces in their fight for national self-determination. Referring to the GDR's foreign policies of *Annäherung* and *Abgrenzung*, Thomas Barnett remarks, "In essence, the South supplied East Germany with much of what it needed to maintain its two-track policy of 'drawing together' with the Soviet Union and 'delimitation' with West Germany."[5]

Historical Background

Unlike the superimposed Communist regime in the GDR, China's Communist movement started soon after the October Revolution in Russia and built a mass base in the populace through its fight against the Japanese and against Chiang Kai-shek's Kuomintang (KMT). Therefore, China could serve as an "ideological mirror" and an exhilarating success story of Communist struggle for East German propaganda purposes years before the 1960s national liberation movements in many Latin American, African, and Middle-Eastern nations.[6] The revolutionary precedent of China and its staunch commitment to Marxism-Leninism reassured East Germans of the correctness of their own Socialist path and served as a form of self-validation. With regard to the foreign policy of the GDR in Africa, Thomas Barnett views the South as providing ersatz revolutionary pathos for East Germany: "If East Berlin could not generate any true revolutionary spirit at home, surrogates had to be found in the South. The vicarious thrills of precipitating revolutions abroad were thus substituted for the bastard legacy of the East German state."[7] China's revolutionary history was borrowed to rally support and create enthusiasm for socialism in the

GDR. Moreover, the DEFA depictions of the epic struggle of Chinese Communists under Mao would evoke the fight of German Communists against the Nazis and thereby corroborate the East German founding myth.

For China, on the other hand, the GDR was a Germany freed from Western imperialism. Mao promised full support for the GDR's struggle toward a unified, independent, democratic, and peaceful Germany. China's first Premier, Zhou Enlai, paid a state visit to the GDR in July 1954, where the two countries signed a joint German-Chinese communiqué. Zhou described the GDR as a bulwark against Western capitalism and endorsed a peaceful reunification of Germany under Socialist auspices. In return, the GDR's first prime minister, Otto Grotewohl, visited China in 1955 and emphasized China's significance in the resolution of international problems. Both sides spoke out against the remilitarization of West Germany and Japan. The GDR supported China's demands for a withdrawal of U.S. troops from Taiwan as well as for the admission of China into the United Nations.[8] Both the GDR and China resisted Khrushchev's de-Stalinization campaigns. China also helped the GDR with material goods to overcome some of the shortages that led to the workers' revolt on 17 June 1953.[9] Under the leadership of Walter Ulbricht, a GDR delegation attended the Chinese Communist Party's (CCP) 8th Party Congress in October 1956, where the very first direct conversation between the two government leaders, Ulbricht and Mao, took place.[10] It was the GDR rather than Moscow that supported the CCP's most prominent initiatives—the Great Leap Forward of 1958 to 1960 and the People's Commune—because the GDR hoped to learn from China's collectivization measures so as to solve its own agricultural problems.[11] This demonstrates that the GDR maintained, when possible, some independence from the USSR in its foreign policy. It also reveals how much knowledge from the Third World was integral to the GDR's own domestic policies.

However, when the alliance between China and the Soviet Union fractured and the Soviet Union recalled all its experts in 1960, the GDR was compelled to avow its allegiance to the Soviets. Fundamental ideological disagreements lay at the basis of the Sino-Soviet Split, according to Lorenz M. Lüthi. However, the Split could also be seen in real-political issues such as the socioeconomic development model, de-Stalinization, and Khrushchev's policy of peaceful coexistence with the United States.[12] The GDR tried to mediate between the two large Socialist powers with "a genuine desire to maintain socialist solidarity and prevent the formation of a Beijing-Bonn axis."[13] Yet in the face of the Sino-Soviet dispute, the GDR did not really have a choice but to side with Moscow. The tension between China and the GDR built up in 1960 as the ruling Socialist Unity Party (SED) adopted the Soviet take on the People's Commune. A public break came during the SED's 6th Party Congress in January 1963. However, couched in every criticism of China voiced by the GDR leaders was the hope that Moscow and Beijing would reconcile. China, on the other hand, continued to declare its support for the GDR in the latter's competition with the FRG. In the early 1970s though, China modified its foreign policy and began to seek allies in the West. Bloody clashes with Soviet troops near the Usuri River in March 1969 and in Xinjiang in August 1969 precipitated China's political reorientation toward the West. Subsequently, China succeeded in establishing diplomatic relations with many Western countries, including the FRG in October 1972. East Berlin saw this new development with great concern because China also supported NATO, Western European integration, and finally German reunification. China's open attempts at strategic cooperation with the West reached their climax with the forming of a worldwide "anti-hegemonic" and "anti-Soviet" united front including the United States, Japan, and Western Europe. By that time, realpolitik had trumped the ideology of Communist internationalism, or rather that ideology had been revised to better serve national interests. As a result, the relationship between China and the GDR in both political and cultural spheres was broken until the end of the 1970s, except when it came to formal contacts on official occasions.[14]

In the early 1980s, the European détente deteriorated, which prompted the Soviet government to signal readiness to reconnect with China by stopping all military actions on the Soviet-Chinese border. The GDR jumped at this sign and rekindled its friendship with China; subsequently, exchanges in various areas, above all in culture and trade, picked up in speed and volume. The rapprochement was highlighted by Erich Honecker's visit to China in 1986 and the return visit a year later by the general secretary of China, Zhao Ziyang. The resumed friendship between the GDR and China, brief due to the GDR's collapse in 1989, ended in a notorious political maneuver. Since both governments remained politically conservative and dogmatic, they rejected Mikhail Gorbachev's liberal politics as causing destabilization to the system. The SED was one of the few foreign governments that endorsed the Chinese government's military suppression of the democratic movement on 4 June 1989.[15] This scandalous endorsement is mentioned as one of the reasons for the mass exodus of GDR citizens across the Austrian-Hungarian border, one of the key developments that finally culminated in the bringing down of the Wall.[16] Shortly before reunification, the first democratically elected People's Chamber revoked the previous support for the crackdown on the Chinese student movement.[17]

DEFA's China Documentaries of the 1950s

This essay explores this bilateral history through the lens of the rarely screened DEFA documentaries on China. The 1950s China films were doomed to oblivion due to the onset of the Sino-Soviet Split around 1960. Moreover, these films were made before the International Week for Documentary and Short Films in Leipzig was revived in 1960. They have since been eclipsed in recent scholarship on DEFA documentaries of Vietnam and Latin America (especially Cuba and Chile), as the latter documentaries enjoyed a favored presence at this film festival. The essay correlates this neglected film history with state relations shaped by political events, the most significant of which being the Sino-Soviet Split. The two-decade-long Split in the 1960s and 1970s left only brief windows of opportunity for joint film projects. Nevertheless, DEFA films on China outnumber by far all the films about other East Asian countries combined, a fact that certainly has to do with the overriding geopolitical significance of China in Asia.

This essay observes a trajectory in the roles that ideology and propaganda play in these films spanning four decades. The early DEFA films on China usually account for how socialism liberated the country from the clutches of feudalism and colonial imperialism and show how the Chinese were now building a Socialist state. A strong ideological agenda determines the films' aesthetics and content. In the late 1970s and 1980s, the films shifted from being ideologically pronounced to focusing more on economic, technological, and consumerist achievements of China's modernization. This shift reflects the rise of globalized capitalism and shows how, over the course of decades, the GDR lost much of its revolutionary energy. Ideology gradually gave way to realpolitik. By way of examining the films, the essay addresses the fundamental relationship between ideology and realpolitik. Given the ideological imperatives of the Cold War, transnational identification based on ideological consensus was inevitable and often translated into real political and economic gains. However, there exists a constant tension between historically transcendent themes—such as solidarity, internationalism, socialism—and real-political expediency for which ideology is counterproductive and thus self-defeating within the realist paradigm of bilateral relations. Especially after the Sino-Soviet Split, realpolitik often took precedence over ideology, which became more moderate and was less emphasized. The later technologically and ethnographically oriented films of the 1980s avoid some of the tendentiousness of earlier propaganda by focusing on economic and sociocultural issues. Although the films of the 1980s still conform to the conventions of Socialist Realism, the anti-colonial and anti-imperialist tone is generally less strident, reflecting the fact that the GDR had been accepted into the United Nations in 1973 and faced a new political reality, domestically and internationally.

Before the first DEFA documentary devoted to China—Bruno Kleberg's *Starke Freunde im fernen Osten* (Strong Friends in the Far East, 1956)—appeared, the Dutch documentarist Joris Ivens, employed by DEFA at the time, made two multinational anthology films with significant Chinese episodes. His 1954 productivist hymn, *Das Lied der Ströme* (The Song of the Rivers), uses six rivers—the Mississippi, the Ganges, the Nile, the Yangtze, the Volga, and the Amazon—as a poetic metaphor and revolutionary trope to parallel man's conquest of nature and the international Socialist struggle.[18] The Chinese episode focuses on the building of a dam across the Yangtze River with the assistance of Soviet machines and tractors from Leningrad. The "dam" was the era's common hydrological metaphor for Socialist nation building.[19] The episode starts with "lives were so cheap on the river banks of Yangtze" and ends with "nothing is more valuable than a human being." The argument that socialism allows human lives to become valuable is typical of the rhetorical strategy within the Socialist humanist paradigm. Not a documentary per se, Ivens's *Die Windrose* (The Compass Rose, 1957) was made for the Women's International Democratic Federation and depicts the intertwinement of class and gender struggles. It consists of five segments from five countries—Brazil, the Soviet Union, France, Italy, and China—each an independent story about a woman's battle for change.[20] In the Chinese segment, Chen Hsiu Hua, the first female brigade leader in her village, overcomes difficulties in her fight against the agricultural collective's patriarchal biases against women. Despite the divide of language and culture, women in the West and East are shown to share the common goal of defying sexism and patriarchal domination. The film attempts to unify people around the globe in the cause of socialism, and the appeal for gender equality strengthens the case for socialism's ability to achieve a just society.

Not until 1956 did DEFA make its first full-length film about China. Many factors contributed to this belated beginning. In the first half of the 1950s, both the GDR and China were preoccupied with their own specific domestic issues. The geographical distance and transportation difficulties due to the lack of an international seaport in the GDR did not make China an easy destination. However, the Rostock harbor was expanded into an international port during the second half of the 1950s.[21] In 1956, then, DEFA set its own record in terms of international documentaries, making ten documentaries that deal with foreign subjects, with only one of them concerned with the West German adversary but two of them with China: *Strong Friends in the Far East* (1956) and Joop Huisken's prizewinning color film *China—Land zwischen gestern und morgen* (China—A Country between Yesterday and Tomorrow, 1956, premiered in 1957). From then on, foreign reportage was firmly established within DEFA's annual production plan. It turned out that DEFA needed such "exotic backdrops" in order to refresh its industry films, whose aesthetics had become stagnant.[22] Within a few years (1956–61), DEFA produced six documentaries on China. These documentaries also served in part as ethnographical travel reportages. They demystified China and provided East Germans with a means to travel vicariously with the camera. However, such virtual travels came with an ideological package that aimed to convince domestic viewers of the legitimacy of their country's political superstructure. Thus, in addition to ethnographical

representations of the people abroad, the political and ideological agendas of
these films determine the choice of stories, images, soundtracks, and the voice-
over narration. The pervasive rhetoric of the Cold War is embedded in the
ubiquitous "voice of God" commentary. It plays an instrumental role in these
documentaries, which, as Bill Nichols points out, "[rely] heavily upon narrative
or expository codes."[23] The burden lies on the narrator to contextualize the
images and extract the ideological and political significance of the represented
reality.

Usually starting with the feudal and semicolonial history of the Old China,
these films then highlight felicitous changes in the New China. The revolutionary history of the CCP is sketched while visiting major Chinese cities. Historic
and touristic sites such as the Forbidden City and the Temple of Heaven in
Beijing are included so as to provide virtual tours of China for East German
viewers, but the narrative voice reminds them that these imperial places were
not accessible to the average Chinese people until the PRC was founded. In
Nanjing, the films pay respect to the mausoleum of Sun Yat-sen as the founding father of the first Chinese Republic. Shanghai's colonial past is invariably
evoked when the famous promenade—the Bund, with its Western architecture—is shown. In Shanghai, the house in which the CCP was founded is a
recurring shot in the films. Sites in Canton that commemorate revolutionaries
are accompanied with a salutary voice-over, for example in *Strong Friends in
the Far East*: "The victims of the revolution will never die!"[24] Ideological affinity compels DEFA to place China's Communist revolution in its historical context and to emphasize the difference the new government has made.
Critical engagement does not occur with regard to any aspect of the Chinese
revolution under Mao or the government policies. Besides the revolutionary
aspects of China, these films also focus on economic and technical-scientific
achievements, such as building infrastructure like dams, bridges, railroads, and
transportation systems, thus stressing the role technology plays in developing
Socialist modernity. The dam is the symbol of the New China and is compared
to the Great Wall as the symbol of the Old China.

Strong Friends in the Far East was occasioned by a state visit. In December 1955, a GDR delegation led by Otto Grotewohl toured China, North Korea, and Mongolia, Socialist countries that "offered a secure ideological backdrop for waving the East German flag."[25] Bruno Kleberg, who was in charge
of propaganda films at the DEFA studio and was one of the most in-demand
directors in the early 1950s, accompanied Grotewohl to China and made
Strong Friends in the Far East as a result.[26] During his official address Grotewohl hands over volumes of the *Yong Le Encyclopedia*, which was compiled
during the Ming Dynasty, and flags from the Boxer Rebellion to Zhou Enlai:
"As German socialists, descendants of Marx and Engels, we place these flags in
your hands." Returning what was "looted by German imperialists" underscores

the GDR's attempt to present itself as "the German country with no 'stain' of past colonialism," and its rival as "unrepentantly reviving the kind of imperialist, Machiavellian foreign policy associated with Germany's evil past."[27] The return of the Boxer Rebellion flags reveals East Germany's sympathetic view of the rebellion as a peasant revolution against feudal and imperialistic oppression, the official interpretation of the controversial revolt in the PRC.[28] The GDR's friendly gesture endorses the rebellion as an emancipatory act, a spiritual and political predecessor of the Socialist revolution, thus symbolically marking its severance from Germany's imperial past.

In 1956, Ivens's student Joop Huisken shot *China—A Country between Yesterday and Tomorrow* with two Chinese camera assistants in cooperation with the French studio Procinext.[29] The temporal metaphor in the title already makes clear that this documentary portrays present-day China as a land in transition. The film describes accomplishments and points out deficiencies but the tone always remains positive: "Small factories exist next to big ones; this is necessary in a period of transition." In a scene where laborers are hauling a ship upstream, the voice-over confidently anticipates future change: "Manpower precedes machines; there are no other alternatives; but it will change." A similar scene of towing a boat appears in Bertolt Brecht's pre-revolutionary didactic play *Die Maßnahme* (The Measures Taken, 1929–30). However, Brecht uses the image of physical labor in the context of political agitation: through their plight the coolies should achieve political consciousness and at least demand more robust shoes that can resist the slippery riverside. Huisken's film predicts that with the advancement of technology the Socialist state will soon relieve the boat trackers from physical toil. The positive outlook the film holds toward China reflects the headstrong optimism of the Marxist-Leninist worldview that socialism paves the way for humankind's bright future.[30]

China—A Country between Yesterday and Tomorrow reflects the influence of the director's mentor, Joris Ivens, who inclines to let individual protagonists emerge from the anonymous masses to tell collective stories.[31] In this vein, Huisken's film also zooms in on and selects its semi-protagonists—a solderer in the city, a couple from the countryside who is soon to be wedded, and a female engineer who leads a railroad construction project—thereby creating mini-vignettes within the flow of the film. Resembling techniques employed in ethnographic films, which commonly "depict individual characters, but … focus their attention upon a level of abstraction beyond the individual," Huisken maintains this level of abstraction and does not personalize the narrative to the degree that a fiction film does.[32] The episodes surrounding these characters all portray them in the context of their work and thus emphasize the productive capacity, both industrial and agricultural, of the New China. The film also uses Ivens's strategy of reconstructing events by restaging them after they have already taken place, treading a fine line between documentary and fiction.[33]

On the side of a road in Beijing, the solderer establishes his "mini-factory" to repair a cracked pot. In a moment of exemplary montage accompanied by oriental string music, the fire the solderer makes in his melting pot transitions to sparks in a steel mill, contrasting the solderer's simple, low-tech, and improvised work station with a large-scale industrial site. The solderer carries his gear to an industrial complex, takes a break, and smiles at what he sees; his smile seems to acknowledge the humbleness of his artisan craft and appreciate the Socialist achievement of industrialization. In this moment, tradition meets modernity, and the two exist side by side in the period of transition (Figure 5.1). As the narrator comments, "Truly, he stands with the melting pot in his hand in the midst of the melting pot of the times."[34]

On one level, the melting pot of the times ("Schmelztiegel der Zeit") refers, in Ernst Bloch's term of "the simultaneity of the non-contemporaneous" (die Gleichzeitigkeit des Ungleichzeitigen), to the coexistence of traditional and modern means of production.[35] On another level, it also implies, perhaps unconsciously, the different development phases that the GDR and China find themselves in. Whereas China is just making its first steps in the industrial direction, the GDR can boast an advanced, modern Socialist state. Thus the film betrays an orientalist tinge, despite the fact that the shared Communist ideology makes the filmmakers greatly receptive to Chinese history and culture.

Figure 5.1. *China—A Country between Yesterday and Tomorrow* screenshot: © DEFA-Stiftung/ Robert Ménégoz, Jean Penzer, Joop Huisken.

In the rural sequence, the bride-to-be and her two bridesmaids are seen harvesting rice. A little subplot is staged, in which the girlfriends poke fun at the bride-to-be for absentmindedly threshing empty straw, because she is thinking about her groom and the upcoming wedding. The film uses a country wedding to point out that the old custom of arranged marriages has been abolished in the New China: "In this way, the old forms were kept, but the content is new; the coercion is gone; the bride is not sold off anymore; the marriage is no longer a business; the bride and the groom have chosen each other themselves. And out of free will they choose their own path, which leads them into the future." A marriage based on free choice becomes an emblematic representation of the happiness inherent in Socialist life (Figure 5.2).

The increased gender equality is further demonstrated in the episode of the female engineer leading a railroad construction, as well as by images of women tractor drivers and steel workers. The film portrays heroic achievements in production with a gender-conscious choice of stories.

The travel reportage *Von Wismar nach Schanghai* (From Wismar to Shanghai, 1958) by Rudolf Schemmel about the maiden voyage of a 10,000-ton freighter named "Friendship" to Shanghai does not focus on international trade per se and does not even mention what GDR products are on the East German vessel. It only mentions Chinese specialty goods that the efficient and hard-working

Figure 5.2. *China—A Country between Yesterday and Tomorrow* screenshot: © DEFA-Stiftung/ Robert Ménégoz, Jean Penzer, Joop Huisken.

stevedores upload for the journey home. China routinely exported foodstuffs and raw materials to the GDR whereas the GDR traded with machinery and high-tech products. As William Gray notes, officials in East Berlin ordinarily preferred to trade by barter. Very much like the West Germans, they also favored technical assistance programs over substantial financial commitments in the Third World.[36] Following the Soviet Union's footsteps in supporting China's industrialization and modernization, the GDR as well as some other Eastern European countries sent specialists to China and launched projects, many of which were abandoned halfway after the Soviet Union pulled out all its experts in 1960, a manifestation of the Soviet penchant for "punishing" the Global South when it did not conform to the whims of the USSR. The reason for the film to be evasive about the trade might be, as Thomas Barnett observes, that the GDR preferred highlighting differences from West Germany, while in fact the GDR's export pattern resembled that of the FRG.[37] Henceforth, in the DEFA films of the 1950s, the preoccupation with political and ideological solidarity overshadowed concrete economic transactions between East Germany and China. *From Wismar to Shanghai* likewise deemphasizes trade so as to highlight its main interest, the construction of a political and propagandistic narrative.

During the voyage recorded in the form of journal entries, the narrator of *From Wismar to Shanghai* laments Algeria's and Yemen's continuing colonial status: "Over there lies the coast of Algeria. A French gunship; how much longer will they cruise here? The most beautiful island of Malta; how much longer will Malta be the bomber base for the US fleet and NATO's marine headquarters?" The voice-over points to the Algerian National Liberation Front's (FLN) anti-colonial struggle against the French, which is the focal point of another DEFA documentary, *Flammendes Algerien* (Algeria in Flames, 1958). When passing Indonesia, the voice-over hails Indonesia's recent national sovereignty from "Dutch imperialism," reflecting the Socialist camp's position on this issue. As Young-sun Hong puts it, "While the United States and its allies opposed anti-colonial and liberation movements in Indochina, Algeria, Cuba, and the Congo during this period, both China and the Soviet bloc supported these movements in their struggle against 'racialized systems of oppression.'"[38] Especially after the FRG joined NATO on 9 May 1955 and the GDR became a Warsaw Pact member in January 1956, DEFA documentarists endeavored to antagonize the Cold War enemies.[39] Criticism of West Germany's rearmament and its new status as America's junior partner became staple subjects in DEFA documentaries until the end of 1950s.

With three films made in a row, Gerhard Jentsch's accounts of China capture the Zeitgeist at the time of the Great Leap Forward of 1958 to 1960 and the People's Commune, and are valuable *Zeitdokumente*, products of the time. *Wir berichten aus Pan Yü* (We Report from Pan Yü, 1959) visits Pan Yü as one example out of tens of thousands of communes in China and witnesses its operations and achievements. The film explains to its viewers at home the rationale of the Chinese government for introducing the People's Commune: "The Party said, 'how much easier must it be if we overcome the difficulties together and do everything together,' thus came the People's Commune into existence." To the soundtrack of Chinese propaganda songs in praise of the CCP, the German voice-over relays the official rhetoric of the Chinese government, e.g., "China will become an industrial country and will even catch up with England before 2062," echoing a famous slogan at the time, "Surpass Britain, Catch Up with America" (超英赶美). The visual sequences show paintings of larger-than-life corns, beets, and pigs, bearing witness to the hyperbolic claim "You can harvest as much as you dare" (人有多大胆，地有多大产). The small backyard steel furnaces that were made to produce steel out of scrap metal—another disastrous mass campaign Mao started—were also recorded, but the voice-over fails to point out the lack of a scientific basis for such primitive means of steel production, which resulted in unusable steel. Instead, it uncritically promotes the official statistics: "In China the steel production doubled from 1957 to 1958." With montages of collective work scenes depicting harvesting, brick making, and house building, this DEFA documentary aims to show the power of the collective at a time when the GDR itself was in the process of agricultural collectivization and nationalization (Figure 5.3).

Figure 5.3. *We Report from Pan Yü* screenshot: © DEFA-Stiftung/Peter Sbrzesny.

In a euphoric tone, the narrator gives voice to his belief that the work ethic and collective wisdom of the Chinese will enable them to overcome whatever difficulties there might be in the future: "650 million people have freed themselves from colonialism and exploitation. With diligence and ingenuity, they work hard to remove the dirt of the past. Although machines and tools are still lacking, they will be here tomorrow, because the strength of the people who are on the march to socialism is inexhaustible. The People's Commune is good, says Mao Zedong. We saw Pan Yü, one of approximately 26,000 People's Communes, led by the Party and its great idea of making the leap forward." In retrospect, the whole question of the People's Commune appears as a tortured one in the GDR. Ulbricht's above-mentioned journey to the CCP's 8th Party Congress to learn about how the Chinese approached agricultural collectivization and industrialization suggests that the GDR at the time was really interested in acquiring new ideas from China. Jentsch's films in support of the People's Commune were thus in keeping with SED policy. In 1960, however, the policy changed so as to follow Soviet criticism of the Commune.[40] As a result, the newly made films became instantly outdated and "politically displaced," a fate common to propaganda in politically volatile times.[41]

East Germany not only sent scientists, technicians, and students to Socialist brother countries, but also artistic ensembles "to spread the word about the 'first workers-and-peasants-state on German soil.'"[40] Jentsch's 1959 documentary *Wir sangen und tanzten in China* (We Sang and Danced in China) follows the Erich-Weinert Ensemble of the People's Army as it tours the PRC (Figure 5.4).

These East German army performers relish the genuine, spontaneous, and hearty receptions from the Chinese everywhere, as the imagery and voice-over attest to: "It was like this; wherever we went, sincere and cordial friendship welcomed us." In an act of friendship, German performers even sing songs in Chinese. As in the other two Jentsch films, the praise of the narrative voice for China's recent achievements has an ideological spin. Speaking of the bridge straddling the Yangtze River in Wuhan, the narrator strikes an anti-imperialist tone: "One cannot build any bridge that is 1,700 meters long across the Yangtze, so said the imperialists. The People's China built it within 15 months." While visiting a warship in southern China in the wake of the Second Taiwan Strait Crisis, which occurred in August 1958, the narrator remains wary of the threat from Taiwan: "Taiwan, the last refuge of Chiang Kai-shek, is still far away, but near enough that its airplanes can still disturb our celebration of friendship. China has had its experience. China is alert." As the film attests to the interstate "friendship," one of the "state-socialist buzzwords" that circulate endlessly in these films, a song about friendship is required:[41]

Oh Communism, oh happiness;
No, no one is above us, who could separate us.

Figure 5.4. *We Sang and Danced in China* screenshot: © DEFA-Stiftung/Peter Barthel, Peter Sbrzesny.

> You don't need to speak Chinese;
> They don't need to understand German.
> When they see your hand, a worker's hand, this is what unites us.
> Two Workers' and Peasants' States,
> Brothers, on the path to socialism,
> Armies of People,
> Friendship, friendship we will achieve when we stand together.

The fact that all vows of friendship ended as soon as the political climate changed shows that a tension between ideology and realpolitik lay at the core of Cold War politics. The relationship between China and the GDR started to worsen in 1960 as the SED accepted the Soviet view on the People's Commune. However, on the eve of the Sino-Soviet Split Gerhard Jentsch made a third documentary—*Genosse Sziau erzählt* (Comrade Xiao Narrates, 1960)—for DEFA's studio for popular scientific films that delineates the genealogy of Communist China and explains the building of the New China. It is not surprising that the film would soon be politically obsolete.

In *Comrade Xiao Narrates*, Jentsch creates a first-person narrative to justify communism in China by recounting the country's history from the perspective of a coolie who once lived in semicolonial China and had to work fourteen hours a day in exchange for a handful of rice. Commenting on rare historical footage, the German-speaking "coolie" familiarizes East German viewers with the recent history of China's humiliation and exploitation at the hands of the colonizers. Presented in flashback as the "coolie's" indelible and haunting memories, the documentary footage switches back and forth between the slaving coolies and the overbearing, hedonistic Westerners. The scenes of the coolies, tinted a sepia or greenish color, are accompanied with pentatonic percussion music created by xylophone, drums, cymbals, and a gong. The music underscores the speed and drudgery of the coolies' work. These scenes alternate with brightly lit ones of the Westerners, with rock 'n' roll and popular Western music from the early 1950s on the soundtrack. The montage sequence functions as the "coolie's" accusation of the imperialists who became "rich and fat" at the cost of "us" and "our children." The narrator brings up the dehumanizing sign "Chinese and Dogs Not Permitted" in Shanghai parks, but he triumphantly announces that "this sign has disappeared, just as those who erected it." He resorts to the familiar Socialist humanist rhetoric when he states that in the PRC he can finally feel "I am a human being." The narrator then uses a generational metaphor to dramatize the country's progress, a "father" taking pride in "his son" who is a brigadier at the An'shan steel plant, a symbol of China's industrialization and modernization (Figure 5.5). The importance of steel for the Socialist economy is prevalent in all these films about China.

Figure 5.5. *Comrade Xiao Narrates* screenshot: © DEFA-Stiftung/Peter Sbrzesny.

By using the nondiegetic song "In China Rises Mao Zedong" as leitmotif, the film not only captures the objective truth of the personality cult of Mao in China, but itself also resembles a tribute to Mao as the savior of the Chinese, the sun that rises in the East. From the perspective of a lowly former coolie, history is personalized and experienced as lived subjective truth. The film presents China's choice of socialism as hard-fought and morally superior and its alternative of a nationalist rule as complicit with the imperialist powers: "Now you understand why the blood in China is so red. You cannot buy a people, only a man; that man's name is Chiang Kai-shek." The Chinese civil war from 1945 to 1949 and the resulting division of mainland China and Taiwan resonate strongly in these DEFA documentaries. Such national division, be it in China or on the Korean peninsula, mirrors Germany's own split. DEFA's condemnation of the U.S.-backed Kuomintang regime as thwarting China's desire for national unity implicitly also places the blame on West Germany and its imperialist patrons for Germany's division. Such rhetoric draws a too simplistic analogy along Cold War lines and disregards the historical differences that produced these national divisions.

The Films of the 1980s

During the time of the Sino-Soviet Split, no more documentaries about China came out of the DEFA studio. Moreover, when the Dutch documentarist Joris Ivens brought out a twelve-hour-long documentary cycle about China, *Comment Yukong déplaça les montagnes* (How Yukong Moved Mountains, 1976), which offers a close-up look at everyday life in China after the Cultural Revolution, the film was not screened in the GDR. All the reviews in the press archive at the Academy for Film and Television (*HFF*) "Konrad Wolf" in Potsdam-Babelsberg are by West German newspapers.[42] The political alienation from China kept Ivens's documentary saga out of East German cinemas.

Not until Erich Honecker's visit to China in 1986 did DEFA start making documentaries about China again. Produced during the GDR's final years, these films were mainly travel reportages commissioned by GDR state television.[43] They bear witness to a modern China that had experienced waves of radical campaigns but had refocused on economic development as the country's first priority. The majority of these films are of an ethnographical nature, admiring Chinese scenery, people, culture, and traditions, including martial arts, acrobatics, local operas, etc. A Socialist worldview continues to underpin the commentary. At the Temple of Heaven, the narrator in *Zwischen Großer Mauer und Perlfluss* (Between the Great Wall and the Pearl River, 1986) comments, "Only in Socialist China has it become possible to feed all people—today a quarter of the world's population. The 317 emperors of the thirty-five dynasties prayed for an abundant harvest once a year here in the Temple of Heaven, but the gods could never help." In 1987, Uwe Belz made an eight-episode television series, *Stromabwärts nach Shanghai* (Downstream to Shanghai), tracing the Yangtze River from its origin in the highlands of Tibet to its estuary in Shanghai. Tibetans, in Belz's depiction, appear as liberated from their past lives of serfdom and as enjoying a better standard of living thanks to state subsidies: "If the Tibet of former times, kept in bondage, hungry, and ignorant, now belongs to the past, then—we hear this everywhere—thanks to the Chinese government. So far they provided seven and a half billion yuan to develop the autonomous region. We heard very telling statistics: in the past five years the peasants' income here has doubled. And most people here are peasants." In Chongqing, *Downstream to Shanghai* visits the Memorial of Liberation and the prisons where revolutionaries were murdered. In the last episode, the way in which Shanghai's Bund is depicted exemplifies continuation of the anti-colonial and anti-imperial language: "Bund: On the promenade we still see stone witnesses of British and American foreign rule to which China was subjected."

The reports abstain from critical language regarding China and, with the exceptions of *Leben in China* (Life in China, 1989) and *China—Mein Traum, mein Leben: Eva Siao—Ein Porträt* (China—My Dream, my Life: Eva Xiao—A Portrait, 1990), even refrain from any reference to past political campaigns, such as the catastrophic Cultural Revolution. In Nanjing, the films never mention the Nanking massacre; the omission cannot have been an oversight, but rather must have had to do with the official treatment of the massacre by the pragmatic Chinese government, which often prioritized its vital trade with Japan over historical justice to the victims.[46] Such evasions reinforce the very distinct agenda of realpolitik of the DEFA films during this time period. The fact that the Chinese government often cosponsored the film projects placed added pressure on the filmmakers to adhere to official policies.[47]

Although the films from the 1980s conform to Socialist politics, they have toned down the ideological language. They attest to further technological progress, and the market scenes repeatedly affirm improved living standards and China's success in its modernization after Deng Xiaoping's economic reforms. One wonders how East German viewers might have reacted to the abundance of consumer goods on Chinese markets. Facing severe domestic problems, the filmmakers seem to use China as a success story—of a different kind this time—that testifies to socialism's capability of creating economic prosperity. It is left unsaid that whereas China could choose a Socialist path with its own characteristics, this had been impossible for the GDR due to its dependency on the Soviet Union. If in the 1950s China offered ideological confirmation for the GDR, China in the late 1980s provided an admirable example of tailoring Marxist theories to its own specific needs. In previous films, DEFA had downplayed the GDR's export of technology. A trade event, which *From Wismar to Shanghai* should have documented, became merely an opportunity to reiterate East German ideology. However, in the 1980s the trade between the GDR and China is mentioned whenever the chance arises. For instance, *Downstream to Shanghai* contains a lengthy episode about the city of Wuhan's purchase of refrigeration wagons (*Kühlwaggon*) from VEB Waggonbau Dessau in an exchange of know-how. The filmmakers appear to take pride in the GDR's role in exporting high-tech to China and thus contributing to its modernization.

Conclusion

By looking at DEFA's Cold War documentaries on China, this essay has examined how ideology and realpolitik played out in the bilateral relationship between the GDR and China. At the height of the Cold War, ideology was a decisive factor in determining policy and the two were inseparable. However, East Germany's revolutionary aspirations gradually took a back seat to realpolitik. The priority of "economics over politics," which manifested itself during the European détente and in the *New International Economic Order* (NIEO) movement, gradually came to dominate the country's international relations.[48] Filmmakers with an uncompromising Socialist *Weltanschauung* faced the challenge of being perceived as too ideologically rigid, while also having to keep up with the swerves and reversals in the party line, as reflected in the changing policies regarding the People's Commune and China in general. Given the limitations to which these politically driven documentaries were subjected, it is easy to label them propaganda, which they undoubtedly are to a great extent. Yet, as propagandistic as they may be, they should be placed in the historical context of the postfascist era where socialism appeared as a viable alternative to capitalism with all its attendant ills of colonialism and imperialism.

Moreover, the merits of the films—cultural and historical—exceed that of mere propaganda. They attest to an episode of unusual openness to the world that overcame the hierarchical divide between the Second and the Third World, between East and West. Ideological bonding with China also enabled East Germans to overcome their feelings of superiority as white Europeans, brave cultural differences, and withstand, quite successfully, the usual orientalist jargon. Ideological affinity enabled East Germans to appreciate China, which the majority of them had no other opportunity to see than on film. In the post–Cold War context in which we live today, the binary opposition between socialism and capitalism, which these films construct, might appear obsolete to many. As products of the time, they are culturally interesting and historically valuable. Beyond that, their stance against colonialism, imperialism, sexism, and other forms of exploitation and oppression still resonates in the early twenty-first century, and the idealism of the filmmakers is to be understood in its own historical context.

Notes

1. I would like to thank the following archives for allowing me to watch the films and for supplying important materials about them: Bundesarchiv-Filmarchiv in Berlin, Deutsches Rundfunkarchiv in Potsdam-Babelsberg, Pressedokumentation at Die Hochschule für Film und Fernsehen (*HFF*) "Konrad Wolf" in Potsdam-Babelsberg, Deutsche Kinemathek – Museum für Film und Fernsehen in Berlin, and the DEFA-Stiftung. I want to thank DEFA-Spektrum in Berlin for providing stills of the films and for giving me permission to use them. I am also indebted to the DEFA Film Library at the University of Massachusetts Amherst for hosting the 2011 DEFA Summer Film Institute with a thematic focus on "Cold War/Hot Media: DEFA and the Third World" that provided me with an expertly compiled reader and a week of inspiring discussions. I thank Benjamin Robinson, Evan Torner, and Skyler Arndt-Briggs for reading this essay and offering insightful suggestions for revision.

2. Young-Sun Hong, "The Benefits of Health Must Spread Among All: International Solidarity, Health, and Race in the East German Encounter with the Third World," in *Socialist Modern*, ed. Katherine Pence and Paul Betts (Ann Arbor, M.I., 2008), 183.

3. Thomas Heimann, "Von Stahl und Menschen: 1953 bis 1960," in *Schwarzweiß und Farbe: DEFA Dokumentarfilme, 1946–92* (Berlin, 1996), 72.

4. William Glenn Gray, *Germany's Cold War: The Global Campaign to Isolate East Germany, 1949–1969* (Chapel Hill and London, 2003); Thomas Barnett, *Romanian and East German Policies in the Third World: Comparing the Strategies of Ceausescu and Honecker* (Westport, C.T., 1992).

5. Barnett, *Romanian and East German Policies*, 95.

6. Barnett, *Romanian and East German Policies*, 105.

7. Barnett, *Romanian and East German Policies*, 152.

8. Werner Meißner, ed., *Die DDR und China 1949 bis 1990: Politik—Wirtschaft—Kultur: Eine Quellensammlung* (Berlin, 1995), 29–31 and 74–81.

9. Meißner, *Die DDR und China*, 29 and 71; Harald Möller, "Das Beispiel China: DDR und VRCH 1949–1964," in *DDR und Dritte Welt: die Beziehungen der DDR mit Entwicklungsländern, ein neues theoretisches Konzept, dargestellt anhand der Beispiele China und Äthiopien sowie Irak/Iran* (Berlin, 2003), 106ff.

10. Meißner, *Die DDR und China*, 83–91; Möller, "Das Beispiel China," 112–4.

11. Meißner, *Die DDR und China*, 33.

12. Lorenz M. Lüthi, *The Sino-Soviet Split: Cold War in the Communist World* (Princeton, 2008).

13. Gareth M. Winrow, *The Foreign Policy of the GDR in Africa* (Cambridge, U.K., 1990), 19.

14. Meißner, *Die DDR und China*, 12–16; Möller, "Das Beispiel China," 134–141.

15. Meißner, *Die DDR und China*, 17.

16. Jordan/Schenk, eds., *Schwarzweiß und Farbe. DEFA-Dokumentarfilme 1946–1990* (Berlin, 1996), 232.

17. Meißner, *Die DDR und China*, 20.

18. Charles Musser, "Utopian Visions in Cold War Documentary: Joris Ivens, Paul Robeson and *Song of the Rivers* (1954)," *CiNéMAS* 12, no. 3 (2002): 109–153.
19. Gray, *Germany's Cold War*, 85.
20. Heimann, "Von Stahl und Menschen," 71. See also Dennis Hanlon, "*Die Windrose*," *DEFA Film Library Newsletter* (Jan. 2012).
21. Möller, "Das Beispiel China," 104.
22. "exotische Kulissen," see Heimann, "Von Stahl und Menschen," 72.
23. Bill Nichols, *Ideology and the Image: Social Representation in the Cinema and Other Media* (Bloomington, I.N., 1981), 7.
24. All translations are by the author.
25. Barnett, *Romanian and East German Policies*, 149.
26. Heimann, "Von Stahl und Menschen," 58.
27. Barnett, *Romanian and East German Policies*, 102.
28. See Joseph W. Esherick, *The Origins of the Boxer Uprising* (Berkeley, 1987); Paul A. Cohen, *History in Three Keys: The Boxers as Event, Experience, and Myth* (New York, 1997), especially Part 3.
29. Heimann, "Von Stahl und Menschen," 73.
30. Gray, *Germany's Cold War*, 5.
31. Hanlon, "*Die Windrose*."
32. Nichols, *Ideology and the Image*, 238.
33. Joris Ivens, "Repeated and Organized Scenes in Documentary Film (1953)," in *Joris Ivens and the Documentary Context*, ed. Kees Bakker (Amsterdam, 1999), 261–272.
34. "Da steht man wahrhaftig mit dem Schmelztiegel in der Hand mitten im Schmelztiegel der Zeit."
35. Ernst Bloch, *Heritage of Our Times* [*Erbschaft dieser Zeit*], trans. Neville and Stephen Plaice (Berkeley, 1991).
36. Gray, *Germany's Cold War*, 116.
37. Barnett, *Romanian and East German Policies*, 105.
38. Hong, "The Benefits of Health," 186–187.
39. Heimann, "Von Stahl und Menschen," 59.
40. Meißner, *Die DDR und China*, 33.
41. "politisch deplaciert," see Heimann, "Von Stahl und Menschen," 50.
42. Barnett, *Romanian and East German Policies*, 100.
43. Hong, "The Benefits of Health," 194.
44. For examples: "Yü Gong versetzt Berge: Der Filmzyklus über China von Joris Ivens and Marceline Loridan," *Süddeutsche Zeitung*, 5 June 1977; "Sich China nähern: Ein Filmzyklus von Joris Ivens und Marceline Loridan," *Der Tagesspiegel—Berlin*, 4 June 1977; "Eine Reise nach China: Das Außerordentliche an dem Yukong-Film von Joris Ivens und Marceline Loridan," *Frankfurter Rundschau*, 7 September 1976; "Yü Gung versetzt Berge: Eine Dokumentarfilmreihe über den Alltag in der Volksrepublik China," *Stuttgarter Zeitung*, 22 September 1976.
45. *Zwischen Großer Mauer und Perlfluss: Begegnungen in der Volksrepublik China* [Between the Great Wall and the Pearl River: Encounters with the People's Republic of China], Redakteur: Antje Geyer (GDR, 20 October 1986); *Stromabwärts nach Shanghai* [Downstream to Shanghai], dir. Uwe Belz (GDR, 1987); *Hallo, wie gehts? Wang Ling in Peking* [Hello, How Are You? Wang Ling in Peking], dir. Uwe Belz (GDR, 1988); *Ni hao—heißt Guten Tag* [Ni Hao—Means Hello], dir. Uwe Belz (GDR, 1989); *Kai-*

serkanal China [The Beijing-Hangzhou Grand Canal], dir. Uwe Belz (1989); *Leben in China* [Life in China], Gestaltung: Horst Mempel (GDR, 1989); *China—Mein Traum, mein Leben: Eva Siao—Ein Porträt* [China—My Dream, my Life: Eva Xiao—A Portrait], dir. Gitta Nickel (GDR, 1990).

46. Takashi Yoshida, "A Battle over History: The Nanjing Massacre in Japan," in *The Nanjing Massacre in History and Historiography*, ed. Joshua A. Fogel (Berkeley, 2000), 70–132. Also see my article, "Revisiting the Wound of a Nation: The 'Good Nazi' John Rabe and the Nanking Massacre," *Seminar: A Journal of Germanic Studies* 47.5 (November 2011): 661–680.

47. Quite a few films, including *China—Land zwischen gestern und morgen*, mention in the credits the generous support from the Ministry of Culture of the PRC and Chinese filmmakers: "Dieser Film wurde mit großzügiger Unterstützung des Ministeriums für Kultur und der Filmschaffenden der Chinesischen Volksrepublik hergestellt."

48. Barnett, *Romanian and East German Policies*, 105.

CHAPTER 6

China Past, China Present
The Boxer Rebellion in Gerhard Seyfried's Yellow Wind (2008)

MARTIN ROSENSTOCK

In the fall of 1899, an uprising by Chinese nationalists began to sweep the province of Shandong and from there spread across the entire northeast of China. The rebels were mainly destitute peasants and workers whose livelihoods had been destroyed in the recent economic transformations wrought by imperialist powers. The rebels believed that certain exercises would make them invulnerable. These had the appearance of shadow boxing, which is why foreigners began to refer to the rebels as Boxers. Their goal was to expel all foreigners from Chinese soil and to annihilate Chinese Christian communities. The rebels caught the colonial powers off guard, murdering approximately two hundred missionaries, priests, and nuns, mostly in rural areas. In the capital of Beijing on 20 June, a motley group of roughly nine hundred foreigners—staff members of a dozen legations, their wives and children, soldiers, businessmen, and tourists—as well as about three thousand Chinese Christians barricaded themselves in the embassy district. Over the following fifty-five days, Boxer rebels and also regular Chinese troops laid siege to the district, until eventually a British-led force relieved the inhabitants on 14 August 1900. The death toll of the foreigners stood at sixty-six, that of the Chinese Christians in Beijing has been estimated in the hundreds. In all of China, more than 30,000 Chinese Christians died at the hands of the Boxers. After the success in Beijing, the victorious powers launched a number of punitive expeditions. Unlike in the relief expedition, the German Reich took a leading role in these, providing the largest troop contingent and also claiming the post of supreme commander. Hostilities continued well into the following year. Finally, on 7 September 1901, representatives of the warring parties signed a peace treaty, stipulating large Chinese reparation payments, limitations on the country's military capabilities, and various gestures of humiliation.[1]

During the ensuing years, the Boxer Rebellion echoed strongly in German-language fiction, particularly in adventure novels aimed at a male (adolescent) audience.[2] Authors of a more literary bent also responded. In 1901, Arthur Schnitzler worked on what would probably have turned into a short novella entitled "Boxeraufstand" (Boxer Rebellion), but the text remained a fragment and was not published until 1957.[3] The rebellion figures in Elisabeth von Heyking's *Briefe, die ihn nicht erreichten* (The Letters Which Never Reached Him, 1903) and provides the theme of her novel *Tschun* (1914), which chronicles the events from a Chinese perspective.[4] Then, however, the rebellion drops almost entirely from the German literary scene. In 1941, Hanns Maria Lux published *Felix und der Bund der roten Laternen* (Felix and the Secret Society of the Red Lanterns), a young-adult novel about the adventures of two brothers during the Beijing siege. More recently, Günter Grass began his chronicle of the twentieth century, *Mein Jahrhundert* (My Century, 1999), with an episode set during the rebellion. The atrocities recounted serve as harbingers of worse to come over the following decades. In 2008, finally, Gerhard Seyfried published *Gelber Wind oder Der Aufstand der Boxer* (Yellow Wind or The Rebellion of the Boxers), billed on the jacket—incorrectly, even if one only considers *Tschun*—as the first German novel on the Boxer Rebellion.[5]

Seyfried came to novel writing in his mid fifties, after a successful career as a comic book author. While his comics, in humorous fashion, display a strongly, at times even radically, leftist view of German society and arguably target a fringe audience (see, for instance, his 1990 work *Flucht aus Berlin* [Flight from Berlin]), this is not the case regarding his historical novels. His first one, *Herero* (2003), which addresses the genocidal war Germany waged between 1904 and 1908 against native peoples in German Southwest Africa, today Namibia, is highly critical of German policies and behavior, but not polemically anti-bourgeois. The genre of the historical novel does not lend itself to satire in the way that a comic book does with its opportunities for visual puns and jokes. Perhaps Seyfried was also trying to reach a large audience. If that was the case, he succeeded: *Herero* became a commercial success. Seyfried's second historical novel on a colonial theme, *Yellow Wind*, was almost certainly written with an eye toward the market, as a piece in the *Tagesspiegel*, which appeared two months before the novel, suggests.[6] This is not to say that *Yellow Wind* is solely an attempt at a profitable book, but rather that the novel constitutes an endeavor to tap into the German cultural mainstream and ought to be considered in this context. Most obviously, this mainstream, then, would appear to carry with it an interest in German colonialism, and to investigate why that is the case would make for a larger study. The goal of this essay is narrower. It proposes to investigate Seyfried's historical novel within the context of current German feelings on China. *Yellow Wind*, while no bestseller, was reasonably successful and remains in print to this day. The Eichborn Verlag, where the book appeared, ran into financial trouble in 2010 and ultimately failed in 2011. By then, however, the Aufbau Verlag had acquired the rights for *Yellow Wind* and—testimony to its continuing commercial potential—had reissued the novel.

During an interview Seyfried gave the *Tagesspiegel* after the book had appeared, his interlocutor at various points tries to draw the author into a discussion of how his novel's themes relate to current political and social debates, be they the role of the military in Germany or even Islamic radicalism. Seyfried, rather strenuously at times, rebuffs these attempts, stating ultimately that the book "is written in the style of the times and references the then current manners of thinking. Thus, it is not a modern book."[7] This is true as far as it goes. In terms of structure and prose, *Yellow Wind* is indeed a rather traditional historical novel. However, the text is inevitably a product of its time and place. The notion that it exists solely in a historical space untouched by the culture out of which it emerged is untenable, even though the author may well in all sincerity hold this opinion. The following reading therefore constitutes an attempt to follow D.H. Lawrence's injunction never to trust the artist, but to trust the tale,[8] and to consider *Yellow Wind* as a symptom and product of the "political unconscious" of contemporary German culture.[9]

The title deserves comment. Within the narrative there rises a literal yellow wind, a sandstorm with "yellow-grey clouds," which enables the abduction of a child, one of the small-scale dramas that unfolds before the backdrop of the rebellion.[10] But this reading is only available after having made quite some headway into the text. To a prospective reader picking up the volume at a store the paratextual information will suggest the rebellion itself as referent of a metaphor. In fact, this interpretation remains compelling throughout the narrative, and obviously such a metaphor carries racial connotations. It also echoes the term *gelbe Gefahr*—"yellow peril"—which came into usage during the 1890s. Hermann Knackfuß's 1895 painting *Völker Europas, wahrt Eure heiligsten Güter* (Peoples of Europe, Preserve Your Most Holy Possessions) is occasionally cited as the point of origin. He created the work after a design of Kaiser Wilhelm's, who was responding to a sense of East Asian ascendancy after the Japanese victory over China in 1895. Knackfuß's canvas depicts the archangel Michael gesturing for the benefit of various allegorical figures of European nations toward a Buddha shrouded in dark clouds. The painting suggests that Christian Europe must stand united against the threat of a heathen culture of radical alterity. The term "yellow peril" went on to achieve widespread popularity after the release of such works as Matthew Phipps Shiel's spectacularly chauvinist and racist bestseller, *The Yellow Danger* (1898), which chronicles how a half-Chinese, half-Japanese mastermind, hailed as a reincarnation of Confucius, incites war between the European nations with the intention of bringing about Chinese world domination. At the close of the novel, only English pluck can save the West, since "screaming Chinese" are playing ball with "bodiless heads and arms" in the streets of Paris, before ultimately even indulging in canni-balism.[11] By the time of the Boxer Rebellion at the turn of the century, the term's semantic field indicated a general unease in Western societies regarding the population sizes of East Asian countries and their increasing technologi-cal prowess.[12] This sense of threat animated much of the Western propaganda during the rebellion and found its most well-known expression in the so-called "Hunnenrede" Kaiser Wilhelm delivered before soldiers departing for China on 27 July 1900. In this speech he warned of a "sly, brave, well-armed, and grue-some enemy," before enjoining his soldiers to behave like "huns" in the defeat of this foe. Given all these historical echoes, Seyfried's title of *Yellow Wind* appears unfortunate, to a degree that one might doubt whether he knew of the entire range of connotations. Yet he must have known. The novel is thor-oughly researched regarding all possible areas of interest, from German party politics to military technology and from journalistic practices to lady's fashion. Seyfried provides a list of sources, characters in the novel discuss the "Hun-nenrede,"[13] and one of them even reflects upon the term "gelbe Gefahr."[14] The title thus appears as the most pronounced symptom of a blind spot the novel has with regard to itself.

A number of questions arise, then, when considering *Yellow Wind*: Why does the text appear at this point in time? How does this fictionalized treat-ment of the Boxer Rebellion relate to current German perceptions of China? And finally, does this historical novel respond, as is typical of the genre, to issues surrounding the concept of nationhood, in this context most notably current efforts to craft a European identity? Topical questions such as these can produce a strong, not to say a tendentious, reading. Their narrow range therefore deserves emphasis. This essay, for instance, merely suggests the novel's approach to militarism, racism, and gender relations—regrettably so, since the-matic complexity remains underappreciated. However, the above-mentioned questions demand focus on pertinent aspects of the text.

A paradigm Georg Lukács introduced in his classic 1937 study on the historical novel still provides a compelling explanation for why the theme of the Boxer Rebellion should again find its way into German-language fiction in 2008: "Without a felt relationship to the present, a portrayal of history is impossible. But this relationship … does not consist in alluding to contempo-rary events … but in bringing the past to life as the prehistory of the present, in giving poetic life to those historical, social and human forces which, in the course of a long evolution, have made our present-day life what it is and as we experience it."[15] By its very nature a historical novel creates its own kind of dramatic irony. The reader may not know the fate of the (fictional) characters, but in most cases he or she does know the outcome of the larger historical drama in which they are involved. He or she may also know the history of the ideas, be they religious or political, scientific or philosophical, that the characters expound or live by. If the reader can trace a line of continuity between the world of the fiction and the present, chances increase that he or she will find the narrative compelling. This line of continuity can be less exclusively defined by causality than Lukács may have envisioned. Not every reader will be able to insert mentally all intermediate steps that connect the "prehistory of the present" to the present. At least, however, the historical fiction ought to echo concerns of the reader's world so as to achieve stimulation and absorption. The Boxer Rebellion constitutes precisely such an echo chamber.

China's rise as an economic and political power over the past two decades has received much attention in Germany (and virtually all Western countries). Public and academic debates as well as publications on China have addressed issues such as job losses, transfer of technological expertise, and a shift of power in the international arena. Konrad Seitz, for instance, concludes his overview of Chinese history, *China: Eine Weltmacht kehrt zurück* (China: A World Power Returns, 2000), with a future scenario and an emphasis on how high the stakes are: "China 2020 has achieved the goal that has driven the Chinese elite since the movements of self-invigoration of the 1860s. Once again, China is 'rich and powerful' (fuqiang)," and he continues: "To integrate the new superpower China into the world system in a peaceful manner, and that also means making room for China, is the most important task for peace of the 21st century."[16] With so much attention paid to the implications of the country's increasing stature, it seems only logical that mainstream German fiction writing should also pick up on the theme of China. In this context, the imperialist era in general, with its iniquitous economic relations, and the Boxer Rebellion in particular as an instance of confrontation between China and Germany (as well as other powers) would appear as subject matter with deep resonances for a twenty-first century public.[17]

The historical novel frequently registers a national discourse, namely of the nation whose (pre-)history the novel addresses. The connection runs even deeper since the ascent of the novel as a form depended on social and economic transformations in the seventeenth and eighteenth centuries linked to the creation of a modern national consciousness. These transformations reached from the constitution of a civic bourgeois identity to the establishment of national public spheres and the codification of national languages. "Well, the nation-state … found the novel," Franco Moretti declares with an eye toward the British novel of the early nineteenth century. "And viceversa: the novel found the nation-state. And being the only symbolic form that could represent it, it became an essential component of modern culture."[18] In a time of limited mobility on the part of most readers, this form, Moretti argues, could depict the newly developing structures in all their complexity and heterogeneity. The novel allowed readers to conceive of themselves as part of a larger entity that exceeded their immediate experience. The historical novel then furthermore added chronological depth to the portrayal of the nation. The genre's pedigree is longer than commonly assumed, reaching back to French *nouvelles* of the seventeenth century, but these generally existed in an ill-defined space between historiography and historical fiction and concerned themselves with the "secret histories" of high-placed personages.[19] The "genre's second life" begins with Walter Scott's efforts of the early nineteenth century, which have very different concerns.[20] Scott's historical novels depict an emotionally charged, strife-ridden past, dramatize the sublation of religious, ethnic, or social differences in the national project, and inscribe a common man—and usually it is a man—into a set of events that in retrospect show themselves to have been of national significance: a formula whose social significance has led Moretti to call Scott's invention "the key genre of the century."[21]

The reborn historical novel served European societies as *the* genre capable of affirming dominant cultural and political beliefs. Small wonder, then, that it became so popular. In the second half of the century, these beliefs culminated in global imperialist ambitions on the part of most major Western European nations and an ever more fervent nationalism.[22] By that time, however, the genre's golden age had passed. John Marx has posited a link between the increasing heterogeneity Western societies developed in the course of the nineteenth century and the historical novel's slippage from its peak of dominance in the sphere of popular literature: "One associates bourgeois individuality with a late-eighteenth-century rise and a mid-nineteenth-century fall. Decline sets in as both the genre of the historical fiction and an ethos of individuality cease to be capable of representing national populations in their entirety."[23] In societies riddled with class tensions the narrative of a historical proto-bourgeois individual whose life story contains the centrifugal forces of the national project no longer resonated with large segments of the reading public. With others, however, arguably mostly middle class, the genre retained its popularity and has done so to this day. A logical line of inquiry therefore suggests a consideration of what a German historical novel like *Yellow Wind* articulates in the early twenty-first century as regards nationality and nationhood, within a vastly changed political and cultural environment.

Seyfried's novel is composed of four main plot-lines, each organized around a central character. The first plot-line follows Arletta Lind, a twenty-seven-year-old school teacher, who in the fall of 1899 successfully applies for a position as private tutor to the son of a German businessman based in Tsingtau, the German leasehold on the coast of northern China. Shortly thereafter, hostilities break out in full force, and Arletta becomes one of the foreigners trapped in the Beijing embassy district. Another one of these is the journalist Ferdinand Roeder. Before relocating to Beijing, he had been working in Shanghai as a correspondent for various publications. An unhappy love affair and an attempt to leave behind his opium addiction have brought him to the capital. Max von Reichenow, a naval officer from an impoverished east-Elbian Junker family, provides the romantic counterpart for Arletta. He will participate in the relief expedition that brings the siege of the embassy district to an end. Unfortunately, the officer is engaged to Charlotte Weinhold, daughter of a Berlin cigar manufacturer. The betrothed have, however, not seen each other in two years and both are experiencing doubts about their engagement. Another Germany-based character rounds out the cast and opens up the possibility of a happy resolution. Janus Ballhaus represents the Social Democratic Party in the Reichstag, a capacity in which he is trying to counteract the militarism and expansionary policies of the Kaiser and conservative politicians. Ballhaus is in love with Charlotte, who eventually breaks off her engagement and accepts him as her suitor, thus allowing the romantic union between Arletta Lind and Max von Reichenow to become official. Entirely conventional, the plot's geographical reach and coverage of a wide swath of the social spectrum do allow for the depiction of forces that in the rearview mirror of history appear to have shaped future cultural, economic, and political developments. Folded into the narrative of the Boxer Rebellion lies the "prehistory of the present."

When Arletta considers applying for the position, she, like a character in a Joseph Conrad novel,[24] turns to a representation of the alluring faraway place: "But she cannot tear her eyes from the atlas, from the alien expanse of the vast Chinese Empire, printed in dim yellow."[25] China represents many things to her: release from the restrictions of class-bound Wilhelmine society, escape from a profession that condemns her to spinsterhood (the law prohibited female schoolteachers from marrying), and economic achievement. Once she is sailing eastward, this latter factor rises to full consciousness: "Gone is the grey, drab school building, the past has gobbled it up, including headmaster, bell, and beadle. One student instead of fifty, almost twice the salary, and a voyage half around the world to boot. She feels like dancing around on deck."[26] Not unlike today, China to the Westerner appears as a place where one can make fast and easy money. This aspect of Arletta's set of motivations is only a minor instance of Western economic aspiration. Her employer Arthur Lenck's projects are of a large-scale entrepreneurial nature. Within this context lie possibilities for equitable alliances with the Chinese: Lenck is considering making his Chinese agent a partner in the firm. In addition, the text suggests that human attachments may improve a relationship prone to antagonism: Lenck's daughter and the agent's son will fall in love. The prospect of their union allows for the contemplation of a hybrid German-Chinese identity, though, as will be shown, the text's faith in the viability of such a romance proves small indeed.

Yellow Wind in many passages locates the causes of the rebellion in the behavior of Western powers, particularly during the Opium Wars (1839–1842 and 1856–1860) in which Great Britain and France deliberately humiliated the Chinese elites. The novel also shows the adverse consequences of Western actions with less malign intentions: technological innovations, for instance steamboats and railroads, are undermining established work relations, giving rise to unemployment and societal dislocations. By analyzing the rebellion's origins the text works toward eliciting the reader's sympathies with those Chinese aiming to throw off the yoke of Western imperialist exploitation. These passages, together with depictions of Western racism and, later in the narrative, of atrocities committed by Western military personnel, constitute a layer of meaning that is in accord with the author's liberal policies. They also echo the prevailing view of the imperialist era today as a shameful and inexcusable phenomenon, with greed as its motivator and doctrines of white supremacy as a supporting discursive formation.

A reading of Seyfried's text along these lines is appropriate and readily available. It is, however, also reductive and amounts to taking the text at face value. The thematic elements of mutually beneficial economic activity, transcultural personal attachments, and analysis of the conflict's roots in abusive Western practices compete with others for dominance of the narrative. These themes, in turn, point to a sublayer of meaning that suggests more ambivalent, perhaps disavowed, feelings regarding China and its people. This is the layer of interest here. *Yellow Wind* over long stretches foregrounds difference and suggests irreconcilable conflict. The rebellion swiftly quashes any tentative efforts toward coexistence, and at the height of the hostilities the Chinese combatants seem barely human:

> Now fear grips him [Roeder]. He closes the suitcase in a wild rush and exits the house through the courtyard into the small alley. At the corner he almost runs into a sailor, is pulled along by a group of men. Smoke and dust cloud the street, commands are bellowed, and from the Austrian embassy the horrifying Sha-Sha-Sha of the Boxers arises. The machine gun hammers, and the bellowing changes into howls of anger. Roeder reaches the Legation Street, comes to a halt in the shadow of the French wall, and gasps for breath. The Chinese have overrun the Austrian barricade, but for a hair's breadth they would have gotten him in his house.[27]

The embassy district constitutes a beleaguered Western enclave, the rebels appear as a ferocious, alien mass that only superior technology can repel. Seyfried's text codes the territory together with its inhabitants as pan-European: a German journalist takes cover behind a French wall after an Austrian line of defense has been smashed. Repeatedly, the text emphasizes the interdependence of the district inhabitants: they will either survive together or all be annihilated by the anti-Western enemy at the gates. The novel imagines a community whose depiction, while certainly accurate, is also charged with affect and symbolic meaning. However, this is not the national community of Benedict Anderson's theorizing,[28] but one delineated by civilizational affiliation. The narrative constructs the image of a (European) West united in a common defensive cause against an enemy with whom—at this point at least—even communication has become impossible. (Notably, the Japanese inhabitants of the district hardly figure in the ad hoc community Seyfried depicts, though they played a vital role in the defense of the district;[29] the same goes for the Russians.) Such an image resonates with current projects toward European integration and the perceived need of a response to Chinese political and economic aspirations. In a speculative mode, one might even argue that the text's emphasis on European homogeneity compensates for the fact that today unity of purpose does not exist in many areas of European politics: a desired sense of unity would thus appear projected backward onto a historical event that dramatizes the need for European solidarity. Before, however, considering further the text's contemporary resonances, a look at the novel's strategy for defining a European identity against a Chinese foil is necessary.

Yellow Wind, in its portrayal of the hostilities, taps into a charged discourse when dramatizing the confrontation between European forces and Boxer rebels who are not targeting Westerners alone. Early on in the siege, the rebels force their way into the part of the city that contains the legations: "They brandished swords and torches and attacked everyone in the street, merchants, beggars, children, no matter."[30] Shortly afterward, the text provides the reason for this indiscriminate violence: the Boxers are attacking every Chinese who in some form or another is connected with the foreigners. In this case, the rebels pay dearly for their behavior: "The Italian guard let the fleeing people through and repulsed the pursuers with warning shots, and when they tried it again, the Italians and the French, who had come to their aid, shot a volley into them that tore half a dozen off their feet."[31] When at the close of the hostilities the besieged finally venture out from the district, they encounter evidence of how the rebels treated those of their compatriots they believed to have sided with the foreigners and whom no Western soldiers could protect: "Others have probably fallen victim to vengeful fellow countrymen. To the left and right of a circular moon gate hang the chopped off heads of Chinese, nailed to the wall by their queues, the eyes pecked out by birds.... In the courtyards behind, corpses, half-eaten skeletons pulled about by feral dogs."[32]

Atrocities at the hands of the Boxers are documented;[33] however, in a historical novel the author exercises a degree of choice regarding the inclusion of details and emphasis on facets of the events. Gruesomeness has been a staple feature in Western imaginings of China since at least the middle of the sixteenth century,[34] though even in Marco Polo's writings certain passages suggest an Eastern expertise in refined cruelty.[35] These constructions became standard tropes of Western culture through such works as George Henry Mason's *The Punishments of China* (1801), which in its preface applauds the "wisdom of the

Chinese Legislature" and by implication suggests that at least in procedural terms the Chinese legal system may be more advanced than that of many Western countries, while also decrying "the custom of attending to fallacious information extorted on the Rack" and suggesting in fact quite literally unspeakable forms of punishment.[36] Literary culture absorbed these influences, leading eventually to such works as Octave Mirbeau's *The Torture Garden* (1899), which blends a critique of European bourgeois values with depictions of oriental sadism. In passages such as the one just quoted, *Yellow Wind* might thus be said to inscribe itself into a literary tradition.

As with the threat embodied by the rebels, though, the depiction of their extreme violence against Chinese civilians also resonates with contemporary political and cultural issues. This is particularly the case because the novel, quite correctly in historical terms, suggests that powerful figures at the Manchu court, most notably Tzu Hsi, the Empress Dowager and de facto ruler of the country, fomented and supported the Boxer Rebellion. The Chinese state itself is thus responsible for the brutalization of those of its own people who are not in line with official policy. Today, Western media regularly charge the country's elites with similar behavior. Human rights violations constitute a key topic in reports on China. For instance, the persecution of the Falun Gong movement in the late 1990s received substantial coverage. Throughout the decade, the Communist Party had begun to perceive the popularity of this meditation movement as threatening the uniformity of the population's ideological orientation toward the state-sanctioned belief system. In 1999, Falun Gong was declared illegal and many of its followers were rounded up, deported to labor camps, and tortured, leading to thousands of deaths. In Germany, as in most Western countries, these events provoked a public outcry and confirmed many observers in their belief that China was a totalitarian state.[37] The controversy around the observance of human rights in China is in fact of long standing, reaching back at least as far as the period of the Cultural Revolution (1966–76) when the behavior of Chinese authorities provided arguments to the opponents of the People's Republic assuming Taiwan's United Nations seat, which occurred in 1971. The violent suppression of the 1989 student protests on Tiananmen Square, questions surrounding the adherence to human rights standards after the return of Hong Kong to China in 1997, frequent usage of the death penalty, and the treatment of political dissidents as well as of ethnic minorities have all contributed to keeping the issue in the Western public's eye. Together with its economic expansion, China's human rights record today provides the main source of friction between China and the West.

Seyfried's novel echoes these topical concerns, but it does so unobtrusively. In fact, it is hard to judge whether the author is aware of how the present will color the manner in which the reader may perceive the novel's depiction of the past. The text appears to guide the reader, but he or she does need to engage with it to construct the parallels. Giving expression to the "felt relationship to the present" requires interpretive work. The gap between the prehistory of the present and the present itself operates much the same way Wolfgang Iser's "blank" operates within a narrative, drawing the reader "into the events and [making him or her] supply what is meant from what is not said."[38] However, *Yellow Wind* does not always allow the reader to engage in this supplementary endeavor. Perhaps the author lacks faith in the reader's capacity to perform the interpretive work and to come to the desired conclusion. Concerning the issue of the disasters resulting from European imperialism the signposting becomes so insistent that it bespeaks a conscious desire to shape the reader's response, even if this requires the stretching of genre conventions.

At various points, the text highlights, with grim irony, the tragic consequences of great power politics. The journalist Roeder, for instance, having accompanied some German officials to a meeting in the British embassy, thinks to himself: "Such a common and friendly demeanor of military brass from eight nations that normally only regard each other with suspicion is certainly a remarkable occurrence. Who knows, perhaps a lasting friendship will develop from such a small occasion, yes, perhaps the basis for world peace, much desired, will be laid here."[39] In the face of the anti-Western enemy, the beleaguered find unity of purpose. Rivalries that have arisen through decades of economic and political competition fade into the background as the forces under siege are compelled into cooperation to face down the Boxers. Another future seems possible, one radically different from the one that did in fact unfold. Roeder is not the most sympathetic character, also not the brightest—the politician Ballhaus is far more clear-eyed about the future—but the journalist's what-if scenario must appeal to Europeans looking back on the twentieth century. His musings, however, appear not to make the point with sufficient emphasis. Perhaps they are too abstract and lack a graphic, dramatized component. The text reinforces them at various points that foreshadow Europe's catastrophe: Ballhaus worries about the consequences of a maritime arms race;[40] a German publisher puts out material that argues against "the violent conquest of markets, which leads to conflicts amongst the competing industrial powers and creates … a growing possibility of war."[41] But the most striking anticipation of futurity is oddly and opaquely personal. The coming disaster already appears to be clouding the dreams of one of the novel's characters, who in all likelihood will end up fighting in World War I: "Reichenow awoke from deep sleep, startled from a dream in which he walked through night-time Vienna, through broad, empty streets without a trace of life, like an abandoned and doomed city. With every step the feeling of eeriness had increased, and this sense of a mounting fear is still lingering within him. His back in pain, he raises himself from his hard bed, brushes some straw from his creased uniform with his hands, and asks himself why he dreamed of Vienna, a city he has never been to."[42] The battles with the rebels have left Reichenow a traumatized man. He is already displaying the pathology that will become a mass phenomenon in the future war, and that will be theorized in the city of his dream. But the psychological in this passage appears to shift into the psychic. Reichenow is a mystery unto himself, which would not be the case if the workings of his unconscious were still bound by what is usually considered their natural limits. Reichenow in fact seems highly attuned to trauma, almost supernaturally so. Much earlier in the narrative, he recalls a childhood episode of him and a friend visiting the ruins, close to his father's estate, of a medieval town that was depopulated by the plague and later pillaged by the Pomeranians; the two boys feel how the "hairs at the nape of their necks stood on end … and a fear full of foreboding touched them."[43] This sensitivity Reichenow has retained as an adult. Were his psyche trying to address the current sense of threat from an Eastern enemy via the historical past, say, the Turkish siege of Vienna in 1683, his waking self would undoubtedly be able to draw the connection. Particularly for a military man, the defense of the Habsburg capital would constitute a salient reference point. In fact, what is surprising is that this does *not* come to his mind. What does is his lack of knowledge of the city he has just dreamed of as a ghost town. He associates dereliction, almost erasure, and senses dread, "a mounting fear." His awareness of the future hovers below the threshold of consciousness, as *Yellow Wind* inscribes the Boxer Rebellion within the prehistory of World War I. The coming disaster, partly a result of the imperialist projects in which the principal European nations are engaged, will destroy the political and social structures of a bygone era. Hence Vienna, representing nineteenth-century culture, both aristocratic and bourgeois, is doomed. Europe stands only a few years away from tearing itself to pieces.[44] The reader knows this; the character senses it. There is, however, an added twist. When fighting a common enemy in Beijing, or when organizing a relief expedition for those beleaguered by Chinese forces, the West, Europe in particular, is capable of setting aside its differences and responding with a joint military endeavor. The text hints at the counterfactual: things could have been different in 1914 had the spirit of 1900 prevailed.

To gauge the manipulation of time as it occurs in the above-quoted passage, it is useful to keep in mind Mikhail Bakhtin's essay "Forms of Time and of the Chronotope in the Novel" (1937–38). In this he describes the relationship between the time of individual and historical life-sequences as "crucial with regard to the historical novel," stating: "Parallel to these individual life-sequences—above them, but *outside* of them—there is a time-sequence that is *historical*, serving as the channel of the life of the nation, the state, mankind."[45] The image of parallelism is key: historical time, in a classic historical novel, exists in a separate stratum, unaffected by the events that impact the lives of the characters, but historical time merely stays abreast of individual time and does not get ahead of it. Bakhtin's beliefs regarding this issue do not contradict the Lukácsian concept of the "prehistory of the present" as the designated topic of historical fiction. The reader, according to Lukács, will be able to perceive the relevance of the events recounted as a result of his or her privileged position in the historical continuum. "Alluding to contemporary events," as Lukács states, is not required.[46] One might add that alluding to events that lie in the future though they are not contemporary with the reader is not required either, or ought to issue organically from the narrative itself (as is the case, for instance, with Roeder's ponderings during the embassy meeting).

Yellow Wind not only knows more than its characters and inscribes into the fictional world epistemic trajectories that lie beyond the ken of those living in the historical moment, but the text in the case of Reichenow's dream also tests the boundaries of realism by making this futurity a component of a character's unconscious life. The specificity of the angst working its way into his dream is unmotivated (he himself wonders at this) and prophetic, delimiting the reader's possible response to the narrative. In passages that foreshadow the coming war, readership consists less in engagement with the text than in reception of it: the "blank" has shrunk considerably as much of what is meant is also said.[47] What is articulated is a condemnation of imperialism, no doubt, but these passages also suggest a didactic point. The contrast between the interdependent relationship of the Western powers that results in their success and the future, already written into the text, that will bring an intra-Western war and the destruction of much of the West's civilization highlights the effects of European division. If one moves to the present and considers the perception of China as a threat to prevailing structures of power as well as to the economic security and stability of Western societies, Seyfried's historical novel might be said to refract the argument that Europe can only succeed in the current global political landscape through a posture coordinated between the nations of which the continent is comprised.

Two of the narrative's three romantic couples, Arletta Lind and Max von Reichenow as well as Charlotte Weinhold and Janus Ballhaus, underscore the theme of civilizational and social homogenization. Arletta, arguably the main character, possesses a pan-European identity. Her mother was Italian, her father German, and the novel repeatedly emphasizes that their daughter's appearance shows her heritage. Both Arletta's parents had somewhat bohemian and intellectual backgrounds, her mother being an actress, her father a theater critic. Reichenow's aristocratic lineage, by contrast, has predestined him for a military career that while fulfilling him professionally has left him rootless. The other couple is similarly notable for the fact that the two parties come from different, not to say opposing, social spheres. Charlotte Weinhold's father is a successful entrepreneur, a representative of conservative high bourgeois culture with aspirations of entering the Kaiserreich's aristocracy. Ballhaus, a left-wing politician, considers this culture a threat to peace and social progress. Both of these romances achieve happy conclusions, without even having to overcome much opposition by societal forces, which might seem surprising in particular as regards Charlotte Weinhold and Janus Ballhaus. In a narrative that drama- tizes a conflict between primarily Western European nations and China, these couples suggest more than the tried and proven opposites attract formula or the fantasy of romantic love prevailing against all other influences shaping a person's identity. Rather, these romances level out national and class differ- ences, implying the possibility of a more homogenous European identity. The third love story, between Julia Lenck and Tschau, the son of Arthur Lenck's Chinese agent, by contrast remains underdeveloped and the viability of their union in question at the conclusion of the narrative: "Tschau stands there si- lently, nothing can be read from his features. Arletta looks at him and then at Julia and thinks: What is going to happen to you two? For a moment, she feels the question on the tip of her tongue, but she does not dare ask. Would the parents let them marry? Very unlikely. And if so, things would not be easy for them as a mixed-race couple."[48] Undoubtedly, Arletta's sympathies lie with the pair, but their story has not been told and her musings suggest tragedy.[49] Yet Arletta's own divided loyalties between two nations with war in their future, Italy and Germany, do not enter the narrative as a potential source of strife, even though the problem might soon be compounded by a husband in the mili- tary. Quite the contrary, Arletta Lind and Max von Reichenow appear as the couple to whom the future belongs. European identity eclipses nationality, but divided civilizational affiliations remain insurmountable.

In the novel's closing pages it falls to the unhappy young woman, whose romantic dreams will probably be thwarted, to draw a résumé: "Such an erup- tion of hatred between East and West must not repeat itself … and the best way is to work together toward orderly relations,"[50] Julia Lenck summarizes the life lesson her father has derived from the rebellion. Considering the magni- tude of the drama in which she has been involved, the sentence appears a little stale and trite. It echoes twenty-first-century received wisdom, conventional political discourse, and also the author's leftist political convictions. Her words belong to the above-mentioned discursive formations that highlight Western culpability and the predatory nature of imperialism. They are what one might expect to find in a novel written about the Boxer Rebellion today. Below the surface, however, this essay has argued, the text displays structures that sug- gest ambivalent feelings and a modicum of unease with regard to the Chinese people and is in that sense symptomatic of a pervasive wariness with which contemporary Germany beholds China. The Boxer Rebellion has reappeared in adult mainstream German literature after over ninety years precisely because a narrative about this historical event resonates with current concerns.

Historiography and historical fiction possess utilitarian functions: revisiting the past can lift a set of current problems out of what is perceived as their threatening immediacy and locate them within a larger context. Contemplation of the past provides a frame of reference for the present. The response *Yellow Wind* suggests to the growth of China's political and economic power pushes the historical novel in a new direction. During its nineteenth-century classic period, this genre constituted itself part and parcel of a national discourse: imagining the nation's past underwrote its legitimacy, charged the idea of nationhood with pathos and affect, and implicitly made the reader—at least the one of the home market—a stakeholder in the national project. In Seyfried's novel, by contrast, the nation has lost its primacy as a value of de facto transcendent quality. In place of the nation the text conceives of a (Western) European civilization as a locus of identity. In the context of the relative decline of Western economic and political power vis-à-vis East Asia as it is already occurring and stands to accelerate in the course of the twenty-first century, *Yellow Wind* advances the notion that only such a supranational entity can increase the stature of the nations in question to a point where they might act as a contender in certain arenas of international politics. Seyfried's historical novel thus responds, perhaps not always consciously, to a sense of anxiety as the West considers its increasingly contested position in the world. The manner of addressing East Asia's ascendancy indicated by *Yellow Wind* engages with political reality in a manner that is different from the one represented by Scott's works. The classic historical novel arose as a response to the Napoleonic wars that had severely tested the Westphalian system of sovereign nation states. In face of the recent continent-wide imperialist aggression, English literary culture celebrated national identity and sovereignty. Europe in the twenty-first century still struggles to move completely beyond the Westphalian system and to embrace a new political order that locates power in supranational institutions. Arguably there has been enormous progress in that direction over the past sixty years, but nonetheless the nation-state still remains the seat of substantial political, cultural, and ideological power. Whereas the classic historical novel thus looks to the past in order to endorse, sometimes to glorify, the present, Seyfried's dramatization of the past comments, with less confidence, upon the present and points a way toward the future.

Notes

1. For a detailed account of the events, see, for instance, Peter Fleming, *The Siege at Peking* (New York, 1959), Egbert Kieser, *Als China erwachte* (Munich, 1984), or Diana Preston, *The Boxer Rebellion* (New York, 1999). In a bibliography attached to the novel, Seyfried cites all three of these accounts as sources.

2. For an evaluation of some of the narratives produced in the immediate aftermath of the rebellion, see Yixu Lü, "German Colonial Fiction on China: The Boxer Uprising of 1900," *German Life and Letters* 59, no. 1 (Spring 2006): 78–100. For an evaluation of the press coverage in three representative German newspapers, see Yixu Lü, "Germany's War in China: Media Coverage and Political Myth," *German Life and Letters* 61, no. 2 (Summer 2008): 202–214. The response to the Boxer Rebellion in Britain appears to have been even stronger. The reason may have been that British colonial history and longstanding structures of power facilitated the literary reworking of the rebellion. It was frequently viewed as similar in kind to the Indian Mutiny of 1857, and writers could thus inscribe the rebellion into a well-established discourse on the "stability of empire and the ultimate supremacy of the 'civilized' over the 'uncivilized,' of discipline over mobbery." See Ross G. Forman, "Peking Plots: Fictionalizing the Boxer Rebellion," *Victorian Literature and Culture* 27, no. 1 (Spring 1999): 20.

3. The Chinese—whether the Boxers or a general "yellow peril" is not clear—also figure briefly in the narrator's stream of consciousness in "Leutnant Gustl" (1900): "All these shysters are Socialists these days. They're a gang.... They'd like to do away with the whole army; but they never think of who would help them out if the Chinese ever invaded the country." Arthur Schnitzler, *Plays and Stories*, trans. Richard L. Simon (New York, 1982), 254.

4. Somewhat surprisingly, considering remarks von Heyking made at other times (see, for instance, George Steinmetz, *The Devil's Handwriting: Precoloniality and the German Colonial State in Qingdao, Samoa, and Southwest Africa* [Chicago, 2007], 427–429), both novels also constitute devastating critiques of imperialism. For instance:

   The tower that stands out boldly in the principal courtyard is decorated on one side with stone relief work, which was taken from an old Bavarian peasant house and which represents St. George, the dragon-slayer. If to-day a dragon legend were to be written, it would have to be quite different from that old tale of handsome chivalrous George, who only went out to free the world from the wicked monster. To-day many puny gnomes sally forth against the dragon, whose home is faraway Cathay, but they don't want to kill it, they merely intend getting fat on it. The modern St. George chains the dragon so that it should remain quiet and allow itself to be milked.

   Elisabeth von Heyking, *The Letters Which Never Reached Him* (New York, 1904), 205–206. For an in-depth reading of von Heyking's novels, see Mary Rhiel, "A Colonialist Laments the New Imperialism: Elisabeth von Heyking's China Novels," *Colloquia Germanica* 41, no. 2 (Summer 2008): 127–139.

5. China, its culture, and its history have of course left deeper traces in German literature. For a reading of the appropriation of the oriental with regard to China as it occurred during the period of Weimar Classicism, see David Kim, "Re-Orienting the Weimar Theater: Enlightenment and Empire in Schiller's *Turandot*," *Colloquia Germanica* 41, no. 2 (Summer 2008): 111–126. The Expressionist period was particularly rich in terms of Chinese themes and motifs; in this context, see, for instance, Ingrid Schuster, *China und Japan in der deutschen Literatur 1890–1925* (Bern, 1977) and Changke Li, *Der China-Roman in der deutschen Literatur 1890–1930* (Regensburg, 1992).

6. http://www.tagesspiegel.de/kultur/pop-stolizei/1188106.html. Last accessed 2 February 2013.

7. http://www.tagesspiegel.de/politik/geschichte/seyfried-der-boxer-aufstand/1257404.html. Last accessed 2 February 2013. All translations from German are by the author, unless otherwise specified.

8. See D.H. Lawrence, *Studies in Classic American Literature* (London, 1971), 8.

9. See Fredric Jameson, *The Political Unconscious* (London, 1981).

10. Gehard Seyfried, *Gelber Wind oder Der Aufstand der Boxer* (Berlin, 2008), 94.

11. Matthew Phipps Shiel, *The Yellow Danger: Or What Might Happen If the Division of the Chinese Empire Should Estrange All European Countries* (London, 1899), 323. Shiel's work belongs to a well-established genre. For an evaluation of another Chinese-invasion narrative, see Eric Hayot, *The Hypothetical Mandarin: Sympathy, Modernity, and Chinese Pain* (Oxford, U.K., 2009), 148ff. Another text worth reading, if only to receive an impression of the paranoia and prejudice in German society at the turn of the twentieth century, is *Die Gelbe Gefahr* by popular adventure novelist and travel writer Stefan von Kotze (Berlin, 1904). Charitably one might describe this text as a political pamphlet, though racist screed would not be inappropriate. Written shortly after the Boxer Rebellion, to which it only alludes in cursory fashion, the text abounds with pseudo-Darwinian speculations, articulates disgust at the notion of miscegenation, and preaches "the pressing need of educating Europe and Germany in particular in the basic tenets of the catechism of race" (36).

12. For a history of the term "yellow peril," see Heinz Gollwitzer, *Die Gelbe Gefahr: Geschichte eines Schlagworts* (Göttingen, 1962).

13. Seyfried, *The Boxer Rebellion*, 489–492.

14. Seyfried, *The Boxer Rebellion*, 234.

15. Georg Lukács, *The Historical Novel* (London, 1965), 53.

16. Konrad Seitz, *Eine Weltmacht kehrt zurück* (Berlin, 2000), 440.

17. In general, the colonial/imperialist era has been the subject of some attention in German (popular) culture over the past decades. An example thereof is also Uwe Timm's 1978 novel *Morenga* and the three-part TV miniseries (1983–84) based on it; more recently, there have been a number of other miniseries with colonial themes, mostly of mediocre quality, for instance, *Momella—Eine Farm in Afrika* (2006) or *Afrika, mon Amour* (2007).

18. Franco Moretti, *Atlas of the European Novel 1800–1900* (London, 1998), 17. The *locus classicus* for an evaluation of the transformation the reading public underwent in the eighteenth century is Ian Watt's *Rise of the Novel* (1957), a study that undoubtedly influenced Moretti's research.

19. See Richard Maxwell, *The Historical Novel in Europe, 1650–1950* (Cambridge, U.K., 2009), in particular chapter 1.

20. Maxwell, *The Historical Novel in Europe, 1650–1950*, 3.

21. Moretti, *Atlas of the European Novel 1800–1900*, 38.

22. Awareness of the historical novel's relationship to conceptions of nationhood and nationality—and also, by one remove, to imperialism—has led many postcolonial writers to focus their efforts on transforming and troubling the genre's conventions. V.S. Naipaul's *A House for Mr Biswas* (1961) or Salman Rushdie's *Midnight's Children* (1980) and *The Moor's Last Sigh* (1995) are prime examples of this trend. Fictions by postcolonial writers have in turn resonated in critical work. See, for instance, Homi K. Bhabha, "DissemiNation: Time, narrative, and the margins of the modern nation," in *Nation and Narration*, ed. Homi K. Bhabha (London, 1990), 291–322.

23. John Marx, "The Historical Novel after Lukács," *Georg Lukács: The Fundamental Dissonance of Existence*, ed. Timothy Bewes and Timothy Hall (London, 2011), 190.

24. For instance, Marlow in *Heart of Darkness* (1899) when he recounts that "when I was a little chap I had a passion for maps. I would look for hours at South America, or Af-

rica, or Australia and lose myself in the glories of exploration." Joseph Conrad, *Heart of Darkness* (New York, 2006), 7–8. The difference between Marlow and Arletta is of course that the desires of Conrad's hero focus on what he shortly after calls the "blank spaces on the earth," (8) while Arletta's ambitions can only find fulfillment in a somewhat Europeanized context.

25. Seyfried, *Gelber Wind*, 10.
26. Seyfried, *Gelber Wind*, 31.
27. Seyfried, *Gelber Wind*, 343–344.
28. See Benedict Anderson, *Imagined Communities: Reflections on the Origin and Spread of Nationalism* (London, 1983).
29. See, for instance, Diana Preston, *The Boxer Rebellion*, 155 and 165.
30. Seyfried, *Gelber Wind*, 217.
31. Seyfried, *Gelber Wind*, 217.
32. Seyfried, *Gelber Wind*, 548.
33. See, for instance, Paula von Rosthorn's eyewitness account, *Peking 1900* (Vienna, 2001), a text Seyfried lists as one of his sources. "Our outrage against them [the Boxers] was continuously fanned by the sight of Chinese Christians who came fleeing to us, begging for protection.… But most appalling was the fact that many of them displayed the scars of the inhuman cruelty of their persecutors. When I think of the horrifying wounds that I saw every day I am struck with terror to this day. For example, I saw a woman whose one side was half roasted because she had been tied to a balcony close to the fire during the conflagration of Tung-Tang and was only able to free herself through the singeing of the cords. A girl showed me her arm from which the flesh had been cut in strips with a saber, and an old man had his neck so badly cleft that one could hardly believe that he was still alive" (36).
34. See, for instance, Jonathan D. Spence's discussion of the narrative of Galeota Pereira, a Portuguese sailor imprisoned and tortured by Chinese officials in the mid sixteenth century, in *The Chan's Great Continent: China in Western Minds* (New York, 1998), 19ff.
35. Polo, for instance, reports that after being defeated and captured, an adversary of the Great Khan, in fact the Khan's uncle, "was wrapped up tightly in a carpet and then dragged about so violently, this way and that, that he died," though in this case there exists a political rationale for the somewhat elaborate procedure: "the object in choosing this mode of death was so that the blood of the imperial lineage might not be spilt upon the earth." *The Travels of Marco Polo* (London, 1968), 97.
36. George Mason, *The Punishments of China* (London, 1801). These elisions have prompted Hayot to read Mason's book as "a trial [of the Chinese legal system] in which the most damning evidence is damning precisely because the text excludes it" (71), but even the evidence that is presented, colored engravings of, for example, "Burning a Man's Eyes with Lime" or "Punishment of a Wooden Collar," testifies to an interest in a putatively Chinese expertise in torture.
37. See, for instance, Manuel Hörth, *Die Verfolgung von Falun Gong* (Hinterskirchen, 2005).
38. Wolfgang Iser, *The Act of Reading: A Theory of Aesthetic Response* (Baltimore, 1978), 168.
39. Seyfried, *Gelber Wind*, 151.
40. Seyfried, *Gelber Wind*, 251.
41. Seyfried, *Gelber Wind*, 387.

42. Seyfried, *Gelber Wind*, 370.

43. Seyfried, *Gelber Wind*, 102.

44. The battles with the Boxers also seem to prefigure the trench warfare that lies a decade and a half in the future: "Reichenow himself feels appalling fear, he is literally shaking, his stomach a painfully cramped lump. To lift the head only a few centimeters can mean receiving a bullet or a splinter right in the face" (341).

45. Mikhail M. Bakhtin, *The Dialogic Imagination: Four Essays* (Austin, 1981), 217.

46. See endnote 15.

47. Despite its manipulation of time, one should emphasize, Seyfried's novel never ventures onto the territory of historiographic metafiction as it has come into fashion since the late sixties with such works as John Fowles's *The French Lieutenant's Woman* (1969) and E.L. Doctorow's *Ragtime* (1975). *Yellow Wind* lacks the theoretical awareness and self-referential structure of these works. To borrow Linda Hutcheon's definition of metafiction, Seyfried's novel does not "enact the problematic nature of the relation of writing history to narrativization and, thus, to fictionalization, thereby raising … questions about the cognitive status of historical knowledge." Linda Hutcheon, *A Poetics of Postmodernism: History, Theory, Fiction* (London, 1988), 93.

48. Seyfried, *Gelber Wind*, 561.

49. The lack of a resolution to this plot-line is even more surprising if one considers that the narrative had implicitly promised one. Much earlier, Arletta had said to Julia with reference to her romance: "'Your parents will surely not be thrilled. We will have to think of something. Chin up, I'm sure things will work themselves out. I'm just not sure yet how'" (236).

50. Seyfried, *Gelber Wind*, 612.

PART III

Negotiating Identity in Multicultural Germany

CHAPTER 7

Anna May Wong and Weimar Cinema
Orientalism in Postcolonial Germany

CYNTHIA WALK

Among ethnic actors in Weimar cinema, Anna May Wong was one of very few with Chinese heritage and the only Chinese American.[1] Wong first came to Germany in 1928 after an early Hollywood career limited to minor ethnic roles. Anti-miscegenation laws in America at the time made mixed-race marriage and interracial sex illegal in thirty of the forty-eight states. Asian roles were most often portrayed by white actors through the practice of yellowface in Hollywood films. With the exception of playing the lead in *Toll of the Sea* (1922), an adaptation of the Madame Butterfly myth set in China, Wong was confined to secondary characters and bit parts. Like Josephine Baker, Paul Robeson, and other nonwhite performers in the American entertainment industry of the 1920s, Wong went to Europe, where a reputation for racial tolerance offered the promise of broader opportunities. She arrived in Berlin under contract with German producer-director Richard Eichberg to star in a series of films intended for distribution on the international market.

As Tim Bergfelder has shown, Wong's transatlantic career has to be placed in the context of Weimar cinema's engagement in a pan-European effort to compete with Hollywood, during the late silent and early sound period, through an integrated transnational film initiative known as the "Film Europe" project. Wong promised to be a good fit as an actress already familiar to European audiences as the Mongol slave girl opposite Douglas Fairbanks in *The Thief of Baghdad*, an internationally successful orientalist fantasy that played in Britain and across the Continent after its release in 1924. The Chinese-American actress offered the validated image of an exoticism that was widely exportable and consumable in countries throughout the West, articulating a "complex hybridity … capable of appealing successfully across national and cultural boundaries

… in the different markets that made up the pan-national distribution networks central to the Film Europe project."[2]

Reactions to Wong's film career as a purveyor of orientalism have vacillated inside and outside the Asian-American community between admiration and embarrassment.[3] To recuperate her legacy from the stereotypes of Madame Butterfly and Dragon Lady, Yiman Wang has proposed that she deployed these clichés as an ironic ethnic masquerade, a deconstructive "yellow yellowface" performance to subvert the stereotypes through exaggeration. Comparing the actress with her fictional character in *Piccadilly* (1929) by German director E.A. Dupont, the most successful film Wong made abroad, Wang construes Wong/Shosho's strategic manipulation of her role as a performer as "an allegory of how Wong negotiated her status as a Chinese in the Euro-American cinema of the 1920s and early 1930s."[4] The view that Wong's performance was deliberately ironic and subversive offers postcolonial criticism a way to salvage the actress from exploitation and recast her as a less compromised ethnic pioneer.

Focusing on Wong's career abroad between 1928 and 1930, this chapter considers the three films Wong made with Eichberg in the title roles of *Song* (*Show Life*, 1928), *Großstadtschmetterling* (*Pavement Butterfly*, 1929), and *Hai-Tang* (*The Flame of Love*, 1930), as well as Dupont's *Piccadilly*.[5] To what extent did her collaboration with Film Europe—in particular the roles Wong played in these Anglo-German coproductions—allow her to move beyond her Hollywood career? What did her putative Chinese authenticity mean to German film spectators at the time? What did the engagement with Weimar cinema mean to her? Did Wong's performance in these films indeed critique the pervasive orientalism of her roles? This chapter addresses these questions in the context of larger historical issues they involve concerning European colonialism, Western views of China, and orientalism in Weimar cinema, as well as censorship and the representation of interracial desire.

Mitigating Colonial Loss and War Trauma: *Song* (Eichberg, 1928)

Richard Eichberg was a director of popular genre films in Weimar Germany with a reputation as a starmaker of several actresses, notably Lilian Harvey in a series of romantic comedies. Known as the "most American" of European directors, he also worked with established actors of the period like Paul Wegener, Heinrich George, and Hans Albers in melodramas and action films.[6] Using his industry expertise, Eichberg created a marketing campaign for Wong fit for a Hollywood star as the main attraction. Wong's image and name in large letters dominated ads in the trade papers like the cover and photo montages in the illustrated brochures for all three films published by *Film-Kurier* (see Figure 7.1).[7]

Figure 7.1. *Hai-Tang* premiere notice, *Film-Kurier*, 1 February 1930. Deutsche Kinemathek.

The Berlin premieres were staged in major movie theaters where the silent films were accompanied by live orchestras playing specially arranged musical compilations.[8] When *Hai-Tang*, an early sound film recorded with synchronized music by Hans May, opened at the Capitol am Zoo, the premiere was covered by the press as a prominent social event attended by dignitaries from the German film industry as well as a delegation from London led by the president of British International Pictures.[9]

Designed as star vehicles for Wong, the Eichberg films feature her as a performer, showcasing her body in exotic costumes and dance sequences, as she rises from poverty to wealth and success in tales of upward mobility. This motif is combined in the scenario with a central recurring theme: the unrequited love of an Asian woman for a white Western man in variations of the Butterfly story that entail self-sacrifice and end with her death or exile. The Butterfly narrative conventionally represents a colonial fantasy that projects Euro-American male desires and fears onto the oriental female. In the Eichberg films this produces what Bergfelder has called a "sado-masochistic gender dynamic" with punitive male violence inflicted on the long-suffering innocent female.[10]

From the zenith of its power in the nineteenth century, European colonialism was dismantled in an extended process of decolonization that began when Germany lost its colonial empire in Africa and the Pacific by the terms of the Versailles Treaty in 1919. Yet after World War I, the German colonial imagination survived even without colonies. Nostalgia for the lost territories and in some quarters outrage over the "colonial guilt lie" fueled an ongoing public discourse of power and appropriation during the Weimar Republic. Colonial revisionism had broad support in the Reichstag and was promoted by popular writers like Hans Grimm in *Volk ohne Raum* (People without Space, 1926), one of the bestselling novels of the interwar years. Colonial loss echoed the larger traumatic loss of hegemony for German national identity, in the context of military defeat and the collapse of the Wilhelmine Empire. The colonial romance motif in the Eichberg films mitigates this loss through an East-West relationship that symbolically reimposes Western hegemony.

This subtext emerges in the opening sequence of the first Eichberg film, *Song*. The setting is introduced as an "Eastern harbor," where the eponymous title character appears as "one of Fate's castaways," a homeless refugee who survives by foraging for food at the beach. Song spears a crab in the water only to become easy prey herself for two sailors who try forcibly to abduct her. She is rescued by a stranger who scares them off with a knife, John Houben (Heinrich George), who turns out to be a professional knife thrower looking for a partner in his variety act at a local tavern. Secretly auditioning her, without warning Houben rapidly throws several knives that etch an outline of her body in the wall. When he asks, "Are you afraid?" she both nods and shakes her head, terrified but eager to please. Despite reservations about serving as a human target, she gratefully accepts the job (see Figure 7.2).[11]

The geographic indeterminacy of the "Eastern harbor" setting in the first intertitle comes into focus with documentary footage of a famous landmark in the opening image. An aerial shot of the Hagia Sophia with its distinctive dome and four minarets places the story on the Bosporus in Istanbul. Known in the popular imagination as the city where East meets West, the bridge linking Europe with Asia, the Istanbul setting invites an allegorical reading of the encounter between Song and Houben. Although the Asian refugee is not assigned a specific ethnic identity, the Weimar German audience would likely have been aware of news reports about the revolutionary turmoil in China that brought many activists to Germany after the expulsion of the Communists from the Kuomintang in 1927.[12] Among them Song Qingling, widow of Sun Yat-sen and herself a former executive member of the Kuomintang, spent several years in Berlin exile. While the name of Wong's fictional character thus recalled one of China's most important political figures of the early twentieth century then living in Germany, she is the opposite of a revolutionary political activist. With Song vulnerable, in need of protection and hopelessly enamored of the strong white Western man

Figure 7.2. *Song* production still. Deutsche Kinemathek.

who rescues her from danger, her relationship with Houben replicates the reassuring orientalist fantasy of a dependent and gratefully submissive East, resonating with the memory of the former German leasehold of *Deutsch-Kiautschou* (the Kiaochow Bay concession in China, 1898–1914) often profiled as a model colony.[13]

After Song's "audition," the knife-throwing act is shown twice (edited each time to include the rapt attention of the diegetic audience at the Blue Moon Café) and becomes an ominous phallic motif throughout the film. Knife throwing has a long history as a sport. As a performance art in modern times, it was popularized in vaudeville, and during the late nineteenth century Bill Hickok's Wild West Show toured Europe with an impalement act in Western dress. Thus it is not surprising that Houben appears for the variety act decked out as an American cowboy in a Western hat and bandana, boots, chaps, and a leather belt with a pistol holster. However his female assistant is not portrayed as a Native American Indian, as one might expect. Instead the target girl, dressed in a grass skirt with beads and flowers in her hair worn open and long down her back, conjures a native island woman. The two costumes in the Blue Moon variety act introduce an eclectic stage version of the East-West scenario aimed at a broad audience (see Figure 7.3).

Figure 7.3. *Song* screenshot.

Since Paul Gauguin the South Seas had inspired a pervasive Euro-American escape fantasy, including a popular Hollywood film genre in the 1920s culminating in F.W. Murnau's *Tabu* (1931). *Deutsch-Neuguinea* (German New Guinea, 1884–1914) and *Deutsch-Samoa* (German Samoa, 1900–14) were Pacific territories of the former German colonial empire, and postwar Germany's fascination with the exotic became tinged with postcolonial anxiety.[14] The knife-throwing act in *Song* expresses a phallic impulse to dominate and (re)impose control. The alluring tropical woman appears as an overdetermined image representing the triple threat of a sexual, racial, and colonial Other that must be contained or eliminated.

In all the Eichberg films the colonial romance is challenged on both sides by male and female rivals, and conflict ensues in multiple overlapping mixed-race love triangles. In *Song* complications develop when Houben's ex-girlfriend comes to town. The man in the middle is unusually vulnerable, a refugee marked by a traumatic past. When Gloria (Mary Kid), Houben's earlier partner on the variety circuit, dumped him for another lover, he snapped. A flashback offers glimpses of rejection, jealousy, and a fight with his competitor that left them both for dead. As a survivor who returns from the dead burdened by traumatic memories, Houben recalls other troubled revenants in Weimar Germany, veterans of World War I who suffered from shell shock (*Kriegsneurose*). His brooding presence conceals a temperament given to impulsive anger and violent outbursts. Discovering Gloria's rise in the entertainment world as the prima ballerina of a touring ballet company, Houben tries to make quick money to impress her; instead he becomes disabled in a bungled robbery, temporarily losing his sight. Blindness combines another psychosomatic symptom of shell shock with symbolic castration.[15] Through the association with wounded war veterans, Houben's injured masculinity makes him an object of sympathy despite a violent attack on Song, who now plays a critical role in his recovery. She not only nurses him back to health but also consoles him by concealing Gloria's abandonment, masquerading as his former lover and even enduring an embrace intended for her.

Blindness and masquerade serve here as the alibi for otherwise taboo gestures of interracial sexuality. In addition to the embrace, the script for *Song* had included an exchange of kisses in this scene: "Reluctant and ashamed to pass herself off as Gloria, at the same time however happy to be caressed by J[ohn]. J[ohn] kisses her eyes and her mouth … Song returns his kiss and cuddles up against him … then her expression suddenly becomes sad. She realizes for whom the caresses were intended."[16] These intimacies in the script were not filmed, presumably to avoid censorship. While neither Germany nor Britain had laws prohibiting miscegenation, film censors in both countries were wary about the depiction of mixed-race relationships.[17] For distribution in the American market where state anti-miscegenation laws were common, the producers could anticipate that censorship of onscreen interracial kissing was inevitable. In this area *Song* sets a pattern for Wong's Film Europe projects: the script in each case is more daring than the released film, which withholds any depiction of explicit interracial sexuality.[18]

Paradoxically, Song is compromised by becoming too capable. To finance Houben's recovery, she accepts help from a wealthy impresario while rejecting his advances to find a job in an upscale night club. Her professional success (like Gloria's) once again leaves Houben behind, further challenging his masculinity. Song's final performance in the film, a sword dance in which she appropriates the phallus, is fatal. Just before the *coup de grâce*, Houben recognizes Song's devotion and his own repressed feelings for her, but it is too late. Mortally wounded in an accident onstage, Song's last words evince her endless capacity for selflessness: "I am so glad your eyes are better." Phallic penetration of the woman coincides with phallic healing. The affirmation of Houben's regained (in)sight points to a resolution of his psychic trauma and inhibition that she enabled, yet there is no time to consummate their relationship, as the final shot closes on Song's face in a death mask that fades into a black silhouette with the erasure of her image. Carefully lit close-ups of the actress's face at melodramatic high points are a consistent feature of the cinematography of Heinrich Gärtner, the cameraman with whom Eichberg collaborated on all three films. Here the soft-focus close-up at the end of *Song* glamorizes her death and with it the disappearance of the multilayered sexual, racial, and colonial threat she poses.

Outsider in the Metropolis: *Pavement Butterfly* (Eichberg, 1929)

Like Song, Mah (a common surname in China) is introduced as an ethnic outsider living on the margins of society in *Pavement Butterfly* (1929). At a street fair in Paris, the Chinese immigrant ekes out a living with a short turn in a variety show, performing a fan dance under the stage name Princess Butterfly. Framed for murder by a vindictive suitor (Alexander Granach), Mah runs away and finds refuge in the studio of a young artist Kusmin (Fred Louis Lerch), with whom she falls in love even after he accuses her of theft, unaware that she has acted under duress to protect him from danger. First blackmailed by a man she fears, then misunderstood, taunted, and turned out by the man she loves, Mah finds herself back on the street, abandoned and destitute with no place to go. A recurring image in the film shows Mah alone on the dark city street at night. Captured in a poster made to advertise the film, it is emblematic of the central conceit: the ethnic outsider (see Figure 7.4).[19]

Figure 7.4. *Butterfly* poster. Deutsche Kinemathek.

Eventually Mah is rescued by Baron de Neuve (Gaston Jacquet), an older aristocratic admirer who becomes her fatherly protector. After many adventures, some filmed on location, that take the action across Paris and down to the gambling tables at the Monte Carlo Casino on the French Riviera, he intervenes to resolve the misunderstanding between Mah and Kusmin. Yet this (explicitly titled) *Butterfly* narrative culminates in a formal act of renunciation, when, watching the budding romance between Kusmin and a new love interest, Mah defers to her rival in the final scene, handing over the white man she cannot have to the other woman. The mise-en-scène constructs the love triangle in a three-shot, then isolates and definitively excludes Mah. The ethnic outsider is now also an intruder in this new romantic relationship. A lingering close-up shows Wong's face in a restrained performance, expressing anguish in a single tear. German critics praised the subtlety of Wong's acting, reporting that her tears were so famous that people actually drove out to the set in Neubabelsberg just to watch her cry.[20] Fascination with abject Asian suffering has a long history in Western culture. According to Eric Hayot, silence/endurance under torture has been a major feature in the European representation of Chinese people since the seventeenth century.[21]

Wong's wardrobe changes in *Pavement Butterfly*, linked to her character's trajectory, tell the story of an immigrant's failed attempt at assimilation. Mah's Chinese stage costume in the variety show is replaced by plain Western street clothes until the Baron steps in. For the ball in Monte Carlo he has her outfitted for the occasion in a high-fashion evening gown with a train reminiscent of Erté designs in the period, a low-cut black dress trimmed with sequins, a long silver cape, and a tiara. The script specifies: "Mah looks like a queen in her costume."[22] Mah's regal costume signifies the nobility of her renunciation, legitimizing her exclusion. Saying farewell, Mah claims: "I don't belong to you [*Ich gehöre nicht zu euch*]." In the script she has one more line of dialogue that does not appear in the film intertitles: "I want to return to my country [*Ich will zurück in meine Heimat*]."[23] Lip-reading the silent image, it is nonetheless possible to see Wong mouthing the words in English, "I want to go home." Bearing witness to Mah's intent, the Baron affirms its wisdom with a gesture in the script that is preempted in the film by Gärtner's close focus on her face: "De Neuve stands at the door, carefully following the scene, he simply nods his head: he has to agree that she is right."[24]

Pavement Butterfly asserts the impossibility of assimilation. While Song died for violating the taboo against miscegenation because she caused a white man to embrace her, Mah survives by relinquishing her claim. But *die Fremde* (the foreigner, as she was called in a working title for the film) is defined—both narratively and visually—as an outsider who does not belong in the West and must emigrate. Gärtner's final shot of Mah's exit through the layered shadows of a portico into endless depth has been hailed as an exemplary model of German camera work in Weimar cinema during the 1920s (see Figure 7.5).[25]

Figure 7.5. *Butterfly* screenshot.

For the Asian Other in Eichberg's melodramas, the options are limited and resolution of the colonial romance leads only to death or exile. Although German critics generally ignored these implications, one Socialist reviewer of *Pavement Butterfly* nailed its sexist and racist hypocrisy: "Following the American scheme, the Chinese woman has to rescue a young white man, a painter, and at the end—because the white race is so sky-high superior to the yellow one—she gets the usual boot."[26]

Fetishized Spectacle and Victimized Heroine:
Hai-Tang (Eichberg, 1930)

Rewarding virtue with insult takes on new dimensions in *Hai-Tang* (1930), Wong's final project with Eichberg and her first sound film.[27] It was a multilingual production in which she played the leading role in three different language versions, shot separately in German, French and English. The plot, set in 1912 pre-revolutionary Russia, centers on a thwarted interracial love affair between Wong as the Chinese dancer Hai-Tang and Boris (Franz Lederer in the German and John Longden in the English version), a young lieutenant in the Czarist army. Their romance is initially challenged by a jealous female rival and then compromised by the imperious Grand Duke, Boris's superior officer, who takes a fancy to the exotic dancer and commandeers her for his own plea-sure. Hai-Tang tries to resist his advances but relents in order to save Boris's career. When her brother intervenes to rescue her but is caught and sentenced to be executed, she again submits to the Grand Duke's advances to save his life. The act of female self-sacrifice, implicit in the earlier Eichberg films, is invoked several times and ritualized here. In a meeting with other members of the Chinese troupe, Hai-Tang is tasked with gaining a pardon for her brother from the Grand Duke at any cost. Confronted with her duty to family and community, she consents, and they acknowledge her selfless gesture, bowing in respect. What the script subsequently calls a "sacrificial journey [*Opfergang*]"[28] leads from the Grand Duke's bedroom to death by her own hand through poi-son. "The road to dishonor" in the subtitle of the film links Hai-Tang's death with the sine qua non of the Butterfly myth, ritual suicide. Better to die with honor than live without it: the colonial mantra that ennobled the self-sacrifice of Asian women for white male privilege. When Hai-Tang kneels in front of a shrine to Buddha as she prepares for the end, echoing Butterfly again, she sanc-tions the mantra through religion (see Figure 7.6).

Figure 7.6. *Hai-Tang* screenshot.

Critics at the Berlin premiere complained about the chasteness of the film lovers who were more polite than passionate. Ernst Jäger of the *Film-Kurier* dryly observed how well Eichberg managed to capture the British sensibility: "Eroticism without sex appeal, exoticism without miscegenation."[29] In the opening scene after Hai-Tang invites Boris into her living room for a cup of tea, he sings a Russian soldier song at the piano and then takes his leave with a crisp military salute. Ironically the lyrics of what becomes a theme song in the film have a refrain that invokes what never happens there: "From Moscow down to Astrakhan/You'll hear love tales from every man/Some girls can't kiss, but some girls can." Hai-Tang's tryst with Boris contrasts with her violation by the Grand Duke, and the narrative alternates between scenes of love and abuse. As in the earlier Eichberg films, the most compelling moments center on Wong as fetishized spectacle or victimized heroine. After Song rescued John Houben, she was unjustly accused, attacked, thrown out, and abandoned by him. Mah was not only misunderstood by the man she loved, but also framed, slandered, robbed, blackmailed, and pursued relentlessly by another jealous and vindictive suitor. The sado-masochistic gender dynamic that informs these films serves to defend white Western masculinity by excluding the exotic foreigner.

The three Eichberg films passed censorship without incident and were licensed for exhibition in both Britain and Germany, where they fit into a tradition of cinematic orientalism. The orientalism contingent of Weimar cinema favored adventure films in exotic settings with white actors cast in Asian roles. Lil Dagover built her career playing the eroticized woman of color in the early 1920s, when she was virtually typecast for roles in ethnic drag, including the lead in Fritz Lang's adaptation of the Butterfly story, *Harakiri* (1919).[30] Although the size of the Chinese communities in Hamburg and Berlin had increased through immigration after World War I, few ethnic actors appeared in German films, where yellowface (such as Werner Krauß in the role of Nung-Tschang in Robert Reinert's *Opium* of 1919) was the norm. Cast in the Eichberg films alongside Wong in minor roles are also Nien Sön Ling (Mr. Wu in *Pavement Butterfly*) and Ley On (Wang Hu in *Hai-Tang*). German reviews typically describe Wong as the Chinese woman (*"die Chinesin"*), the Asian artist (*"die asiatische Künstlerin"*), the Mongolian from Hollywood, (*"die Mongolin aus Hollywood"*), or even the Yankee-Chinese (*"Yankee-Chinesin"*), imputing racial authenticity to her performance of Asian roles.[31] Her acting is praised for its expressive subtlety and restraint. Wong herself is compared with the great artists of the silent cinema, Asta Nielsen and Lillian Gish: "One recognizes it was not only the appeal of the exotic that has made Anna May Wong famous here. This Chinese woman has a mesmerizing, fascinating aura similar to the first films of Gish."[32] Among other early Gish films where she plays the role of suffering innocence, perhaps the critic Hans Sahl was thinking of *Broken Blossoms* (1919), a miscegenation narrative in an orientalist setting that features a sympathetic view of Chinese culture albeit with a different alignment of race and gender. The German critics' emotional favorite was *Song*. They sentimentalized the childlike demeanor of Wong's submissive character and the tragedy of her sacrifice invoked in the subtitle, "Die Liebe eines armen Menschenkindes" (The love of a poor human child). On the other hand, Wong's vocal performance in *Hai-Tang*, her first sound film, was considered inadequate, and Eichberg did not sign her for any further projects.

Benjamin and Weimar Berlin

Reports about Wong's offscreen presence in Berlin mostly correspond to her onscreen image as an orientalist fantasy. Among those who met her in the first spring of 1928 was one of Weimar Germany's leading cultural critics, Walter Benjamin. He interviewed her at a friend's house and published a profile in *Die literarische Welt*. Born in Los Angeles as a third-generation Asian American, Wong's bicultural heritage is invoked in Benjamin's title, "Conversation with Anne [sic] May Wong: A Chinoiserie out of the Old West," a conceit that conjures a playful combination of East Asia and the American West.[33] Yet this differentiated view of Wong's ethnicity in the title disappears in Benjamin's text, where numerous references to Chinese culture focus only on her Asian heritage. The profile is punctuated with putative Chinese proverbs as well as lines of poetry quoted directly from the *Dschung-Kuei* (a text based on a mythical figure in Chinese folklore) and another book identified as the *Ju-Kia-Li*. Through a series of quotations and analogies (Wong's name is like tea leaves, her face like the spring wind, her long hair like tumbling dragons, etc.), Benjamin imbues her image with the literary aura of ancient China.[34] The initial allusion to Wong's cultural hybridity shifts into an essentialist preoccupation with her Chineseness. Unlike the darker version in the Eichberg melodramas that reveals the latent violence of projective exoticism, here an iconic Weimar German intellectual succumbs to orientalism in an ostensibly flattering portrait.[35]

To the European audience Wong did not appear at odds with her orientalist environment. The young Hollywood celebrity was greeted with curiosity on the set and off. A well-known photo by Alfred Eisenstadt shows her in evening dress at the Berlin press ball in 1928 with Marlene Dietrich and Leni Riefenstahl. Wong stands between them at the center of the image as the guest of honor and the most prominent of the three at this stage in their respective careers (see Figure 7.7).[36]

Another photo—Wong's portrait by the English photographer Paul Tanqueray in 1929—shows her glancing to the side, a flower tucked behind one ear, with her hand held like a fan in front of her face in a pose that suggests the demure Butterfly. The handwritten dedication reads: "To Ruth Jannings: May

Figure 7.7. Alfred Eisenstadt photograph of Marlene Dietrich, Anna May Wong, and Leni Riefenstahl. Patrice Petro, "In the Wings," in *Idols of Modernity: Movie Stars of the 1920s*, ed. Patrice Petro (New Brunswick, 2010), 270.

you always remain as charming as the day I met you." Signed "Orientally yours, Anna May Wong."[37] Wong bows here to the wife of Emil Jannings, perhaps the most well-connected and internationally successful German actor of the period, having just returned from Hollywood, where he won the first American Oscar in May 1929. Her note expressly affirms the star image in the publicity photo with a flourish that conveys a posture of diplomatic deference toward power in the industry.

Wong's public persona served Weimar as a projection of orientalist fantasies. In this respect, although her brief career abroad was more successful and glamorous, it remained bound by limitations similar to those she experienced in Hollywood. To argue that Wong engaged in an ironic ethnic masquerade to subvert orientalism ignores the circumstances under which she performed abroad. Coming to Germany at age twenty-three on her first extended contract, nothing suggests that Wong used her new position in a foreign film industry to adopt a critical posture toward its practice that might jeopardize her opportunity there to star in a string of back-to-back leading roles. Moreover it is unlikely that Eichberg—who produced and directed at least three films

a year—would have allowed such leeway, given the pressure in his new coproduction arrangement with B.I.P. to deliver viable films for the international
market.[38] Yiman Wang posits that appreciation of Wong's career has been ob-
scured by a mistaken view of her acting as mimetic rather than performative.
While it may be true that German filmmakers and critics tended to essentialize
Wong and thus implicitly undervalue her acting in Asian roles by treating them
as a natural expression of her putative Chineseness, neither her performance
in the Eichberg films nor her behavior offscreen suggests irony and subversion.
On the contrary, the evidence indicates that Wong embraced and promoted
orientalism as the strategic key to her success. Wong's performance in *Piccadilly*
supports this view.

Shosho and the Vamp: Miscegenation Fantasies in *Piccadilly* (Dupont, 1929)

Filmed between the two later Eichberg projects, *Piccadilly* (like *Hai-Tang*)
was produced at the new B.I.P. studios at Elstree in London, where Dupont
imported his German team (art director Alfred Junge and cinematographer
Werner Brandes) to collaborate with the international cast of this film. Based
on a story by the English novelist Arnold Bennett, Dupont's script for *Piccadilly* brings forward a similar constellation of figures as the Eichberg films.
Wong's character is engaged in multiple overlapping mixed-race love triangles,
but the rivalries here form and harden into opposing white and Asian dyads,
foregrounding confrontation along the axis of racial difference in a scenario
that addresses colonialism from a different perspective. While the Eichberg
films mostly treat the solitary colonial subject abroad, the historical context
for *Piccadilly* is the migration of colonial subjects to the metropole. Not a lone
Asian refugee in the East or a visiting performer in the West, Shosho is part
of an established community of immigrants in a major European city. Though
she works in the kitchen at the Piccadilly Club in the fashionable entertainment district of London's West End, Shosho lives on the other side of town
in Limehouse, London's Chinatown. When her break comes with the opportunity for a stage career at the club, Shosho sends her white boss, Valentine
Wilmot (Jameson Thomas) to Limehouse to buy an exotic costume for her
performance. A tracking shot ominously follows him from behind, as he enters
alien territory through a labyrinth of closed doors. On another occasion later
in the film, during a night together on the town, Shosho brings him to a pub
in the East End and then back to her apartment, where she is killed after their
tryst under mysterious circumstances. As a space of ethnic alterity in the film,
Limehouse offers the white middle-class male visitor business, pleasure, and

the lure of transgressive adventure, where interracial desire implicates him in murder. While Shosho is punished for the threat of miscegenation, he will be exonerated.[39]

Piccadilly incorporates elements of the sensationalist Chinatown myth in British popular culture. *Nachtgestalten* (*The Alley Cat*, 1929, another Anglo-German film in production at the same time at the B.I.P. studio in Elstree directed by Hans Steinhoff) is a crime film also set in London that features a slumming visit to the East End, where a shady Chinese bar becomes the site of an attempted rape and a bloody showdown with the police.[40] Chinatown served as a locus of widespread anxiety about immigrant ethnic communities in large cities throughout the West, like the increased Chinese presence in postwar Berlin, where the working-class district around the Schlesischer Bahnhof (today's Ostbahnhof) in Friedrichshain was known as "the Chinese quarter."[41] In the racialized metropolis of the postcolonial era, miscegenation became a threat to traditional white European identity. *Piccadilly* addresses this highly charged topic head on in the pub sequence, where racism is subjected to a startling critique.

Shosho's sensational debut at the Piccadilly Club earns her a contract and celebrity. It also seems to offer the promise of acceptance in a mixed-race relationship with the West End nightclub owner, Val, when she takes him across London to a working-class pub in the East End: "This is *our* Piccadilly," she says, emphasizing class allegiance and the complementary spaces between which she moves with greater ease now. However, social mobility does not exempt her from restrictive attitudes toward race. Standing at the bar, Shosho and Val witness a disturbance on the dance floor, where a white woman is bounced from the pub for dancing with a black man, mirroring the taboo of their own mixed-race relationship. "I think we better go," Val warns, and they make a quick exit. But first they watch a remarkable standoff between the Vamp (as the white woman is called in the credits) and the bar owner (see Figure 7.8a,b).

When he reproaches her for violating the prohibition against mixed dancing, she stands her ground and talks back, holding the center of the screen for almost a full minute. Filmed at close range in medium shot, her lips form words so demonstratively that they invite us as spectators of this silent film to "read" them. The Vamp, a cameo role played by the character actress Ellen Pollock, is introduced with a sight gag that puns on the idea of spectacle(s). Standing outside the pub she peers in through the name on the glass door; a close-up of her eyes behind the double "o" in the word "saloon" creates the playful effect of eyeglasses. A reversal of this joke then turns the subject into the object of spectacle in the Vamp's altercation with the bar owner. "How dare you!" she shouts fiercely in his face. Pointing to herself and others nearby, her gestures suggest a principled defense in terms of her right to consort with whomever she pleases.

Figure 7.8a. *Piccadilly* screenshot.

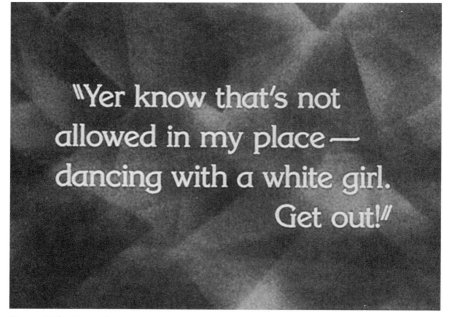

Figure 7.8b. Intertitle.

If her defiance seems to offer a glimmer of hope that power might yield and resistance triumph, in fact it does not when she is forced to leave under protest. The Vamp's expulsion is a warning to Shosho.

Piccadilly was marketed as an original screenplay by Arnold Bennett, with the cachet of originality enhanced by association with a popular British novelist of the period. No doubt promoting British authorship was a B.I.P. pitch for national recognition, though it seems the reality in this case was more complicated—as it usually is in the collaborative enterprise of filmmaking. The shooting script for *Piccadilly* was written in German.[42] Evidently the screenwriting process involved at least two authors and many drafts. It appears that Bennett provided the initial story and Dupont adapted it for the screen, a view supported by internal evidence. Briefly: Bennett's story is available in print, published by Readers' Library in London as an illustrated photoplay with frame enlargements from the film to commemorate its release in 1929. His text lays out plot, character, and dialogue in twenty-five chapters written in conventional narrative form like a novel, Bennett's forte. Dupont's adaptation selectively integrates these elements into a list of shots, numbered 1–555, with technical notes on camera direction, scene transitions and intertitles. The change in format is accompanied by a shift in emphasis on visual effects. A signature feature of Dupont's work, evident also in the scenario for *Piccadilly*, is his emphasis on spectacle: all the performance scenes are amplified and a new one is added. The pub scene is not in Bennett's story. The contribution of a different author, it is introduced in Dupont's adaptation as a new episode in the narrative, an embedded spectacle, "*eine kleine Tragikomödie,*" as he characterizes it in the scenario. The little tragicomedy features an object lesson in the power of social convention that crushes transgression and punishes it with exclusion.[43]

Bennett's story portrays race relations in terms of British colonialism. There Shosho criticizes the arrogance of her rival for Val, the Englishwoman Mabel Greenfield, as a legacy of British colonial policy in Asia:

> I know you look down on me because I'm Chinese and you're English, and because I was a scullery-maid, and because I've lived here in Limehouse and don't talk English like you do ... And supposing I was a scullery maid—me a Chinese girl? Why was it? It was because of all that you Europeans did in China. Why didn't you leave us alone ... But my family was ruined, and my father and mother came to England, and when they died I had to be a scullery maid, and you look down on me.[44]

Dislocation, class loss, and humiliation: the postcolonial subaltern voices a list of grievances and then Shosho threatens Mabel with a dagger in part to avenge the historical insult. Dupont's adaptation drops all reference to British colonialism in the women's confrontation, reducing their conflict to romantic rivalry, and shifts it to the pub scene where colonial racism and white racism toward blacks echo and are framed by an allusion to American culture. The pub scene highlights the common plight of Asians and blacks as outsiders in white European society, subject to exclusion if they cross the color barrier. In effect Dupont's script moves beyond Bennett's story, reframing the racial argument to address not only British colonialism in Asia but also race relations in the United States. This argument in the script is amplified in the film through the casting, costume, and performative acting style of the Vamp and her black dance partner. Like the Vamp, he is casually dressed in street clothes except in one respect. He wears a top hat—not a cap or a derby like other working-class male customers in the pub, but a topper that sets him apart. With its crown bent and beaver skin beaten up and crushed, this top hat cannot be confused with the upper-class accessory of London gentlemen who frequent the Piccadilly Club. It alludes instead to the American tradition of blackface minstrelsy and the distinctive costume of the would-be dignified character, Jim Dandy (see Figure 7.9).[45]

Figure 7.9. *Piccadilly* production still. Deutsche Kinemathek.

Piccadilly's allusion to African American performance resonates with another contemporary theatrical event. In 1928, at the same time the film was in production, the young African-American actor Paul Robeson made his London debut at the Drury Lane Theatre. Like his contemporary Wong, whom he knew and with whom he socialized abroad, Robeson was part of the outmigration of American performers of color to Europe during the interwar period. At Drury Lane he starred in a revival of *Showboat*, the musical by Oscar Hammerstein that thematizes interracial sexuality in the context of black-white racial conflict in the American South. There, in what has become known as the "miscegenation scene," the sheriff expels a mixed-race couple from town for violating the legal ban on race mixing. As we have seen, *Piccadilly* stages a similar scenario in which the pub owner takes over the role of enforcer. The treatment of miscegenation as a serious social subject in both musical and film melodrama is a significant departure from tradition that represents movement toward the integration of racial themes in modern popular entertainment.[46]

Western society has historically privileged whiteness with the agency to speak in public. It is symptomatic that while Shosho is a stage performer, her dance is silent. In the pub scene she turns away from the disturbance and remains voiceless, like the black man who is dismissed and leaves the dance floor without protest. Instead the Vamp speaks for them both as their proxy. In this way the two interracial couples in the scene are linked by the dynamics of identification and projection. Shosho eventually will have her say too, but only later and in private. For now, because of the disturbance, she has become afraid of exposure. The high fur collar of her evening coat (an index of assimilation through Paris fashion)[47] serves as a cover behind which Shosho can hide her face to conceal her racial identity. That allows a safe exit but leads to a poignant missed opportunity in an epilogue to the pub scene. Bounced from the pub the Vamp finds a sympathetic audience outside. Several people gather around to hear her story, and the debate she initiated inside continues on the street with a diverse crowd of outsiders who, like her, have been excluded. Meanwhile Shosho's covering strategy is so effective that even the Vamp is fooled. Misrecognizing her double, she mocks the hasty departure of what appears to be an officious upper-class couple slumming in the East End. But the scene is not yet quite over. The camera tracks down the street to Shosho who slips her house key into Val's hand. As a truck passes, the mixed couple is erased from the screen and disappears from view. What is not sanctioned in public will now continue out of sight in private.

The innovations in Dupont's script decisively broadened the appeal of *Piccadilly* to international audiences beyond Europe and the British Empire. The privileging of America in particular as a market for the film is evident in the in-

troduction of black characters in the pub scene. That is consistent as well with
cuts undertaken to accommodate the restrictive attitude toward miscegenation
in American cinematic culture at the time, laid out in cautionary guidelines
known as the "Don'ts and Be Carefuls." Thus the forbidden interracial kiss in
Dupont's script was evidently staged and shot but then edited out of the seduction scene in a preemptive act of self-censorship to advance the release date and
facilitate distribution in America.[48] Interracial desire still suffuses the film in
the aura surrounding Shosho, and when she engages with Val by stepping out
in public as a couple, a boundary is crossed where voyeuristic fantasy becomes
social reality. Dupont ventures furthest in the pub scene when the social taboo
is challenged in the Vamp's pushback. A white woman facing down a white
man is especially dangerous, because it fractures traditional patriarchal power.
However, what she says is not reproduced and validated in the intertitles. For
the film spectator the Vamp's credibility is undercut by her status as a street-
walker, a bit drunk and unsteady on her feet, whose words remain largely unintelligible. Any notion Shosho may have about reversing the power structure
is exposed in the pub sequence as a naive illusion. The "little tragicomedy" provides a sobering corrective, an object lesson in the futility of resistance. It has
implications for Wong herself too. Shosho's proxy in the embedded spectacle
can also be seen as Wong's cautionary double or evil twin. The Vamp demonstrates the high price of transgression—to avoid exclusion, do not be like her!

For distribution in Germany *Piccadilly* was retitled *Nachtwelt*, conjuring a
provocative vision of urban nightlife. A notice for the Berlin premiere emphasizes the ascendancy of racial difference, where the white woman is displaced
and marginalized by the looming presence of her Asian rival at the center of the
image (see Figure 7.10).

Then there is the racy poster designed in Austria by Josef Bottlik in 1929
showing Wong bare-chested in an image borrowed from an earlier Hollywood
film, *Across to Singapore* (1928), and doctored to make her look topless (it now
appears on the cover of the Milestone DVD box for *Piccadilly*). The marketing campaign appealed to voyeurism with the promise of interracial sex in an
era when it was taboo not only in the film industry. In the gathering climate
of extremism during the late Weimar period in postcolonial Germany, *Piccadilly*'s miscegenation theme—especially in the agitated pub sequence face-
down—also potentially triggered anxieties about political activism and racial
pollution through historical associations with yellow peril demagoguery ("*Die
gelbe Gefahr*")[49] as well as the notorious Black Shame campaign ("*Die schwarze
Schmach*") during the post-World War I occupation of the Rhineland.[50] Of
course the end of the film dispels such anxieties with the murder of Shosho by
her jealous Asian boyfriend in a conclusion that eliminates the racial Other and
restores the dominance of whiteness.

Figure 7.10. *Piccadilly,* Berlin premiere notice, *Film-Kurier,* 16 February 1929. Deutsche Kinemathek.

Wong, Baker, and the Performance of Ethnic Identity

The famous African-American entertainer, Josephine Baker, provides a useful comparison to Wong in the discussion of performativity. Like Wong and Robeson she joined the outmigration of performers of color and found the celebrity and success that had eluded her in America in a career on the Continent, including Berlin. Baker was known for the kind of camp excess and irony Yiman Wang attributes to Wong. The emblem of Baker's career abroad was the iconic skirt of bananas she wore onstage. Marketed in Paul Colin's poster for the *Folies Bergère*, she used this costume to the hilt, an example of her skill as a comic performer and self-promoter. Her exuberant representation of primitivism onstage and in four French feature films called out the racist stereotype. The 1927 film *Siren of the Tropics* is a Cinderella story featuring Baker as Papitou, a native of the French Antilles islands, who pursues a colonial visitor back to Paris, where she loses him but becomes a star on the music hall stage.[51] The narrative culminates in a farewell scene where she renounces her white lover, a sequence that contrasts with a similar moment at the end of *Pavement Butterfly*. While Wong plays the scene as straight melodrama, Baker's performance complicates the act of renunciation. When Baker/Papitou announces her departure ("Me leave now…go far…real far…America"), she does not simply walk out the door and leave. She turns back and asks for a personal souvenir of André to remember him by, a token she receives with trembling fingers and embraces with tears and elaborate gestures of affection, as if the cherished object were the man himself. The memento is a prayer book that opens in her hands to a passage idealizing the "joy" of altruistic sacrifice. However, Baker's highly stylized pantomime of pain and loss undercuts that sentiment and puts the lie to the self-serving colonialist myth it represents. The excess in her characteristically over-the-top performance produces a campy exaggeration that both expresses and invites ironic distance.

Scholars emphasize that Baker began her career in stage comedy with a star image that endured as a comic performer. Nancy Nenno observes, "Baker's performances could be read as consistently and openly mocking precisely those who most praised her."[52] Biographer Benetta Jules-Rosette sees a political motive in Baker's identity construction: "Through parody and innuendo, she molded stereotypical roles that she was commissioned to play into a form of social criticism."[53] Their view is not simply a retrospective assessment beholden to tenets of postcolonial criticism. When Baker first appeared in Berlin on tour with the *Revue Nègre* at Rudolf Nelson's Theater am Kurfürstendamm in 1926, the writer Max Hermann-Neisse characterized her primitivist performance as a self-parody (*Selbstpersiflage*) that resonated in Germany with a tradition of racist caricatures in the illustrated weekly, *Fliegende Blätter*.[54]

By contrast, no contemporary critics of the Eichberg films saw any irony in Wong's performance—even those who deplored their racial bias and would likely have been receptive to such tendencies. Instead Benjamin, who spoke with her during the shooting of *Song*, reports Wong's delight with her role as the first film character that was conceived and written specifically for her talents: "The role … is perfect, it's My Role like none ever before." For Benjamin the darkness of its suffering and misfortune suited her stated preference as an actress for the sad scenes of melodrama.[55]

Austrian scriptwriter, Adolf Lantz, author of the Eichberg scripts for both *Song* and *Pavement Butterfly* as well as a collaborator on the script for *Hai-Tang*, spoke with remarkable candor about the constraints of the film industry on these projects that he ascribed to repressive censorship in the international market:

> A happy ending is downright forbidden only in one circumstance: when a black woman, an Indian woman, or as in our case, a Chinese woman plays the leading role. Then … we portray this 'foreign-race female' not among her own people (we wouldn't even be able to find so many Chinese), but in the milieu of white people and in conflict with them. A happy ending could only involve marriage with a white man. But such a thing would never pass American censorship.[56]

When Wong left Hollywood in 1928, the "Don'ts and Be Carefuls" guidelines that circulated informally in the American film industry warned against miscegenation in film production. By 1930, that warning had escalated under the Production Code into an outright ban that lasted until 1956. Although the wording of the Code's miscegenation clause forbade only the depiction of "sex relationships between the white and black races," the prohibition was generally construed more broadly to include Asians and other people of color. Nonetheless it is one of the open secrets of American film history that classical Hollywood cinema thrived on what Susan Courtney has described as "miscegenation fantasies," especially the spectacle of white women under assault by men of color as in D.W. Griffith's *Birth of a Nation*, and more to the point here Cecil B. De Mille's *The Cheat*, both 1915. Courtney interprets the charged interracial scenario as a symptom of racial and gender anxiety among white men in turn-of-the-century America and a displacement of male vulnerability onto the female body.[57] Gina Marchetti, on the other hand, views Hollywood's interest in taboo sexuality, aside from its commercial appeal, as a way for film to offer both "forbidden pleasures" and maintain "existing, unequal racial, gender, and class hierarchies."[58] These analyses of the topic in American cinema suggest intriguing analogues for the Eichberg films under different historical circumstances in the countries of Film Europe.

Eichberg's scriptwriter lamented the limits imposed by censorship: "It is … terrible for the scriptwriter to lead this wonderful, poor sufferer through so many dramatic adversities and yet never be able to make her happy. On the other hand: you can't run your head through the wall. It's better to choose the lesser evil. Better not to insist on the 'happy ending' than deprive a hundred million people of experiencing this unique actress."[59] Lantz crafted three film roles for the star persona of Wong, whom he admired as an actress, but whose characters in his scenarios were subjected to the agonies of melodrama without achieving fulfillment. The prohibition against miscegenation in Hollywood also impinged upon production and distribution in Film Europe. Calculating that resistance would be futile and self-defeating, Lantz chose accommodation to further his primary objective. Play according to the rules in the industry, he reasoned, so that your work can reach as large an audience as possible. In *Piccadilly* as well her other Anglo-German films abroad, it appears that Anna May Wong did too.

Notes

My thanks to the organizers of the German Film Institute on "Unknown Weimar: International Connections," hosted by the University of Michigan in 2006, where I was introduced to the European film career of Anna May Wong, and to the editors of this volume for their insightful comments. I am also grateful to the staff at the Deutsche Kinemathek Berlin and the British Film Institute London for their help in providing access to relevant unpublished material and for permission to reproduce many of the images that accompany this chapter.

1. Notable ethnic Chinese actors in Weimar cinema include Henry Sze (*Die Herrin der Welt 1–4, Die Sonne Asiens*), Nien Sön Ling (*Die Freundin des gelben Mannes, Großstadtschmetterling*), Ley On (*Hai-Tang*), and Grace Chiang (*Melodie der Welt*).

2. Tim Bergfelder, "Negotiating Exoticism: Hollywood, Film Europe and the Cultural Reception of Anna May Wong," in "*Film Europe" and "Film America": Cinema, Commerce and Cultural Exchange 1920–1939*, ed. Andrew Higson and Richard Maltby (Exeter, 1999), 321. This essay builds on Bergfelder's pioneering work.

3. Edward Said's study of orientalism informs the academic debate, sometimes explicitly as in Anthony B. Chan's monograph, *Perpetually Cool: The Many Lives of Anna May Wong* (Lanham, M.D., 2007), 218–223. Wong's controversial film legacy is debated in "A Twentieth Century Actress: A Conversation with Yunah Hong and Peter X. Feng," *Quarterly Review of Film and Video* 23 (2006): 37–44. Feng's posture here is telling: "I'm ambivalent. Is there a film where you enjoy Anna May Wong's performance even though the film makes you cringe?" See also Graham Russell Geo Hodges, *Anna May Wong: From Laundryman's Daughter to Hollywood Legend* (New York, 2004), 234: "For practitioners of Asian American history, Anna May Wong was a dilemma that had to be solved."

4. Yiman Wang, "The Art of Screen Passing: Anna May Wong's Yellow Yellowface Performance in the Art Deco Era." *Camera Obscura* 60, vol. 20, no. 3 (2005): 174. More recently, see also Yiman Wang, "Anna May Wong: Toward Janus-Faced, Border-Crossing, 'Minor Stardom,'" in *Idols of Modernity: Movie Stars of the 1920s*, ed. Patrice Petro (New Brunswick, N.J., 2010), 159–181.

5. The Eichberg films are currently available only as archival prints: *Song* and *Großstadtschmetterling* at the Bundesarchiv-Filmarchiv Berlin and the English version of *Hai-Tang* under the title *The Flame of Love* at the British Film Institute London. A

beautifully restored version of *Piccadilly* has been released on DVD (Milestone Film & Video, 2005).

6. Hodges, *Anna May Wong*, 75.

7. My thanks to the Deutsche Kinemathek Berlin for permission to reproduce the premiere notices for *Hai-Tang* (Figure 7.1) and *Piccadilly* (Figure 7.10), the poster for *Großstadtschmetterling* (Figure 7.4), and the production stills for *Song* (Figure 7.2) and *Piccadilly* (Figure 7.9).

8. Herbert Birett, *Stummfilm-Musik: Materialsammlung* (Berlin, 1970) documents the compilations of Paul Dessau (for the premiere of *Schmutziges Geld* a.k.a. *Song* at the Alhamabra Theater, 127) and M.A. Pflugmacher (for *Großstadtschmetterling* at the Universum am Kurfürstendamm, 140). Pflugmacher's *Musikaufstellung* (available at the Deutsche Kinemathek Berlin) is a numbered list of themes from diverse sources including melodies from Puccini's opera, *Madama Butterfly*, cued to accompany each scene in the film.

9. "Das Capitol stand gestern im Zeichen eines 'großen Abends.' Die äußerst wirksame und festliche äußere Aufmachung der Hai-Tang-Premiere … bildete den Rahmen eines gesellschaftlichen Ereignisses, das die Berliner Prominenz aller Schattierungen vereinigte. Dazu die prominenten Gäste aus London, an ihrer Spitze Mr. Maxwell, der Präsident der British International. Die Köpfe vieler bekannter Theaterbesitzer Berlins und aus dem Reiche bemerkt man in dem festlichen Hause, das den kommenden Ereignissen erwartungsvoll entgegenblickt." Hans Wallenberg, "*Hai-Tang*: Eichberg Ton-Film der B.I.P.," *Lichtbild-Bühne*, 27 February 1930.

10. Bergfelder, "Negotiating Exoticism," 316.

11. Not unlike the dilemma Wong herself faced, given the problematic roles she was assigned to play in the Eichberg films.

12. See the chapter by Weijia Li in this volume.

13. The German Sinologist Richard Wilhelm (1873–1930) served as a missionary in the colonial city of Tsingtao. Among other influential publications, his 1923 translation of the *I Ching* shaped Weimar German views of China's spiritual heritage in the 1920s. See also the comparative analysis of ethnographic discourse in the German colonies in George Steinmetz, *The Devil's Handwriting: Precoloniality and the German Colonial State in Qingdao, Samoa, and Southwest Africa* (Chicago, 2007).

14. Jared Poley, *Decolonization in Germany: Weimar Narratives of Colonial Loss and Foreign Occupation* (Bern, 2005). On postcolonialism and sexuality in the writings of Hanns Heinz Ewers, Poley observes that colonial encounters that had previously been pleasurable became threatening and dangerous.

15. Anton Kaes's analysis of shell shock in postwar Weimar cinema opens with this motif in *Dem Licht Entgegen* (1918). *Shell Shock Cinema: Weimar Culture and the Wounds of War* (Princeton, 2009), 8–14.

16. "Befangen und beschämt, sich als Gloria auszugeben, gleichzeitig aber beglückt von J[ohn] liebkost zu werden. J[ohn] küsst ihre Augen und ihren Mund. Song schlägt fast beschämt die Augen nieder, dann huscht ein seliges glückliches Lächeln über ihre Züge. Song erwidert seinen Kuss und schmiegt sich an ihn … Song atmet beglückt auf; dann wird ihr Ausdruck plötzlich traurig. Es wird ihr klar, wem die Liebkosungen gegolten haben." Adolf Lantz and Helen Gosewisch, script for *Schmutziges Geld* (working title for *Song*), scenes 81b–82, pp. 50–51. Deutsche Kinemathek Berlin.

17. James C. Robertson, *The British Board of Film Censors: Film Censorship in Britain, 1896–1950* (London, 1985).

18. By contrast *Java Head* (1934), the last film Wong made abroad with British producer Basil Dean, thematizes miscegenation, albeit in a moralizing object lesson about the impossibility of colonial marriage.

19. Bottlik, Prodag, Ritter, poster for *Großstadtschmetterling* (1929). Reproduced in Michael Wedel, *Kolportage, Kitsch und Können: Das Kino des Richard Eichberg* (Berlin, 2007), 117. Reprinted here with the permission of the Deutsche Kinemathek Berlin. See a series of frame enlargements from the film online at http://www.stummfilm konzerte.de/glossar/stummfilme/grossstadtschmetterling.html. Last accessed 31 December 2013.

20. "Ihr Weinen ist unter den Kollegen berühmt. Man fährt nach Neubabelsberg heraus, um es zu sehen." Walter Benjamin, *Gesammelte Schriften*, IV, 1, ed. Tillman Rexroth (Frankfurt, 1972), 524.

21. Eric Hayot, *The Hypothetical Mandarin: Sympathy, Modernity, and Chinese Pain* (Oxford, U.K., 2009), 48.

22. "Mah steht in dem Kostüm wie eine Königin." Adolf Lantz, script for *Asphaltschmetterling* (like *Die Fremde*, a working title for *Großstadtschmetterling*), scene 152, p. 114. Deutsche Kinemathek Berlin.

23. Lantz, script for *Asphaltschmetterling*, final scene 170, p. 128.

24. Lantz, script for *Asphaltschmetterling*, "An der Portiere steht de Neuve, die Scene aufmerksam verfolgend, ganz leicht nickt er bloß mit dem Kopf: er muss ihr recht geben!"

25. Thomas Brandlmeier, "'Rationalization First.' Deutsche Kameraschule im britischen Film," in *London Calling: Deutsche im britischen Film der dreißiger Jahre* (Munich, 1993), 74.

26. "Die Chinesin muß nach amerikanischem Schema einen jungen Weißen retten, einen Maler, und bekommt zum Schluß, weil die weiße Rasse der gelben so himmelhoch überlegen ist, den üblichen Fußtritt." Anon., *Sozialistische Bildung*, May 1929.

27. The name, Hai-Tang, recalls a character with the same name in Döblin's Chinese novel, *Die drei Sprünge des Wang-Lun* (1915). It also resonates with Chang Hi-Tang [Tschang Haitang], the role Wong played in a Basil Dean production of *The Circle of Chalk* by Klabund [Alfred Henschke] at the New Theatre in London from 14 March through 20 April 1929.

28. Ludwig Wolff, Monckton Hoffe, and Adolf Lantz, script for the German version, *Hai-Tang. Der Weg zur Schande*, scene 52, p. 62. Deutsche Kinemathek Berlin.

29. "Erstaunlich wie der Producer Eichberg die englische Mentalität ergriffen hat, Erotik ohne Sex-Appeal, Exotik ohne Mischlingsneigung." Ernst Jäger, "Hai-Tang." *Film-Kurier*, 27 February 1930.

30. Tobias Nagl, *Die unheimliche Maschine: Rasse und Repräsentation im Weimarer Kino* (Munich, 2009), 13, 431–441.

31. Fritz Olimsky, "Großstadtschmetterling," *Berliner-Börsenzeitung*, 12 April 1929; Hermann Linden, "Anna May Wong, das asiatische Wunder," *Frankfurter Zeitung*, 4 May 1929; Anon., [Review of *Song*], *Internationale Filmschau* [Prag], 25 September 1928; Ernst Jäger, "Song," *Film-Kurier*, 21 August 1928.

32. "Man erkennt, daß es nicht nur der Reiz des Exotischen war, der die Anna May Wong bei uns berühmt machte. Von dieser Chinesin geht eine ähnlich betörende, faszinierende Wirkung aus wie von den ersten Filmen der Gish." Hans Sahl, "Großstadtschmetterling," *Der Montag Morgen*, Nr. 15, 15 April 1929.

33. "Gespräch mit Anne [sic] May Wong. Eine Chinoiserie aus dem alten Westen," in Benjamin, *Schriften*, 523–527.

34. See Birgit Tautz, *Reading and Seeing Ethnic Differences in the Enlightenment: From China to Africa* (New York, 2007).
35. Contemporary Chinese American artist, Patty Chang, recently made a two-channel video installation about the meeting between Wong and Benjamin as well as his published interview: "The first video alternates between three people each individually translating Benjamin's German text into English. This illuminates the ease with which mistranslation occurs in Benjamin's 'reading' of Wong. The performance of translation gives distance to Benjamin's text and allows the viewer space to reconsider Benjamin's contextualization of Wong. On the other screen, two Chinese actors portray Benjamin and Wong's meeting as an imaginary, intimate encounter. The installation restages and recontextualizes this meeting as a porno in China with Chinese television actors—a reversal of sorts, turning a Chinoiserie into a Western." Handout, Mary Boone Gallery (New York, 2009). One provocative implication of Chang's installation, called "*Die Ware Liebe*/The Product Love," is that Wong exploited the commercial power of orientalism to captivate/seduce Benjamin and sell herself in the film market.
36. Patrice Petro, "In the Wings," in *Idols of Modernity*, 270.
37. Paul Tanqueray, "Anna May Wong, mit Autogramm 1929," in *Glamour! Das Girl wird feine Dame—Frauendarstellungen in der späten Weimarer Republik*, ed. Verena Dollenmaier and Ursel Berger (Berlin, 2008), 104.
38. Mostly romantic comedies and melodramas (four in 1928, three in 1929, and three in 1930 including German-French and English versions of *Hai-Tang*, Eichberg's first sound film). See the annotated filmography in Wedel, *Richard Eichberg*, 113–124.
39. Thus in Karen Leong's astute analysis "*Piccadilly* ultimately presents a cautionary and cynical version of the Hollywood narrative of white heterosexual romance." Leong, "Anna May Wong and the British Film Industry," *Quarterly Review of Film and Video* 23 (2006): 18.
40. My thanks to Philipp Stiasny for this reference. See his analysis of the film in program notes for a screening by StummfilmKonzerte at Babylon Berlin in 2006, "Ein grundanständig gemachter Reißer: Drei Gründe für die Wiederentdeckung von *Nachtgestalten*," in *StummfilmKonzerte Programmheft*, ed. Stefan von Bothmer (Berlin, 2006).
41. "Im Chinesenviertel," *Tägliche Rundschau*, 23 April 1925, cited in Dagmar Yü-Dembski, *Chinesen in Berlin* (Berlin, 2007), 20–24.
42. E.A. Dupont, "*Piccadilly*": *Adaptation and Scenario*. Unpublished typescript, 129 pages in German, at the Deutsche Kinemathek Berlin. An English translation of this text with notable Germanicisms is also available as an unpublished typescript at the British Film Institute London.
43. The films of Dupont, a German Jew, often dealt with ethnic outsiders and their attempts to assimilate. See my analysis in "Romeo with Sidelocks: Jewish-Gentile Romance in E.A. Dupont's *Das alte Gesetz* (1923) and Other Early Weimar Assimilation Films," in *The Many Faces of Weimar Cinema: Rediscovering Germany's Filmic Legacy*, ed. Christian Rogowski (Rochester, N.Y., 2010), 84–101.
44. Arnold Bennett, "*Piccadilly*": *Story of the Film Illustrated with Scenes from the Photo-Play* (London, 1929), 169–170.
45. My thanks to Camille Forbes for this reference on minstrelsy. Camille F. Forbes, *Introducing Bert Williams: Burnt Cork, Broadway, and the Story of America's First Black Star* (New York, 2008).
46. Linda Williams, *Playing the Race Card: Melodramas of Black and White from Uncle Tom to O.J. Simpson* (Princeton, 2001), 158–186.

47. Wong's wardrobe in *Piccadilly* (as in the Eichberg films) uses Western dress as a marker of her characters' efforts to assimilate. Here Shosho wears a high-fashion contemporary design. Compare the evening coat with fur collar and hem by Annemarie Selter, "*Abendmantel*, Berlin, 1928," in Adelheid Rasche, *Pailletten, Posen, Puderdosen: Modezeichnungen und Objekte der Zwanziger Jahre* (Berlin, 2009), plate 61. On the other hand, Wong's stage costumes in all these films share the fashion aesthetic of Art Deco Orientalism, a prevalent design style in films of the period. See especially the discussion of Garbo's costume for the exotic dance in *Mata Hari* (1931) in Lucy Fischer, *Designing Women: Cinema, Art Deco, and the Female Form* (New York, 2003), 96–100. On the relationship between film and fashion in Weimar Germany, see Mila Ganeva, *Women in Weimar Fashion: Discourses and Displays in German Culture, 1918–1933* (Rochester, N.Y., 2008).

48. For a closer examination of the seduction scene and the evidence for self-censorship, see my article "31 January 1929: Limits on Racial Border Crossing in Film Europe Exposed in *Piccadilly*," in *A New History of German Cinema*, ed. Jennifer Kapczynski and Michael Richardson (Rochester, N.Y., 2012), 185–189.

49. Hans Gollwitzer, *Die gelbe Gefahr: Geschichte eines Schlagworts* (Göttingen, 1962). In postwar Berlin, while working-class Chinese merchants, street peddlers, and circus performers lived in Friedrichshain, middle-class Chinese university students lived mostly in Charlottenburg. Some of these students were political activists in exile from China who also became involved in local politics and agitated for the Communist Party and other left-wing causes in Germany. See Yü-Dembski, *Chinesen in Berlin*, 26–27, 40–44. For example, already in 1920 the Chinese Student Union protested the racist depiction of Chinese characters in *Die Herrin der Welt* and lobbied successfully for changes in the film series. See Nagl, *Rasse und Repräsentation*, 129–142.

50. Tina M. Campt, *Other Germans: Black Germans and the Politics of Race, Gender and Memory in the Third Reich* (Ann Arbor, M.I., 2004), 50–62. See Nagl's extensive discussion of the "*Schwarze Schmach*" film campaign in *Rasse und Repräsentation*, 159–308.

51. For an analysis of this master narrative and its variations in Baker's films, see Benetta Jules-Rosette, *Josephine Baker in Art and Life: The Icon and the Image* (Urbana, I.L., 2007), Chapter 3: "Celluloid Projections," 72–113. These films have all been released on DVD by Kino International.

52. Nancy Nenno, "Femininity, the Primitive, and Modern Urban Space: Josephine Baker in Berlin," in *Women in the Metropolis: Gender and Modernity in Weimar Culture*, ed. Katharina von Ankum (Berkeley, 1997), 145–161.

53. Jules-Rosette, *Josephine Baker*, 71.

54. Max Hermann-Neisse, "Braunes und weisses Parodietheater," cited in Nagl, *Rasse und Repräsentation*, 657.

55. "'[D]ie Rolle … ist vollendet, ist Meine Rolle [sic] wie noch keine bisher.' … Und weil dem so ist, wird es viel Leid und Mißgeschick geben, denn sie liebt die traurigen Szenen." Benjamin, *Schriften*, 524.

56. "Nur in einem Fall ist das glückliche Ende geradezu verboten: wenn eine Negerin, Indianerin, oder wie eben bei uns, eine Chinesin die weibliche Hauptrolle spielt. Da … zeigen wir diese 'fremdrassige' Frau nicht unter ihresgleichen (wir würden auch nie so viele Chinesen auftreiben) sondern im Milieu der Weißen und im Konflikt mit ihnen. Ein glückliches Ende könnte also ausschließlich in der Heirat mit einem weißen Mann bestehen … Aber durch die amerikanische Zensur passiert so etwas überhaupt nicht." *Tempo*, Berlin, Nr. 83, 10 April 1929.

57. Susan Courtney, *Hollywood Fantasies of Miscegenation: Spectacular Narratives of Gender and Race, 1903–1967* (Princeton, 2005), 19–23.

58. Gina Marchetti, *Romance and the "Yellow Peril": Race, Sex, and Discursive Strategies in Hollywood Fiction* (Berkeley, 1993), 5.

59. "Es ist … schrecklich für den Manuskriptschreiber, diese wunderbare, arme Dulderin durch so viele dramatische Fährnisse hindurchzuführen und sie doch niemals glücklich machen zu dürfen. Aber anderseits: man kann nicht mit dem Kopf durch die Wand rennen. Lieber das kleinere Übel wählen. Lieber auf dem 'happy end' nicht beharren, als hundert Millionen Menschen von dem Erlebnis dieser einzigartigen Schauspielerin auszuschließen." Lantz, *Tempo*.

CHAPTER 8

Rewriting the Face, Transforming the Skin, and Performing the Body as Text
Palimpsestuous Intertexts in Yōko Tawada's "The Bath"

MARKUS HALLENSLEBEN

Yōko Tawada's "The Bath" (Das Bad; 「うろこもち」)[1] can be read as an intermedial palimpsest of body images and text. Tawada's critical depiction of a female protagonist, who imagines herself as a hybrid being in between human and fish, follows the literary motif of metamorphosis in a cross-cultural manner and constitutes a textual and narrative technique best described as palimpsestuous intertextuality.[2] Based on the notion of the palimpsest as spatial metaphor for identity and memory, the aim of this essay is not only to show how the narrator's body images of transparent skin and letters reflect the "body as text" metaphor,[3] but also how the protagonist's transcultural ethnic identity has to be understood as performative and her gender as a textual and bodily image space.[4] "The Bath" forms a nexus of various allegories of biopower that have mapped the world as a patriarchal text, and, consequently, the female body as a territorial intertext.[5] It can be considered a playful, postmodern deconstruction of Foucault's biopolitical allegory of the body as historical text,[6] "where the body is figured as a ready surface or blank page available for inscription, awaiting the 'imprint' of history itself."[7] However, the text also fosters a materially feminist perspective, which goes beyond Foucault by pointing to a spatial, palimpsestuous connection between tissue (as organic material) and text (as environmental medium).

Awareness of the Asian cultural tradition of keeping face and of European images of nature as a faceless woman furthermore allows one to cross-map

Tawada's text with recent body performances in bio art. While contemporary body artists (e.g., Aziz+Cucher, ORLAN)[8] often deal with strategies of "de-facialisation" (Deleuze/Guattari) on a visual, medial level, and thus remediate the blank page of a papyrus, Tawada, as an intercultural writer and cultural hyphenate,[9] whose metamorphic writing style has been described as "hyper-literal,"[10] utilizes language as an imaging technique. This strategy turns post-colonial literature into a posthuman cultural affair, where there is no longer the desire to make a distinction between self and other, human and animal, tissue and text. Finally, one has to take into account the etymological double bind of tissue and text, and conceive of the body as a transcultural image and intertextual space. The cross-mapping of avant-garde literature and bio art here provides a novel approach for Tawada scholarship by suggesting that her writings deconstruct the biopolitical territorialization of gender images, and thus can be seen in analogy to current body art performances. I demonstrate that from the biopolitical code of *mapping* the world as text only one performative step separates the Western European history of colonization and the alteration of human tissue as material in bio art. Hence, the performative character of Tawada's work not only lies in representing physical experiences, but also in a corporeal understanding of literature as an enactment of the human body as alterable text.

Tawada holds a Ph.D. in modern German literature with a doctoral thesis entitled *Spielzeug und Sprachmagie: Eine ethnologische Poetologie* (Toys and Language Magic: An Ethnological Poetology), supervised by Sigrid Weigel, in which she analyzed texts by E.T.A. Hoffmann, Franz Kafka, and Paul Celan with an ethnographic approach. She frequently incorporates references to theorists such as Walter Benjamin, Jacques Derrida, and Jacques Lacan into her own fictional works,[11] the intertextuality usually hidden, but sometimes explicit. Furthermore, Tawada herself considers her writing rhizomatic, a never-ending text that "is a weird and wonderful plant that has grown in all directions out of a single word knot."[12] For "The Bath" in particular, she adapted Roland Barthes's *Camera Lucida* and the etymology of photo-*graphy* as a *written* image. Employing Barthes's writings on ethnicity and Aleida Assmann's concept of "spaces of cultural memory" (*Erinnerungsräume*), I illuminate how the hybrid body images in "The Bath" question cultural spaces as fixed categories. By taking Tawada's own "ethnographic poetology" of a metamorphic writing style as a starting point,[13] I reconsider this story as the centerpiece of her work, which as a whole does not distinguish between body and text, or—as has been noted before—between hybrid ethnicity and multilingual cultural spaces.

"The Bath," which was republished in a bilingual Japanese-German edition in 2010, was originally written in Japanese and first published in German in a translation by Peter Pörtner with the author as collaborator (*Das Bad*, 1989).[14] The new edition, for the first time, unveils the Japanese text, which the author had previously mythicized as nonexistent, claiming that there was no original text but only copies in multiple languages.[15] The print layout of both editions—both of them art books—plays with the work's multilingual, palimpsestuous structure. The first edition is printed without page numbers on yellowish paper covered with watermarks. The page design includes photographs of naked female bodies as background, so that the text appears as if written on skin, thus visualizing and mediating the story's leitmotif of the body as a canvas. The bilingual edition in turn includes facsimiles of ten pages and the cover of the first edition embedded into the text. Since the new edition can be read in two directions, forward (in German) and backward (in Japanese) one could also interpret these self-referential book images as the appearance of the German edition out of the Japanese text. The ambiguous identity of the protagonist and her hybrid body image therefore find an analogy in the imagery and physical reality of the book itself.

"The Bath" tells the story of a simultaneous translator and typist, who finds herself not only between two cultures, post-World War II Japan and pre-unification West Germany, but also between animal and human (fish and woman), and between the techniques of analog photography and digital text processing. Her Japanese identity finds expression in her double role as German language student from Japan and Japanese photo model for a German photographer named Xander, who is also her lover and language instructor. On the inside of the book jacket, her double identity as human and animal is foregrounded by a reference to the opening scene, though the cultural context is elided: "A woman sits in front of a mirror and compares her image with a portrait photograph of herself. She enters a bathtub, travels as a woman with scales ('Schuppenfrau') through dreamlike and everyday life sequences."[16]

The loosely connected scenes include a Japanese fairy tale of a fish woman, who sacrifices her life in order to stop the starvation of her village (chapter one), a photo session, in which Xander stylizes the protagonist as a geisha (chapter two), and a business lunch, during which she, as a Japanese-German interpreter, begins to stutter and then faints (chapter three). After she comes to, she finds herself in the rat-infested basement suite of a woman who appears to be heavily burned and dead. The mysterious woman not only takes the protagonist's tongue (chapter four), but also turns her skin into fish scales, although it never becomes clear whether or not this is just the protagonist's imagination (chapter six). She then follows a classified ad for a "scale bearer" (*Schuppenträgerin*) and joins a circus as a scaly woman (chapter seven), visits her mother in Tokyo where she finds the remains of her pet rat in her abandoned room (chapter eight), and becomes a typist who records ghostly voices at night, including the voice of the burned woman. Finally, Xander who has taught her German with hand puppets (chapter five) builds her a bed that looks like a transparent coffin. This then turns into a birdlike, flying sarcophagus, with which she, mute and deaf, travels over the earth (chapters nine and ten). Just like the mysterious woman, who is thought to have been murdered, the protagonist lives in the past and the here and now, is absent and present, dead and alive at the same time, and speaks with multiple voices and transforms into different identities and bodily shapes.

"The Bath" is replete with literary, cultural, and autobiographical references. The opening scene deploys the same image of an aging woman in front of a mirror, whose face reminds herself of a "terrible fish,"[17] as in Sylvia Plath's poem "Mirror," though the reference remains oblique. References to the *Undine* myth in German Romanticism as well as to "Urashima Tarō," a Japanese fairy tale that deals with the origin of (Japanese) human beings in the sea, are quite obvious to a reader familiar with Japanese and German mythologies, especially in terms of their sexual connotations.[18] In addition, the recently published Japanese title 「うろこもち」 (*urokomochi*) suggests that "The Bath" presents not only the transformation of a woman into an "animal with scales" (*Schuppentier*),[19] but also references the Japanese New Year's tradition of remembering one's ancestors. The Japanese neologism うろこもち literally means "having scales" while *mochi*, as part of the compound noun, alludes to the sweet Japanese rice cake (*mochi*) that is served during the New Year's holidays and symbolizes how the family sticks together. While the German and English titles refer only to the first and last chapters, in which the protagonist compares her mirror image with a photograph of herself and discovers that part of her body "is already a corpse"[20], the Japanese title also alludes to the presence of the ancestors, be they the mysterious dead woman in chapters four, six, seven, nine, and ten, or the mother in chapter eight. It remains unclear whether the burned woman is an alter ego of the protagonist or if she is her mother, whether the protagonist has killed herself, or whether she is an amalgam of all three identities simultaneously. The last possibility perhaps also constitutes a reference to Ingeborg Bachmann's *Malina* from her unfinished novel-cycle project *Todesarten* (Death Styles). The burned woman could furthermore be read as an allegory of the suffering inflicted by the U.S. air raids on Japan at the end of World War II, including those on Hiroshima and Nagasaki, and might possibly even allude to any victims of wartime, including victims of the Shoa.

All these allusions notwithstanding, the story loosely follows the genre of the traditional Japanese ghost story (*kaidan*),[21] and when the protagonist remains invisible in a photograph taken by her lover Xander,[22] one is reminded of the motif of a faceless woman (*nopperabo*).[23] However, "The Bath" is anything but a simple modern renarration of early Japanese literature in the vein of, for example, Ryōi Asai's collection of *kaidan* stories, *Otogi Bōko* (Hand Puppets). Rather, the story constitutes a postmodern collage that partakes of various narrative traditions and pre-texts, including Ovid's *Metamorphoses*[24] and Kafka's *The Metamorphosis*.[25] Tawada's play with different myths of metamorphosis[26] amalgamates the literary corpuses of different cultures into one polyphone text or, one might say, into a bodily palimpsest.[27] All these stories from various traditions are burned into the protagonist's skin in the form of scales,[28] a process that culminates in her transformation into a text and dead body at the story's end. When she then flies over the earth, the Melusine myth is embodied as modern allegory of the world as text, or of nature as female figure, being betrayed and disfigured.[29] Finally, the protagonist's struggles with her own self-image also recall the motif of the mirror in Japanese literature and society, beginning with the myth of the goddess Amaterasu and leading to the notion of loss of face and voice as an inherent problem in contemporary Japanese culture.[30]

In chapter two, the first person narrator is modeling for her German lover and language teacher, the photographer and carpenter Xander, whose name is a short form of Alexander, but literally stands for the "other" (read as a combination of "X" and the German pronoun for other, "ander–", originating in the Greek χενοσ ανδροσ or *xenos andros*).[31] He has her masquerade as a stereotypical Japanese woman with a white painted face. Only as the embodiment of a Western stereotype of an exotic woman can she become visible in his photographs. According to Tawada, "The body that wants and has to be seen is a European body … this need is based on the fear that something that cannot be seen can disappear at any time."[32] The first edition emblematizes this (literal) photo-*graphic* play with the in/visibility of the "other," with the appearance and disappearance of the body as sign, through the exoticizing images of naked Asian women.[33]

Furthermore, the text addresses this theme discursively via the symbolic erasure of the protagonist herself. She suggests multiple times that Xander kills her when shooting her picture by "pulling a trigger"[34] and might have even driven her to suicide by burning her with his flashing camera. In one scene, the flash digs into her flesh and marks her skin with an "X": "It stopped the light from playing and crucified the image of a Japanese woman onto the paper."[35] The German version here, again, comes much closer to the metaphor of the palimpsest by using the word "etching": "und die Gestalt einer Japanerin war auf Papier geätzt."[36] Ironically, the "X" here stands for an ambivalent cultural identity, being "*durcheinander* (mixed up)" and "*miteinander* (together)" at the same time.[37] The letter also symbolizes different semiotic traditions: whereas in Japanese an "X" is used to signify that something is not correct, in German it is used to mark something as correct or to select something. Caught in this ethno-*graphic* linguistic uncertainty, the protagonist's "eyes turned into fish made of light."[38] While her individuality disappears in the ghostlike photographic images dissolved in water, it is only Xander's image of her performing the role of geisha that can last on paper. When he claims that she, as an individual, is invisible in the photographs, he causes her, as a woman with/out (Japanese/human) identity, to lose face completely. At the same time she is also losing her own language when he teaches her German,[39] and she has already lost her tongue to the burned woman.[40]

Thus, Tawada's transcultural and multimedial image of a faceless woman in "The Bath" cannot only be traced to the *kaidan* genre, but can also be interpreted as a form of (re)*writing* the author's own Japanese-German bio-*graphy* by extending the bodily image of the protagonist into a transcorporeal space,[41] the empty canvas of her photo-*graphed* face on which the society leaves its markings. In Tawada's *Ein Gast* (A Guest) the narrator, when confronted by a book vendor with the statement that she, as a foreigner, is similar to a book with an unfamiliar script, answers with a gesture that brings the metaphor of Freud's "Wunderblock"[42] and the process of (de)facialization[43] as (re)membering one's identity together: "I rubbed my forehead from left to right, as if rewriting my face."[44] The surrealist act of rewriting,[45] however, is not only one of gestural, but also one of failed intercultural communication. It turns her face into a surface with no depth, a blank wax board on which others can inscribe their memories and cultural preconceptions. Correspondingly, the protagonist's mother in "The Bath" describes her daughter's face as from a foreigner's perspective typically "Asian": "You've started to have one of those faces like Japanese people in American movies."[46] This is an obvious reference to the chapter "The Written Face" in Barthes's *The Empire of Signs*, where he defines the face as "the thing to write"[47] and illustrates his thought with opposing images of Western and Japanese actors and journalists within, respectively, Eastern and Western cultural contexts. It is the mass media aesthetic that makes the Japanese face appear as Western and the Western face as Japanese. Tawada, in one of her poetics lectures, has described this phenomenon of citing and thus altering physiognomy: "The expectations of the observer produce masks and they grow into the flesh of the foreigner. The constant gaze of the other is inscribed into one's own face."[48]

Face and body become overexposed, composed of erased and rewritten/inscribed cultural identities. Similarly, skin is no longer a signifier of race,[49] but a remediated performance space.[50] Here, the text indeed constitutes a Barthesian "multi-dimensional space" and a "tissue of quotations drawn from the innumerable centres of culture."[51] Furthermore, Tawada presents skin as an alterable textual space, a surface that merely reflects the light that hits it.[52] Skin becomes a "kind of color-neutral canvas or blank sheet, a tabula rasa," to quote Claudia Benthien's definition of skin as a cultural medium.[53] "The Bath" can therefore be understood as a remediation on two levels. First, the special book layout of both editions allows for reading the text as bodily inscription, as an overwriting of the original body of the text, as well as for reading it backward and forward, by following both languages, German and Japanese. This shows its hypermediacy by crediting the old medium of the palimpsest.

Second, the text follows Bolter and Grusin's logic of "transparent immediacy"[54] by taking the metaphor of the palimpsest to a literal level (i.e., as etched skin). Whereas the first technique makes the reader aware of the medium tissue that underlies the text, the latter one aims at making the reader forget this medial aspect.[55] This ambiguity corresponds with the image of the protagonist's body as a "transparent coffin" or of the protagonist as a living corpse at the end of the story[56] when she is presumably dead and described as "a four-legged bird covered with scales that was called Sarcophagus."[57] These images can be read at both the symbolic and semiotic levels. Kersting not only correctly interprets the appearance of the burned woman as an embodiment of the German proverb "eine Leiche im Keller haben" (hiding a corpse in the basement), but also argues that the "transparent coffin" constitutes a hidden reference to the fairy tale "Snow White" and its adaptation in Ingeborg Bachmann's *Der Fall Franza* (The Case Franza).[58] Tawada's narrative, enriched by intertextual references, is the story of a woman who is dead alive, whose body carries the inscription of the environment, and whose gender represents the societal order.

In the beginning of "The Bath," the dead skin of the woman, pictured as fish scales, symbolizes her origins in Japanese *and* European mythology, then her blank face signifies her loss of identity within Asian *and* German culture, and, finally, when at the end her skin as "a membrane separating this world from the other one" becomes "transparent"[59] her last words can be understood in the context of Barthes's "The Death of the Author." Her erasure, her passage into transparent invisibility, allows for the overcoming of even *inter*-cultural communication patterns. In other words, by losing her ethnic and professional identity the protagonist and simultaneous translator/narrator extends the transcultural and intertextual image of the *living corpse* to the notion of a *transcorporeal* authorship. The image of the fish scales here serves as the *tertium comparationis* between text and skin: "When I became a fish and tried swimming around in the sea I experienced many things I wanted to write about. It was best for me to physically feel the condition of languages through my scales."[60] As Tawada further states in an interview with Antje Mansbrügge, "For me, the text is actually the place for which one does not need to have a national identity, not even a sexual identity.... If we could only find a place, perhaps even multiple places, within our thinking where so much comes together that fascinates us."[61]

With regard to Tawada's collection *Überseezungen* (Transatlantications), which can be read either as *Über Seezungen* (About Soles [as a kind of fish]; literally *About Sea Tongues*), or as *Übersee-Zungen* (Foreign Languages; literally *Oversea-Tongues*), or as an allusion to *Übersetzungen* (translations),[62] Kraenzle has pointed out that this fascination with transformations is also reflected in a linguistic journey, "a physical transformation that takes place when switching from one language to another." For Tawada, speaking in another language transforms the body: "Words are imagined as living creatures.... Vowels and the signs of punctuation permeate the body, transforming the speaking subject."[63] Tierney therefore sees the bodily instability of Tawada's protagonists, who often seem to have a semipermeable membrane as skin/text, in analogy to the fluidity of the transcultural writer in between continents: "Fish scales, along with Tawada's other privileged images of the skin's pores and mesh nets, are ones that present numerous openings and call forth a design comprised of multiple repetitions that are not centered around any one single instantiation of the pattern. This dispersion of foci and the permeability it produces extends to Tawada's interest in the membranes and orifices of the human body."[64] And with reference to Tawada's lectures on *Verwandlungen* (*Transformations*; *Metamorphoses*), Michiko Mae summarizes the author's aesthetic strategy as "merging language and sensual perception, that is language and body, as closely as possible," so that writing can be understood as a "bodily act" and language can be experienced in its corporeality.[65] It is not surprising that Tawada's avant-garde poetics, her ability to work with the materiality of language and to bring letters to life by enacting the sounds of a foreign language in the form of a corporeal alienation technique and performative speech act, even made scholars of cognitive visual studies point to her writings as performance art.[66]

In her essayistic text "Erzähler ohne Seelen" ("Storytellers without Souls") Tawada finds her own allegory of the body as text in the image of a cell, which plays with the German homonym "Zelle,"[67] a word that can refer to the biological cell as well as to any confined space, such as a "booth for simultaneous translators." The fact that the protagonist in "The Bath," who is a simultaneous translator, can switch not only languages but also identities appears consistent with the view of the human body in "Storytellers without Souls," where it is described as containing "many booths [cells] in which translations are made. I suspect that these are all translations for which no original exists. There are people, though, who assume that everyone is given an original text at birth. They call the place in which these texts are stored a soul."[68] Notably, Tawada labels the place in which the original text is stored a "soul" and not a gene, the content of a biological cell. For her, "the soul is a fish whose name is also a 'sole': thus the soul is related to water, or to the sea."[69] The transformation from human to animal, from woman to fish, has shamanic roots, with the narrator appearing "to be soulless because my soul is constantly in transit."[70] She distances herself from any kind of essentialist biology and seems closer to the social construction of the protagonist in "The Bath," who has also lost her original identity (or soul) and appears as a translational space without an original text.[71]

Read in the context of Tawada's transcultural poetics of transformation,[72] "The Bath" is nothing less than a fictional adaptation of her theories of transformation or metamorphoses in literature. These theories in turn are based on those of textual and bodily performativity in Barthes, Benjamin, Julia Kristeva, and her doctoral advisor Sigrid Weigel, among others.[73] Tawada's narrative is, in short, a perfect example of a theory of "plurilingual" translation studies,[74] or in her words represents "a multilingual web."[75] Correspondingly, the scene with the simultaneous translator is narrated as an intercultural encounter with programmed miscommunication. Linguistically correct communication during the German-Japanese business dinner fails and exchange of information is only upheld through bodily expressions. The dinner culminates with the interpreter figuratively and literally losing her balance during an attack of nausea caused by the meal she has been served. Unfortunately, she was not able to order her favorite dish, a fish called "sea tongue" in German ("Seezunge") and "sole" in English. The German version stresses the fish's *nomen est omen*—if needed, it gives the interpreter another tongue[76]—while in the English version eating a "sole" ensures that she does not "*lose* [her] *soul*" and thus that her "*soles* stand on a *solid* footing."[77] Instead, a large fish with no tongue is carried to the table, looking like "a wounded person on a stretcher," whose "white swollen belly ... looked like a fat woman's thigh."[78] The surrealist image of the tongueless fish as a woman's body goes together with the description of "interpreters as prostitutes that serve the occupying forces" with the "German entering my ears [as] something like spermatic fluid."[79] This image echoes the history of post-World War II Japan as a U.S.-occupied country and merges this notion with the contemporary reality of the protagonist in pre-unification Western Germany, while simultaneously foreshadowing the disturbing vision at the end of the story where the earth as a woman's body is raped.

The narrator has, as the reader learns multiple professions. Besides being a photo model and a simultaneous translator, she claims to be a typist and finally a "mechanical writing doll,"[80] which medially mirrors her loss of the Japanese language, her tongue, and her human identity. The multiple professions and self-images go hand in hand with her multiple voices and identities. According to the sociologist Shingo Shimada, the Western European concept of identity, which sees the body as part of the I, or even the body as I, does not apply to Japanese culture, in which the voice of the body is considered a polylogue that also carries the voices of the ancestors.[81] The image of such a "polyphone body" helps one understand the structure of Tawada's work, where intertextuality is extended from a solely textual to a bodily category, where Kristeva's aesthetics of polyphony (or *chora*)[82] approach surrealist automatic writing.[83] The academic reader might also associate *écriture féminine*,[84] but "When Tawada Yoko herself was asked, in the mid-1990's, if she sees her writing as part of *l'écriture féminine*, her response was that it did not seem necessary to identify bodily interested writing with one particular gender. Her response did not dismiss the insights and possibilities produced by the intensity of experimental writing about, and through, the specifically female body, but suggested that the benefits of such work could now be gleaned by both male and female writers."[85] In fictional form, as well as in the layout, "The Bath" presents readers with a theoretical and practical approach to what one might call transgendered *écriture* or a transcorporeal literature, comparable to the queer technique of a critical palimpsestuous writing style that constructs body and text as interchangeable spaces.[86]

The unusual publication history of "The Bath" is also remarkable. Tawada herself used this history as an example of Barthes's theses in "The Death of the Author" when presenting "an academic paper on the nonexistence of the writer Tawada Yōko" in 2004.[87] In her paper, she tells the fictional (and quite comical) story of a foreign language student from the United States, who, a thousand years from today, unsuccessfully tries to track down the original manuscript of "The Bath," published in numerous languages, but without a handwritten source. Tawada's talk points to the rhizomatic structure of textual production in the digital age, thus undermining the author's authoritative role even more radically than Barthes did. For the student, lost in the global search for a text that exists in multiple languages and versions, "The Bath" no longer can help to trace the author in reality. Tawada not only rejects an autobiographical reading, but also the ethnic implications that come with it. Indeed, it remains impossible to determine whether the English version of "The Bath" from *Where Europe Begins* was translated from German or Japanese (and by which of the two translators listed). Thus the question who wrote the text, a Japanese or German or even Spanish-American author, as Tawada humorously suggests, can likewise not be resolved.[88]

In her talk Tawada also plays with the metaphor of the text as palimpsest or rhizomatic body. With the computer as copying tool, which has replaced analog writing, "the body of the text, the style in the form of scars and traces etched like ditches onto the paper, is gone. Not even the traces of ink exist in any place any longer."[89] Despite the loss of materiality, Tawada here seems to draw a direct line between the written work of art in the age of digital reproduction and the tradition of the text as bodily (analog) palimpsest. Elements of the body have long been viewed as texts, most prominently the human brain by Thomas de Quincey as a palimpsest and as a "Wunderblock" by Sigmund Freud.[90] Such metaphors of memory originate in images like the wax board in Plato's *Theaetetus*.[91] But the notion of body as text has wider bearings, especially when reversed. In research on intertextuality, literary and cultural texts have often been read as bodily figurations of palimpsests, the city as physical image space, for instance, in Benjamin's media theory. Other trajectories reach from the archeological discoveries of a plant's body (*papyrus* as texture) to Gérard Genette's theory of the "body" of literature as *palimpsest*,[92] from the biological hybridity (*hybrid* as crossbreed) of a plant to *hybridity* of culture,[93] and from the performed gender of a socio-*contextual* and therefore hybrid body to the intermedial and transcultural body in performance studies and anthropology.[94] These theoretical writings can be considered medial reflections of the human body on different levels. Body and text are seen as performative entities, which constantly represent and simultaneously act as media of spatial memory.[95] Both record time not only in a metaphorical and figurative sense, but also in a material sense. Any text/body thus constitutes a spatial act instantiating the ritual of a (cultural) performance of memory,[96] or is, in other words, a living corpse that combines past and present.

As Aleida Assmann in her study on *Spaces of Memory* has shown with reference to Walter Benjamin, there is a close connection between palimpsest and analog photography, since both are bound by the chemical process of making "an invisible script readable" and "an invisible image visible."[97] In this sense "The Bath" not only employs palimpsest and photography as spatial metaphors of identity and memory, but may also be said to adapt Barthes's *Camera Lucida*. When Tawada closes her story with the words, "I am a transparent coffin",[98] it recalls Barthes's notion of the photograph as "horrible … because it certifies, so to speak, that the corpse is alive, as *corpse*: it is the living image of a dead thing."[99] One could even describe Tawada's story in Barthes's own words, as when he speaks of the photographic self-image as one in which "'myself' never coincides with my image."[100] Tawada's protagonist also suffers "from a sensation of inauthenticity, sometimes of imposture (comparable to certain nightmares)."[101] Her body follows Barthes's description of being "simultaneously living and dead … with the painted face" of Asian theater.[102] Ultimately, Barthes compares a photograph with "a living organism…. Attacked by light, by humidity, it fades, weakens, vanishes," since the perishable "fate of paper" makes it "mortal."[103] What links Barthes's medial though subjective analysis of analog photography with Tawada's narration of the "myth of the Woman without a Shadow"[104] is a semiotic understanding of image creation that goes beyond language as a simple tool of communication.[105] Both authors, in their own ways, follow an etymology of photo-*graphy* as written image and textual body space. Photo-*graphy* stands for an *engraved* image that is to be understood in a certain cultural, ethnographic context.[106] The photograph becomes a textual body space in which the past can be narrated for the viewer as contemporaneous and in which the absent person can become present, as can be seen, for instance, in Barthes's description of the Winter Garden Photograph of his mother.[107]

The symbolic becomes the semiotic, and vice versa. In short, the body of the woman is the *graph*, and the photo-*graph*, as text, assembles the body of a woman, who is at once dead and alive. This can be seen in analogy to the human body, which is neither exclusively essential nor only socially constructed, but represents natural as well as social categories of collective memory and can be considered a medium that combines both. Since *text* is likewise not assembled by the mind alone, and always has, though it is sometimes heavily remediated, a material, spatial quality, it represents cultural as well as biological categories, including its archeological origin in the cell cultures of plant tissue. Thus the metaphor of the *palimpsest* blends the artificial and the natural realms of texts. The point of departure, both for Tawada and Barthes,[108] as well as for contemporary body artists, is a mythological worldview that does not distinguish between real material (cloth, tissue) and fictional material (text): "Based on the etymological analogy of tissue and text there is no objective, un-metaphorical, non-textual understanding of the body.... If the meaning of the Latin *textus* as connectivity or web has its origins in the performative execution of the verb *texere*—to weave—then text and tissue are metaphorically related figures of speech, having in common the notion of a tissue structure."[109] The etymological double bind of tissue and text thus unveils two prerequisites: a material and a medial understanding of the body as biological and therefore also as an alterable, palimpsestuous text.[110] Tawada herself points to the Japanese *kanji* for "body" which consists of the radicals "human" and "book": "does this mean that a body is a book which pretends to be a human?"[111] By combining Japanese and European myths of textualized bodies (and stereotyped women's bodies in particular), she was certainly not only able to point ahead to the hybridity of today's body modifications, where body tissue is altered as text, but also back to the history of mapping the world as a gendered text. In conclusion, I will therefore briefly cross-map her writings with the biopolitics inherent in those forms of twentieth-century avant-garde and body art that also deal with a de-territorialization of gender images. There are three hypotheses on which this cross-mapping of art and literature is based.

First, "The Bath" combines and utilizes Barthes's reflections upon photo-*graphy* and bio-*graphy* by presenting body images and the narration of life (*bio*) as *written* categories, both etched onto skin and paper, thus reminding us of the etymological relation of *tissue* and *text*.[112] Second, in accordance with Eastern and Western mythology, Tawada's narrative blurs animal (*zoē*) and discursive life (*bios*) by making no distinction between fish scales and human skin tissue. Third, it also shows that, "wherever the body is depicted as palimpsest, that is: penetrated by language,"[113] it mirrors gender discourses of biopower.[114] With her description of the final metamorphosis, during which the protagonist becomes a "four-legged bird covered with scales that was called Sarcophagus" and flies over the earth, which is compared to a woman's body, Tawada also reintroduces centuries-old allegories of mapping the world as female.

Tawada plays with an allegorical tradition of nature as woman, which went hand in hand with the territorialization of the so-called motherland (*matria*)[115] and can also be found in depictions of the woman's body as landscape in European avant-garde art, based on Gustave Courbet's *L'Origine du monde* (e.g., Marcel Duchamp, André Masson).[116] It is important to note that in these images the female body has become part of an artificial understanding of nature as landscape and that the two metaphoric fields nature and woman, which are inscribed into this personification, have become interchangeable.[117] These images often depict the origin of the world in the woman's pelvis. They also present an ongoing alienation process from nature, or more precisely, from *man* as part of nature. In more recent feminist body art, patriarchal gender images have been subjected to irony and satire (e.g., by EXPORT or ORLAN),[118] but the ongoing process of (de)territorialization as a reaction to mapping the world as (wo)man can still be observed in many examples of body and bio art, where "defacialisation" and hybridity have become an issue. Seen as a recurrence of the *terra incognita*, here the underlying religious imagery of the "alien," unknown world as female body exposes the human body as a territorial, patriarchal text.

In chapter nine, during the woman's transformation into a coffin, the depiction of a flying airplane turns into a nightmarish war scene, perhaps in reference to the Melusine myth, as well as to the protagonist's mother's fear of flying due to her traumatic experience of the Tokyo air raids at the end of World War II.[119] The scene begins with a description of a map of the earth dominated by the spread of the human population and caught up in the net of their communication and transportation lines: "On the map, the water has suspended any motion, so all cities look as if they're always in exactly the same place. Countless red lines, perhaps air routes or fishnets, run from city to city. The earth's face is caught in this net."[120] Then the text invokes the first scene of the story, in which the protagonist applies makeup to her face in front of a mirror: "Everyday, human beings adjust the face with makeup, using the map as their model."[121] Thus the face of the woman is set in analogy to the image of the earth, and the world map and the photograph of the protagonist taken by Xander, which she uses as model of herself in the first scene, collapse into one. The metaphor of the earth as woman, however, here provides a grim outlook:

> After a war, everything you eat tastes of ash.
> In the desert, someone builds a factory in which the woman, now dressed in work clothes, has sex with a handsome man. Behind him, an even more handsome man is waiting his turn. And behind him stands a man twice as handsome as the last, and so on, all of them in a long, long line.[122]

Afterward, the hair of the woman is turned into script, into "letters" to be precise, which are then used as "illegible" toilet paper by policemen who shoot the woman in the head "every time" she leaves the bathroom: "More and more holes appear in the woman's head, but she never falls down. She appears to be a mechanical writing doll."[123] What reads like a surreal movie scene, is in fact a nightmare from which the protagonist soon awakens and discovers that her voice is that of the burned woman,[124] which can be seen as a reference to the post-World War II period in Japan, and possibly also in Germany, including the victims of the Shoa. But it also has wider connotations in terms of a general allegory of the world as text. The communicative "net," in which the face of the world and the fish-scaled woman are caught, is then the patriarchal, violent text.[125]

It is the same net in which physiognomy was caught when reading faces as imprints of different types of characters,[126] and in which bio art might be caught too when altering tissue as text based on the tradition of mapping the world as woman. In short, one has to be aware that this worldview, which binds the (material) world and the (physical) human body, is mythological and follows a textual understanding. When the terminology of *palimpsest* is applied, it further includes, within this particular metaphor of cultural memory, an interpretation of body images as textual spaces, no matter whether one looks at the organic body in tissue engineering or at figurative images of the body in literature. With media studies, one can even assume an organic connection between tissue (as material) and text (as material). However, from the common code of *mapping* the world as text it is only one performative step backward to the cultural text of the Western European history of colonization and from there to human tissue as material, which may be altered as any image of the world has been altered before—through a religious, patriarchal, and territorializing understanding of the ("alien," female) world as (malleable, "gendered") text.

Tawada's critical approach to this tradition shows us where the technique of *mapping the world* can lead, at least from the Kafkaesque point of view of a traveler who does not understand the language of the country he visits, or relies only on the images he sees, as in the case of Barthes and the *Empire of Signs*, or from the ethnological point of view of a Japanese woman who has lost her face and tongue:

> Once, in the supermarket, I bought a little can that had a Japanese woman painted on the side. Later, at home, I opened the can and saw inside it a piece of tuna fish. The woman seemed to have changed into a piece of fish during her long voyage. This surprise came on a Sunday: I had decided not to read any writing on Sundays. Instead I observed the people I saw on the street as though they were isolated letters … and thus, briefly, formed a word…. I might have read this foreign city like a text. But I never discovered a single sentence in this city, only letters and sometimes a few words that had no direct connection to any "cultural content." These words now and then led me to open the wrapping paper on the outside, only to find different wrapping paper below.[127]

This humorous scene illustrates the technique of *mapping* the world as text, as a palimpsestuous technique of un-*wrapping* paper, and it might not be a coincidence that normally wrapping paper is not only made of plant *tissue*, but also sometimes is even called so. Analogously, script can be understood as the ribbon around the wrapping paper, with the text being the package to be unwrapped. In Tawada's ethnographic poetology this deconstructionist understanding of language as a never-ending signifying process is based on an ideogrammatic tradition, in particular the adaptation of Chinese *kanji* into Japanese culture, by which "signs are delivered as packages of meaning."[128] Ironically, when the image of a foreign person is wrapped up in this way, it is almost certainly a canned image, a stereotype, causing a layering-on of other stereotypes, with an empty center in the middle. For further explanations, one might open the "canned foreign" in *Empire of Signs* using Freud's *uncanny* as a can opener; or follow Tawada's palimpsestuous, intertextual, and transcultural word plays even further and understand Kafka's *Metamorphosis* as a "translation from a non-existent language,"[129] of "an ideogram, perhaps of a certain Egyptian hiero-glyph, which has the form of a beetle."[130] The protagonist's story in "The Bath," finally, could be read as the translation of another ideogram from this "non-existent language" of transcorporeality. It has the form of a fish and embodies the fluidity of language, gender, identity, ethnicity, society, and history.

Notes

1. Yōko Tawada, "The Bath," in *Where Europe Begins*, trans. Susan Bernofsky and Yumi Selden (New York, 2002), 1–55; reworked German-Japanese edition: *Das Bad = Uro-komochi*「うろこもち」, trans. Peter Pörtner (Tübingen, 2010).
2. For a definition of the term palimpsestuous, see Sarah Dillon, *The Palimpsest: Litera-ture, Criticism, Theory*, Continuum Literary Studies (London, 2007), 4f.
3. According to Bernard Benoun, "When one understands to what extent fabrics and texts are semantically brought together in Tawada's imagination, it becomes impossible to downplay the importance of these images." Bernard Benoun, "Words and Roots: The Loss of the Familiar in the Works of Yoko Tawada," trans. Joshua Humphreys, in *Yōko Tawada: Voices from Everywhere*, ed. Doug[las N.] Slaymaker (Lanham, M.D., 2007), 131.
4. Since Jeremy Redlich has analyzed the performative aspect of race in Tawada's "The Bath," here I will concentrate on the aspect of gender as performative space. Jeremy Redlich "Reading Skin Signs: Decoding Skin as the Fluid Boundary between Self and Other in Yoko Tawada," *Critical Studies* 33 (2010): 75–88.
5. See Sigrid Weigel, *Topographien der Geschlechter: Kulturgeschichtliche Studien zur Lite-ratur* (Reinbek, 1990).
6. Michel Foucault, "Nietzsche, Genealogy, History," trans. Donald F. Bouchard and Sherry Simon, in *Language, Counter-Memory, Practice: Selected Essays and Interviews*, ed. Donald F. Bouchard (Ithaca, 1977), see p. 148 in particular.
7. Judith Butler, "Foucault and the Paradox of Bodily Inscriptions," *The Journal of Philoso-phy* 86, no. 11 (1989): 603.
8. ORLAN, *Le Plan du Film: Poster The Kiss*, 2001 (Illustration in *ORLAN: A Hybrid Body of Artworks*, ed. ORLAN, Simon Donger, and Simon Shepherd (London; New York, 2010), 154; Aziz+Cucher, "Dystopia," http://www.azizcucher.net/1994.php. Last accessed 30 September 2010.
9. See Linda Koiran, "'Offen und ent-ortet': Anmerkungen zur Gestalt von Yoko Tawa-das Werk," *Text+Kritik* 1991/2 (2011): 17, with reference to Byun-Chul Han, *Hyper-kulturalität: Kultur und Globalisierung* (Berlin, 2002), 32.
10. See Susan C. Anderson, "Surface Translations: Meaning and Difference in Yoko Tawa-da's German Prose," *Seminar: A Journal of Germanic Studies* 46, no. 1 (2010): 51.
11. See Tawada, "Der Schriftkörper und der beschriftete Körper," in *Zuerst bin ich im-mer Leser: Prosa schreiben heute*, ed. Ute-Christine Krupp (Frankfurt am Main, 2000), 73ff. See also the bibliography of her dissertation *Spielzeug und Sprachmagie in der*

europäischen Literatur: Eine ethnologische Poetologie (Tübingen, 2000), 231–238. As further theoretical references, she lists Barthes, Baudrillard, Foucault, Freud, Leiris, Lévi-Strauss, de Man, Schechner, and Weigel.

12. Quoted in Bettina Brandt, "The Postcommunist Eye: An Interview with Yoko Tawada," *World Literature Today: A Literary Quarterly of the University of Oklahoma* 80, no. 1 (2006): 43–45.

13. See Tawada, *Spielzeug und Sprachmagie*, 14f., with reference to Benjamin's concept of *Sprachmagie* ("theory of language magic"), in which, according to Tawada, the nonverbal "language of things" can be articulated as artistic language.

14. According to Tawada in a Skype interview with my Germ 390 course at UBC Vancouver on 4 February 2011. I am grateful to the author and the students, respectively, for granting and conducting the interview.

15. See Tawada, "Tawada Yōko Does Not Exist," trans. Doug[las N.] Slaymaker, in *Yōko Tawada: Voices from Everywhere*, ed. Doug[las] N. Slaymaker (Lanham, M.D., 2007), 13–19.

16. My translation. For a psychoanalytic analysis of the entrance scene in front of the mirror, utilizing Lacan's mirror image, see Sabine Fischer, "*Wie der Schlamm in einem Sumpf*: Ich-Metamorphosen in Yoko Tawadas Kurzroman *Das Bad*," in *Interkulturelle Konfigurationen: Zur deutschsprachigen Erzählliteratur von Autoren nichtdeutscher Herkunft*, ed. Mary Howard (Munich, 1997), 64–66.

17. Sylvia Plath, *Collected Poems*, ed. Ted Hughes (London, 1981), 173f.

18. "The Story of Urashima Taro, the Fisher Lad," in Thomas A. Green, *Asian American Folktales*, Stories from the American Mosaic (Westport, C.T., 2009), 148–176. For further references to narrative images taken from German Romanticism, Japanese fairy tales and German and Japanese creation myths, see Tawada, "Tawada Yōko Does Not Exist," 13f., 19, fn.3f., and Florian Gelzer, "'Worte von Gedanken trennen': Schreibweisen und Sprachprogrammatik bei Yoko Tawada" (Lizenziatsarbeit, University Basel, 1998), 30.

19. See Yumiko Saitô's retranslation of the title in her "Synchronopsis of Yoko Tawada's Book Publications in Germany and Japan," in *Yoko Tawada: Poetik der Transformation, Beiträge zum Gesamtwerk*, Stauffenburg Discussion, ed. Christine Ivanovic (Tübingen, 2010), 485. Saitô lists the text as "reworked" and as a "novel." Technically too short for a novel at fifty-nine pages in the original edition, the text is also sometimes labeled a short novel.

20. Tawada, "The Bath," 8.

21. The publisher advertised the first German edition as "Ich-Findungs-Gruselroman," i.e., "Self-Discovery-Gothic Novel," quoted in Ruth Kersting, *Fremdes Schreiben: Yōko Tawada* (Trier, 2006), 133. In addition, Tawada often refers to *kaidan* stories, such as "The Story of Mimi-Nashi-Hoichi" in her essay "Der Schriftkörper," 77ff. Lafcadio Hearn, *Kwaidan: Stories and Studies of Strange Things* (Champaign, I.L.; Boulder, C.O., [1904]), 3–8.

22. Tawada, "The Bath," 11.

23. See "Mujina," in Hearn, *Kwaidan*, 19f.

24. Tawada often interweaves cultural traditions, such as Ovid's *Metamorphoses* and Sei Shōnagon's *The Pillow Book* (枕草子, *Makura no Sōshi*). See her comment in "Der Schriftkörper," 77, and Tawada, *Opium für Ovid: Ein Kopfkissenbuch von 22 Frauen* (Tübingen, 2000).

25. See Tawada, *Verwandlungen: Tübinger Poetikvorlesungen* (Tübingen, 1998).

26. Monika Schmitz-Emans, without further analysis, adds the Melusine myth, *Poetiken der Verwandlung* (Innsbruck, 2008), 189, and Linda Koiran mentions Andersen's "Little Mermaid," among others. *Schreiben in fremder Sprache: Yoko Tawada und Galsan Tschinag,* Studien zu den deutschsprachigen Werken von Autoren asiatischer Herkunft (Munich, 2009), 297.

27. This is similar to the reading of Tawada's *Ein Gast* (Tübingen, 1993) as palimpsestuous intertext, done by Schmitz-Emans, "Rausch und Rauschen: Yoko Tawada tanzt mit Thomas de Quincey," *Etudes germaniques* 65, no. 3 (2010): 607–626.

28. I am thankful to one of the peer reviewers for the valuable reminder that Melusine is not only a variation of the mermaid myth, but also a more complex hybrid figure between human, fish, snake, and flying dragon, and therefore the scales cannot be interpreted just as fish scales.

29. Within the context of German speaking Romantic literature, Inge Stephan has pointed out the connection between the patriarchic image of nature as women and the "subtle violence" inherent to the male projections of Undine, Melusine, and mermaid myths. "Weiblichkeit, Wasser und Tod: Undinen, Melusinen und Wasserfrauen bei Eichendorff und Fouqué," in *Weiblichkeit und Tod in der Literatur,* ed. Renate Berger and Inge Stephan (Cologne, 1987), 138.

30. For this aspect, in reference to Rita Nakashima Brock, see Winnie Tomm, *Bodied Mindfulness: Women's Spirits, Bodies and Places* (Waterloo, O.N., 1995), 93–96. See also Tawada's remarks that faces are stored in a mirror to keep them from being forgotten (quoted in Fischer, *"Wie der Schlamm in einem Sumpf,"* 66).

31. See Christiane Ivanovic and Miho Matsunaga, "Tawada von zwei Seiten: Eine Dialektüre in Stichworten [Tawada–Glossar]," *Text+Kritik* 191/2 (2011): 109. In addition, Xander reminds one of the German *Zander* or pikeperch.

32. Tawada, "Eigentlich darf man es niemandem sagen," *Talisman* (Tübingen, 1996), 47 (my translation). Tawada's reflection upon the European gaze (see 45f.) begins with a citation of the scene from "The Bath" in which Xander and the protagonist talk about the color of the skin (11).

33. Kersting, who reads "The Bath" as an allegory of Kristeva's *Revolution in Poetic Language*, has closely analyzed the illustrations in the book and refers to the publisher's comments that these are probably based on images by a Chinese photographer from the 1920s and 1930s. Kersting assumes that these illustrations were supposed to be "dreamlike allusions" to the reception of exotic images of Japanese women in the West. Kersting, *Fremdes Schreiben,* 133, (my translation).

34. Tawada, "The Bath," 12.

35. Tawada, "The Bath," 12.

36. Tawada, *Das Bad*, 35.

37. Tawada, "The Bath," 9.

38 Tawada, "The Bath," 30.

39. Tawada, "The Bath," 30.

40. Tawada, "The Bath," 26.

41. Transcorporeality can be defined as a space in between nature and culture, by which there is no distinction between the human body and the environment. See Stacy Alaimo, *Bodily Natures: Science, Environment, and the Material Self* (Bloomington, I.N., 2010), 2–3.

42. Sigmund Freud, "Notiz über den 'Wunderblock,'" *Studienausgabe,* vol. 3, ed. Alexander Mitscherlich (Frankfurt am Main, 1989), 363–369.

43. See Gilles Deleuze and Félix Guattari, *A Thousand Plateaus: Capitalism and Schizophrenia*, trans. Brian Massumi (Minneapolis, 1987), 210.
44. Tawada, *Where Europe Begins*, 154.
45. For an interpretation of this scene as an act of surrealist imaging, see Brandt, "The Unknown Character: Traces of the Surreal in Yoko Tawada's Writings," in *Yōko Tawada: Voices from Everywhere*, 117f. Brandt also stresses the various connotations of the German word *umschreiben* used in the original edition of Tawada's *Ein Gast*, 9, and suggests, "that the narrator is 'delineating her face' while 'altering' it by 'paraphrasing' and 'transcribing' it." Brandt, "The Unknown Character," 118 (my translation).
46. Tawada, "The Bath," 44.
47. Roland Barthes, *Empire of Signs*, trans. Richard Howard (New York, 2005), 88–90.
48. Tawada, *Verwandlungen*, 53 (translation by Redlich, 79).
49. Redlich, "Reading Skin Signs," 80–83. See also his dissertation on *The Ethnographic Politics and Poetics of Photography, Skin and Race in the Works of Yoko Tawada* (University of British Columbia, 2012), https://circle.ubc.ca/handle/2429/43452. Last accessed 12 December 2012.
50. David Bolter and Richard A. Grusin define remediation as "the representation of one medium in another," *Remediation: Understanding New Media* (Cambridge, M.A., 1999), 45.
51. Roland Barthes, "The Death of the Author," in *Image, Music, Text*, trans. Stephen Heath (New York, 1977), 146.
52. Tawada, "The Bath," 11.
53. Claudia Benthien, *Skin: On the Cultural Border between Self and the World*, European Perspectives (New York, 2002), 48.
54. Bolter and Grusin, *Remediation*, 53.
55. See also Chiel Kattenbelt's summary of this "double logic" of remediation, described by Bolter and Grusin as transparent immediacy and hypermediacy, "Intermediality in Theatre and Performance: Definitions, Perceptions and Medial Relationships," in *Cultura, Lenguaje y Representación/Culture, Language and Representation*, vol. 6 (2009), 25, http://www.e-revistes.uji.es/index.php/clr/article/viewPDFInterstitial/30/30. Last accessed 29 June 2011.
56. Tawada, "The Bath," 55.
57. Tawada, "The Bath," 49. This is another allusion to one of Plath's poems, "Last Words." *Collected Poems*, 172.
58. See Kersting, *Fremdes Schreiben*, 149. Tawada's allusions to Bachmann's *Todesarten*-project are yet to be fully investigated.
59. Tawada, "The Bath," 54.
60. エクソフォニー: 母語の外へ出る旅, *Ekusophonii: bōgo no soto e deru tabi* [Exophony: Traveling Out of One's Mother Tongue] (Tokyo, 2003), 5, quoted in Robin L. Tierney, "Japanese Literature as World Literature: Visceral Engagement in the Writings of Tawada Yoko and Shono Yoriko" (Ph.D. diss., The University of Iowa, 2010), 40.
61. Quoted in Karl Esselborn, "'Übersetzungen aus der Sprache, die es nicht gibt.' Interkulturalität, Globalisierung und Postmoderne in den Texten Yoko Tawadas," *Arcadia*, no. 2 (2007): 260 (my translation).
62. See, among others, Schmitz-Emans, *Poetiken der Verwandlung*, 188, and most recently, Yasemin Yildiz, *Beyond the Mother Tongue: The Postmonolingual Condition* (New York, 2012), 135, who sees this as an example for a "globalized linguascape," 109ff., and rightly states that Tawada's "ethnographic lens, enabled by a bilingual perspective,

functions to destabilize the familiar linguistic behavior by reinterpreting it in a new, unexpected framework," 128.

63. Christina Kraenzle, "Traveling without Moving: Physical and Linguistic Mobility in Yoko Tawada's *Überseezungen*," in *Yōko Tawada: Voices from Everywhere*, 98.

64. Tierney, "Japanese Literature as World Literature," 40.

65. Michiko Mae, "Tawada Yokos Literatur als transkulturelle und intermediale Transformation," in *Yoko Tawada: Poetik der Transformation, Beiträge zum Gesamtwerk*, ed. Christine Ivanovic (Tübingen, 2010), 381 (my translation).

66. "At a deep level, her work is concerned with kinesthetic sensations.… The displacement of Yoko Tawada's body in shuttling continually between different countries mirrors the changes undergone by familiar objects mobilized in unfamiliar words.… Tawada's demonstration that action is material communication reveals the propensity of mind and world to interpenetrate." Barbara Maria Stafford, *Echo Objects: The Cognitive Work of Images* (Chicago, 2007), 93.

67. Tawada, *Talisman*, 16–19.

68. Tawada, *Where Europe Begins*, 104.

69. Tawada, *Where Europe Begins*, 106. "In meiner zweiten Vorstellung ähnelt die Seele einem Fisch. Das Wort 'See-le' zeigt, daß sie mit dem 'See' oder überhaupt mit dem s zu tun hat." Tawada, *Talisman*, 21.

70. Tawada, *Where Europe Begins*, 106. "Ich sehe aus wie ein seelenloser Mensch, weil meine Seele immer unterwegs ist." Tawada, *Talisman*, 21.

71. "When did everything actually begin? We cannot say when the original text was written. Each text arises as the second one, as a by-product. And so it seems as if man had never begun to write but rather had always written." Tawada, "Der Schriftkörper," 70, trans. Benoun, 135, fn. 24).

72. See Mae, "Tawada Yokos Literatur," 382.

73. As sources for her lectures *Verwandlungen*, Tawada lists, besides Kafka's *Verwandlung* (Metamorphosis), Ovid's *Metamorphoses* and Akinari Ueda's *Unter dem Regenmond* (Tales of Moonlight and Rain), Kristeva's *Die Chinesin* (About Chinese Women), Benjamin's *Einbahnstraße* (One-Way Street), and Roland Barthes's *Das Reich der Zeichen* (The Empire of Signs).

74. See, with reference to Tawada's "Das Fremde aus der Dose" ("The Canned Foreign"), Brian Lennon, *In Babel's Shadow: Multilingual Literatures, Monolingual States*. Minneapolis, M.N., 2010: 1, 10, 20–21, 48. I thank one of the outside reviewers for pointing out the difference between translation and multilingual studies.

75. Tawada, "Writing in the Web of Words," in *Lives in Translation: Bilingual Writers on Identity and Creativity*, ed. Isabelle De Courtivron (New York, 2003), 148. This main aspect of Tawada's work has been analyzed extensively; see, among others, Esselborn, "'Übersetzungen aus der Sprache, die es nicht gibt.'"

76. Tawada, *Das Bad*, 41.

77. Tawada, "The Bath," 14.

78. Tawada, "The Bath," 16.

79. Tawada, "The Bath," 14.

80. Tawada, "The Bath," 47, 51.

81. See Christine Ivanovic, "Exophonie, Echophonie: Resonanzkörper und polyphone Räume bei Yoko Tawada," in *Gegenwartsliteratur: Ein germanistisches Jahrbuch / A German Studies Yearbook*, ed. Paul Michael Lützeler and Stephan K. Schindler (Tübingen, 2008), 229.

82. See Kersting, *Fremdes Schreiben*, 130–157.
83. See Miho Matsunaga, "Zum Konzept eines 'automatischen' Schreibens bei Yoko Tawada," *Etudes germaniques* 65, no. 3 (2010): 445–454. With a reference to Lautremont, Bettina Brandt also shows the influence of Surrealism on Tawada's *Ein Gast*: "The body in Tawada's text is never a mere object; it is itself a site of transformation that, with the help of the senses, converts mere sensitiveness into sense and sensibility.... This is the case in *A Guest*, where the recorded voice of the book-on-tape, effectively blowing away the letters of the alphabet, soon starts to become a (invisible) physical presence that matters." Bettina Brandt, "The Unknown Character: Traces of the Surreal in Yoko Tawada's Writings," in *Yōko Tawada: Voices from Everywhere*, 111, 116).
84. See Florian Gelzer, "Sprachkritik bei Yoko Tawada," *Waseda Blätter* 7 (2000), 98f.
85. Tierney, "Japanese Literature as World Literature," 98f.
86. See in particular Dillon's adaptation of Genette's theory in her literary analysis of H.D. *The Palimpsest: Literature, Criticism, Theory*, Continuum Literary Studies (London, 2007), 102–126.
87. Tawada's contribution was delivered at the University of Kentucky in March 2004 during the first conference that was solely dedicated to her work. "Tawada Yōko Does Not Exist," 13.
88. Tawada, "Tawada Yōko Does Not Exist," 19.
89. Tawada, "Tawada Yōko Does Not Exist," 16.
90. See Sarah Dillon, "Reinscribing De Quincey's Palimpsest: The Significance of the Palimpsest in Contemporary Literary and Cultural Studies," *Textual Practice* 19, no. 3 (2005), http://www.informaworld.com/10.1080/09502360500196227. Last accessed 11 June 2010.
91. See Aleida Assmann, *Erinnerungsräume: Formen und Wandlungen des kulturellen Gedächtnisses*, C.H. Beck Kulturwissenschaft (Munich, 1999; reprint, 2003), 209f.
92. Gérard Genette. *Palimpsests: Literature in the Second Degree*, trans. Channa Newman and Claude Doubinsky (Lincoln, 1997).
93. Homi K. Bhabha, *The Location of Culture*, Routledge Classics (London; New York, 1994).
94. Judith Butler, *Bodies that Matter: On the Discursive Limits of 'Sex'* (London; New York), 1993; Erika Fischer-Lichte and Christoph Wulf, "Vorwort," in *Theorien des Performativen*, ed. Erika Fischer-Lichte and Christoph Wulf, *Paragrana: Internationale Zeitschrift für Historische Anthropologie*, vol. 10 no. 1 (Berlin, 2001), 9.
95. Performance here is used as a term of theatrical ritual and refers to social acting rather than solely to Austin's speech act theory. For further definitions of the term performance in this context, see, for instance, Erika Fischer-Lichte, *The Transformative Power of Performance: A New Aesthetics*, trans. Saskya Iris Jain (London; New York, 2008).
96. See Assmann, who defines "kulturelle Akte des Erinnerns" as techniques of *storing*, as an *art* (*ars*) of memory, and distinguishes it from the *process* (*vis*) of remembering. *Erinnerungsräume*, 28.
97. Assmann, *Erinnerungsräume*, 157.
98. Tawada, "The Bath," 55.
99. Roland Barthes, *Camera Lucida: Reflections on Photography*, trans. Richard Howard (London, 1981), 78f.
100. Barthes, *Camera Lucida*, 12.
101. Barthes, *Camera Lucida*, 13.

102. Barthes, *Camera Lucida*, 31.

103. Barthes, *Camera Lucida*, 93.

104. Barthes, *Camera Lucida*, 110.

105. For a comparison between Tawada's *Talisman* and Barthes's *Empire of Signs*, see Gelzer, "'Worte von Gedanken trennen,'" 61–68.

106. For an analysis of this aspect as tool for imaging the East-West-German borderland after reunification in Tawada's "Das Leipzig des Lichts und der Gelatine" ("The Leipzig of Light and Gelatine," published in 1991 in a German translation from the Japanese in *Wo Europa anfängt*, 7–26), see Katharina Gerstenberger, "Writing by Ethnic Minorities in the Age of Globalisation," in *German Literature in the Age of Globalisation*, ed. Stuart Taberner, Studies in German Literature, Linguistics, and Culture (Birmingham, 2004), 220f.

107. Barthes, *Camera Lucida*, 72.

108. "*Text* means *tissue*." Roland Barthes, *The Pleasure of the Text*, trans. Richard Miller (New York, 1989), 64.

109. Markus Hallensleben and Jens Hauser, "Performing the Transfacial Body: ORLAN's *Manteau d'Arléquin*," in *ORLAN: A Hybrid Body of Artworks*, 139.

110. For a further adaptation of the term palimpsest in art history and aesthetics see Klaus Krüger, "Bild—Schleier—Palimpsest: Der Begriff des Mediums zwischen Materialität und Metaphorik," *Archiv für Begriffsgeschichte*, Sonderheft, ed. Ernst Müller (2004), 106.

111. Tawada, "Bilderrätsel ohne Bilder," in *Nur da wo du bist da ist nichts* (Tübingen, 1997), 33 (my translation); quoted in Christiane Ivanovic and Miho Matsunaga: "Tawada von zwei Seiten," 132.

112. In *Verwandlungen*, Tawada speaks about the "trace of a pencil, which reminds one of an old scar on skin." 42 (my translation).

113. Hanna Eglinger, *Der Körper als Palimpsest: Die poetologische Dimension des menschlichen Körpers in der skandinavischen Literatur der Gegenwart* (Freiburg, 2007), 45 (my translation).

114. For a comparable reading of *Ein Gast* as palimpsest with rhizomatic structure see Margret Brügmann, "Jeder Text hat weiße Ränder: Interkulturalität als literarische Herausforderung," in *Postmoderne Literatur in deutscher Sprache: Eine Ästhetik des Widerstands?*, ed. Henk Harbers (Amsterdam, 2000), 351.

115. Weigel speaks of a "colonization of 'female nature,'" *Topographien der Geschlechter*, 140 (my translation).

116. Gustave Courbet, *L'Origine du monde* (*Origin of the World*), 1866 (Musee d'Orsay, Paris); Marcel Duchamp, *Given: 1. The Waterfall, 2. The Illuminating Gas*, 1946–1968 (Illustration in *ORLAN, A Hybrid Body of Artworks*, 161); André Masson, *L'Origine du monde* (Landscape), 1955 (Gallery Louise Leiris, Paris, Illustration in Weigel, *Topographien der Geschlechter*, 147).

117. Weigel, *Topographien der Geschlechter*, 141. For the influence of Weigel (and Unica Zürn) on Tawada, see her essay "Der Schriftkörper," 76. Tawada's writing in general could be traced back to the avant-garde aesthetics of fragmented body parts and the technique of photomontage, as explored in Hans Bellmer and Unica Zürn's surrealist notion of the body as anagrammatical text, and as summarized by Peter Weibel when curating the exhibition *Der Anagrammatische Körper: Der Körper und seine mediale Konstruktion*, Zentrum für Kunst und Medientechnologie (Cologne, 2000).

118. ORLAN, *The Origin of War*, 1989 (Illustration in *ORLAN: A Hybrid Body of Artworks*, 163); VALIE EXPORT, *Identitätstransfer B/Identitätstransfer I*, 1972–73 (Barbara Gross Gallery, Munich), http://www.artnet.com/artist/26012/valie-export .html. Last accessed 5 January 2013.

119. Tawada, "The Bath," 41, 46.

120. Tawada, "The Bath," 50.

121. Tawada, "The Bath," 50.

122. Tawada, "The Bath," 51.

123. Tawada, "The Bath," 51.

124. Tawada again uses a proverbial phrase to express the exchange of voices: "You gave a dead person your tongue." "The Bath," 52.

125. This, again, alludes to the Melusine myth. For a wider discussion of the net metaphor originating in the Western European notion of *text* (*Gewebe*, tissue), see, for instance, Hans Staub, "'Der Weber und sein Text:' Das Subjekt der Dichtung," in *Festschrift für Gerhard Kaiser*, ed. Gerhard Buhr, Friedrich A. Kittler and Horst Turk (Würzburg, 1990), 533-553, http://nbn-resolving.de/urn:nbn:de:bsz:21-opus-40067. Last accessed 14 June 2010.

126. See Tawada's distinction between Lavater's and Benjamin's understanding of physiognomy. Whereas Lavater applied moral standards, Benjamin tries to decipher the images of the past, which have been inscribed into the skin as "net." Tawada, *Spielzeug und Sprachmagie*, 166.

127. Tawada, "The Canned Foreign," *Where Europe Begins*, 89f.

128. Tawada, *Verwandlungen*, 28 (my translation).

129. See Esselborn, "Übersetzungen aus einer Sprache die es nicht gibt" (my translation).

130. Tawada, *Verwandlungen*, 39 (my translation).

CHAPTER 9

Love, Pain, and the Whole Japan Thing

Dancing MA in Doris Dörrie's Film Cherry Blossoms/Hanami

ERIKA M. NELSON

MA means to be IN BETWEEN. MA is the moment just at the end of a movement and before the beginning of the next one. MA is like standing on the riverside watching the water floating along. You want to reach the other side but the other side means death. You want to finish your life on this side but not yet, you are half here and half over there. Your soul is waiting for the last step—completely calm—without breathing—completely quiet—not dead and not alive—this is MA.
—Tadashi Endo, Butoh master

In her film *Kirschblüten/Hanami* (Cherry Blossoms/Hanami, 2008), German filmmaker Doris Dörrie grapples with the Japanese Zen Buddhist concept of MA,[1] understood both as "emptiness" and "the space between the things."[2] While juxtaposing German and Japanese culture, Dörrie bridges the perceived gap in between through the shamanic elements encapsulated in the Japanese dance form of Butoh, considered by its masters to be "a way to make the invisible visible" as well as a "point of fusion,"[3] capable of traversing both the spiritual and human realms, to reveal that the apparent void or "nothingness" of MA between the disparate landscapes and cultural settings is not empty, but rather a "no-thingness," lacking materiality yet nonetheless an unexpected source full of rejuvenating creative power and potential. Central to Dörrie's exploration of the MA is the German play on the word: "MA," understood also as "MAMA," or mother, thereby invoking archetypal potentials of feminine creativity but also realistic portrayals of mothers. In the film, Dörrie links the "emptiness" of the Zen concept to the loss of and mourning for a mother and wife. Through this alternative lens, the lines of division suddenly shift to other perceived opposites—including the film's backdrops of the chaotic big city versus the idyllic countryside, as well as its exploration of generational conflicts caught between tradition and modernity, clichéd ideals and unseemly reality, life and death, health and sickness—while similarities of motherhood experienced in both German and Japanese society bring the cultures into closer proximity.

Dörrie's piece thus offers a movingly incisive meditation on distinct, yet shared paradoxes of human life, with Butoh giving expression to the jarring, disjointed, often awkward, random, and disorienting, yet nonetheless meaningful "danced" encounters between the self and the familiar, here specifically the familial, as well as the exotic Other, and finally the unknown at the threshold between the living and the dead. The term "Butoh," as Sondra Fraleigh writes, "is one of several words for 'dance' in Japan,"[4] and in Dörrie's film, this dance is understood as a universal form of dance, in spite of its Japanese trappings. The film follows the main characters' dance movements in and out of various situations and predicaments, through diverse human experiences, such as trying to find their balance, their sense of self, or a feeling of peace with their surroundings, only to then lose their way and all sense of hope when faced with unexpected tragedy and the darkness of the unknown. As Alice Kuzniar suggests in her article "Uncanny Doublings and Asian Rituals," the "white European protagonist is 'dis-oriented' (to borrow from a play on words that Sara Ahmed uses in her book *Queer Phenomenology*) only to find resolution by participation in Asian custom."[5] The tragicomic as well as the humorous twist, Dörrie underscores, is part of Butoh dance, and this, too, is MA.

Butoh—or rather Butoh-MA, as Tadashi Endo, the professional Butoh performer featured in Dörrie's film, calls the form he practices—is a hybrid form of dance theater, considered a collective expression of a wide range of contemporary styles and influences, from German expressionist dance forms to movements inspired by the avant-garde "hippie" Ankoku-Butoh movement and Japanese dance legends Tatsumi Hijikata (1928–86) and Kazuo Ohno (1906–2010). As Fraleigh points out in her groundbreaking study on this particular dance form, entitled *Butoh: Metamorphic Dance and Global Alchemy*, Butoh "is not filtered through classical or folk forms, but its basic material is the body itself in its changing conditions."[6] What makes Butoh stand apart from many other dance forms in Fraleigh's opinion is "its shape-shifting potentials and its somatic shamanistic basis, not marking race so much as metamorphic change."[7] Butoh's strong gestural and hyper-controlled motions express both playful and grotesque imagery, while embodying taboo topics and extreme experiences, such as death, loss, and disorientation. Fundamentally, however, Butoh is, as Tatsumi Hijikata suggests, "an exploration of the frightening depths of the body itself."[8] Traditionally performed in white body makeup, with or without an audience, Butoh has its roots in post-World War II Japan and in social protest movements against Western materialism. Known also as "the dance of darkness," Butoh reflects "older values of pre-modern Japan," and evokes, as Fraleigh suggests, "the original face of Japan beneath the fast-paced surface, and the timeless austerity of Zen, awash with mystical emptiness and nature's evanescence."[9] But as she also points out, Butoh has gone global, and there is no set style. It may even be purely conceptual with no movement at all.

Butoh, with its curious interplay of exaggerated portrayals of happiness and grief, demands an intense inner search for expression of that which usually remains unconscious and silent. "Be a stone" was, for instance, one of the first instructions of Kazuo Ohno to his students in Butoh workshops in order to encourage them to understand the dance's potential for healing both the self and the environment. When Ohno first visited Auschwitz, Fraleigh explains, he "wanted to dance there for healing, but couldn't—not until he saw the pain in the stones. Ohno saw the hidden morphology: that stone carries human history as well as geologic."[10] For Butoh performers like Ohno, as for shamans, everything in the universe is alive with awareness or consciousness, including the spirits of our ancestors. Butoh dancers, similar to shamans, seek to connect to that energy, resonate with it, and transform it by shifting through various states of awareness either through meditative movement or the "embodiment of surreal imagery that stirs the unconscious."[11] Ultimately, Butoh appears in this capacity in the film, evoking an unfamiliar dream/dance space of the shamanic dream body, as a force of liberation and transformation in the film, allowing both of the main characters, the wife and the widower, to engage and express their suppressed hopes, fears, and sorrows through the movement of the "otherworldly" Japanese dance. Indeed, the Japanese overlay of the Butoh tradition helps root and anchor this dance in a realistic setting and the film's storyline in a plausible modern-day experience. Here Dörrie exploits what is to her German audience the "exotic" nature and foreignness of Japanese culture to her advantage, in order to highlight difference, expand imaginative potential, and bring the audience into contact with the unknown, while bridging the cultural and creative gap with an altered appreciation, not simply appropriation, of the Other.

Dörrie's affinity to Japan is palpable in much of her previous work, which has repeatedly introduced aspects of Japanese culture into typical German stories and settings, with the intention of celebrating these foreign influences. In none of Dörrie's films is this Japanese presence more apparent however than in *Cherry Blossoms/Hanami*. Far more than merely offering a cultural sightseeing tour or a theatrical celebration of difference, Dörrie's endeavor envisions cultural similarities and differences in more subtle, nuanced, metaphysical terms, encapsulating the encounters and exchanges with the Other as an ever-widening and simultaneously unwinding inner dance at the threshold of the familiar and the unknown. This delicately crafted film, partly inspired by Yasujiro Ozu's seminal Japanese film *Tokyo Story* (1953), tells a story of love, loss, and spiritual healing after bereavement. When the film was released in 2008,[12] a review in the German newspaper *Die Welt* sought to offer its readers insight into "why Dörrie dances in Japan."[13] Her personal and professional relationship with the country spans two decades, going back to the very beginnings of her career,[14] when, as she describes, "I stumbled into this country as one stumbles into a dream."[15] The filmmaker asserts that "there are again and again points where Japan and Germany always directly touch"[16] beyond the obvious parallels in the countries' histories as "defeated nations in WWII, rebuilt economic powers, and lands torn between traditions."[17] Early on in her career, Dörrie already recognized that "Germans and Japanese are really very much alike—incredibly repressed and very irrational at the same time."[18]

Dörrie's work has been enthusiastically embraced by Japanese audiences. Indeed, apart from Dörrie's native Germany, her films are typically better received in Japan than in any other country.[19] She has responded by continuing to feature Japan in her work. Nevertheless, *Cherry Blossoms/Hanami* is by no means the product of a simple love affair between Germany and Japan. Dörrie's fascination with Japanese culture stems from her perception of it as a "strange mixture of great familiarity and great strangeness."[20] The country remains a disorienting place, particularly in the hectic inner city of Tokyo, perplexing and impenetrable to outsiders. At the same time, it is a place to find oneself. Dörrie returns repeatedly to Japan's majestic Mount Fuji as a site of orientation for all things beautiful and to the monastic life in the Buddhist temples, which she offers as examples of incomparable sanctuaries of serenity and peace, for instance in *Enlightenment Guaranteed* (2000). The various aspects of Japanese culture allow for encounters not only with the self, but also with the perceived "Other"—an Other, more specifically, that in terms of mentality shares deep similarities with Germany, yet also offers a cultural and experiential perspective that is radically alien. There is, as Dörrie notes, ample opportunity for misunderstanding Japan: "it does not become any more familiar, the more I get to know it; it withdraws again and becomes even stranger then."[21]

The cross-cultural blending, or dancing of MA, this chapter addresses resembles not only a dance of opposites, but also an exchange between opposites, where each partner at times appears separate, culturally distinct, and, as Dörrie suggests, strange. Yet, in their encounter within the dance, they also come together, combine, and merge into something larger. The result is a blending of differences that moves beyond culturally inscribed norms and boundaries. Such ideas draw upon the theoretical works of Marcel Mauss and Douglas Davies, which consider the interplay of embodiment, exchange, and material culture not only as social phenomena, but also as analytical concepts.[22] Each of the three themes functions as a representation of reality as well as an instrument for its analysis. Together they work in an organic relationship with each other and combine, as Davies suggests, "basic information and the analysis of information," thus achieving their full potency.[23] Mauss's ideas on exchange theory, as formulated in *The Gift*, and on issues of embodiment and the social nature of the body, its representation and the revealing of inner states, which he presents in "Techniques of the Body," describe how embodying actions of a given culture both articulate and communicate culturally specific approaches to social life. Through meaningful encounters with others, these bodies mingle or "dance," and visible and invisible gifts are exchanged. Dörrie's work resonates with such gifts and displays, gratefully, the enriching potential of meaningful cultural exchange.

As one of Germany's most renowned and prolific filmmakers and "arguably one of the most important cultural voices in Germany, both in film and across several other cultural forms,"[24] Dörrie has enjoyed both national and international recognition. She has made several successful feature films, including for instance her international hit *Männer* (Men, 1985). A list of other notable films includes *Mitten ins Herz* (Straight through the Heart, 1983), *Im Innern des Wals* (Inside the Belly of the Whale, 1984), *Paradies* (Paradise, 1986), *Ich und er* (Me and Him, 1988), *Geld* (Money, 1989), *Happy Birthday, Türke!* (Happy Birthday!, 1992), *Keiner liebt mich* (Nobody Loves Me, 1994), *Bin ich schön?* (Am I Beautiful?, 1998), *Nackt* (Naked, 2002), *Der Fischer und seine Frau—Warum Frauen nie genug bekommen* (The Fisherman and His Wife—Why Women Never Get Enough, 2005), and *Die Friseuse* (The Hairdresser, 2010). She has also made children's films, for example *Paula aus Portugal* (Paula from Portugal, 1979), and documentaries, for instance *Von Romantik keine Spur* (Not a Trace of Romanticism, 1980), which is a portrait of a young shepherdess, and *Wie man sein Leben kocht* (How to Cook Your Life, 2007). She is often credited with having introduced a more entertaining and commercially oriented form of filmmaking to Germany after the New German Cinema.[25] In addition, she is also a very productive novelist, short story writer, opera director,[26] and a practicing Zen Buddhist, intent on developing wisdom, compassion, and greater understanding in her life.

Much of Dörrie's work focuses on the interpersonal—relationships, love, and human caring—but not in conventional ways. As Birgit Rühe points out in her biographical sketch, fantastical extravagance is "exemplary for Dörrie's philosophy," as is the tendency to "play, dress up, think against the grain, transgress boundaries, transform the serious into something light-hearted, seek out unconventional paths, be in transit."[27] In her children's book *Lotte will Prinzessin sein* (Lotte Wants to Be a Princess, 1998), Dörrie has Lotte and her mother wear beautiful dresses and crowns to preschool and work, after Lotte complains in the morning: "The blue skirt is too blue and the red sweater is too red.... I want to put on the princess dress."[28] Dörrie enjoys presenting an eclectic mix of characters in complex relations and exploring the ensuing challenges they face, particularly in terms of negotiating their cultural and social identities. Travel constitutes a recurring theme in Dörrie's work, often playing itself out as journeys of self-knowledge and the Buddhist concept of "human revolution," typically ending in a celebration of the fullness of life. Her focus narrows in on the transformative potential of such journeys of personal development, character evolution, and emotional growth. Often, one senses, she speaks from personal experience.

Dörrie was born in Hanover, Germany, in 1955 and has traveled much since then: she studied theater arts, philosophy, and psychology at the University of the Pacific in Stockton and the School for Social Research in New York City, hitchhiked through the Soviet Union, explored South America, and made many trips to Asia, especially to Zen Buddhist monasteries in Japan. She also studied at the College of Television and Film (Hochschule für Fernsehen und Film) in Munich, where she now teaches, among other things, creative writing, something she felt was missing in the German academic curriculum. In particular, she focuses on Joseph Campbell's understanding of the monomyth of "the hero's journey,"[29] which emphasizes the stages a protagonist must pass through on his or her heroic quest. As Campbell summarizes in *The Hero with a Thousand Faces*: "A hero ventures forth from the world of common day into a region of supernatural wonder: fabulous forces are there encountered and a decisive victory is won: the hero comes back from this mysterious adventure with the power to bestow boons on his fellow man."[30]

Joseph Campbell's work focuses not only on the hero's journey, but also on the cultural significance of comparative religions and storytelling, aspects Dörrie similarly emphasizes in all her work. In one of his interviews with Bill Moyers, Campbell retold the story of an American delegate at an international conference on religion who had difficulty trying to figure out what Japanese Shintoism was about and commented: "We've been now to a good many ceremonies and have seen quite a few of your shrines. But I don't get your ideology. I don't get your theology." Campbell explained that the Japanese priest paused for a moment, as though deep in thought, and then slowly shook his head. "I think we don't have ideology," he said. "We don't have theology. We dance."[31]

Clearly, Dörrie has taken note. Not only is the "mythic" dimension present throughout her work, particularly in the development of her protagonists, but also the understanding of life's essence as a cosmic and often tragi-comic dance. Butoh's fusion, much like the completed hero's journey, occurs as Fraleigh indicates at the "end of assimilation; it represents a synthesis or result and sometimes even an aesthetic or psychological transformation. It speaks of something that has been accomplished."[32] Dörrie's camera faithfully follows her protagonists as they embark on personal quests toward something greater than themselves—be it true love, inner peace, or the coming to terms with death and grief—and also how they stumble and slowly find their footing again. Dörrie likes unconventional, typically reluctant heroes who ultimately defy the odds, everyday people in commonplace jobs, facing a variety of challenges, often with less than heroic grace and grandeur. Typically, it is the very dilemma the hero faces that propels him or her to seek answers to life's most vexing questions. Dörrie repeatedly shows the hero's life as messy and unpredictable, but also as dynamic, funny, touching, beautiful, and full of potential. *Cherry Blossoms/ Hanami* is no exception.

Cherry Blossoms/Hanami tells the story of a widower's grief at the unexpected loss of his beloved wife, mother to their three children. In memory of her long-time dream of visiting Japan, he travels to the country. The themes of loss and impermanence, as embodied in the transitory beauty of cherry blossoms, lead into an exploration of the questions of life and death—topics Dörrie has dealt with again and again in her work and sums up succinctly in the title of her 1989 quartet of short stories as *Love, Pain, and the Whole Damn Thing.*[33] In her director's statement, Dörrie poses Butoh-esque[34] questions about love and loss that occupied the team while filming: "does impermanence teach us to see things the way they really are? Is it possible to enjoy the present moment in the face of death? What makes us blossom? What makes us wither? How can we water our seeds of joy?"[35] At the heart of these questions lies the desire "to discover beauty in each moment and let it pervade the story," even if this at times blurs the boundaries of reality.[36]

The film draws on Dörrie's own experiences not only of Japan, but also of bereavement. Her husband, cinematographer Helge Weindler, died unexpectedly during the shooting of *Am I Beautiful.* It was not until six years later that Dörrie was able to lend words to her grief in the novel *Das blaue Kleid* (The Blue Dress, 2002), which—as she is quick to point out—is not a book of mourning, but rather one of consolation: wit and imagination helped lead her out of the maze, and the taboo-breaking depiction of unfamiliar funeral rituals in Bali gave death a face. Dörrie categorically maintains: "Humor and self-irony are absolutely necessary for survival."[37] In *Cherry Blossoms/Hanami* she shares insights gained from her personal experiences with "loss and grief, death and dying": "Now, 12 years later, I think I do know what it feels like when you overcome grief, when you come out on the other side of this process, so that's why I wanted to talk about it now."[38]

Cherry Blossoms/Hanami also explores how emotional, physical, and linguistic distance shapes instances of transnational difference. Throughout the film, Dörrie utilizes dual perspectives structurally, thematically, and geographically; they are repeatedly brought together to carve out a space of non-duality. Even the film's title places the German word for "cherry blossoms" side by side with the Japanese term "Hanami," thereby suggesting that the film bridges cultures and translates difference. The title seems to present equivalents. Yet the Japanese term is nuanced: "Hanami" refers specifically to the Japanese custom of enjoying the beauty of cherry blossoms, or *ume*, and the term evokes the annual spring celebrations throughout Japan of the blossoms' ephemeral beauty. People usually experience this in parks, together with coworkers, friends, or family. This ritual marks the beginning of spring and serves as a reminder of the cyclical and transitory nature of life, underscoring how quickly things can change from one day to the next. The cherry blossom is "one of the most significant symbols in Japanese culture associated not only with awakening, but also with the idea that life consists of various stages and that it is transient. The older a cherry tree, the more blossoms it bears."[39] These allusions might easily be overlooked by a German viewer, yet they are central to the film's theme of recognizing life's inherent beauty in every unfolding, passing moment. The title demonstrates that even in the simplest instances of contact between the cultures there emerges the possibility of valuable exchange and expanded insight and understanding, of an enriched experience of shared humanity.

In an interview, Dörrie explains that she chose the film's double title explicitly to highlight cultural difference:

> I wanted to have "Hanami" in the title in Germany because it means "to *watch* the cherry blossoms," which is an active way of remembering impermanence. It's really the exact translation of "memento mori," which means "remember dying;" it's an activity, it's something that you do, which in the West we don't do much anymore. In the West, our goal is to consolidate things and make them permanent, like plastic surgery, and not wanting anything to change. We don't want things to change, we want them to stay the same—that's our credo—which is very different training to the East, where they're taught that everything is imperfect and everything changes all the time. So that's why we have these two sides, two titles, two languages, two countries, two color gradings. It's very different in Japan and Germany, the mountains, the sea.[40]

Cherry Blossoms/Hanami captures the mountains and the sea, but also a couple, their children, their dreams, their disappointments, and the complexities of the human condition—first in Germany, then in Japan. The comparison strikes familiar and unfamiliar chords. A German encounter with Japanese culture emerges in which aspects of Japanese culture serve as counterpoints to stereotypical German ideas about the country. As in a musical score, such contrapuntal moments lend expression to harmonic interdependence between the two seemingly independent expressions. As unfamiliar as the Japanese landscapes in Dörrie's film might initially appear to her German viewers, deep similarities and human connections between the two cultures emerge. The images of Japan become the means of mediating different emotional experiences, sometimes even their absence.

The film begins with paintings of Japan's iconic Mount Fuji, accompanied by a woman's voice-over, explaining: "I always wanted to go to Japan with him. Just to see Mt. Fuji once. With him. Because seeing it without my husband, I can't even imagine that. That would be like not really seeing it." The woman, Trudi Angermeier, played by Hannelore Elsner, is then shown in close-up as she peers at her husband's x-ray, while the doctors explain to her that he is dying, although the symptoms of his illness might be slow to manifest. The doctors have chosen to reveal the illness to her first, so she can decide the best course of action. Then they encourage her to undertake a trip with her husband, perhaps even a small adventure, to which Trudi responds immediately: "My husband hates adventures" and elaborates: "He'd prefer it if nothing changes. Ever. Nothing. At all." Indeed, Rudi, the protagonist and unassuming, not to mention unwilling, hero, played beautifully by Elmar Wepper, dressed throughout much of the film in his beloved Bavarian coat and hat, loves German orderliness and dutifully maintains an easy, yet regimented routine: he goes to work every day on the same train, precisely places his Tyrol hat in the overhead bin, reads the newspaper and then on cue trades sections of it with his colleague. His wife, the very embodiment of the antiquated German *Hausfrau* ideal,[41] meanwhile is at home, ironing his handkerchiefs and preparing dinner, and, when he returns from work, she welcomes him home, helps him slip on a comfortable sweater and slippers, and serves him dinner.

In these opening scenes, the film revels in its German-ness, specifically in its provincial Bavarian setting, captured with a great deal of affection and a sense of humor in clichéd forms of *Gemütlichkeit*. The long-married couple enjoys the peaceful familiarity of their predictable life in their quaint, picturesque Allgäu town. In fact, they blend into their environment perfectly, embodying the deep desire humans have to find a home and fit into it, described by Neil Leach as "camouflage."[42] Clearly, over the span of many years, the couple has conformed and grown into their built environment to such an extent that they find themselves perfectly connected, and "camouflaged," in their home there.

Their quiet, harmonious, secure little place in the world is disturbed by what in Campbell's terminology is the hero's "call to action," the beginning of the hero's journey. Here, the call comes in the form of the unpleasant news of the doctor's prognosis from the "outside," less familiar world of the cold, sterile office with its medical equipment. Once the news is shared privately with Trudi, it looms like a dark shadow over their Bavarian idyll. Unwilling and perhaps unable to deal with this disturbance, Trudi finally decides to hide the information of the terminal disease from her husband and the rest of the family. However, she does set out to change the rhythm of their lives and also his heart and to encourage Rudi to set out on a journey with her. She suggests they visit their son Karl in Japan to see Mount Fuji, whereupon Rudi exclaims: "Mt. Fuji is also just a mountain," arguing that there are plenty of beautiful mountains where they are in Bavaria. Trudi is finally able to convince him at least to take a trip to see their daughter and other son who live in Berlin, understanding that this might be his final opportunity to see his children.

From this point on, the film closely resembles Yasujiro Ozu's cinematic masterpiece *Tokyo Story*, a film generally regarded as "particularly Japanese" but also praised for its "universal appeal"[43] and its poignant insights into the human condition, specifically in its depiction of the generational divide between parents and their children. The film's German title, *Die Reise nach Tokyo* (The Trip to Tokyo) emphasizes the importance of the journey itself within the larger story of an older couple and their relationship with their estranged children.[44] Ozu, called "the poet of family life," is known for his quiet art of slow pacing, which focuses attention on the seemingly trivial and thereby makes it significant. (Dörrie's presentation of the Allgäu, the close-ups of the couple, and the lingering focus on Trudi's compassionate gestures of concern and care for her husband, captured in the early part of the film, clearly mimic Ozu's style and pacing.) *Tokyo Story* explores the problems of ordinary modern family life and draws upon key aspects of Japanese tradition, including religious and socio-cultural systems that are often misperceived by Westerners. Nonetheless, through the intimate portrayal of his characters, his work is able to cross most boundaries, as issues of generational alienation, relational disconnect, and the passing of time carry relevance for any culture.

In *Tokyo Story* an elderly couple from a seaside resort town in southwest Japan takes a daylong journey to Tokyo to visit their estranged grown children. Upon arriving, the parents are deeply disappointed and find themselves neglected, as their children are too busy with their own lives. The children send their parents off for a cheap stay at a noisy hot springs resort. The couple realizes they are a burden and do their best to smooth things over; the children guiltily complain about the failed visit. Ozu shot his film with a sense of balance, rendered through minimal camera movement. *Tokyo Story* condemns neither side, but displays reality with resigned and unflinching sadness. The couple then visits the widow of another son, who treats them far better than their own children do and even takes the pair on a sightseeing tour. On the train journey home, the wife becomes ill and dies shortly afterward. The children dutifully attend the funeral, but then rush back to Tokyo. The film's last sequence portrays the old husband alone in his seaside home, followed by an exterior shot of the rooftops of the town and a boat passing by, as if simply to express that life continues even amid the sense of emptiness.

Dörrie acknowledges *Tokyo Story* as a key source of inspiration for her own work, especially in this film, as well as for her initial encounter with Japanese culture: "I saw that a lot of what I thought was Ozu was really Japan. Then I wondered what would happen to the couple from *Tokyo Monogatari* if you placed them in the 21st Century in the West, which is something that Ozu did backwards, because his film is based on an American movie [Leo McCarey's *Make Way for Tomorrow*]. That I found interesting, because it was *not* so Japanese, and in the end it was something that came from the West, traveled to the East, and I took it from the East to the West—but made the main character go to the East, to Japan."[45] Dörrie recasts *Tokyo Story* in modern-day Germany, paying homage to the Japanese filmmaker with many recognizable borrowings from Ozu's film (from the introductory depiction of Mount Fuji at the beginning of the film to the daughter's sudden and selfish claim to the mother's kimono after her death, to the film's pacing, unique camera angles, and the general plot-line itself). Like Ozu, she is able to capture moments of deep resonance and remembrance. As Alice Kuzniar suggests:

> Indeed, the film's entire aesthetic borrows from Ozu's stationary shots and calmly paced montage. Like Ozu, Dörrie jump-cuts to images captured by an immobile camera, an editing technique that endows both films with a concentration and focus on place, making the fleeting moment a precious one. It is a way of commemorating the mutability of life, whether symbolized by the movement of a train, the flow of a river, or the vista of the sea. Once they are repeated in the film, the images recall that the mother is no longer alive to also witness them; we then see reality differently through the lens of loss.[46]

The couple travels from their scenic Bavarian town to the big city of Berlin, where their children greet them with a polite but annoyed air of civility. The children's estrangement from their parents becomes more obvious at every turn: awkward silences dominate the scene, broken only by the sound of the grandchildren's electronic games.[47] The grandchildren themselves can scarcely bear to move their attention away from their Gameboys to acknowledge the grandparents' arrival. In private, the adult children whine and bicker about their parents, about the stress and demands of the unexpected visit, about not having time for the parents, and finally about old childhood jealousies revolving around their other sibling, Karl, who lives in Japan, and who, they believe, was the only one the parents ever truly loved. Rudi and Trudi find their children's uncomfortable civility difficult to bear. In spite of their best efforts, they cannot fit into their children's urban lifestyles and landscapes. It is especially difficult for the sensitive Trudi, whose lesbian daughter and working daughter-in-law distance themselves from her, unable to measure up to and/or relate to the example Trudi has set of being a "good mother and good wife," who bakes cakes (rather than purchasing baked goods) for her family and guests. During their first night in Berlin, Trudi confides in her husband, voicing her frustration at not being able to bridge the generational gap: "I can remember them so well as children, but now, as adults, I simply don't recognize who they are. I just don't know them anymore."

The only real connection the parents can establish is with their daughter Karolin's lesbian girlfriend, Franzi, who ends up being much more sympathetic and appreciative of Trudi and Rudi than their own children. Franzi is the one who spends the most time with the older couple while they are in Berlin. She takes them on an impromptu car tour of the city and does her best to point out various sights while navigating the traffic with colorful profanity. She also accompanies Trudi to a Butoh performance when Karolin cannot and sees firsthand how much Trudi loves this expressive dance form. Trudi immediately finds herself at home in the theater and in the dark anonymity of the audience, entranced and brought to tears by the beauty of Butoh dancer Tadashi Endo's performance and the haunting Japanese musical accompaniment. In his slow, meditative depiction of life's stark hardships, Trudi enters MA and is able to slow down, connect, self-reflect, and perceive her own suppressed sorrow. Fraleigh describes Butoh's ability to conjure up this experience of space as follows: "As in mediation, Butoh offers a slow contemplative space within consciousness, somatically transforming: one pace, one synapse, and one cell at a time. This space of passage is known as ma. We have no Western term for *ma*. It is a middle, a hyphen in-between in any case."[48]

The experience also gives Trudi the ability to let go, and in the dark theater, she weeps. Franzi offers her a tissue. This act of consideration brings the two closer, and even without exchanging words creates a shared experience of intimacy between the women. Franzi has witnessed and responded to Trudi's vulnerability as no one else has.[49] The two share this moment, captured by Dörrie in a close-up, as they watch Endo dance, crawl, and writhe through life's depicted raw moments. A jump shot to Rudi shows him standing in the foyer, looking around uncomfortably at the walls covered in grotesque modern art, depicting expressionistic figures of humans and angels. He reads the graffiti heading above the figures that proclaims: "Im Himmel ist viel Glück" (In heaven there is much happiness). He peers into the theater itself, catching a glimpse of the performer through the dark curtains, but decides to sit down and wait things out.

The two scenes reveal a notable divide between the couple. As Rudi waits uncomfortably and impatiently in this unfamiliar setting, it is clear that he is obviously outside his element. He is unable and unwilling to blend into this foreign landscape, the place where his wife feels most at home, most herself, and most importantly where she finds much desired solace. The stark contrast reveals an unexpected gap between the two.

Nonetheless, the next scene quickly restores a sense of the familiar order, as the two stand together overlooking the sea, the next stop of their shared journey. Having brought forward their scheduled departure in order to avoid causing their children and themselves any further discomfort, the couple leaves Berlin early the next morning and heads for the Baltic Sea, a place they have not visited in many years. In this particularly moving scene, as they look out over the water on a cold day, Trudi teases Rudi about his constant complaints, including his complaint that the Baltic Sea is no longer what it once was. She then cozily shares one sleeve of her sky-blue cardigan with Rudi, so that they wear it together and in a comfortable embrace. Rudi then voices—much to Trudi's surprise and dismay—his desire to have his ashes scattered into the sea. As they begin to speak about death, Trudi cautiously asks Rudi what he would do if he only had a short time left to live. Rudi assures her that he would not change a thing about his life: "I'd go to work and come home to you."

Yet the peace of this moment is short-lived. In the evening, Rudi is restless and unable to sleep "because the sea is so loud." Trudi distracts him, and, dressed in her coral flower kimono, she seductively dances, swaying her hips back and forth, twirling and beckoning him to join her. Initially, he protests, saying: "This is silly. Dancing in the middle of the night." Yet slowly and awkwardly he surrenders to his wife's gentle urgings, and the two dance together, first swaying back and forth in Western dance motion. Then Trudi raises his arm and moves behind him, embracing him dramatically. She then begins to move his body like a marionette, stretching his arm in unfamiliar ways to mimic Butoh gestures and postures. Her gaze follows the arm, and looks out as if into the distance. She pulls him close, caught up in her own emotion. She encircles his arm again and stretches it off to the side, pauses as they see themselves reflected in the mirror, then embraces him tightly as the two kiss. Rudi, unused to this unusual display of intimacy, asks his wife: "What's with you?" To which she replies, "Nothing, nothing at all." Yet, in the brief movements of this dance, Trudi finds a way to communicate her abiding love to her husband, without words. She also is able to express *herself* through her dance, and her deep love of Butoh allows her to reveal a greater depth of genuine emotion, which she has kept carefully under wraps. She has also begun to instruct her husband in the art of Butoh as "a discovery of the heart," giving him a sense of how to dance with her in the space of MA. And finally, for the first time since their journey began, Trudi is able to sleep peacefully.

The next day, as the couple strolls together comfortably on the beach, at peace in the unfamiliar, yet tranquil setting, it becomes clear that Rudi, too, has changed and softened. Against the backdrop of the sea, he appears more open, more willing to communicate his feelings. He speaks of the true happiness they share, simply because they have each other. His contentment fills him, and he announces that he is ready to go home, as they have accomplished all they set out to do. Trudi hesitates on the beach for a second, standing alone and looking out over the water, and tries to catch her breath, overwhelmed with emotion. The camera then pans to show her shadow dancing alone on the sand until Rudi's shadow comes to her, reaches out to her, and the shadows of the two figures merge. This "foreshadowing" is also a foreboding. Later that evening, unable to sleep, Trudi gets up as she has numerous times before in the middle of the night. A vision of herself dancing Butoh in a white nightgown, face painted, resembling a ghost beckons her in the mirror and Trudi stands off to the side, staring at this apparition. When it approaches her in the mirror, she smiles knowingly. The ghost seems unfamiliar and haunting, yet Trudi welcomes it as a guest. Trudi's dancing self articulates her anguish and sorrow at her husband's imminent death in ways she could never put into words. In retrospect, this dance scene proves to be pivotal to the story. As she views herself, there is a sense of homecoming that is soothing and exhilarating. Then the camera simply pans back to the sea and the sound of the waves crashing onto shore.

The next morning, as the sun shines on the beautiful quiet blue sea, Rudi tries to awaken Trudi, only to find that she has passed away in her sleep. All three children come to the Baltic Sea, including Karl, who travels from Japan. Karolin suddenly requests of her siblings her mother's coral flower kimono, which she remembers her always wearing in the kitchen when they were young. Rudi, however, carefully guards Trudi's clothes, her blue cardigan, black skirt, and in particular her kimono. They will reappear again and again throughout the film and function as a vivid *memento mori* for him. There is a sense that his daughter, who had little time for her mother when she was alive, could never appreciate the kimono as fully as he could. The alienation between the family members grows, as the children are painfully unable to relate to their father's present grief, preferring instead to hold on to the childhood memories they have of their mother. Indeed, it seems that only in memories of the past can they find common ground.

The familial estrangement results from the changed circumstances of each person's life and finds a visual echo in the film's depiction of the change of seasons from summer to fall. The children's priorities become even more apparent at Trudi's funeral in Bavaria, which only Franzi attends. Without his wife, Rudi clearly has no idea what to do with himself. He is painfully alone. As he and Franzi sit together at the dining room table, he thanks her for her kindness. She simply shares what Trudi had shared with her during the Butoh performance in Berlin: "She told me about how she always wanted to dance, to become a really good Butoh dancer, more than anything else in her life, and how she would have liked to go to Japan so much to study it there and how everything turned out differently and that it was a good life but.... Not that you think she wasn't happy. Maybe there was another woman in her that nobody saw and I saw that other person. That's all."

Thus, Rudi hears from his daughter's girlfriend that his wife forwent her own dreams and desires out of love for him and the children. This is not completely new to him. He disappears into the bedroom and comes back with a small book of photographs of Trudi, dressed in black, her hair disheveled, with a white-painted face and red lipstick, performing Butoh. He explains to Franzi: "I didn't like it. It was so … so extreme. It embarrassed me. I didn't want her to keep it up." Indeed, Butoh is often seen as a tortured and disturbing dance, with grotesque elements that evoke disdain and denial. The dance's powerful expressiveness confronts reality directly, inspired by the basic Buddhist values of compassion and truth. As Rudi grapples with this realization, he begins to understand that the woman he thought he knew was nothing like he imagined: Trudi's intriguing and passionate, yet faded, dream of Japan, which includes Mount Fuji, cherry blossoms, and the enigmatic and beguiling art of Butoh, then takes center stage and appears in photos and pictures decorating their quaint Bavarian home. Rudi begins to understand how he thwarted her great desire in life to travel to Japan, and he vows to make up for her lost dream in a belated, life-altering journey of atonement and reconciliation. This vow takes him to Japan—to Tokyo, specifically, in the midst of the cherry blossom festival, Hanami, and the celebration of beauty, impermanence, and new beginnings. Rudi finally begins his hero's journey, responding to the initial, unheard call to action with a sincere sense of mission. His journey mirrors the shaman's journey into "other worlds" of experience to be explored in search of healing after experiencing a "shamanic wounding." This recurring motif is a precursor to shamanic rituals and practices, which are said to crack the shell of the lesser self to reveal one's true nature and place in the world. Yet before Rudi can experience the boons gained from such a journey, he must undergo ordeals, face his own shadow, experience the death of his old self, and focus on inner realities in order to find healing, harmony, and wholeness for the self and others and learn to embrace the wide emotional spectrum in the dance of human life.

Rudi's first experiences of this "other world" of Japan hardly differ from those in Berlin, or from a clichéd and sentimental sightseeing tour. He is lost, uncomfortable, out of his element, and unable to find his way, even when the camera slyly closes in on a map that indicates "You are here," like a gentle reminder from his environment calling for him to be more present and alert. He spends a whole day in his son's small apartment, then the next day in a bar, until he cannot stand it any longer. Dörrie captures Rudi's grief-stricken confusion as he stumbles around the city, at one point tying a handkerchief to a pole as a reminder of where he is. Seeking solace and shortcuts to a new sense of happiness, he goes to a strip club, then a geisha bath-house, but breaks down once the two young female attendants notice his wedding band. Unable to find his son's name on the plate outside the apartment building, he sleeps in front of the door until Karl comes out. Upset, his son creates a sign for him with his name written in Japanese and his son's phone number. Moments like these recall Sophia Coppola's *Lost in Translation* (2003). However, Dörrie is less interested in how out of place Rudi feels in Japan than in exploring how he comes to fit in. After depicting his initial failures and tribulations on the path of his personal journey, the film dramatizes his potential to transform. Ultimately, *Cherry Blossoms/Hanami* is not about Rudi dying, but about him learning to deal with death and his life. Through all these experiences, he begins to gain an appreciation of the value of human care and love and to understand how small actions can have lasting effects.

Rudi is an unlikely hero, one who against his own inclination finds himself on this journey: from the comfortable surroundings of his Bavarian home to the big city of Berlin, then to the even more unfamiliar cityscape of Tokyo, with its frantic pace and—at least for a Westerner—incomprehensible geography, and finally to serenity and a sense of home in the obscure dance form of Butoh. One afternoon, Rudi watches Japanese TV, which resembles the many mindless programs on German TV. But all of a sudden he stumbles upon a Butoh performance. His melancholy returns. He puts on his wife's sky-blue cardigan, pearl necklace, and black skirt over his own clothes so as to express his grief and embody his memories of her, and then looks at himself in the mirror. Rudi's ritual borders on the pathological, yet the film portrays it with compassion. Perhaps he needs to feel close to her, maybe he senses his own impending death. The clothes give him comfort. At night, he lays them out next to himself, so he can imagine her presence. Dörrie sees this as a natural part of Rudi's journey: "grieving is a process of integration," she states, "there is this infinite pain, caused by the physical separation and the knowledge that one will never be able to encounter the other one again physically. But then it also becomes a successful, internal integration when one suddenly carries the other one inside one's self."[50] Rudi tries to explain what he is going through to his son: "I don't understand where Trudi is. Where her body is. My memories of her are in my body but when my body is no longer here, where will Trudi be then?"

The relationship between father and son remains strained. They go to the park together to celebrate Hanami with Karl's colleagues. Karl drinks heavily and lashes out at his father for always having been so self-absorbed. Rudi, however, is changing. His wife's demeanor emerges in him: he listens to his son, gently makes him go to bed. In the middle of the night, Rudi checks on him. The next day he returns to the park to see the cherry blossoms and, more importantly, a young Butoh dancer he spotted the day before. He observes her from a distance as she dances without an audience near the water and under the cherry trees in full bloom, with a pink telephone that has receivers on both ends of a long cord. But the cord is not attached—there is no one on the line.

Motivated to make a connection to that which reminds him of his wife, Rudi slowly gathers courage and approaches her, asking in English whether she is a Butoh dancer. She answers in broken English: "Butoh is dance of shadow. Not me dance, shadow dance," as her shadow is shown dancing on the ground. His next lesson in Butoh-MA begins as the dancer then teaches him how to watch his shadow dance, explaining: "I do not know who is shadow." She bends over to speak to the ground, asking: "Hello, hello! Who are you?" but receives, as she indicates, "No answer." She clarifies further, showing him how to extend his hands and feel the air around him: "You feel the memory, the wind," she says and encourages him to "hold, hold, hold" and "catch the shadow and feel the shadow. Everybody has shadow. Women, men. Alive, dead." Then, as if answering his deepest questions, she states: "I dance with the dead." When he asks who is dead, she explains: "My mother. She loved the telephone. Pink telephone. Always on the phone with family. Now I am on the phone with my mother all the time. She is in me." She hugs the telephone as if holding a baby. The other end of the phone line is shown dangling from the tree trunk, open to the air and wind. The dancer looks dreamily at the cherry blossoms, which then fade into a majestic shot of Mount Fuji. Rudi and the Butoh dancer's lack of a common language matters little. Their shared experience of loss and grief bridges their differences more successfully than language ever could.

Rudi walks with the young dancer through the park, once she has packed up her things, and asks her for more information. She patiently explains the mysterious movements of Butoh. When Rudi asks for her name, she stumbles to find the right words, then insists, "I am Yu," clearly to be understood also as the statement "I am you." He has met his double and his shadow in this Other named Yu. The encounter is both jarring and emancipating. Yu comes to teach Rudi the ability to see and understand himself through the "the dance of shadows," known also as "the dance of the senses."[51] Through his experiences he begins to access the places in his life that have been shrouded in darkness. Rudi begins to dialog inwardly with Trudi and to reconnect not only with the part of her he knew, but also with a part he never really understood. He begins to sense her through the dance she loved so much. At the heart of Butoh lies the notion that the body can serve not merely as "an abstract instrument or a tool for aesthetic figuration, but rather as a tool to find and reveal deep, dark and impenetrable layers in the body that had once been imprinted there."[52] By connecting with these unconscious traces, one becomes open to experiencing life, death, and memories free from the mind's conscious control over the body.

Interestingly enough, Dörrie first came across Butoh not on one of her many visits to Japan, but rather in Germany. First she saw a TV documentary by Peter Sempel and later met the world-renowned Butoh dancer Tadashi Endo, who lives and teaches in Göttingen. This is not as surprising as it might seem, as some of Butoh's roots lie in expressive dance forms, or *Ausdruckstanz*, which originated in Germany. The white face paint and stylized movements combine various aspects of Japanese dance and German expressionist dance theater, but also of many other dance forms from across the world. Butoh's vocabulary of gestures ranges from the meditative and graceful to the grotesque and disturbing. In Butoh, it is "the dancer himself or herself who, with his or her imagination, creates the technique of the dance."[53] As Dörrie explains, she became fascinated with the dance, as it appeared to be "something altogether different, something that I had never seen before: it was the visual portrayal of the presence of the dead within each of us."[54] Indeed, Tadashi's teaching asks that one begin to see and sense the connection to one's ancestors in all of one's movements, indicating, as he told Dörrie, "that the dead are dreaming of us."[55]

According to Fraleigh's accounts, another great Butoh performer, Atsushi Takenouchi, similarly emphasized the need to "dance and be danced and keep dancing"[56] until perceived barriers disappear. In his piece *Yin Yang Butoh*, which focuses on "embracing souls that have been excluded or pushed away by society, or suffered from mental and physical disturbances," his dancers are said to "encounter the suffering of the dispossessed and keep dancing until they change their darkness into light."[57] Butoh's shamanic properties, Fraleigh suggests, have an alchemical "power of enchantment and transformation," which enables its dancers to "attend to metamorphosis and healing through the body."[58] By embodying the shamanic idea of "shape-shifting" and dancing Butoh through the changing conditions of experience, the transformative and therapeutic aspects of shamanic alchemy can come to the fore.[59] As Fraleigh explains, these are not "the paranormal or supernatural but rather the very real ability of the body to manifest healing through dance and movement," as shamans do through repetitive movement, such as shaking, stamping, leaping, and whirling, to "pass between conscious and unconscious life, finally distilling this in various forms of dance and theater."[60] As she also acknowledges, "this might be said of other kinds of dance as well, but Butoh methods cultivate this passage in-between in unique ways, one of which is called *ma* in Japanese."[61] Butoh is able to capture great contradictions: it portrays light and shadow, birth and death, joy and pain, and imbues each moment and each movement with spiritual presence.[62] It captures the body in motion as well as the body in grief and makes visible the inner landscape of the soul in its experiences of beauty, joy, and pain. The great Butoh master Kazuo Ohno maintained the preeminence of physical and emotional impulse over rational or cerebral reactions, seeing the former as the body's connection to nature's cycles of birth and decay, and the dancer's body itself as a flower able to communicate with the living and the dead. For Rudi, Butoh is a means through which he can begin to find a sense of peace and purpose.

At the same time, he finds himself on new ground, isolated from much of what he has known in this life. As Dörrie emphasizes in her notes, Butoh dancers "are complete outsiders; even in Japan, only very few people who are into art and culture know about this form of dance. The masses don't know about Butoh."[63] As Rudi learns to appreciate Butoh as much as his wife did, he begins to behave in ways that, if they knew, would alienate those around him. Rudi secretly puts on Trudi's cardigan, necklace, and skirt over his own clothes before leaving the house each day wrapped in his heavy coat. With Trudi's clothes

208 ~: *Erika M. Nelson*

thus hidden, he occasionally opens the coat at a striking aspect of Japan, for instance a pink cloud of cherry blossoms, and says: "Trudi, this is for you."

When he returns home one day, Rudi overhears a conversation between Karl and one of his sisters, in which the son complains about the father's mood swings, unpredictable behavior, and extended stay. Rudi simply requests that his son allow him a little more time. Rudi also begins to care for others actively: he sweeps, cleans, and cooks for his son, just as his wife had done for him. He learns the "mindfulness" Trudi possessed instinctively and which Japanese culture prizes so highly. Dörrie explains this "mindfulness" in the following way: "There is even a name for this mindfulness: *Mono no aware.* There are many translations for *Mono no aware* but the ones that best capture the meaning, at least in my mind, are: to be delighted and wistfully touched; to be moved by things; and the self becoming one with the outside world. Maybe it's just a more pronounced awareness of the transient nature of things, resulting in a much more focused enjoyment of even the simplest things in life."[64]

Mono no aware also refers to compassion, experienced through one's vulnerability, not one's strength, which makes one keenly aware of the impermanence of all phenomena. This care and compassion leaves lasting results in Rudi's environment. The taste of cabbage rolls, one of his mother's specialties, brings tears to Karl's eyes. He does not know how to respond to his own reaction. Ultimately, he breaks down and openly shares with his father for the first time his grief over his mother's death.

Rudi also brings some of the rolls to Yu, who moves the cabbage rolls with her chopsticks so that they line up next to each other, side by side. She speaks of them being like Rudi and his wife, once separated and now reunited. She then rolls herself up in her blue tarp like a cabbage roll and Rudi follows suit. The two lie there, wrapped up tightly in opposite ends of the blue tarp, and take in the sensation of togetherness.

The most striking technical deviation from *Tokyo Story* is Dörrie's choice of a mobile camera: as one interviewer suggests, it is "incredibly fluid and vibrant," even "loose,"[65] which Dörrie associates with her own way of seeing as a woman director and her rejection of the male heritage of filmmaking, as well as with her feeling of non-belonging as regards this heritage.[66] *Cherry Blossoms/ Hanami* engages the viewer both emotionally with its intimate feel and moving narrative and aesthetically as a visually striking and sometimes almost experimental film. Dörrie shot *Cherry Blossoms/Hanami* digitally, with a crew of only ten people, for the most part on location "by going with the flow and by not trying to control the sets, by not letting the story meander but letting reality come in and serve the story."[67] The lead actor, Elmar Wepper, was in character from morning to night. He also had to wash and maintain his own clothing, as he does so meticulously in the film. At times he got lost in the Tokyo streets and subway system, and occasionally he would improvise, for instance the unscripted "free hug" scene, when Dörrie "asked Elmar to just walk up to them [i.e., the group holding the "free hug" placard] and see what happened. Because he was always in character, it turned out to be a very nice miniature scene to illustrate that a total stranger is the only person who gives him a hug, when it should be his son doing that. But we could only do this because we were so sure what we wanted to talk about and how to tell the story."[68]

As Dörrie suggests: "Maybe it's my advantage as a woman filmmaker: I'm so used to not being taken seriously that I love not being recognised as a film director on the set. I love just behaving like a tourist with a video camera and nobody pays any attention to me. That's my sandbox to play around with."[69] At the same time, she did stick to a "very fixed screenplay," and she suggests that the film's feeling of fluidity, spontaneity, and immediacy came out of a paradox: "the trick was to stay very close to the screenplay and simultaneously be completely open. That was something that we rehearsed, that there were no guarantees."

One day, Rudi follows Yu home, only to find out that she is homeless and lives in a tent. He is overwhelmed at this reality. He packs up all his things and asks her to take him to see Mount Fuji. On the train ride, Yu explains that there is a chance they will not be able to see the mountain: "I say to you. He is very shy." Indeed, Mount Fuji is often shrouded in fog.[70] When they arrive at their destination, Mount Fuji is nowhere to be seen. Days pass without a sighting. One early morning, Rudi is unable to sleep. He opens the curtains and finally sees Mount Fuji. He paints his face, dons Trudi's nightgown and kimono, and dances Butoh outside in front of the elusive mountain. With Trudi as his shadow, Rudi faces his loss. In his dance, his wife rematerializes and dances with him, and a poetic, fantastical moment enters unexpectedly into this realistic film. After the bittersweet dance, Rudi falls down and dies, having completed his life's journey, his heroic and shamanic journey, boon in hand.

Upon hearing of Rudi's death at the foot of Mount Fuji, Yu dons his coat, hat, and the sign with his name on it as a gesture of appreciation and acknowledgement of his significance to her life. The next scenes follow Rudi's body to its burial site. As is tradition in Japan, the eldest son—in this case Karl—takes care of the funeral arrangements. Rudi is cremated according to Japanese traditions, revealing how differently Germans and Japanese face death. The cremation incorporates, as Hiroko Nakata explains, "a unique mixture of religion, tradition, culture, ritual and geography that to the outsider may appear perplexing."[71] In Japan it is custom for the family to witness the sliding of the body into the cremation chamber and, once the cremation is complete, to retrieve the body by picking the bones out of the ashes and transferring them to the urn using large chopsticks. This is the only time when Japanese etiquette allows for two people to hold the same item with chopsticks at the same time. The retrieving of the bones is regarded as a sacred act to be carried out by family members and those closest to the deceased. Inside the crematorium, Karl and Yu stand next to Rudi's cremated body and pick up his remains piece by piece and place them into an urn. The scene brings Karl and Yu into strained and silent proximity, another unlikely bridging of the gap and an opportunity to experience MA. Yet, Karl is noticeably uncomfortable during this hands-on confrontation with death and distances himself, while Yu—clearly more familiar with notions of mortality—focuses on honoring the dead with this ritual.

Rudi's remains are returned to Bavaria, where the children all gather for the funeral, still unable to leave behind their own self-centeredness and to understand their father and what they view as a scandalous end: caught with an eighteen-year-old homeless girl in a hotel, wearing women's clothing. They cannot see Rudi and Yu's relationship as anything other than one of mutual exploitation, not as one based on camaraderie and compassion. The children's myopia serves as a critique of modern German society and its values, of its superficial appearances, and its distorted expectations about relationships. Poetic justice prevails, since Yu apparently ends up with Rudi's life savings, which he withdrew before flying to Tokyo. She has more need of them than his children, just as she had more need of Rudi. The film portrays the experience of death as requiring the ability to enter and inhabit a world that is very different culturally and socially from one's day-to-day reality. This space is defined by dance, inner presence, pain, anguish, and loss.

Cherry Blossoms/Hanami emphasizes the significance of cultural influences, of the arts, and of the inward journey of self-knowledge. The film is infused with quiet, subtle moments and gentle revelations, as well as with tenderness— whether it is Trudi's concern for her husband or the delicate relationship that develops between Rudi and Yu, who comes to be closer to him and more like a daughter than his own flesh and blood.[72]

The film's intermedial and intertextual aspects, which blend conventions of dance and film, of romantic comedy and road movie, as well as of travel narrative and East-West identity discourses, help shape this peculiar odyssey. Dörrie captures a Buddhist sense of life's fleeting nature, of the impermanence of things, and of the inevitability of death. The film portrays the significance of simple, often unexpected gestures, which make life meaningful, as for instance when Yu takes Rudi to the subway station and leads him to the right train. The film embraces such moments, as they bring humanity to life. The film's slow pace, just like the patient wait for Mount Fuji, ultimately proves worthwhile, as it allows for a depiction of Rudi's transformation from oddly grumpy, typical, middle-class Bavarian homebody to cosmopolitan Butoh-dancing world traveler, compassionate husband, and more complete human being.

Dörrie's interweaving of German and Japanese cultural tropes exemplifies her ability to decenter cultural norms by dramatizing encounters between cultures. Rudi's journey and his exchanges with people of an "exotic" East Asian culture enable him to break out of stereotypical, learned behavior and experience a greater sense of himself beyond his familiar cultural parameters. Dörrie follows, with reserve and respect and without belaboring her point, a typical Westerner in his encounter with difference and chronicles the cultural, psychological, and social effects of such an encounter. Rudi stands in a long line of Dörrie heroes who acquire a greater sense of their humanity through a slow, conscious inner human revolution and grow into champions of life, a benefit to the societies they inhabit—all by learning how to dance, in this case Butoh, with MA.

Notes

1. The concept of "MA" is taken from Zen Buddhism, as explained in the introductory comments found on the Butoh master's website, "The Official Website of Tadashi Endo–Butoh–MA," http://www.butoh-ma.de/index.php?option=com_content&task=view&id=2&Itemid=5. Last accessed 4 January 2013.
2. Tadashi Endo's website.
3. Sondra Fraleigh, *Butoh: Metamorphic Dance and Global Alchemy* (Champaign, I.L., 2010) 25.
4. Fraleigh, *Butoh*, 4.
5. Alice A. Kuzniar, "Uncanny Doublings and Asian Rituals in Recent Films by Monika Treut, Doris Dörrie, and Ulrike Ottinger," *Women in German Yearbook: Feminist Studies in German Literature & Culture*, vol. 27 (2011): 178.
6. Fraleigh, *Butoh*, 11.
7. Fraleigh, *Butoh*, 11.
8. *Cherry Blossoms: A Film by Doris Dörrie Presskit*, Mongrel Media, http://www.mongrelmedia.com/data/ftp/Cherry%20Blossoms/CHERRY%20BLOSSOMS%20-%20English%20(Mongrelized)%20press%20kit.pdf. Last accessed 20 June 2011, 4. This is the English translation of the German *Kirschblüten Presseheft* from Majestic Filmverleih, http://www.majestic.de/presse/kirschblueten/Presseheft/kirschblueten%20presseheft.pdf. Last accessed 20 June 2011, 7.
9. Sondra Fraleigh, *Dancing Into Darkness: Butoh, Zen, and Japan* (Pittsburgh, P.A., 1999), 3.
10. Fraleigh, *Butoh*, 38–39. Also see chapter 4 of Sondra Fraleigh and Tamah Nakamura, *Hijikata Tatsumi and Ohno Kazuo* (London, 2006), in which Yoshito Ohno explains his father's exploration of "Be a stone" and his experience of dancing pain in the stones of Auschwitz.
11. Fraleigh, *Butoh*, 13.
12. The quotes from the film are all taken from the dubbed English version of *Kirschblüten/Hanami*, http://www.imdb.com/title/tt0910559. Last accessed 20 June 2011. The film won three Lolas at the Berlinale in 2008.
13. Peter Zander, "Warum Doris Dörrie in Japan tanzt," *Die Welt*, 7 February 2008. http://www.welt.de/kultur/article1641536/Warum_Doris_Doerrie_in_Japan_tanzt.html. Last accessed 20 June 2011.
14. In her early days as a filmmaker, Dörrie was invited to Tokyo with her first feature film, *Straight through the Heart*, in 1982.

15. *Cherry Blossoms: A Film by Doris Dörrie Presskit*, 4.

16. Zander, "Warum Doris Dörrie in Japan tanzt."

17. Zander, "Warum Doris Dörrie in Japan tanzt."

18. David Noh, "Cherry Blossom Time: Germany's Doris Dörrie Ventures to Japan for Drama of Aging and Rebirth," *Film Journal International*, 30 Dec 2008. http://www .filmjournal.com/filmjournal/content_display/news-and-features/features/movies/ e3ic8de2356a5754927491aefe2b76a8f1a. Last accessed 20 June 2011.

19. See in particular Klaus Phillips, "Interview with Doris Dörrie: Filmmaker, Writer, Teacher," in *Triangulated Visions: Women in Recent German Cinema*, ed. Ingeborg Majer O'Sickey and Ingeborg von Zadow (Albany, 1998), 179.

20. Zander, "Warum Doris Dörrie in Japan tanzt."

21. Zander, "Warum Doris Dörrie in Japan tanzt."

22. The most pertinent works include Marcel Mauss, *The Gift: The Form and Reason for Exchange in Archaic Societies* (London, 1990) (originally1923) and "Techniques of the Body," *Economy and Society* 2 (1973): 70–88, and Douglas Davies, *Death, Ritual and Belief: The Rhetoric of Funerary Rites* (London, 2002) and *Anthropology and Theology* (Oxford, U.K., 2002).

23. Davies, *Anthropology and Theology*, 19.

24. Nick Dawson, "Doris Dörrie, Cherry Blossoms," *Director Interviews. Filmmaker Magazine*, 16 January 2009. http://www.filmmakermagazine.com/news/2009/01/doris-Dörrie-cherry-blossoms/. Last accessed 20 June 2011.

25. For those critics who see either the New German Cinema or feminist avant-garde film as the pinnacle of postwar German cinema, Dörrie is damned for this, not praised.

26. In 1989, along with some friends, Dörrie founded Cobra Filmproduktions GmbH, the company that has produced all of her numerous subsequent films. In 1987, Dörrie also began to write short stories, which have received numerous awards. Many of her films are based on her fiction: for example, the drama *Happy* became the film *Nackt* (Naked, 2002) and the collection of short stories *Für immer und ewig* (Forever and Always) was made into the film *Keiner liebt mich* (Nobody Loves Me, 1993). Dörrie has directed opera productions, including *Cosi Fan Tutte* (Staatsoper Berlin, 2001), *Rigoletto* (Münchner Staatsoper, 2004–05), *Madame Butterfly* (Münchner Staatstheater, 2005), and *La Finta Giardiniera* (Salzburger Festspiele, 2006).

27. Birgit Rühe, "Biography: Doris Dörrie," trans. Rebecca van Dyck. http://www.fembio .org/english/biography.php/woman/biography/doris-doerrie. Last accessed 20 June 2011.

28. Doris Dörrie and Julia Kaergel, *Lotte will Prinzessin sein* (Ravensburg, 1998).

29. Joseph Campbell. *The Hero of a Thousand Faces* (Princeton, 1949).

30. Campbell, *The Hero of a Thousand Faces*, 23.

31. Bill Moyers's "Introduction" in Joseph Campbell and Bill Moyers, *The Power of Myth* (New York, 1988), xx.

32. Fraleigh, *Butoh*, 28.

33. Doris Dörrie, *Liebe, Schmerz und das ganze verdammte Zeug. Vier Geschichten* (Zurich, 1989). The English version, *Love, Pain and the Whole Damn Thing*, was published in 1989 by Alfred A. Knopf.

34. In her writings on Butoh, Fraleigh continually poses similar questions, aimed to provoke deeper self-inquiry and evoke a more authentic movement in her dance.

35. "Director's Statement," *Cherry Blossoms: A Film by Doris Dörrie Presskit*, 2.

36. *Cherry Blossoms: A Film by Doris Dörrie Presskit*, 2.

37. Dawson, "Doris Dörrie, Cherry Blossoms."
38. Dawson, "Doris Dörrie, Cherry Blossoms."
39. *Cherry Blossoms: A Film by Doris Dörrie Presskit*, 8.
40. Dawson, "Doris Dörrie, Cherry Blossoms."
41. The vanishing image of the German *Hausfrau* ideal has repeatedly been discussed, as for instance in a *Time Magazine* article, "West Germany: The Vanishing Hausfrau," *Time*, 17 August 1962. http://www.time.com/time/magazine/article/0,9171,870027,00 .html. Last accessed January 4, 2013. The piece laments: "Ah, the German *hausfrau*. There she stands in front of her beloved stove. Her mind untarnished by thoughts that do not concern the care of her family or the future of her soul, she is cheerfully dedicated to producing heartier dinners, cleaner floors, and more babies. From a life tightly bound by *Kinder, Kirche* and *Küche*, she gazes fondly up at her worldly husband. This is a picture comforting to any German male—but these days he is likely to find it only in an old movie. In fact, the traditional hausfrau is no more." Also see Nancy R. Reagin, *Sweeping the German Nation: Domesticity and National Identity in Germany, 1870-1945* (New York, 2007).
42. Neil Leach, *Camouflage* (Cambridge, M.A., 2006).
43. David Desser, ed., *Ozu's Tokyo Story.* Cambridge Film Handbooks (Cambridge, U.K., 1997), i.
44. In contrast, Ozu never depicts any of the actual journey to and from Tokyo; *Tokyo Story* is an anti-road movie where the inner journey completely displaces the outer.
45. Dawson, "Doris Dörrie, Cherry Blossoms."
46. Kuzniar, "Uncanny Doublings," 184–185.
47. Trudi and Rudi's three children's names, Karl, Karolin, and Klaus, are all very similar in sound. In fact, Karl and Karolin are etymologically the same name. Thus, the children's names tie them together as a group in opposition to Trudi and Rudi, whose names are similar at the end rather than at the beginning (like an *Endreim* rather than *Stabreim*).
48. Fraleigh, *Butoh*, 16.
49. There lies sly humor in the fact that Dörrie chose a lesbian character who uses profanity to perform a role that functions analogously to the one performed in Ozu's film by Setsuko Hara, the impossibly virtuous "virgin queen" of classic Japanese cinema who retired upon Ozu's death.
50. *Cherry Blossoms: A Film by Doris Dörrie Presskit*, 9.
51. *Cherry Blossoms: A Film by Doris Dörrie Presskit*, 7.
52. *Cherry Blossoms: A Film by Doris Dörrie Presskit*, 7.
53. *Cherry Blossoms: A Film by Doris Dörrie Presskit*, 7.
54. *Cherry Blossoms: A Film by Doris Dörrie Presskit*, 6.
55. *Cherry Blossoms: A Film by Doris Dörrie Presskit*, 6.
56 56. Fraleigh, *Butoh*, 39.
57. Fraleigh, *Butoh*, 40. The dance here expresses the metamorphic and alchemical potentials and processes of the Buddhist practices of "changing poison into medicine" or transforming grief, sadness, and pain, i.e., "darkness," into something of value and benefit, i.e., "light."
58. Fraleigh, *Butoh*, 12.
59. Fraleigh, *Butoh*, 11–12.
60. Fraleigh, *Butoh*, 12.
61. Fraleigh, *Butoh*, 12.
62. Fraleigh, *Butoh*, 202.

63. "Butohtänzer sind noch heute komplette Außenseiter, auch in Japan kennen das nur Leute, die sich um Kunst und Kultur kümmern. Die Masse kennt das nicht. Butoh hat viel mit Entstehen und Vergehen zu tun: mit Geboren werden und Sterben. Die Vergänglichkeit ist das Thema von Butoh und ist auch das Thema des Films." *Kirschblüten Pressheft*. http://www.majestic.de/presse/kirschblueten/Presseheft/kirschblueten%20presseheft.pdf. Last accessed 20 June 2011.
64. *Cherry Blossoms: A Film by Doris Dörrie Presskit*, 4.
65. Dawson, "Doris Dörrie, Cherry Blossoms."
66. In Dawson, "Doris Dörrie, Cherry Blossoms," Dörrie elaborates on what she means, stating:

    Dörrie: That's a long discussion about form and content and the male relationship to form, which I have thought about a great deal. When I went to film school, there were people there like Wim Wenders who were older than me. He had already made his first film and kept saying, "I use shots by John Ford and I set up the camera *exactly* the same way," and he saw himself as such a direct heir to that tradition of filmmaking. As a woman, I could never see myself in a direct ancestry; it's something you don't do because you don't feel part of that heritage.

    Filmmaker: Was that because there are not nearly so many women film directors to look back to?

    Dörrie: It's not even that. It's something that you just don't do as a woman because it's so completely out there to be making films at all that you don't *dare* put yourself in this line of famous ancestors. It took me about 20 or 30 years and then I said, "OK, what is *my* connection to film history?" I don't connect through style and form, I connect through content and theme. That is where it brings me very close to Ozu and his themes, his sensibility of how to talk about relationships. And I would never dare to adopt his style; I have to come up with my own style. I have to find ways of portraying this world through *my* eyes.
67. Dawson, "Doris Dörrie, Cherry Blossoms."
68. Dawson, "Doris Dörrie, Cherry Blossoms."
69. Dawson, "Doris Dörrie, Cherry Blossoms."
70. In her interview with Nick Dawson, Dörrie also speaks of the challenges of filming Mount Fuji, stating:

    Kurosawa nearly hung himself because of Mount Fuji—he waited and waited for weeks—and because of that famous story of Kurosawa who almost gave up on Mount Fuji, and because I had never been able to see it in 25 years—not once—I knew that you cannot take 100 people in the crew and then wait for Mount Fuji. No producer in the world would allow you to do that, so I knew I had to work very differently, be very flexible, and the second we saw a little sun on top of Mount Fuji on the weather forecast, we just hopped on the train and went and that was the whole style [of shooting]. We had also to catch the cherry blossoms—which are *impossible* to catch—and shoot zillions of other scenes, so it was a different way of approaching things. Whenever the weather was calling to us, we would shoot the scene. (Dawson, "Doris Dörrie, Cherry Blossoms.")
71. Hiroko Nakata, "Japan's Funerals Deep-rooted Mix of Ritual, Form," *Japan Times*, 28 July 2009. http://www.japantimes.co.jp/text/nn20090728i1.html. Last accessed 11 November 2011.
72. In the second part of the film, Yu thus takes over the "Setsuko Hara-function" fulfilled by Franzi in the first part, and again briefly at the end.

PART IV

Trade, Travel, and Ethnographical Narratives

CHAPTER 10

Hairnet Manufacturing in Vysočina and Shandong 1890–1939
An Early Globalizing Home Industry

CHINYUN LEE and LUCIE OLIVOVÁ

Introduction

Hairnets, which hold hair in place while still revealing it and allowing air to circulate, can be traced back to at least the eleventh century. They were widely worn in the Middle Ages and in the Renaissance (see Figure 10.1). At the end of nineteenth century, hairnets again became fashionable in the Western world, giving rise to the first modern hairnet manufacturing facilities in the region of Vysočina in Bohemia. Later, in the early twentieth century, Shandong province in China developed as a center for hairnet manufacturing. Until now, this history of hairnet production in Central Europe and China has not been documented. This essay gives an account of how the techniques and business of hairnet production came to link China with the Austro-Hungarian Empire and later nascent Czechoslovakia in the period of 1890 to 1939 (when the Czech hairnet business was ruined by the Nazis) by looking at the cases of several manufacturers and merchants. In doing so, one discerns a globalized economy with distinct geographic centers for the collection of raw materials, production, and retail sale of this item.

Though it has only risen to a prominent position in critical and historical literature since the 1990s, globalization is not a new phenomenon. Between 1870 and 1914, a period we refer to as early globalization in this chapter, the world saw the emergence of new commodities, speedy transportation (steamers replacing sails, the Panama Canal, etc.), and rapid communication (telegraph, transoceanic cables), as well as of the first global marketplace for commodities and their production. The second wave of globalization, from 1950 until today,

has seen not only newly developed technologies enabling an expansion in the scale of economic activities, but also a shift of their center from the West to East Asia, in recent decades particularly China and India.[1] Disparate regions have become knit together through production and sale, and international trade has come to dominate the world.

And yet, this phenomenon only extends a centuries-old commercial connection between China and Europe. Already during the Middle Ages, merchants transported Chinese silk, porcelain, paper, and tea over deserts and oceans to Europe. In modern times, the transmission of goods and techniques grew faster and more extensive, so that even small products, such as hairnets, became connected with and affected by colonization and war. The lives of Czech Jews, Austrians, Germans, and Chinese intertwined in the workshop industry of producing hairnets for over half a century. Geopolitical developments exerted powerful influences: German colonial merchants brought the knotting techniques to China in furtherance of their commercial interests; World War I cut off China from its usual purchasers of raw materials, promoted Chinese industrial power, and made it more competitive in the global marketplace; the German hyperinflation in the 1920s also had an impact. During this entire period, hairnets went from being decorative goods for the upper classes to mass consumer items, and the market grew considerably.

The vast Habsburg Empire was a miniature of Europe: the economic and social structures of its western territories—the Czech lands, the Danube basin, and the Alpine regions—resembled those of Western European countries, while the social structures and localized markets of its eastern parts resembled those of Eastern Europe. In spite of this disparity, the economy of this Empire was rising since the *Ausgleich* (Compromise) of 1867: "The evolution of extensive communications and financial networks broke down the barriers separating the local and regional markets of the sprawling multinational realm. The late nineteenth century was a period of increased interregional exchange of commodities as well as financial and human capital. Associated with these exchanges was a significant trend toward the equalization of commodity prices, interest rates, and wage rates on a regional level. Economic integration was under way."[2] In line with this trend, isolated Vysočina during these years connected the markets of the Monarchy and of the world via the hairnet business. Statistical data show that in 1869 in the Czech lands and the Archduchy of Austria the economy was on par with that of Germany.[3] Between 1867 and 1913, the Monarchy's foreign trade increased at the surprising rate of 340 percent and most years saw export surpluses.[4] In 1526, the Czech lands (or Bohemia) had become part of the Hereditary Lands (or Crownlands) of the Habsburg dynasty. Czech people enjoyed basic education, political reforms, and the economic advantages that the Monarchy offered to native Austrians. Around 1850, the Czech lands contributed 28 percent of the realm's industrial production, although only 19 percent of the population lived there. The Czechs greatly benefited from the German-speaking population surrounding them, but also suffered anti-Czech rhetoric and occasional discrimination. In 1866, ethnic Germans in Bohemia enthusiastically greeted the Prussian army during the Austro-Prussian War, a prelude to the events of 1938.[5] Regional economic development frequently fostered the growth of nationalism.

Archival materials relevant for this essay are located in the Czech Republic, in Shandong, China, and in Taiwan. Unfortunately, many of the sources elucidating the role Jews had played in this globalizing market disappeared during World War II. The limited nature of the resources compelled us to rely heavily on unconventional ones.[6] This research also profited from several books. C. Ernest Fayle and Simon P. Ville provide a clear and vivid description of maritime and shipping developments from the nineteenth century onward. Timothy Brook analyzes six paintings by Vermeer, so as to draw conclusions about the golden age of the Dutch East India Company and trade between China and Europe. In their book *The World that Trade Created*, Kenneth Pomeranz and Steven Topik trace the processes of globalization as reflected in commodities, transportation technologies, and the world market over the past centuries. John E. Schrecker shows how the Germans in the leasehold of Qingdao carried out tax reforms, reforestation and education programs, and urban construction projects (sewage system, water utilities, and road construction), and how the share of German goods in their import trade at Qingdao did not justify the German government budget of 110 million Marks. Finally, the Chinese scholar Wang Jinyu (汪敬虞) shows how Western gunboats destroyed the traditional Chinese economic order and way of life.

Vysočina

Vysočina was the center of the hairnet industry in Bohemia (see Figure 10.2).[7] In the nineteenth and the first half of the twentieth century, Vysočina's economy was overwhelmingly local and agricultural. It is a hilly and barren region with a relatively rough climate. People farmed cabbage, potatoes, and beets on two or three acres of land and sold their produce in the towns. It was a life of

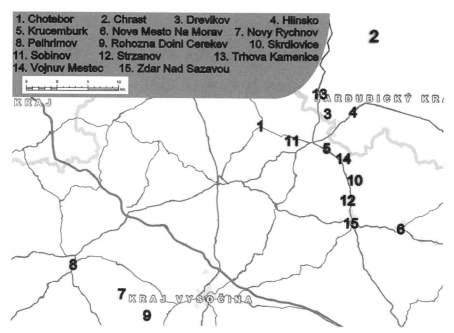

1. Chotebor   2. Chrast   3. Drevikov   4. Hlinsko
5. Krucemburk   6. Nove Mesto Na Morav   7. Novy Rychnov
8. Pelhrimov   9. Rohozna Dolni Cerekev   10. Skrdlovice
11. Sobinov   12. Strzanov   13. Trhova Kamenice
14. Vojnuv Mestec   15. Zdar Nad Sazavou

Figure 10.2. Hairnet production centers in Vysočina, designed by Claire Chien.

poverty—basic needs such as butter were out of reach for even those families considered better off. Women ploughed the land, doing the horse's job, because horses were unaffordable.[8] Struggling to make ends meet, the peasants sought ways to supplement their income by making nets, quarrying, and lumbering. The long winters made knotting nets an ideal choice. Hairnet manufacturing became a popular cottage industry because it provided a higher income than agriculture.

Vysočina's traditions encouraged the development of the industry. In the Middle Ages, nets for hunting and fishing, curtains, altar cloths, and hairnets were produced in the region. In Czech the technique is called *sít'kování* or *necování*;[9] in this article, we shall use the English terms "knotting" and "net-knotting." Net-knotting with artistic designs was done by hand and was not replicable by machine. Before discussing the specific impact on this region of hairnet production, let us first provide an overview.

The Origin of Hair Used for Knotting

Before 1890, hairnets were made of silk; businessmen, however, were seeking cheaper alternatives. Some materials, such as wool and horsetail hairs, were tried, but proved unsuitable. It was discovered that, ironically, some human hair made excellent hairnets. Chinese hair became the preferred raw material, although it required chemical treatment to render it supple enough for knotting.[10]

Practically all hair used in making hairnets came from China. No other hair possessed the right degree of coarseness and resilience to give the peculiarly elastic spring to the mesh that a good hairnet required. The lighter hair of northern European people was too fine and soft for the purpose. The darker hair of southern Europeans, Italians and Spanish, tends to be a little coarser and was therefore more suitable, but it was not possible to obtain it in sufficient quantities. Japanese hair was too stiff and coarse.[11] It is not known for certain when Chinese hair began to be exported as a raw material, but in the second half of the nineteenth century the quantity was already noteworthy. As early as 1887 Chinese hair had become a commodity significant enough in volume and value for the Canton customs office to note rises and falls of demand for hair as an export item in its reports.[12]

During this period of intensive net-knotting in Vysočina, Chinese production of hair was at its zenith. Hair exports increased suddenly after 1910. Following the fall of the Qing Dynasty in 1911, a resolution was adopted in favor of abolishing the queue, the traditional hairstyle of men enforced by the ethnically minded Manchu Qing Dynasty since 1644. Thus the fall of the dynasty was

marked by the wholesale cutting of queues, although not to the extent generally imagined. As a matter of fact, the queue had disappeared from men's heads
in southern and central China already before 1911, but in northern China the
bulk of the population still wore it.[13] There, itinerant barbers and peddlers had
been cruising villages, markets, and fairs and diligently collecting the so-called
"combings."[14] The commodification of Chinese hair during this era increased
to the point at which women stored every fallen hair to exchange it for needles,
thread, and matches from peddlers,[15] who then channeled the hair to the big
cities, from which it was exported. Besides hairnets, Chinese hair found usage
in wigs, switches, bandeaux, foundations, lace, etc.

Beginning in 1909, much of the hair was classified according to developing
market standards. It was sorted by length into lots between 10 to 12 inches and
up to 36 inches in length, the commercial limit; the longer lots brought better
prices.[16] Hair intended for knotting hairnets had to be 16 to 27.5 inches long.
Large quantities of combings, weighing from 123 pounds (about 55.8 kg) to
130 pounds (about 59 kg) per bale, were packed in cases, wrapped in straw, and
shipped to the Austro-Hungarian port of Trieste (now in Italy) or the German
port of Hamburg.[17]

According to Figure 10.3, hair exports jumped in 1910 when men began cutting the queue in the south and again in 1912 and 1913, following the above-
mentioned resolution, but fell during the war. In 1923, hair exports exceeded
prewar levels and in 1926 reached a staggering 2,154.61 tons. After 1932, exports decreased so radically that they can reasonably be disregarded.[18]

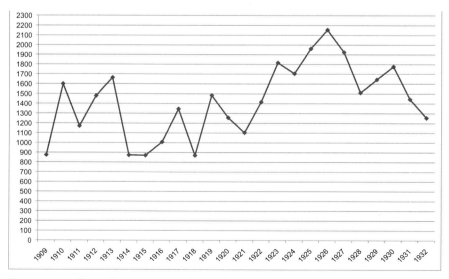

Figure 10.3. Chinese hair exportation (in tons), 1909 to 1932.

Chemical Preparation of the Human Hair

A portion of the hair collected in China and shipped to Europe was treated there in preparation for its use as hairnets. The chemical processing was not easy, but was crucial as it rendered the hair pliable for knotting. The main advantage and disadvantage of Chinese hair was its thickness, making it a more durable material for hairnet production. However, this characteristic also made Chinese hair too stiff for easy knotting. Thus, a technique for softening the hair without reducing its strength was essential and became a trade secret.[19] The softening was done with acid, and expert judgment was necessary to remove the hair from the chemicals at exactly the right time to strike a balance between softness and strength. The hair could be bleached to absolute whiteness with hydrogen peroxide or ammonia or boiled in dye, becoming darker the longer it was left in the vat. Again, good judgment was necessary to obtain the exact shade desired.[20]

This chemical processing and dyeing was normally carried out in Europe or the United States. In China the skill of dyeing did not develop until World War I. When Austria and Germany stopped importing hair because of the war, the Chinese had to develop dyeing techniques of their own. They carried out these processes using inferior chemicals from Japan, resulting in damaged hair and easily fading colors; the nets made of it soon changed color and often broke. Such inferior products were often sent back, and significant damage was done to the trade. By 1918, after a period of trial and error, the quality of the Chinese products became as good as that of any from abroad.[21]

We shall briefly compare the situation in Shandong with the situation in Vysočina. Chinese production was centered in three province towns: Chefoo (芝罘),[22] Jinan (濟南), and Qingdao (青島). The focus of this article will be on Chefoo. In this town alone, there were nine Chinese companies engaged in the hair dyeing business. Not surprisingly, a German company, Arnhold, Karberg & Co. (Ruiji 瑞記), was also present.[23] In Vysočina, entrepreneurs such as Josef Heisler played the crucial role in developing processes for hair dyeing. Around 1879, he built a chemical factory in Chrast u Chrudimi, which produced paper and medical goods in addition to engaging in activities in the hairnet industry. His family consisted of both Jews and Christians. Heisler controlled the dyeing industry in the region, and by the end of the century was obtaining hair from China, Russia, and Moravia.[24] Another important personage in the history of Vysočina's hairnet industry was Bedřich Bondy (1864–1943). He developed the industry in the town of Chotěboř, after inheriting a wig company that originally served theaters. At first he relied on Heisler to provide the material, either dyed hair or silk.[25] Later he obtained the secret of chemical processing from František Jehlička (1879–1939), whose parents had worked for Heisler. Bondy paid Jehlička well to reveal the key processes and employed him from

1915 to 1926. As the director of Bondy's factory, Jehlička completed the entire dyeing process with only 30 workers.[26] Gradually, Bondy came to dominate the hair industry in Vysočina. Both Heisler and Bondy were Jews, and Bondy's influence in this market made Jews critical to the hairnet industry in Vysočina, as they came to represent a significant proportion of those involved in the production and distribution of hairnets.

Net Processing: Organization of the Handicraft and Trade

With the hair properly treated and dyed, it could now be distributed for knotting. Making hairnets is not difficult, but requires patience. Unlike the weaving of a cloth, with vertical and horizontal strands crossing each other, hairnets are made with only one strand, using a rod or dowel and a needle to make a net by tying knots[27] (see Figure 10.4).[28]

The industry was organized as a workshop system with three layers: *Fabrikanten, Faktoren,* and individual laborers working out of their homes. This tiered system was by and large established by Bondy and became common practice for other *Fabrikanten* throughout Vysočina. *Fabrikanten* obtained hair from China, sorting it by length if need be, and usually performed the chemical procedures. Thus prepared, the hair was then passed on to *Faktoren.* The *Faktoren* distributed hair bundles to farmhouses and usually on a weekly basis collected the hairnets. In most cases *Faktoren* maintained working relationships with certain farmhouses. For example, the father of Bohumil Hospodka (who gave us an interview) was a *Faktor* who maintained connections with twenty to thirty female workers. The finished nets then went back to the *Fabrikanten,* who exported them. While workers included both Jews and Czechs, *Faktoren*

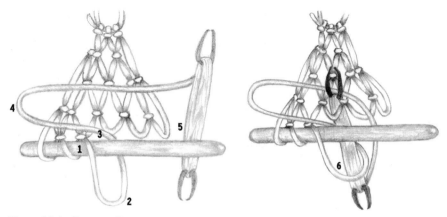

Figure 10.4. Process of Netting, designed by Claire Chien.

and *Fabrikanten* were mostly Jews. One might go so far as to say that they dominated the trade and were largely responsible for its organization in this region.[29]

Hair-netting spread quickly and extensively throughout Vysočina after the 1890s, when Bondy innovated the hairnet trade. During the peak of the industry there were over 150 *Faktoren* in Trhová Kamenice, a town of less than two thousand inhabitants. *Fabrikanten* competed with one another to contract as many *Faktoren* as possible. They paid them commissions and sometimes offered gifts as well. When a subordinate left for another *Fabrikant*, his former employer lost workers.[30] Some successful *Faktoren* established their own shops. In the town of Žďár nad Sázavou, three *Faktoren* owned their own shops: Mořic Bergmann, active around 1900; František Krupař, active from around 1900 to 1914; and a female *Faktor*, Elsa Ecksternová, active in 1919 and the 1920s.[31]

According to an Austro-Hungarian government survey conducted in the 1900s, over 50 percent of the local population was involved in hairnet production throughout Vysočina. Often, several family members participated.[32] In the small town of Nové Město na Moravě, a government survey lists no less than 1,446 adults and 1,080 children as involved in hairnet production, working on average nineteen hours per day. Adults earned 2 crowns and children 0.5 to 0.8 crowns per day. The industry clearly represented an important source of income not only for individuals and families, but for the entire region.[33] In fact, the hairnet industry, with its comparatively high wages and quickly acquirable skills, even caused other industries to suffer a lack of manpower.[34] Children constituted an important labor source (see Figure 10.5). Intelligent and dexterous children could even support a family. Children as young as six began to tie hair together, end to end, to make one long strand. (Hair could not be spun into yarn on a wheel.) When they were about ten, they started knotting nets. Throughout the region, it was not uncommon that a third to a half of all children in a town or village were involved in the industry. These child laborers rose at four o'clock to start work at five, before they went to school. On holidays they worked from five in the morning until ten or eleven at night. This impacted their health and development, and some were unable to finish school.[35]

Grade	Total students	Number making hairnets	Male	Female
1st	70	11	4	7
2nd	75	33	12	21
3rd	54	41	17	24
4th	80	40	13	27

Figure 10.5. Schoolchildren at Nový Rychnov working in the hairnet industry in 1907, organized by grade level.

However, women, not children, always provided the majority of laborers, and they were well paid. In Trhová Kamenice a street named Damenstrasse (today's Okružní ulice)—"Ladies's Street"—was lined with new houses in the early 1920s, the achievements of female hairnet labor.[36] In 1921 the export of hairnets reached its peak at 720 million Czechoslovak crowns, of which 69.44 percent, 500 million crowns, went to labor costs.[37] The percentage spent on labor costs in China was practically the same at 68.57 percent.[38] Hairnet manufacturing should therefore not be regarded as exploitation. Globalization offered advantages to the people of two hardscrabble, largely agrarian regions; hairnet production improved the standard of living for entire communities.

Market Expansion

The major markets for the finished product were in the United States, England, France, and Germany, consuming 90 percent of the output, either for cosmetic or practical uses (see Figure 10.6).[39] The U.S. market was especially important. In 1913, many shipments for Hamburg or London eventually found their way to the United States. Changing U.S. demand eventually caused a steep fall in hair prices and put many Chinese combers temporarily out of business.[40] Due to the lack of Czech records, Chinese customs returns are used to demonstrate the importance of the American market for hairnets between 1923 and 1931.

Bondy, the *Fabrikant* who largely developed the industry in Vysočina, had branch offices in Berlin[41] and Vienna as footholds in the German and Austrian retail markets. Already in the late nineteenth century, he also maintained an office in London[42] and from there distributed his products throughout the world. The blockade of the Habsburg Monarchy during World War I restricted the export of Bondy's products, yet he was able to recover financially after the war. Despite fierce competition from the Japanese, who established a foothold in the German market in the 1920s, Bondy was able to maintain his business while others in Vysočina folded. He achieved great success and amassed significant wealth. However, his Jewish background would spell disaster for his business and his family. Between 1939 and 1942 the Jewish inhabitants of the Protectorate of Bohemia and Moravia were gradually moved out of their dwellings, deprived of their civil rights, robbed of their property, and ultimately deported to the extermination camps in the east.[43] Without the Holocaust, hairnet production in Vysočina could possibly have endured longer than it did, with Bondy at the helm. The death of the Bondy family essentially put an end to the industry.

The demand for hairnets rose to new heights by the end of World War I, when their use had spread all over the globe. Hairnets made from new types of yarns and from polyester were now in production.[44] Perhaps most importantly, the hairnet found myriad new applications. Consumers ranged from motorists

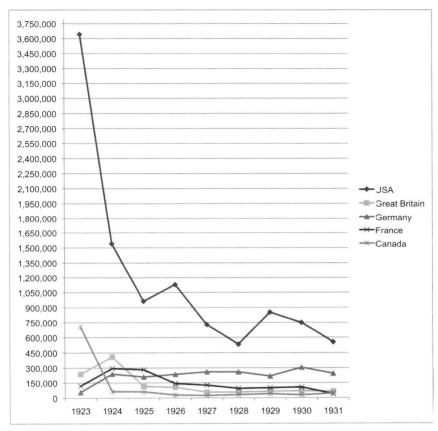

Figure 10.6. Important world markets for Chinese hairnets (Unit = Hk. Tls.).

and sportsmen to factory laborers. The largest group of consumers, however, were women, whose usage of the item originated in the workplace[45](see Figure 10.7[46]): "Of interest is the fact that on the entry of the United States into World War I, the army medical staff advised nurses to wear nets or elastic bands to keep their hair in order. Acting on these instructions, nurses took to wearing invisible hairnets constructed from human hair. It gave the first real impetus to popular demand for hairnets in America. They have since become an indispensable article in the daily toilette of women who desire to maintain a neat and well groomed appearance at all times. The factory girls in Europe and America, too, form a large percentage of the demand for hairnets."[47]

Hairnets thus went from being decorative to being practical goods, which significantly expanded the market to new consumers and countries (see Figure 10.8).

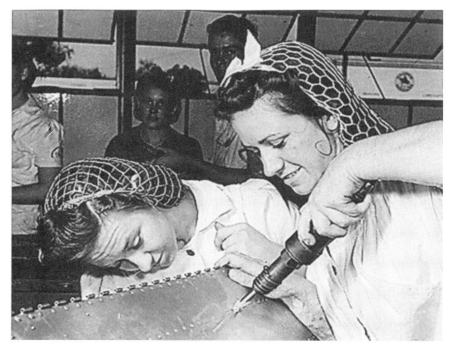

Figure 10.7. Women workers at a Texas naval air base in 1942 with hairnets. Franklin D. Roosevelt Library & Museum, Library ID: 65716 (8).

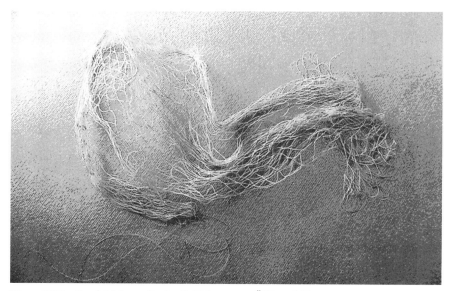

Figure 10.8. Czech Hairnet, Regionální Muzeum at Žďár nad Sázavou.

The Decline of the Vysočina Production

According to data collected by Petr Adam and Bohumil Hospodka, the failure of the Czech hairnet industry was caused by the Japanese undercutting market prices. Chinese competition also played a role. In 1924, Japanese merchants started using Hamburg as a hairnet warehouse, from which they provided whatever the European market demanded. The extremely low wages of their workers made the hairnets of Japanese manufacturers up to 75 percent cheaper than their counterparts produced in Vysočina. Czech hairnets immediately lost 98 percent of the German market, despite being of superior quality. In 1923 the German Mark collapsed, further facilitating the penetration of the cheaper Japanese hairnets into the German market. In Vysočina, production essentially stopped, and hundreds of thousands of families faced financial ruin. Most *Fabrikanten* went bankrupt; the primary exception was Bondy (as mentioned above), whose capital was relatively strong.[48] During the Depression of 1929, only some two hundred women in the Chotěboř district still produced hairnets at home, a mere shadow of what the industry had once been.[49] As recorded in the customs returns, from 1928 on Czechoslovakia began importing hairnets from China. This trade was unstable, however, and for several years sank almost to zero, but returned to significant levels in the period from 1936 to 1939, with 1937 as the peak with 32,694 gross.[50] Chinese hairnets had been encroaching upon the market of Czech *Fabrikanten* from the end of World War I onward. The blockade of their markets during the war had forced the Chinese to treat, dye, and knot their own hairnets instead of simply exporting the raw materials to Europe or the United States. The situation effectively shifted the European market toward importation of the final product for domestic consumption.

However, this was not the end of the Vysočina hairnet industry. In the 1950s, Vavřín Krčil (1895–1968)[51] almost single-handedly caused a transformation of the industry, spurring a new period of development. Starting in 1921, at the peak of the hairnet trade, he began to work for the Jaro J. Rousek Company which dealt in metal goods, including tools for fishing, and Krčil was responsible for introducing fishing nets. In 1922, he stormed the market with his own brand, *Marque Saarense* (literally, "the trademark of Žďár"), exporting nets to Germany and later to France and Austria under the same brand name. Krčil also tried, and achieved success with, knotted handbags. By using the hairnet knotting technique with cotton, he created handbags (in Czech, *síťovka*) that soon became fashionable. In 1938, he patented his technique and expanded his business, building a branch in northern Italy.

Hairnets in Shandong

It is quite natural that a hairnet industry also developed in China, since it was the major source of hair. According to Qu Chengmin (曲拯民), who was engaged in the business in Chefoo until 1945, hairnet manufacturing was introduced by a German engineer known only by his last name, Schröder, in about 1909.[52] Schröder cooperated with Wang Huating (王華亭), one of his colleagues at Northern Telegram, a Danish company. They decided to set up a hairnet firm named Hair-Industry Co. (Faye gongsi 髮業公司). Later Schröder returned to Europe as an agent of this company and stayed at least until the outbreak of World War I. The company itself lasted until 1939.[53] The hairnet business achieved great importance in Shandong province, which became practically the sole supplier of finished products to Europe (mainly Germany and Austria) and America, supplanting Germany and Austria. While records show that most Chinese provinces exported hair, Shandong was the most successful in hairnet manufacturing. Similar efforts were also made in Canton, but the labor costs could not compete with those in Shandong.[54] Hair for Shandong nets mostly originated in Hunan (湖南) and Henan (河南),[55] but these two provinces did not develop their own industries.

Traditionally, girls in northern China helped support their families by working at home in lace and embroidery. They quickly acquired the knotting techniques. Here, as in Vysočina, children and adolescents contributed significantly to production, and the pay was also good. A young girl could earn 170 coins per day, while a male worker made 150 to 200 coins for a day's work.[56] With this income they were able to help their families and gain self-confidence. An oversupply of female laborers in villages meant that small children rarely took part in the trade, unlike in Vysočina. According to the customs returns, the market went up and down after 1922, but hairnet manufacturing in Shandong lasted until the end of World War II. From 1946 to 1948, the hairnet exports were 332,463 gross, 518,765 gross and 390,130 gross, respectively (see Figure 10.9).[57]

Almost every year after 1911 there was either a natural disaster or war in Shandong, and the thriving international hairnet market contributed greatly to alleviate the effects. The heavy drought of 1920 and 1921 coincided with a worldwide hairnet boom. The hairnet trade in Zhili (直隷) and Shandong grew. Relief officials trusted merchants with loans to build up hairnet companies in the drought-stricken area. Free month-long courses were offered to teach girls knotting as long as there were at least sixty to seventy-five who could attend. After class the girls went home and taught others, quickly spreading the skills throughout the region. Similar to the workshop system in Vysočina, companies regularly sent hair to villages and collected the finished nets.[58] It is

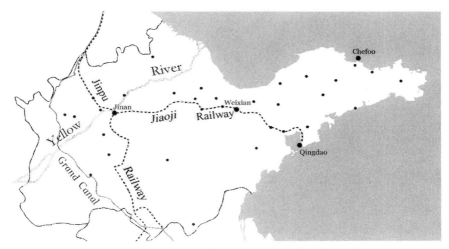

Figure 10.9. Hairnet producing centers in Shandong, designed by Claire Chien.

estimated that about three million people were involved in handicrafts such as hairnet-, lace-, and tablecloth-production during World War I.[59] As in Vysočina, Shandong's hairnet industry offered tremendous financial advantages, tiding the population over in hard times.

Qingdao vs. Chefoo

Another important center was Qingdao, which had become a German concession in 1898. When the Jiaoji railway (from Jinan to Qingdao, see Figure 10.9) was built in 1904, Shandong came within the German sphere of influence. Qingdao, however, never surpassed Chefoo—which had as many as seventy-eight hairnet companies of various sizes in 1936—as the center of the industry.[60] Lightweight lace and hairnets were not dependent upon a railway. Moreover, Chefoo was the first treaty port in Shandong, and it had accumulated rich foreign trade experience from 1862 onward. The following table shows the considerable difference in the fortunes of the two cities, especially at the time of the 1921 peak (see Figure 10.10).

Unlike Bondy's monopoly in Vysočina, there were several companies and businessmen who developed the industry in Shandong province. Many foreign companies, British, Greek, Russian, and American, were based in Chefoo,[61] for example the Jewish-owned and U.S.-based Rieser Company, which distributed the popular Venida hairnets and other products. Its Chefoo branch opened in 1920 and at first handled only hairnets (see Figure 10.11).[62]

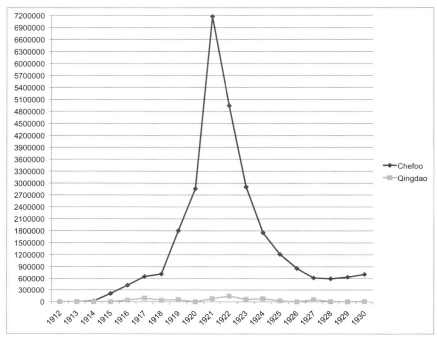

Figure 10.10. Hairnet exportation in Chefoo and Qingdao: 1912–30 (Unit = 100,000 Hk. Tls.)

Other hairnet manufacturers in Chefoo included three companies of particular interest. Wilhelm Niggemann and August Boerter started their firm in 1913 and exported hairnets primarily to the United States, but also to Europe. The hairnets, sold under the Gimbel brand name in the Gimbel Brothers department stores in the United States, were actually produced by Boeter in Shandong. Despite the economic challenges facing the company during World War I, it was able to survive. Boeter was crowned "the hairnet king of Shandong," and he sold his shares ten years after founding the company.[63] Niggemann continued and founded his own company, W. Niggemann & Co. (Wanfeng yanghang 萬豐洋行) in 1922. At first, he produced only hairnets and lace, but later successfully expanded his business and also processed peanuts.[64] C. Dau & Co., established in 1929, exported hairnets, lace, and related items. The owner Carl Dau had lived for many years in the interior district of Weixian (濰縣), building up the local hairnet industry and training thousands of workers. What is interesting is that this company was a cooperative venture between Dau and three Chinese, a rare occurrence.[65] The Dau and Niggemann companies both lasted until World War II.

Figure 10.11. Packaging for the Venida line of hairnets produced by the Rieser Co., *Advertising & Selling* 30, no. 10 (1921): 6 (detail).

Chinese Efforts and Adaptation

Chinese hairnet firms were in operation at almost the same time. Hairnet manufacturing was an ideal choice for starting an enterprise because it did not require huge capital, complicated skills, or expensive facilities, and therefore offered quick returns on investment.[66] The Chefoo Hair Net Co. (Yizhong 億中), one of the few Chinese firms in Chefoo that traded directly with foreign countries—England, Germany, and Australia—was established in 1914. Initially it concentrated on the manufacturing and export of hairnets, but later added lace, pongee silks, embroideries, handkerchiefs, and so on. Under the leadership of B.W. Sen (Sun Bo'e 孫伯峨), whose specialties were mathematics and chemistry, the company overcame the challenges involved in dyeing hair.[67] By 1933, however, the Chefoo Hair Net Co. had closed its Berlin office, and its Australian and Cairo branches followed suit before the beginning of the Pacific War.[68]

Factories inspected nets for flaws and made up for breakage. Careful inspection became the rule after a painful lesson in 1919. The sharp rise in demand in the United States in the spring of that year caused prices to more than double by the year's end, driving hairnets out of reach for many English and French women. Unprincipled agents began bypassing Chefoo and going inland, where they offered workers high prices for any kind of product. As a result, quality was greatly reduced and large quantities of substandard products sold to the United States. Inevitably these would be returned, and buyers came to take great care in inspecting delivered goods.[69] In response, manufacturers introduced thorough quality controls: only one gross could be properly inspected by each worker in a ten-hour day.[70] In the following year, returns greatly increased. The industry seemed to offer the Chinese a promising future, if they could only develop and adhere to quality-assurance measures.[71]

Conclusion

This case study demonstrates how two very distant regions became linked through hairnet manufacturing. Hair was exported from China and made into hairnets by peasants in the impoverished region of Vysočina. There were other similar connections. Shandong was not the only Chinese province to export hair, and Vysočina was not the only recipient. The technique of knotting was also known in various places. These facts are, however, not what made this market—and the relationships it created—unique. In order to develop this industry, it was necessary to organize production networks and trade across countries and continents, to create centers for the collection of raw materials, to establish manufacturing sites, marketing facilities, and ultimately outlets for the finished product. This research has revealed that certain factors were always crucial in the development of the industry: techniques transmitted through unofficial networks, traditional business channels, merchants' organizations, and the accumulation of expertise in foreign trade, all of which served to connect local workshops and international markets. Surprisingly, the workshop system survived well into the first half of the twentieth century, despite massive industrial development in the production of other goods during this period. In the hairnet industry, women and children were able to work at home, both in Vysočina and Shandong, protected by their families and by local rules. Through hairnet manufacturing these two regions joined the global market, although they persisted in using old-fashioned methods. In the small towns of Vysočina, the income from making hairnets was enough to renovate or even build a house. In remote Shandong villages, knotting was often the primary source of family income, and it became crucial for survival in times of famine and other disasters. Despite the fact that knotting was by no means a comfortable or easy job and could undermine a worker's health, it was still a positive factor in the lives of families in both areas.

Jewish entrepreneurs made a great contribution to regenerating this old trade and fostering international commerce. Heisler acquired the hair-dyeing skill, Jewish *Faktor* Bondy replaced silk with cheap human hair as the raw material and set up the *Fabrikanten* system. Under his organization, he gathered a majority of Czech villagers as participants in this trade, including many Jewish people. It is accepted that the entrepreneurial spirit was generally dormant in Austria,[72] but exceptions can be found, such as the successful Bondy. The Nazis eventually ruined his enterprise and destroyed the trade; the Chinese firm, the Chefoo Hair Net Co., coincidentally closed its Berlin branch in 1933. It is true that hairnet production in Vysočina could possibly have endured longer than it did without the Holocaust, but Shandong's hairnet industry would have replaced Vysočina's sooner or later due to its cheaper labor. It is said that the German-Jewish engineer Schröder brought the netting expertise to Shandong. Both American department stores, Rieser Company and Gimbel Brothers, had Jewish owners and sold Shandong's hairnets broadly, contributing to an overall Jewish dominance in the hairnet business.

As demonstrated, Shandong's hairnet manufacturing outlived Vysočina's, even though the Chinese did not innovate the industry in the ways the talented Czech designers had done. World War I, the vagaries of international labor markets, and merchants pioneering new developments all played important roles in the manufacture and trade of this simple product. In Vysočina the availability of Chinese hair in the last decade of the nineteenth century created economic growth. With World War I and the closing of trade routes the relative prosperity dried up. In China hairnet manufacturing was equally dependent upon the dynamics between the two regions. Entrepreneurs from Europe as well as native Chinese recognized the potential of the industry and developed it in Shandong province where they found cheap labor. The decline in Vysočina compelled the Chinese to learn dyeing and knotting techniques. Eventually, this industry contributed substantially to the financial health and stability of Shandong province. The industry required the cooperation of Germans and Chinese. Competition, rivalry, and conflicts were inevitable, yet Chinese merchants nevertheless learned the business, including dyeing, careful inspection, etc. They also adopted new practices to meet the demands of foreign markets. The low cost of Chinese labor ultimately contributed to making hairnets widespread consumer items throughout Europe and North America.

Notes

The contributors would like to express their sincere gratitude to Mrs. Maja Dohnalova, the granddaughter of Bedřich Bondy, who provided us with many materials and much help. Also many thanks to Mr. Stanislav Mikule of the Regionální Muzeum, Žďár n. Sáz., Dr. Hana Řeháková of the Východočeská Galerie (VČG) at Pardubice, Dr. Rudolf Schebesta of the Muzeum Vysočiny Library at Jihlava, Dr. Sylva Tesařová of the Horácké Museum at Nové Město na Moravě, Dr. Cord Eberspaecher, and Professor Shang-sheng Chen (陳尚勝), School of History and Culture, Shandong University. The contributors would also like to thank heartily the following five people, who granted us interviews and provided us with rich information: Mr. Bohumil Hospodka, Mr. Chlubna, Mr. Eduard Kříž, Mrs. Plachá, and Mrs. Stará. Mr. Hospodka, the son of a *Faktor*, is an amateur historian and has been collecting materials and photos on the topic of hairnets for a long time. Mr. Kříž was the owner of Divadelní služba (Theater Services), which had been managed by Heisler as a chemical and dyeing factory. Mrs. Plachá demonstrated how to net, and both Mrs. Plachá and Mrs. Stará described the time they experienced. With the help of these interviews, the contributors were able to arrive at a better understanding of the time and the background of the netting industry.

1. For further reading, see Michael D. Bordo, Alan M. Taylor, and Jeffrey G. Williamson, *Globalization in Historical Perspective* (Chicago, 2005).
2. David F. Good, *The Economic Rise of the Habsburg Empire, 1750–1914* (Berkeley, 1984), 124.
3. David F. Good, "Modern Economic Growth in the Habsburg Monarchy," in *Economic Development in the Habsburg Monarchy and in the Successor States Essays,* ed. John Komlos (New York, 1990), 201–220.
4. Magnus Tessner, "Der Außenhandel Österreich-Ungarns von 1867 bis 1913," Ph.D. Diss. (University of Cologne, Dip-Arb, 1989), 19, 25.
5. Jan Bazant, Nina Bazantova, and Frances Starn, eds., *The Czech Reader: History, Culture, and Politics* (Durham, 2010), 148.
6. Regarding the sources of this article, for two months in 2009, the authors collected oral data and documents in the Czech language. The authors interviewed five persons who still remembered conditions surrounding the hairnet production and distribution in early twentieth-century Bohemia (the historic name of the Czech Republic), and further information was found in six museums and the Czech National Archive. In January 2001, the author Chinyun Lee spent three weeks in libraries and archives that were open to visitors in Jinan and Qingdao and found old Chinese and Japanese reports and surveys.
7. The term Bohemia is a historical toponym, indicating the western part of today's Czech Republic, its eastern part being Moravia. The term "Czech," used in Slavonic languages including the Czech language, has a broader meaning, however. It may indicate Bohemia only, but it may also indicate all the Czech lands, i.e., Bohemia, Moravia, and even Silesia. In this article, the authors use the term Bohemia in the broader sense, i.e., to refer to the Czech lands.
8. Lucie Olivová, interview with Bohumil Hospodka at Trhová Kamenice, 17 July 2009.
9. *Necování* is from the German *netzen,* "to knot a net."
10. Centrum, http://www.sendme.cz/krcil/historie.htm. Last accessed 23 July 2009.
11. "German Hair-Net Industry," *Daily Consular and Trade Reports,* 1912 II, 1072.
12. Apparently an important source of income, hair exports were significant enough to arouse the attention of Chinese customs officials, one of whom worried that "the demand for human hair had lessened" in 1887. *British Parliamentary Papers: China.* Irish University Press Area Studies Series (Shannon, 1971), 16, 210.
13. "Chinese Trade in Human Hair and Hair Nets," *Journal of the Royal Society of Arts* 66 (1918): 631–632.

14. "A General Survey of Hairnet Production in North China" 〈中國北部之髮網業概況〉, *Shenbao* 《申報》, 10 February 1924, 2–3.

15. Qingdao Archives, B0038/003/00231/, 19 January 1948. "General Survey of Hairnet Production," 2–3.

16. "Human Hair Not from Queues," *Daily Consular and Trade Reports*, 1911 I, 920–921.

17. "The Human Hair Industry in Austria," *Journal of the Royal Society of Arts* 58 (1909), 1031–1032.

18. Unless otherwise noted, statistics in tables in this chapter are all from China Inspectorate General of Customs, *Imperial Maritime Customs Returns of the Import and Export Trade* (*Customs Returns*) (Shanghai: Statistical Department of the Inspectorate General of Customs, Jinghua Pub. reprint, 2001).

19. Petr Adam, *The Fate of Ludmila Löwidtová's Family: The Lost Neighbours from Chotěboř* (Chotěboř: Secondary School of Economic and Higher Professional School, 2006), 10.

20. *Customs Returns*, 1915, 68: 469. Lucie Olivová, interview with Eduard Kříž, 17 July 2009, Chrast u Chrudimi.

21. Japanese Consulate at Chefoo, "Yuukan Shifu hatsumou seizougyou" (有關芝罘髮網製造業, "On Hairnet Manufacturing in Chefoo"), *Manmou kenkyuu ihou* (『滿蒙研究彙報』) 25 (February 1918): 1–7.

22. In this essay we use the transliteration Chefoo, rather than Zhifu, or the present name Yantai (煙台), because that is the name used in most old English language documents, much as today people usually say "Amoy" rather than "Xiamen 廈門."

23. "Chinese Trade in Human Hair and Hair Nets," *Journal of the Royal Society of Arts* 66 (1918): 631–632. *Customs Returns*, 1915, 68: 469. Japanese Consulate at Chefoo, "Yuukan Shifu hatsumou seizougyou" (有關芝罘髮網製造業, "On Hairnet Manufacturing in Chefoo"), *Manmou kenkyuu ihou* (『滿蒙研究彙報』) 25 (February 1918), 1–7. The other nine companies were: Fuxinghe (福興和), Fuxianghe (福祥和), Yidong (義東, Jieji 捷記), Dongxing (東興), Dexinghe (德興和), Xingjidong (興記東), Huishengshun (會盛順), Haiquanyong (海全永).

24. www.sendme.cz/krcil/historie.htm. Last accessed 23 July 2009; Olivová, interview with Kříž. In 1919, Josef Vacek bought the company and changed its direction: producing and selling wigs became its primary activity. It was a development that proved quite successful, as wigs were exported across the world. In addition, Josef Vacek opened a beauty parlor in Wenceslas Square (Václavské náměstí), the central commercial area of Prague. In 1951, this company was confiscated by the Communist regime and continued under the name Divadelní služba (Theater Services). The hair was imported from Hong Kong and India.

25. Adam, *Ludmila Löwidtová's Family*, 10. It is said that Bondy's assistants developed the chemical process after lengthy experimentation. The authors believe, however, that the secret of the industry, the chemical process, originated with Heisler.

26. www.sendme.cz/krcil/historie.htm. Last accessed 23 July 2009.

27. www.sendme.cz/krcil/historie.htm. Last accessed 23 July 2009.

28. Source: Iva Prošková, *Síťování*. (Praha: Společnost městské dopravy 1992): 5.

29. Olivová, interview with B. Hospodka, 17 July 2009, Trhová Kamenice.

30. Bohumil Hospodka, *Z historie města Trhová Kamenice* (Glimpses into the History of the Town of Trhová Kamenice), 2nd ed. (Trhová Kamenice, Prague, 1988), 74. Trhová Kamenice had 1,634 inhabitants in 1910.

31. Cited from the manuscript List of Entrepreneurs, the Archives of the Regional Museum (Regionální muzeum), Žďár nad Sázavou.
32. Jaromír Tausch, "O *sítkování (necování) trochu jinak* (The Netting Seen Differently)," *Vlastivědný sborník Vysočiny* (*Transactions on Vysočina's Local History*) XII (2000): 223–236.
33. For more specifics from these statistics: in the town of Pelhřimov, on average four members of every family were involved in net production. The ratio of the people involved in four villages in the Pelhřimov district was as follows: less than 50 percent in Nový Rychnov; more than 30 percent in Dolní Cerekev; less than 25 percent in Vyskytná; and more than 50 percent in Rohozná.
34. Miroslava Ludviková and Jaroslav Orel, *Podomácké síťování na Žďársku* (The Domestic Netting in the Region of Žďár). (Žďár n. Sázavou: Muzeum a galerie Žďárska, 1970), 12; "Yuukan Shifu hatsumou seizougyou," *Manmou kenkyuu ihou* 25 (February 1918): 1–7.
35. Tausch, "O *síťkování*," 223–236.
36. Olivová, interview with B. Hospodka. See note 30.
37. www.sendme.cz/krcil/historie.htm. Last accessed 23 July 2009.
38. *Customs Returns: Decennial Reports*, 1912–21, Chefoo, 156: 208. "The average value of 1 pound of hair may be taken as $11, of 1 pound of nets (about 10 gross) as $35; the added value consists of overhead charges, transport and labor of making and repairing, labor representing about 70 percent (actually 68.57 percent), and this sum goes principally to women and children, who formerly had little employment save slaving about a house."
39. Qingdao Archive, D00014800440039, 23 September 1947.
40. "Exports of Human Hair," *Daily Consular and Trade Reports*, 1914/January–March, 1787.
41. The address was 24 Zimmerstrasse, Berlin.
42. The address was 55 Berners Street, London.
43. Sixteen members of the Bondy family died in the gas chambers of the Auschwitz II-Birkenau extermination camp; only two survived the Holocaust. Adam, *Ludmila Löwidtová's Family*, 15, 20.
44. Adam, *Ludmila Löwidtová's Family*, 10.
45. "Increasing American Market for Hair Nets," *Daily Consular and Trade Reports*, 1914 II, 855–856.
46. http://www.fdrlibrary.marist.edu/archives/collections/franklin/?p=digitallibrary/digitalcontent&id=3810. Last accessed 23 July 2009.
47. A.G. Ahmed, ed., *Pictorial Chefoo: 1935–1936*. (A.G. Ahmed, n.d.), 91.
48. www.sendme.cz/krcil/historie.htm. Last accessed 23 July 2009. Adam, *Ludmila Löwidtová's Family*, 10, 22; Miroslava Ludvíková and Jaroslav Orel, *Podomácké síťování na Žďársku*, 15.
49. Adam, *Ludmila Löwidtová's Family*, 10.
50. *Customs Returns*, 1929, 107: 512; 1931, 111: 550; 1933, 115: 429; 1936, 123: 462; 1937, 135: 536.
51. V. Krčil was born in Aspang, Austria. When he returned from World War I, he obtained the license to sell hairnets and other related goods and thus became a *Faktor*.
52. His first name has been lost.
53. Chengmin, Qu, "Initiation and Development of Lace, Hairnets, and Tablecloths in Chefoo," *Shandong Wenxian* 《山東文獻》 11, no. 4 (March 1986): 8–14; Chefoo

Branch of Maritime Association (航業聯合協會芝罘支部), *Shifu Jijou* (『芝罘事情』 *Chefoo News*) (Qingdao: Maritime Association, 1939), 155. It is also claimed that the Sisters connected with the Catholic Mission were the first ones to introduce hairnet weaving into Shandong Province (Ahmed, *Pictorial Chefoo*, 91).

54. Julean Arnold, *China: A Commercial and Industrial Handbook* (Washington D.C., 1926), 255.

55. Qu, "Initiation and Development," 8–14.

56. As there was no standard currency in China at this time, each province had its own currency based on silver. The British standardized this for trade and tax purposes into the Tael, which was then subdivided into 1,000 coins per Tael. "Yuukan Shifu hatsu-mou seizougyou," *Manmou kenkyuu ihou* 25 (February 1918), 1–7.

57. See the annual *Chinese Customs Returns*. Dots on the map, Fig. 10.9, are major towns where there were net factories distributing hair and collecting and inspecting nets. The net processing itself took place in farmhouses in the surrounding areas. Huang, Zecang 黃澤蒼, *Shandong* (《山東》) (Shanghai, 1935), 46–47.

58. "General Survey of Hairnet Production," 2–3.

59. Archive of the Institute of Modern History, Academia Sinica, Ministry of Foreign Affairs 北洋政府外交部, 03-18-017-06-002, 14 June 1918.

60. *International Trade Report* 《國際貿易情報》, 1936, no. 8, 75.

61. Companies present in Chefoo at the time include the following, organized by nation: the British firms Railton & Co. Ltd. H.E., from Manchester, and James McMullan & Co. Ltd., (Rende Yanghang 仁德洋行), the Greek firm Paradissis Freres Et Cie. (Yongxing Yanghang 永興洋行), the Russian firm L.H. Smith & Co., and the U.S. firm Rieser Company, Inc. (Yuandong Yanghang 遠東洋行).

62. Ahmed, *Pictorial Chefoo*, 63.

63. Regine Oswald, "Postsekretär Hermann Hinzpeters Aufenthalt in China von 1909 bis 1920," (Post Officer Hermann Hinzpeter's Stay in China from 1909 to 1920), *StuDeO—INFO*, September 2010, 7–9; Archive of the Institute of Modern History, Academia Sinica, Ministry of Foreign Affairs 北洋政府外交部, 03-18-017-06-002, 14 June 1918. In 1918, Boeter pleaded with the Chinese government to allow him to continue as manager, although he was German. He also requested a special travel license to purchase materials. His company reached its peak in 1922, with branches in Jinan, Qingdao, Weihai (威海), and Zhengzhou (鄭州 in Henan province).

64. Ahmed, *Pictorial Chefoo*, 88. A comprador was a native servant in a European household who sold his employer's merchandise in the market.

65. Ahmed, *Pictorial Chefoo*, 46.

66. "Yuukan Shifu hatsumou seizougyou," *Manmou kenkyuu ihou* 25 (February 1918), 1–7.

67. Ahmed, *Pictorial Chefoo*, 43, 45.

68. Qu Chengmin, "Initiation and Development," 8–14. Both the Chefoo Hair Net Co. and Feng Shun Xiang (豐順祥) were able to maintain branches in Berlin.

69. *Customs Returns*, 1919, 84: 451.

70. Ahmed, *Pictorial Chefoo*, 93.

71. *Customs Returns*, 1921, 90: 10.

72. Good, *The Economic Rise of the Habsburg Empire*, 248.

CHAPTER 11

Orbiting around the Void
Emptiness as Recurring Topos in Recent German Short Stories on Japan

GABRIELE EICHMANNS

Introduction

"A trip to Japan takes us to an unreal, dreamlike country replete with mythical creatures," Britta Heidemann charges in her newspaper article "Japan: Die Faszination des Fremden" (Japan: The Fascination with the Foreign),[1] thereby pointing to a longstanding cliché that is inextricably intertwined with Japan: Japan as a riddle, shrouded in mystery, a land that cannot be penetrated by the inquisitive gaze of the Westerner, since the magical and the unreal constitute decisive elements of its nature. The more we try to uncover its secrets or attempt to glance behind the all-concealing veil, the more the country seems to elude us, refuses to meet our curious stare and immediately recedes into the distance. Instead of revealing itself, it confronts us with a void, an emptiness we are unable to fill.

Adolf Muschg,[2] too, in his essay "Japan—Versuch eines fraktalen Porträts" (Japan—An Attempt at a Fractal Portrait) emphasizes the alleged incomprehensibility of Japan when he remarks: "There is no host country in the world about which international residents become more fascinated or perplexed the longer they talk about it than the *Empire des signes*, whose signs, it appears, can only be misinterpreted. Japan seems to be an object that, strictly speaking, does not want to materialize.... Churchill's angry bon mot becomes almost true: *a riddle wrapped in a mystery inside an enigma.*"[3]

Muschg reiterates the trope of Japan's enigmatic nature, of its incomprehensible signs that do not conform to Western reasoning. A profound disconnect between sign and meaning appears to exist that defies Western rationalism and, in the end, leads to confusion rather than clarity. This disconnect has to be regarded as a defining feature of the relationship between Japan and the

West. Whereas signs seem easily interpretable in the West, emptiness appears to take the place of clarity in the East and intelligibility is replaced by nothingness. "You only need to capitalize the nothingness in order to immediately be transferred to the center of Far Eastern wisdom," states Muschg.[4] In his introductory comments to the volume *The Empire of Signs: Semiotic Essays on Japanese Culture*, Yoshihiko Ikegami contends that it is the void, "the idea of the 'empty' center," that lies at the heart of things Japanese and "seems to have existed already in the oldest stratum of Japanese culture."[5] Emptiness forms an essential component of Japanese philosophy, comparable to rationalism in the Western world. Thus, it comes as no surprise that in many contemporary narratives that depict the encounter between Japan and the West emptiness plays a key role. Emptiness becomes the center around which the narrative revolves, orbits, yet without the intention of ever filling the void with meaning. The empty center serves as a literary strategy that is employed to point to the seemingly indescribable nature of Japan.

In this chapter, I intend to take a closer look at the topos of the Japanese "void" and examine how it is applied in three short stories by German-speaking authors: "Ich weiß alles über Japan" (I Know Everything about Japan) by Thomas Brussig, "Japanisches Japan" (Japanese Japan) by Sabine Scholl, and "Schatten" (Shadows) by Marcel Beyer. All three stories are taken from the collection *Nach Japan: Reiselesebuch* (To Japan: Travel Writings), which brings together anecdotal stories, travelogues, and experimental essays of German-speaking writers about their time in Japan. Before addressing the three stories, I will delineate Roland Barthes's explorations of Japan in *Empire of Signs*—"a touristic commentary on Japan," Jonathan Culler notes, "with a reflection on signs in everyday life and their ethical implications."[6] I will particularly focus on Barthes's analysis of the sign and its characteristically profound emptiness, as well as on his critique of Western rationalism and of our urge to interpret and infuse foreign artifacts with meaning. According to Barthes, we erroneously attempt to understand Japan by subjecting it to the laws and rules of our own language and reasoning. This is inevitably followed by our lament when the country's incomprehensibility calls our method into question. Using Barthes as my theoretical framework and as starting point for my examinations, I will then discuss Brussig's, Scholl's, and Beyer's intentional play with empty signs that prevent the reader from getting to the core of things Japanese. Instead, their texts highlight the concept of the void as prevalent in the East, a concept that might seem unintelligible to the Western beholder and thus calls for a thorough reconsideration of Western hegemonic approaches to interpreting the world. By examining the notion of emptiness in each respective story, I intend to explore various aspects of the void and cross-link my findings with Roland Barthes's uneasiness regarding the usage of Western rationalism to make sense of Japan.

Roland Barthes's *Empire of Signs:*
The Empty Center of Things Japanese

Roland Barthes's *Empire of Signs* is a fairly small book inspired by the author's lecture tour through Japan in 1966. Yet, as the title indicates, Japan is not the primary focus of Barthes's study, but rather serves as a tool, "a fictive nation," that Barthes employs to convey his own philosophical explorations of the East.[7] Barthes is first and foremost interested in form, not content, in the "signs" of Japan rather than the "meaning" of things Japanese.[8] He postulates at the outset that for him Japan is a semiotic system, an exercise to experience cultural difference on an abstract level. As Rolf Goebel explains, "the real Japan becomes a mere support for the sign, one in which 'the inscription obliterates the wall.'"[9] Barthes does not claim to represent or analyze the reality of Japan. Rather, he is creating his own reality: "I am not lovingly gazing toward an Oriental essence," he states. "To me the Orient is a matter of indifference, merely providing a reserve of features whose manipulation—whose invented interplay—allows me to 'entertain' the idea of an unheard-of symbolic system, one altogether detached from our own."[10]

Japan becomes a foil for Barthes, an "aesthete's utopia"[11] (to borrow an expression from Susan Sontag) to investigate the nature of Japanese signs in relation to the West. However, Barthes does not set out to judge and evaluate Japan, which would inevitably lead to his voicing preconceived notions of places, stereotypes, and fantasies. Instead Barthes advocates the abandonment of all judgment in lieu of "the possibility of a difference" that lies at the heart of his examination.[12] His goal is to explore evenhandedly the difference in greater detail, to characterize and define it.[13] Since "Japan has afforded him a situation of writing," Barthes draws on the power of words in an attempt to cause "a subversion of earlier readings, a shock of meaning, lacerated, extenuated to the point of its irreplaceable void."[14] By writing about the alleged difference between the "fictive nation" and the Occident, Barthes intends to call into question the ingrained values and commonly held beliefs of the West. He wishes to empty out and shake up the very foundation of our Western belief system so that we become open to new ways of viewing the world. Yet, the observations Barthes tries to convey are inextricably bound to his own language, a language very different from the signs of Japan and thus far removed from the truth.

As Michael Moriarty remarks, "the notion of a language as a *découpage*, not intrinsically commensurate with other systems of articulation of thought and sound, does imply that our apprehension of the world is inevitably conditioned by the particular *découpage* to which our language subjects us."[15] Thus, the problem Barthes faces regarding the suitability of his own language to describe and make sense of another culture lies in the fact that language itself is a less than perfect tool, because it restricts our perception of the Other to the specific lens of our own culture, a linguistic system known intimately to us. This system will inevitably distort by assigning false meaning to the unknown object: "How absurd it is to try to contest our society without ever conceiving the very limits of the language by which (instrumental relation) we claim to contest it."[16] To emphasize his point, Barthes in his chapter "The Unknown Language" refers to Edward Sapir and Benjamin Lee Whorf's work on Native American languages, which, like Moriarty, argues that language determines decisively the way we perceive our surroundings. "It is quite an illusion to imagine," Sapir writes, "that one adjusts to reality essentially without the use of language and that language is merely an incidental means of solving specific problems of communication or reflection. The fact of the matter is that the 'real world' is to a large extent unconsciously built upon the language habits of the group."[17] As a consequence, a speaker of Hopi whose language does not include grammatical tenses would have a sense of time utterly distinct from the user of the English language. From this awareness, one might argue, follows the necessity of looking closely at one's own language and exploring its mechanisms before one can even begin to understand another culture.

Yet, Barthes takes his explorations in an altogether different direction: if one's own language does not serve as an appropriate tool to make sense of another culture, then the only way to sidestep the limits of language is to renounce any attempt to make sense of the Other or assign meaning to experience at all. Barthes places himself deliberately in a country whose language he does not speak and whose signs he is not able to decipher. All he can do is observe, never translate or fully comprehend as the tradition of Western hermeneutics suggests he must. However, for Barthes, the incomprehensible reality of Japan does not turn out to be a cause of frustration but a fundamental asset: "The murmuring mass of an unknown language constitutes a delicious protection, envelops the foreigner (provided the country is not hostile to him) in an auditory film which halts at his ears all the alienations of the mother tongue: the regional and social origins of whoever is speaking, his degree of culture, of intelligence, of taste, the image by which he constitutes himself as a person and which he asks you to recognize."[18]

Without words, the author is protected from social conventions and feels no necessity to comply with cultural expectations. He is not privy to details that are being exchanged by the Japanese; nonetheless, he still claims to "grasp the respiration, the emotive aeration, in a word the pure significance, [that] forms around me, as I move, a faint vertigo, sweeping me into its artificial emptiness, which is consummated only for me: I live in the interstice, delivered from any fulfilled meaning."[19] Again, Barthes emphasizes the importance of form, not content, in his encounter with Japan—a form that is characterized by a fundamental emptiness, devoid of all meaning. "For whilst the culture of the Occident is full of connotation and myth," Trevor Pateman charges, "that of Japan is devoid of either. *L'Empire des Signes* constitutes a system where a second level of meaning does not exist, a blissful, innocent world which offers no excuse for paranoia."[20] Barthes is not interested in making sense of Japan and his cultural findings but is determined to accept the prevailing emptiness and deliberately defy the Western urge to comprehend and analyze the unfamiliar.

Emptiness becomes the starting point for all of Barthes's explorations. Whereas Western culture posits deeper implications at the core of just about anything, Japanese culture, according to Barthes, is characterized by a void at its very center,[21] be it food ("The eel … is reduced to a tiny clump of emptiness … all the more provocative in that this emptiness is produced in order to provide nourishment");[22] the city of Tokyo ("The city I am talking about (Tokyo) offers this precious paradox: it does possess a center, but this center is empty. The entire city turns around a site both forbidden and indifferent, a residence concealed beneath foliage, protected by moats, inhabited by an emperor who is never seen, which is to say, literally, by no one knows who");[23] or the elaborate package which "is no longer the temporary accessory of the object to be transported, but itself becomes an object."[24] In the end, there is nothing profound to be discovered, and the curious explorer is forced to acknowledge that signifiers point to an empty signified and that meaning is replaced by the aforementioned void which cannot be penetrated: "From envelope to envelope, the signified flees, and when you finally have it … it appears insignificant, laughable, vile: … to find the object which is in the package or the signified which is in the sign is to discard it: what the Japanese carry, with a formicant energy, are actually empty signs."[25]

Emptiness lies furthermore at the heart of the *haiku*, to which Barthes devotes several chapters of his book. At first glance rather simplistic due to its mere seventeen syllables, the haiku triggers Western ambitions to imitate and emulate the age-old art form. Yet, instead of being content with the plain description of an everyday occurrence, it is the Western fascination with images, metaphors, and morals that comes to the fore and that fundamentally contradicts the very nature of the haiku. "While being quite intelligible, the haiku means nothing,"[26] Barthes explicates. Rather than infusing it with symbolism, the sole task of the haiku is "to suspend language, not to provoke it."[27] Contrary to Western beliefs, the haiku is capturing a fleeting moment that has been put in its proper form, not a deep thought condensed to merely three lines.[23] The challenge, therefore, is to stop all thoughts, not to expand on the content of the haiku, and succumb to the moment: "All of Zen, of which the haiku is merely the literary branch" Barthes postulates, "thus appears as an enormous praxis destined to halt language … to empty out, to stupefy, to dry up the soul's incoercible babble,"[29] thereby reiterating his own method of yielding to the incomprehensibility of the Japanese language while eliminating "incoercible babble" in the form of "stupidity, vulgarity, vanity, worldliness, nationality, normality."[30]

"The literary work tends to turn itself into a monument of reticence and am-biguity," Gérard Genette restates Barthes's viewpoint, "but it constructs this silent object, so to speak, with words, and this work of abolishing meaning is a typically semiological process, liable as such to an analysis of the same order: literature is a rhetoric of silence."[31] Again, language is not an appropriate vehicle to convey meaning; on the contrary, as with the haiku, all words are to be sus-pended as are all forms of commentary that try to analyze and evaluate.[32]

Thus, Barthes's focus, even though it might appear to be Japan at first glance, is ultimately not the "fictive nation" but rather his own Western culture. Ac-cording to Bettina Krüger, Barthes does not want his readers to perceive Japan as a new ideal nation, a counter model to the familiar West, but "he is rather concerned with the depiction of that which can only be disclosed through the encounter with something that eludes our system, that unmasks it, and raises the possibility of questioning what we have formerly taken for granted."[33] Japan serves as a foil, a tool, "a reserve of features," so that we may be able to under-stand our own culture in more profound ways and to free ourselves "from what is perceived as the authoritarian nature of Western subjectivity."[34] By experi-encing the Other it is ultimately our own belief system, our values and view-points, that come into focus and that are called into question. It is Barthes's goal to create a counter-myth to Western culture by casting doubt on Western thought and its strong belief in the ultimate power of language.

In the following part of this chapter I intend to apply my analysis of Barthes's theoretical concept to the examination of the aforementioned three short sto-ries by Brussig, Scholl, and Beyer. I will specifically investigate the topos of the void within these stories and in the process highlight similarities with as well as differences from Barthes's own notion of emptiness.

Thomas Brussig's "Ich weiß alles über Japan"

Thomas Brussig, in his essay "Ich weiß alles über Japan" (I Know Everything about Japan), depicts the deliberate misreading of Japanese signs by blending fact and fiction to the point where they become indistinguishable.[35] Despite the title's announcement of the author's omniscience, the subtitle "Ironischer Essay" (Ironic Essay) makes clear that the author's previous statement cannot be taken at face value. Employed seventeen times over the course of the essay, the phrase "Ich weiß alles über Japan" ironically calls the validity of Brussig's ruminations into question.[36] Rather than providing the reader with verifiable insights into the complex nature of Japanese society, Brussig creates a sophisticated amal-gam of "true" and "false," of "real" and "imagined" regarding things Japanese.

From the beginning, Brussig's strategy is revealed when he sets out to elu-cidate in a rather mocking way the high life expectancy of Japanese people by referring to their daily intake of Yakult: "a fermented dairy drink developed in the 1930s which aids your digestion in a wonderful way: Thanks to lactic acid bacteria resistant to stomach acid and gall … the Japanese enjoy the best digestion, the most pleasant intestinal flora, the highest well-being and therefore also the highest life expectancy."[37] A few sips of this yogurt-like substance taken every morning are, according to Brussig, responsible for the longevity of an entire nation. And he reasons further: "That's why it does not come as a surprise that Japan has been in a crisis for 14 years. The older the population gets, the higher the expenses for health care rise."[38] In the end, Brussig suggests, Japan's financial plight can be traced to Yakult, the reason for both the exceptional well-being of the Japanese people and at the same time the culprit for the economic downfall of the entire nation—an absurd notion that pretends to give an accurate reading of Japanese society but could in fact not be farther from the truth.

Another example where fact and fiction overlap is Brussig's depiction of the origin of Japanese bonsai trees. Due to Japan's inhospitable landscape, its population is forced to reside on a rather small territory without the luxury of enjoying their own garden with a tree. Consequently, according to Brussig, the idea of a miniature tree called bonsai was born: "The Japanese cultivated the tree that fits into every flower pot: bonsai. And because their trees were such a success, the Japanese decided to miniaturize everything else" and created "the tiniest tape players, TVs that are not bigger than an electric razor, cars that fit into every parking space."[39] At first, Brussig's analogy seems to be convincing. Why should bonsai trees not be the result of cramped living conditions in a country whose land area is marked by over 70 percent of uninhabitable space?[40] Yet, a more thorough investigation reveals a slightly different history of the tree: after all, it was the Chinese, not the Japanese who "invented" the miniature plant, which came to Japan via Buddhist monks in the sixth century.[41] Furthermore, practicality and a specific sense of beauty—not a deficit of space—were responsible for the emergence of bonsai trees: a potted plant in a container was easier to transport and, in addition, "appreciated for its form and aesthetic quality."[42] Thus, Brussig's intricate train of thought, so persuasive at first, does not adhere to verifiable data and is reduced to absurdity. Again, it is fact and fiction that are inextricably intertwined and that make it almost impossible for the uninitiated reader of Japan to gauge the validity of Brussig's text. Yet, it is Brussig's goal to lead his reader astray, to create a fictive, yet completely logical argument that turns out to be fundamentally flawed.

Brussig calls into question the belief in rationality that Barthes's *Empire of Signs* notes is so ingrained in Western reasoning and thought patterns but so foreign to other nations like the Japanese. As Barthes emphasizes over and over again, the Western obsession with meaning and rationality is incompatible with the Eastern perception of the world. In his chapter "No Address," Barthes depicts the West's utter bafflement vis-à-vis the complete lack of street names in Tokyo when he postulates: "This domiciliary obliteration seems inconvenient to those (like us) who have been used to asserting that the most practical is always the most rational.… Tokyo meanwhile reminds us that the rational is merely one system among others. For there to be a mastery of the real (in this case, the reality of addresses), it suffices that there be a system, even if this system is apparently illogical, uselessly complicated, curiously disparate: a good *bricolage* can not only *work* for a very long time, as we know; it can also satisfy millions of inhabitants inured, furthermore, to all the perfections of technological civilization."[43] Barthes describes the possibility of effective urban planning that operates beyond Western expectations of efficiency and rationality, a surprisingly well-functioning system that, despite what Western eyes might see as a comical defect, remains unquestioned by its Japanese users.

Brussig likewise shows how the ubiquitous Western ways of reasoning do not lead to genuine understanding but rather to convenient, ready-made explanations that actually frustrate a more in-depth exploration of the respective culture. Indeed, Brussig's essay is replete with clichés and stereotypes that at first appear logical, since they are presented as the truth: the low crime rate due to the unimaginable honesty of the Japanese,[44] the willingness of Japanese managers of ailing companies to commit suicide because of their dedication to their workplace,[45] or the refusal of the Japanese to sign the Kyoto treaty based on their feelings of superiority toward other nations.[46] By allegedly accepting these stereotypes as genuine representations of reality, Brussig uncovers the often condescending attitude of the Western tourist who deems himself capable of fully "understanding" a foreign culture after having been exposed to a mere fragment of it.

In the process, Brussig's declared omniscience—"I know everything about Japan"—turns out to be a hoax, a sophisticated game that points to the fundamental problem of passing judgment on things foreign by misreading its signs. Brussig's use of exaggerated statements ("I, on the other hand, who knows everything about Japan, I certainly know the origin and meaning of 'lean production'")[47] or patronizing phrases ("The fact that every lunch of the Japanese nation destroys numerous acres of rainforest is certainly known to the Japanese—nonetheless they do not eat with knife and fork like we do")[48] should not be mistaken for arrogance but, on the contrary, viewed as ironic illustrations of the fact that tourist and author are in no position to judge since neither of them comprehends the Japanese way of life in its entirety. Hence, it is interesting to note that even the author himself, in the course of his essay, loses his own assertiveness when he surreptitiously transitions from expressions that signal utter certainty such as "it's that simple"[49] or "that should be obvious to anyone who can put two and two together"[50] to more tentative statements that reveal his own hesitations: "And then there are those carps. I forget what they are called even though I know everything about Japan"[51] to outright admissions of puzzlement: "the Japanese behavioral code is a mystery to me."[52] Western logic breaks down, reveals its limits in the face of an unknown entity that cannot be grasped with the help of Western tools.

Brussig's ponderings do not clarify but rather obscure the subject in question. Instead of a clearly marked center where all arguments merge and join together, the reader is presented with an impenetrable void. Despite a plethora of information that appears to be logically connected, mere fragments of knowledge, seemingly incoherent pieces of a puzzle can be detected that do not form a comprehensible whole. Facts follow fictive statements that are interspersed with personal observations. "If I were Japanese I would be unhappy and wouldn't know the reason why," Brussig writes, "I would always have the feeling that something was missing from my life despite the fact that I did everything right."[53] As they stand on their own, refusing to provide the reader with a red thread that guides him or her to the end of the essay, Brussig's sentences seem to function as mere decorations which embellish rather than convey substance. As such, they are reminiscent of Barthes's chapter "Food Decentered," in which the author states: "The edible substance is without a precious heart ... no Japanese dish is endowed with a *center* (the alimentary center implied in the West by the rite which consists of arranging the meal, of surrounding or covering the article of food); here everything is the ornament of another ornament ... food is never anything but a collection of fragments, none of which appears privileged by an order of ingestion."[54] Again, meaning is denied. There is no hierarchy that assigns special significance to an item but only fragments among other fragments. The center is replaced by an endless network of signs that all point to one another. "The fact that there is no ultimate signified" Michael Sheringham remarks, "means that the process of signification involves infinite metaphorical chains where each signified becomes in its turn a signifier in another chain."[55] A decisive endpoint is nonexistent as can be seen again in the Japanese dish of sukiyaki which Barthes calls "an interminable dish to make ... *sukiyaki* has nothing *marked* about it except its beginning (that tray with foodstuffs brought to the table); once 'started,' it no longer has moments or distinctive sites: it becomes decentered, like an uninterrupted text."[56] It is the void that replaces Western thought patterns and rational analysis and leaves the reader with "a strong code but one signifying 'nothing,'"[57] as Barthes interprets to his readers the ritual of Japanese bowing.

In the end, it is not knowledge but uncertainty that characterizes Brussig's essay. Emptiness prevails where genuine understanding should reside. Hence, as has been shown, the parallels between Brussig's short story and Barthes's *Empire of Sings* are easily detectable in spite of the fact that Brussig's diagnosis of emptiness is not an overt one but remains hidden behind his ironic use of omniscience, his alleged ability to explain major societal problems, as well as his self-proclaimed hubris. Unlike Barthes, Brussig does not pretend to be the patient observer who uses the unknown and incomprehensible as his guide through a maze of Japanese signs. Instead, Brussig plays the role of an active participant who comments, evaluates, judges, and provides suggestions for improvements from an all-knowing Western point of view. Yet, the author also stresses again and again that Western reasoning is incapable of capturing the core of Japanese being. Despite the frequent repetition of "Ich weiß alles über Japan," the phrase ultimately comes to communicate the opposite of its alleged meaning: Brussig's acknowledgment that logic and rationality are not always appropriate tools to make sense of a non-Western way of life.

Sabine Scholl's "Japanisches Japan"

Sabine Scholl, too, in her anecdotal story "Japanisches Japan" (Japanese Japan) conflates fact and fiction, the real and the imagined. Yet, her strategy differs considerably from Brussig's. Whereas Brussig displayed interest—as well as feigned expertise—in every aspect of Japan, be it its geography, history, politics, customs, or work ethics, Scholl openly denies the equal significance of all things Japanese. Instead, she meticulously distinguishes between two categories of items she comes across during her stay in Japan: "Japanisches" (Japanese) and "Japanischjapanisches" (Japanesejapanese). Rather ordinary Japanese objects like the milk Scholl consumes, a spoon she uses, or a construction site she walks past are described as "japanisch," whereas items that allegedly correspond to Scholl's preconceived notions of the "real" Japan are admiringly called "japanischjapanisch." As she explicitly points out, it is her desire to encounter those "artifacts" that attest to the genuine nature of the land she is visiting: "I am always glad to find Japanesejapanese in Japan where I tend to be awfully non-Japanese." "Because Japanese by itself is not enough. Since I am already in Japan, I want to see more and more Japanesejapanese."[58] The experience of everyday life does not suffice; she is looking for the "extraordinary" that Japan is supposed to offer the Westerner.

However, as with Brussig, Scholl's rather whimsical differentiations between the real and the ordinary Japan cannot be taken at face value. By posing as a naïve visitor herself, Scholl covertly mocks the average tourist who is determined to verify his or her expectations of the Land of the Rising Sun. Thus, Scholl ironically states that it is her duty to experience "the real Japan" while abroad since "the people who have remained in the West expect that from me."[59] "Japanisch" in itself will not do; only a set of pre-established images and clichés, "Japanischjapanisches," serves as unmistakable evidence of Scholl's encounter with the "real thing." By leaving the rather mundane occurrences of everyday life behind and by venturing into the world of the "japanischjapanische" Japan,

Scholl proves to her fellow countrymen at home that her (and their) clichés are based on reality. Collecting evidence of her endeavors abroad becomes a mandatory part of her travels, and in doing so she appears to conform to the image of the tourist that Hans Magnus Enzensberger critiques in his essay "Eine Theorie des Tourismus" (A Theory of Tourism): "Because the sight is not only worthy of a visit, the sight demands it in an imperative way. A sight demands to be seen. By fulfilling his duty the tourist washes away the guilt he feels for surreptitiously fleeing society."[60]

Scholl ventures into the heart of rural Japan pretending to search for accurate representations of her own imaginings. However, she does not journey on her own, but embarks on a bus tour for tourists. This tour, meticulously prepared and staged to create a sense of authenticity, becomes the vehicle through which the author eventually achieves what she would have her readers believe to be her authentic encounter with Japan—an experience categorically different from her time spent in an ordinary Japanese city. There, in the countryside, she stays at a Japanesejapanese inn, consumes Japanesejapanese food, and is served by Japanese women in Japanesejapanese costumes. Beer is delivered on Japanesejapanese wooden trays to guests in the Japanesejapanese eating quarters, who are wrapped in Japanesejapanese bathrobes after taking a Japanese-japanese bath.[61] Now, Scholl deems her encounter with Japan successful since her expectations have been met and her desires satisfied. And while Scholl professes her eagerness to experience authenticity—thus purposely articulating the desires of the ordinary tourist—she ultimately pretends to feel content with a mere simulation, which she appears to mistake for reality.

Yet, Scholl is aware of this dilemma, and by using a tautological word creation such as "japanischjapanisch," she alerts her readers to the rather silly attempts of the tourist to match reality to his or her preconceptions. As Jean Baudrillard notes in his book *Simulacra and Simulation*, we are unable to differentiate between reality and its representation since no clear point of reference exists anymore. "Simulating is not pretending," he writes. "Pretending, or dissimulating, leaves the principle of reality intact: the difference is always clear, it is simply masked, whereas simulation threatens the difference between the 'true' and the 'false,' the 'real' and the 'imaginary.'"[62] In a similar fashion, Scholl appears unable to discriminate even between her own classifications of Japanese and Japanese-japanese during her bus tour: whereas futons, tatami mats, and sliding doors in her urban apartment, despite their uniquely Japanese origins, are only categorized as ordinarily "japanisch," much more mundane items such as wooden benches, wooden buckets, and even hot water are suddenly elevated to the more prestigious level of "japanischjapanisch."[63] Everything Scholl encounters during her tour she perceives in the light of true authenticity, her experience thus resonating with Baudrillard's notion of the hyperreal,[64] in which signifier and signified collapse into one another. "In such a world, the tourist would not know an 'authentic' experience even if one could be found," note George Ritzer and Allan Liska, thereby delivering a verdict that could serve as an apt description of Scholl's intentionally staged encounter with things Japanese.[65]

Yet, interestingly enough, it is not only the tourists but also the Japanese themselves who in search of "Japanischjapanisches": "At the hot springs, the Japanese residents cook their Japanese cabbage and their eggs while Japanese TV cameras, positioned in the right places, are awaiting Japanese nightfall in order to capture the correct Japanesejapanese shots when the Japanesejapanese water vapors will rise, because even the Japanese need to know time and again what they are, Japanese or—non-Japanese."[66] For the Japanese, the lines between the real and the imagined have become indistinct, and as a result their own Japanese identity has been called into question. This uncertainty creates an ironic state of affairs, in which tourists' expectations and imaginations serve as the yardstick of what *really* constitutes being Japanese, creating a second-order reality that the Japanese themselves accept. One might even say with Douglas Kellner, referencing Baudrillard, that both Scholl and, as she claims, the Japanese are "inserted in a coded system of similarities and dissimilarities, of identities and programmed differences. The society of simulations thus comes to control an individual's range of responses and options for choice and behavior."[67] Hence, it does not come as a surprise that houses with traditional Japanese roofs pretend to look "japanischjapanisch," plants and bushes are constantly cut into "japanischjapanische" shapes,[68] and the Japanese themselves embark on bus tours to find the real Japan in the form of a "japanischjapanisches" farmhouse decorated with hundreds of dried chains of persimmons.[69] Japan, in an attempt to conform to the tourist's expectations, is trying to verify again and again its own authenticity, be it with the help of dozens of TV cameras that are filming "Japanesejapanese temples" or by taking "Japanesejapanese pictures" of oneself in the "Japanesejapanese gardens," while making sure that no foreigner will ruin the photograph "what no-one wants because I am too—non-Japanese."[70]

Simulacra take the place of reality and make it impossible to distance oneself from preconceived notions of Japan. Unlike Barthes, who openly rejects such notions and refuses to familiarize himself with Japan before his departure, Scholl is determined, on the surface, to find an accurate replica of her own images of Japan. She appears to be only interested in encountering what she already knows: she does not travel to discover but to verify her own ideas of what constitutes Japan. Thus, she finds herself unable to appreciate everyday life in Japan, which she considers mundane, ordinary, and slightly disappointing. Since reality does not live up to her expectations, she enlists the services of the tourist industry that caters to the uninformed demands of its Western customers. Yet, all Scholl is left with in the end is an inauthentic experience characterized by an emptiness reminiscent of the one Barthes encounters in

Empire of Signs—an emptiness that ordinary Japanese also appear to embrace. But while the ordinary Japanese Scholl encounters feel comfortable with this ambiguity, both Barthes and Scholl remain in a state of ignorance and orbit around a void that does not yield its secret. Instead of unveiling Japan's mysteries, both authors are forced to return to the familiar: Barthes is reminded that his Western ways of analysis are of questionable value in the context of Japan, whereas Scholl is unable to distance herself from stereotypes about the East. For her, the lines between the real and the imagined are erased, and she and the reader remain caught in a circular structure with no reference point in sight, surrounded by signs that lead to other signs without offering up the "genuine" meaning that she, with her Western sensibilities, seems to demand.

Marcel Beyer's "Schatten"

The last text I intend to discuss is Marcel Beyer's essay "Schatten" (Shadows). Whereas Brussig declares his alleged omniscience of Japan seventeen times over the course of his essay, Beyer's approach is characterized by an outright admission of his ignorance: he profusely apologizes for his limited knowledge regarding things Japanese which, despite his fascination with Japan from an early age on, can be barely called more sophisticated than that of the "child who was amazed by a number of ghost drawings."[71] As a young boy, Beyer chanced upon various Japanese ink drawings of ghosts that left a lasting impression on him, and these drawings become his point of entry into Japanese culture. Only partially visible to the eye due to their multiple shades of darkness, those ghosts could not only be found on the dusky pages of the exhibition catalogue but also came alive at night during their mysterious flights around Beyer's house. The sense of mystery those ghosts instilled in the young boy is still palpable to the author today; it is a mystery Beyer deliberately never tries to unveil, fearing that for the mystery to reveal itself would result in utter disappointment. "After all," he writes, "there are secrets that do not demand disclosure and that are most fascinating to us in their form as secrets."[72] Mystery seems more alluring than knowledge, darkness more intriguing than light. Beyer prefers the Eastern tendency to leave things unexplained and in the dark to Western efforts at enlightenment, which can also be detected in his own writings.

Throughout his essay, Beyer employs the dichotomy of black and white, darkness and light to explain both Japan and the process of creating literature. For Beyer, literature, like the ghostly ink drawings of his youth, is "a matter in black and white: characters or letters against light background, nothing more,"[73] a figure of thought reminiscent of Barthes's emphasis on the significance of form over content. Barthes, too, like Beyer, discusses the "colors" of black and white in connection with both writing and painting in his chapter "The Written Face." Since "*to paint* is never anything but *to inscribe*"[74] for Barthes, paint-ing the theatrical face is synonymous to writing it, with the face becoming "the white of the paper, the black of the inscription (reserved for the eyes)."[75] Yet, writing (or painting) is not necessarily an activity that leads to the conveyance of meaning or to the exchange of profundities; on the contrary, "reduced to the elementary signifiers of writing (the blank of the page and the indentations of its script), the face dismisses any signified, i.e., any expressivity: this writing writes nothing (or writes: *nothing*); not only does it not 'lend' itself … to any emotions, to any meaning …, but it actually copies no character whatsoever."[76] In a similar fashion, Beyer dismisses his own ruminations on his childhood memories when he declares, "I know very well that those thoughts are nothing more than mere fantasies of a writer."[77] The ability to write in order to rep-resent reality becomes questionable since the dark letters seem impenetrable, reminiscent of Barthes's explorations of Japanese signs as riddles that hide their meaning from the curious gaze of the Western observer.

Not only the form of a text but also its content can be marked by white and black, light and darkness, the familiar and the foreign. As Beyer explicates, in his second novel, *Spione*, the narrator tries to reconstruct his family history, which is completely unknown to him, by analyzing pictures in a photo album. Yet the task turns out to be an almost impossible one, not only because the photographs seem to obscure more than to elucidate the past, but also because some of the most important pictures happen to be missing: "On the basis of these photographs the relationship between dark and light comes into focus, the old pictures reveal that light without darkness is not possible. The family history will never be fully illuminated but can only be perceived in shades. Ev-ery single family member conjures up their own picture with patches of higher and lesser degree of brightness, and those different pictures will never be fully congruent."[78] Knowledge of his family, the truth of the past, can only be par-tially revealed; a complete victory of light over darkness remains unattainable. In *Spione*, the missing photographs cannot be reconstructed, and the various family histories remain mere figments of the imagination.

Yet Beyer does not lament the opacity of history but is quick to point out that light and darkness are not necessarily binary opposites. A look at Japanese authors and their sophisticated play with light and darkness is quite instruc-tive, Beyer charges, "because light does not appear as the antithesis of darkness. They do not form complete opposites but rather produce shades, transitions, a relationship."[79] Although European culture perceives light and darkness as an-tagonists, with light signifying the metaphysically good and darkness the meta-physically evil, antagonists that attempt to oppress and conquer each other, Beyer does not share this commonly held point of view. "I am not interested in darkness as the antithesis of light," he writes. "I am interested in how they form a relationship. I am interested in concrete light, in the different levels of brightness, and in the angle of the light. Images not metaphors."[80] Comparable to Barthes, Beyer focuses not on metaphorical readings but advocates a simple acceptance of the way light and darkness operate side by side.

To underline his point, Beyer refers to the Japanese writer Tanizaki Jun'ichiro and his essay collection *In Praise of Shadows*, a book whose elaborate reflections on the interplay of light and shadows had a profound impact on Beyer's awareness of his environment as well as on his perception of literature.[81] In *In Praise of Shadows*, Tanizaki criticizes the alleged superiority of the West with its overbearing emphasis on light and modernization that destroys Japanese tradition and its age-old sense of beauty. Tanizaki even goes so far as to wish for a separate Japanese modernity, independent of Western influence in order for the Japanese to create suitable innovations to preserve their own traditions and unique identity: "The Orient quite conceivably could have opened up a world of technology entirely its own."[82] Many of the latest inventions, be it electric lamps, the radio, phonographs, heating systems, or bathroom tiles do not, according to Tanizaki, reflect Japanese aesthetics and, moreover, do not fit the traditional Japanese lifestyle: "These machines are the inventions of Westerners, and are, as we might expect, well suited to the Western arts. But precisely on this account they put our own arts at a great disadvantage."[83] The same holds true for the craft of writing itself: the enormous popularity of foreign ink and pens has not only resulted in numerous concerns regarding the replacement of the Japanese writing system with Roman letters, but has also led to countless imitations of Western literature.[84] "An insignificant little piece of writing equipment, when one thinks of it," Tanizaki notes, "has had a vast, almost boundless, influence on our culture."[85]

For Tanizaki, this turn of events is particularly threatening because the Western aesthetic is diametrically opposed to the Japanese sense of beauty. "As a general matter," he writes, "we find it hard to be really at home with things that shine and glitter."[86] The dislike of shiny items can be detected in the Japanese aversion to "silver and steel and nickel,"[87] to bathroom tiles,[88] "ceramic tableware,"[89] as well as brightly lit rooms. According to Tanizaki, darkness is preferable to light since darkness smoothes over imperfections and leaves much to the imagination. Darkness brings out the beauty in Japanese lacquer works, temples, and even Japanese cuisine: "Our cooking depends upon shadows and is inseparable from darkness."[90] "We find beauty not in the thing itself but in the patterns of shadows, the light and the darkness, that one thing against another creates.... Were it not for shadows, there would be no beauty."[91] It is the combination of light and dark shadows that creates beauty, not bright but indirect light charms the Japanese eye. As a consequence, the traditional Japanese home is arranged in such a way as to bring about intricate variations of shadows, resulting in the most elaborate display of beauty.

However, Japan's modernization as well as Westernization have infused the country with unnecessary lights and led to the deplorable relegation of darkness to a subordinate position. The dimly lit traditional Japanese toilets, "truly … a place of spiritual repose"[92] "where haiku poets over the ages have come by a great many of their ideas"[93] have been replaced with Western style bathrooms, candles have given way to electric lamps and "light is used not for reading or writing or sewing but for dispelling the shadows in the farthest corners."[94] Yet, as Tanizaki laments, the more one lights the erstwhile hidden and mysterious, the less meaning remains, thereby echoing Beyer's refusal to uncover the mysteries of his childhood encounters with Japan when he states, "Where lies the mystery to this? Ultimately it is the magic of shadows. Were the shadows to be banished from its corners, the alcove would in that instant revert to mere void."[95] Shadows generate a world of their own: they invite meditation, grant spiritual repose, and create an atmosphere of silence and tranquility, often mistaken by the uninitiated Westerner for "uncanny silence."[96] Shadows remove all clarity and even manipulate "all consciousness of the passage of time."[97] However, in a time in which Japan consumes more electricity than most countries in the world and even the minutest shadows are being eradicated from every nook of Japanese dwellings,[98] darkness has to be regarded as a thing of the past.

Tanizaki turns to the realm of literature to re-create with words those shadows that are being removed from the world around him, to salvage the mysterious beauty that is being lost in the glaring light of Western rationalism. "In the mansion called literature," he writes, "I would have the eaves deep and the walls dark, I would push back into the shadows the things that come forward too clearly, I would strip away the useless decoration."[99] It is the act of writing Tanizaki resorts to, thereby foretelling what Barthes will expound three decades later in *Empire of Signs*: as Barthes charges, writing causes previous knowledge to "vacillate: it creates *an emptiness of language*. And it is also an emptiness of language which constitutes writing; it is from this emptiness that derive the features with which Zen, in the exemption from all meaning, writes gardens, gestures, houses, flower arrangements, faces, violence."[100] Out of nothing emerges something, emptiness produces matter which appears to be a paradox at first. Yet, as Susan Sontag points out about Barthes: "Arguments about many subjects have this identical climax: that absence is really presence, emptiness repletion, impersonality the highest achievement of the personal."[101] Previous knowledge or, to put it differently, Western rationality, becomes of questionable use in the face of Japan—be it Japanese aestheticism or the impervious Japanese language. It is not Western clarity that produces universal meaning but darkness and shadows that recreate, through the process of writing, the mystery lost by the glaring light of the West. Hence, the alleged emptiness of things Japanese is being filled, yet not with the lucidity of light but with the shadows of mystery, with the beauty of darkness which defies the "progressive Westerner [who] is determined always to better his lot."[102]

Ultimately, it is the rejection of Western enlightenment that lies at the heart of both Tanizaki and Beyer's works in favor of Eastern "obscurity." The mysterious shadows are not to be dispersed by the curious Western gaze or by seemingly rational explanations. It is the acceptance of the impenetrable, the irrational Beyer, in particular, emphasizes, thus pointing to a profound difference between Eastern and Western thought that lies beyond the realm of analysis or explication. All Beyer intends to do is make visible that difference, the incomprehensible, the void that rationality is unable to fill. And with the help of literature, when putting one's experience into words, that difference comes to the fore. Even though literature as a Western tool is overall insufficient to elucidate Eastern thought, literature is vital in depicting—not necessarily bridging—differences and incomprehensibilities. As Beyer himself writes: "Since literature consists in nothing other than in the circling of objects and in indirect observation, whereby certain areas of darkness are definitely welcome."[103]

Conclusion

As has been shown, all three authors discussed in this chapter keep their readers in a state of partial ignorance since the darkness of the foreign cannot be penetrated and consequently a deeper level of understanding of things Japanese seems beyond reach. In Brussig's essay, Western ways of analysis, inapplicable to Eastern culture and customs, are employed; in Scholl's, a mere simulacrum is taken for reality; and in Beyer's, Japanese culture becomes a shadow play that echoes with the nature of writing itself. Despite the authors' alleged endeavors to illuminate Japan, the results remain similar: the discovery of a void that yields no useful information and in turn demands reflection on Western thoughts and beliefs. But as Beyer stresses specifically, Japan's darkness is a necessary complement to the light that, to the Westerner, is absolutely essential in signifying the true and authentic. Both he and Tanizaki champion this darkness as the source of beauty in Japanese culture.

In the end, none of the three authors attempts to offer a reading of the true nature of things Japanese. On the contrary, all point to the pitfalls for those Westerners who endeavor to understand and judge a culture radically different from their own. Self-comprehension must therefore be regarded as the ultimate goal of these authors. Thus, I would like to end with a quote by Adolf Muschg who in an attempt to explain the seemingly inexplicable, paradoxical nature of Japan points to Katsushika Hokusai's famous woodblock printing "Der Fuji, von Kanagawa aus betrachtet" (Mount Fuji Seen from Kanagawa):

"Being" and "appearance" are hasty and thus incorrect alternatives, constructions of a disturbed point of view. The picture is both pure *action* and complete calm. That's all we see—but what we see is at the same time different from what we see and completely identical to it. Western thought does not have any words for that phenomenon—only sophisticated-mystical terms that want to put things in order where everything comes to an end. Hokusai's popular woodcut explains without pathos that the phenomena that we are unable to express with words are common and taken for granted because of their familiarity. This experience does not detect contradictions in opposition. It perceives in wave and mountain, life and death, being and non-being the manifestation of the mystery of identity.[104]

Notes

1. Britta Heidemann, "Japan: Die Faszination des Fremden," *Der Westen*, 13 June 2009. http://www.derwesten.de/kultur/literatur/Japan-Die-Faszination-des-Fremden-id386850.html. Last accessed 26 December 2013. Unless otherwise noted all translations of titles and quotes are mine.
2. Adolf Muschg is a Swiss writer and former professor of Germanic languages and literature at the Eidgenössische Technische Hochschule in Zurich who has been profoundly interested in Japan for the past forty years.
3. Adolf Muschg, *Die Insel, die Kolumbus nicht gefunden hat. Sieben Gesichter Japans* (Frankfurt a.M., 1995), 36–37.
4. Muschg, *Die Insel*, 37.
5. Yoshihiko Ikegami, "Introduction: Semiotics and Culture," in *The Empire of Signs: Semiotic Essays on Japanese Culture*, ed. Yoshihiko Ikegami (Amsterdam; Philadelphia, P.A., 1991), 12.
6. Jonathan Culler, *Roland Barthes* (New York, 1983), 11.
7. Roland Barthes, *Empire of Signs*, trans. Richard Howard (New York, 1982), 3.
8. See Gérard Genette, who writes in connection with Barthes and semiology: "The semiological discipline stops the vertigo of meaning and authorizes a liberating choice: for it is the privilege of the semiologist to turn away from the signified in order to devote himself to the study of the signifier, and therefore to an exclusive commerce with it." Gérard Genette, "The Obverse of Signs," in *Critical Essays on Roland Barthes*, ed. Diana Knight (New York, 2000), 67.
9. Rolf J. Goebel, "Japan as Western Text: Roland Barthes, Richard Gordon Smith, and Lafcadio Hearn," *Comparative Literature Studies* 30, no. 2 (1993): 189.
10. Barthes, *Empire of Signs*, 3.
11. Susan Sontag, "Writing Itself: On Roland Barthes," in *A Barthes Reader*, ed. Susan Sontag (New York, 1982), xxv.
12. Barthes, *Empire of Signs*, 3.
13. As Annette Lavers remarks about *Empire of Signs*: "It obviously belongs to the tradition represented by Voltaire's book on England and Madame de Staël's on Germany: it aims to castigate one's own country by means of a utopian portrait of another." Even though "castigate" might be too strong a word in this context, Lavers is right in saying that Barthes is not a neutral observer but displays a clear allegiance to Japan and its philosophy of emptiness that he finds superior to the Western obsession with mean-

ing. Annette Lavers, *Roland Barthes: Structuralism and After* (Cambridge, M.A., 1982), 203.

14. Barthes, *Empire of Signs*, 4.

15. Michael Moriarty, *Roland Barthes* (Stanford, C.A., 1991), 84.

16. Barthes, *Empire of Signs*, 8.

17. Edward Sapir, "The Status of Linguistics as a Science," in *Culture, Language and Personality*, ed. D.G. Mandelbaum (Berkeley, C.A., 1958), 69.

18. Barthes, *Empire of Signs*, 9.

19. Barthes, *Empire of Signs*, 9.

20. Trevor Pateman, "Remarks on Roland Barthes' 'L'Empire des Signes.'" http://www .selectedworks.co.uk/EmpireDesSignes.html. Last accessed 26 December 2013.

21. See also Edmund White's article entitled "From Albert Camus to Roland Barthes," in which he charges, "In this fictive Japan, there is no terrible innerness as in the West, no soul, no God, no fate, no grandeur, no metaphysics, no 'pro-motional fever' and finally no meaning." Edmund White, "From Albert Camus to Roland Barthes," *The New York Times*, 12 September 1982, Section 7, Page 1. And in a similar fashion Michael Moriarty writes, "Barthes's 'Japan' is simply a storehouse of features, which he can arrange so as to form the image of a symbolic system quite detached from our own (ES, 7/3), without the latter's metaphysical and theological foundations, and within which signs are empty and never disclose an ultimate signified." Michael Moriarty, *Roland Barthes*, 113.

22. Barthes, *Empire of Signs*, 24.

23. Barthes, *Empire of Signs*, 30.

24. Barthes, *Empire of Signs*, 45.

25. Barthes, *Empire of Signs*, 46.

26. Barthes, *Empire of Signs*, 69.

27. Barthes, *Empire of Signs*, 72.

28. Barthes, *Empire of Signs*, 75. "As a 'vision lacking commentary,' haïku will nevertheless not allow commentary. Haïku cannot be explicated, merely repeated; nor can it be deciphered, analyzed, or developed without subjection to the processes of metaphor or syllogism." Trinh T. Minh-Ha, "The Plural Void: Barthes and Asia," in *Critical Essays on Roland Barthes*, ed. Diana Knight (New York, 2000), 211.

29. Barthes, *Empire of Signs*, 74.

30. Barthes, *Empire of Signs*, 9.

31. Genette, "The Obverse of Signs," 69.

32. Barthes, *Empire of Signs*, 81.

33. Bettina Krüger, "Sehnsucht nach dem ganz anderen." http://parapluie.de/archiv/ sehnsucht/japan/. Last accessed 26 December 2013. See also Trinh T. Minh-Ha, who argues that Barthes seeks not "to decipher Asia, but rather to assess his own position vis-à-vis exoticism, ethnocriticism and above all, to assess his own hermeneutic posture, his role as decoder." Trinh T. Minh-Ha, "The Plural Void: Barthes and Asia," 217.

34. Krüger, "Sehnsucht nach dem ganz anderen."

35. With Japanese signs, I mean not necessarily Japanese characters but primarily cultural signs such as the Japanese smile or the significance of Japanese politeness.

36. Seventeen constitutes an important number: a *haiku* consists of seventeen phonetic units. Since Barthes devotes a substantial part of his essay to the discussion of the Japanese *haiku* whose main characteristic, he claims, is its emptiness, a comparison of Brussig's statement, "Ich weiß alles über Japan" and Barthes's examination of the *haiku*

seems inevitable. Like the *haiku*, whose task is not to convey meaning but to suggest the mere atmosphere of an event, Brussig's phrase is characterized by a void. It has to be viewed as a hoax, a tremendous exaggeration that does not provide the reader with valuable knowledge but, on the contrary, is employed by Brussig to question the genuine understanding of Japanese culture.

37. Thomas Brussig, "Ich weiß alles über Japan. Ironischer Essay," *Nach Japan. Reiselesebuch*, ed. Renate and Peter Giacomuzzi (Tübingen, 2005), 25.
38. Brussig, "Ich weiß alles über Japan," 25.
39. Brussig, "Ich weiß alles über Japan," 25.
40. http://www.facts-about-japan.com/. Last accessed 26 December 2013.
41. Yuji Yoshimura, "Modern Bonsai, Development of the Art of Bonsai from an Historical Perspective, Part 2," *International Bonsai* 4 (1991): 37.
42. Deborah R. Koreshoff, *Bonsai: Its Art, Science, History and Philosophy* (Portland, O.R., 1997), 2.
43. Barthes, *Empire of Signs*, 33.
44. Brussig, "Ich weiß alles über Japan," 26.
45. Brussig, "Ich weiß alles über Japan," 34.
46. Brussig, "Ich weiß alles über Japan," 29.
47. Brussig, "Ich weiß alles über Japan," 28.
48. Brussig, "Ich weiß alles über Japan," 29.
49. Brussig, "Ich weiß alles über Japan," 25.
50. Brussig, "Ich weiß alles über Japan," 29.
51. Brussig, "Ich weiß alles über Japan," 30.
52. Brussig, "Ich weiß alles über Japan," 34.
53. Brussig, "Ich weiß alles über Japan," 34.
54. Barthes, *Empire of Signs*, 22.
55. Michael Sheringham, "All That Falls: Barthes and the Everyday," in *Critical Essays on Roland Barthes*, ed. Diana Knight (New York, 2000), 298.
56. Barthes, *Empire of Signs*, 22.
57. Barthes, *Empire of Signs*, 65.
58. Sabine Scholl, "Japanisches Japan," *Nach Japan. Reiselesebuch*, ed. Renate and Peter Giacomuzzi (Tübingen, 2005), 217.
59. Scholl, "Japanisches Japan," 222.
60. Hans Magnus Enzensberger, *Einzelheiten I. Bewusstseins-Industrie* (Frankfurt a.M., 1979), 196.
61. Scholl, "Japanisches Japan," 219.
62. Jean Baudrillard, *Simulacra and Simulation*, trans. Sheila Faria Glaser (Ann Arbor, M.I., 1994), 3.
63. Scholl, "Japanisches Japan," 219.
64. As stated above, for Baudrillard, reality does not exist anymore; it has been replaced by a gigantic simulacrum Baudrillard calls hyperreality. Signs do neither relate to reality nor do they represent meaning; instead they endlessly refer to other signs, other signifiers—"It is a question of substituting the signs of the real for the real"—rendering reality a rather outdated concept or "[t]he desert of the real itself," Baudrillard charges in *Simulacra and Simulation*. Baudrillard, *Simulacra*, 1–2.
65. George Ritzer and Allan Liska, "'McDisneyization' and 'Post-Tourism': Complementary Perspectives on Contemporary Tourism," in *Touring Cultures. Transformations of Travel and Theory*, ed. Chris Rojek and John Urry (London, 1997), 107.

66. Scholl, "Japanisches Japan," 220.

67. Douglas Kellner, *Jean Baudrillard. From Marxism to Postmodernism and Beyond* (Stanford, C.A., 1989), 80.

68. Scholl, "Japanisches Japan," 216.

69. Scholl, "Japanisches Japan," 218.

70. Scholl, "Japanisches Japan," 221.

71. Marcel Beyer, "Schatten," *Nach Japan. Reiselesebuch,* ed. Renate and Peter Giacomuzzi (Tübingen, 2005), 10.

72. Beyer, "Schatten," 9.

73. Beyer, "Schatten," 10.

74. Barthes, *Empire of Signs,* 88.

75. Barthes, *Empire of Signs,* 88.

76. Barthes, *Empire of Signs,* 89. What Barthes refers to here is the notion that the Japanese face displays pre-coded emotions of love, shame, anger, etc. that the actor is not able to interpret any further. Emotions are culturally encoded and not individually produced. As Barthes remarks himself, "What then is our face, if not a 'citation'?" Barthes, *Empire,* 90. See also Kentaro Kawashima, "dem Lächeln nah. Das photographierte Gesicht in Roland Barthes' *Das Reich der Zeichen,*" *parapluie* no. 23 (Summer 2006). http://parapluie.de/archiv/bewusstsein/barthes/. Last accessed 26 December 2013.

77. Beyer, "Schatten," 10.

78. Beyer, "Schatten," 11.

79. Beyer, "Schatten," 15.

80. Beyer, "Schatten," 15–16.

81. Beyer, "Schatten," 12.

82. Jun'ichiro Tanizaki, *In Praise of Shadows* (London, 1991), 18.

83. Tanizaki, *Shadows,* 20.

84. Tanizaki, *Shadows,* 18.

85. Tanizaki, *Shadows,* 18.

86. Tanizaki, *Shadows,* 21.

87. Tanizaki, *Shadows,* 21.

88. Tanizaki, *Shadows,* 12.

89. Tanizaki, *Shadows,* 25.

90. Tanizaki, *Shadows,* 29.

91. Tanizaki, *Shadows,* 45.

92. Tanizaki, *Shadows,* 13.

93. Tanizaki, *Shadows,* 14.

94. Tanizaki, *Shadows,* 56.

95. Tanizaki, *Shadows,* 34.

96. Tanizaki, *Shadows,* 34.

97. Tanizaki, *Shadows,* 36.

98. Tanizaki, *Shadows,* 47.

99. Tanizaki, *Shadows,* 61.

100. Barthes, *Empire,* 4.

101. Sontag, "Writing Itself: On Roland Barthes," xxiv.

102. Tanizaki, *Shadows,* 47.

103. Beyer, "Schatten," 17.

104. Muschg, *Die Insel, die Kolumbus nicht gefunden hat,* 29.

CHAPTER 12

Discovering Asia in the Footsteps of Portuguese Explorers
East Asia in the Work of Hugo Loetscher

JEROEN DEWULF

Hugo Loetscher (1929–2009) was known as one of the most cosmopolitan Swiss authors, a characterization generally linked to a famous quote from his novel *Der Immune* (The Immune, 1975): "He would have loved to go in all directions, and to return from all directions, until every foreign place became familiar and every familiar place became foreign so that there would be no difference any longer between familiar and foreign."[1] Loetscher's oeuvre is, in fact, deeply marked by the many journeys he undertook as a foreign correspondent for Swiss newspapers and magazines.

Scholars have mainly focused on the importance of Latin America, in particular Brazil, in Loetscher's work.[2] Strongly influenced by Brazilian authors and intellectuals, including Mário de Andrade and Gilberto Freyre, Loetscher introduced a hybrid perspective on culture and identity into German literature. By conceiving a notion of transnational identity that is no longer based on the exoticism of multiculturalism or the diversity of cultures but rather on their interconnections, he anticipated a discussion that only in the aftermath of Homi Bhabha's *The Location of Culture* (1994) became a prominent field of research in German Studies.

After focusing on Lusophone and Hispanic cultures in Latin America for more than a decade, Loetscher broadened his perspective in the mid 1970s by traveling to Asia to study the relics of the Portuguese and Spanish colonial presence. While German literature, according to Lange, is characterized by a tendency to use Asia as a metaphor and a contrast to Europe,[3] Loetscher did not approach the Asian continent in search of the "exotic Other" but aimed his attention at those places where European culture mixed with Asian culture.

This engagement with hybridity characterizes his reflections on Asia in German literature.

I begin this article with a critical reflection of Loetscher's theoretical framework and continue with an analysis of two of his texts. First, I will study his report on Macau from 1977 as an example of Loetscher's focus on hybridity in his encounter with Asia. Then, I will analyze the role of Chinese culture in Loetscher's attempt to elaborate a "global consciousness" in his novel *Die Augen des Mandarin* (The Eyes of the Mandarin, 1999).

On the Reflexivity of Writing

Loetscher's lifelong ambition to contribute to the formation of a "global consciousness" through his writing necessarily implied theoretical reflection on the representation of the Other. Building on Roland Barthes's essay "Écrivains et écrivants" (1960), which distinguishes between a transitive, functional way of writing (that of the *écrivant*) and an intransitive way that focuses on the act of writing in itself (that of the *écrivain*), Loetscher's main concern was not the (intransitive) question "How do I write?" or the (transitive) question "What do I write?" but rather a third aspect of writing: its reflexivity. As he wrote in his essay *How Many Languages Does Man Need?* (1982), "we do not just see what we have in front of our eyes, but also what we bring with us in our mind."[4] Loetscher's question "How do I write myself?" therefore centered on the subjectivity of writing and the fact that there is no way to avoid interference from the describing subject on the described object.[5]

While this "reflexivity" of writing might seem like a truism, it becomes highly problematic as soon as one finds oneself in a situation where one intends to write about a foreign culture, especially when this culture is little known to one's readers and marked in their perception by stereotypes of the "exotic Other." Because of writing's inherent reflexivity, the logical consequence is that an objective representation of the Other through writing is impossible because any type of writing necessarily implies that the writer also "writes him/herself." This reflexivity of writing was traditionally not recognized as a problem in the Western representation of the Other. The Western perspective on the world was not perceived as Eurocentric or biased, but as the logical standard. The fact that the image of the non-Western Other that resulted from this perspective was not realistic should, therefore, also be considered a consequence of the unproblematic authority of the narrative "I."

At the beginning of the twentieth century, the field of anthropology first attempted to tackle this problem. Franz Boas and Bronislaw Malinowski realized that the exclusion of the Other in the interpretation of his/her culture rendered a truly objective representation of a foreign culture virtually impossible. In *Argonauts of the Western Pacific* (1922), Malinowski, therefore, suggested a change in perspective: instead of representing foreign cultures from the anthropologist's perspective, they had to be represented from the perspective of the Other.

While Malinowski's method of "participant observation" revolutionized the field of anthropology, it did not seem to affect literary authors who also had the ambition to write about a foreign culture from a non-Eurocentric perspective. For literary authors, the point of departure was different. The reflexivity of writing could not be considered a problem because it is inherent in literature. Literature is not expected to claim objectivity. The image of a foreign culture presented through literature is, by definition, a subjective image that does not (completely) correspond to reality, nor does it have to (completely) correspond to reality. Despite the fact that this conclusion is self-evident, several authors did not take it for granted and searched for alternatives. Loetscher was one of these authors. Although he never denied that his literary writings on foreign cultures were fictional, he questioned the assumption that the result of his approach was necessarily less true than a scientific study. As is reflected in his desire to become an "ethnographer of his own tribe,"[6] much of Loetscher's approach to this problem corresponds with discussions in the field of anthropology.[7]

One of the crucial problems in anthropology arising after the introduction of Malinowski's method of "participant observation" was the transposition of the "native's point of view" into an understandable language for a non-native audience. By solving the old question "What do we represent?" Malinowski had, in fact, created a new one: "How do we represent?" Consequently, anthropologists became increasingly interested in the literary aspect of ethnographic writing. As the leading representative of the "literary turn" in the field of anthropology, Clifford Geertz shifted the focus from "participant observation" to "participant description" in his book *Works and Lives: The Anthropologist as Author* (1988), acknowledging that the transposition of the "native's point of view" into a book was essentially a creative, imaginary act. While anthropology as a field of science remained obliged to truth, it had to recognize that this truth was necessarily "partial." Geertz denied that ethnographies become more objective by removing all subjective elements inherent to the process of collecting data and the creative transposition of this data through writing. Rather, he argued that including a reflection on these subjective elements in the actual writing process would bring ethnography closer to the truth.

Loetscher drew the conclusion from these theoretical reflections that the best possible way to handle subjectivity in writing about other cultures was not by denying, removing, or hiding it, but rather by making it a topic of reflection in the writing process.[8] Such an approach to the representation of the Other is, however, not without danger. The French sociologist Pierre Bourdieu warned of a risk of "ethnographic narcissism" in *Réponses* (Answers, 1992), in the sense that excessive attention to subjectivity might lead to a situation where the ethnographer/author ends up writing primarily about him or herself, pushing the foreign culture to the background or even reducing it to sheer decoration.[9]

As Beat Mazenauer has shown, Loetscher tried to circumvent this danger through the use of irony. According to Mazenauer, irony forms a constitutive element of Loetscher's writing style and can have different functions.[10] In order to avoid literary narcissism, Loetscher uses self-irony as a stylistic weapon to combat the risk of taking oneself too seriously as an author. Irony, however, also functions as a strategy to deal with human limitations in perceiving, understanding, and representing the Other. It serves as a way to resist narrative arrogance by acknowledging that the representation of (a foreign) reality in words is necessarily limited and imperfect. Loetscher's abundant use of irony reflects the awareness that an author does not have a language but rather possibilities of language at his disposal and that whatever type of language he uses, he will never be capable of capturing the entire complexity of the situation he attempts to describe.[11] Irony thus functions as a way to recognize deficiency and to combat a neocolonialist "monarch-of-all-I-survey" attitude when writing about a foreign culture. But Loetscher also uses irony as a strategy to resist the potential danger of glorifying the Other as a form of escapism or as a naïve way of dealing with twinges of conscience about historical crimes committed by people of one's own culture.

The Indian scholar Anil Bhatti interpreted the importance of irony in Loetscher's work by placing his use of irony in a postcolonial context: "It is fascinating to see how Loetscher, in his travel reports from the 1970s, anticipates an attitude that today is associated with the interest in hybridity and diversity in Postcolonial Studies. He does not exoticize despite the fact that he writes about the exotic. Loetscher's irony gives rise to a sense of the appeal inherent in the traces and ruins of colonialism, which in turn constitutes the source of his text's success."[12] Bhatti's use of the word "hybridity" corresponds with Loetscher's tendency to perceive cultural difference as a variation among variations, combining diversity with universalism. His definition of man as "individuum varietas varietatis,"[13] man as a variety within a variety, implies a strong interest in moments and places when people from different cultural backgrounds came into contact with each other—hence Loetscher's fascination with the sixteenth century, the Age of Discovery. In his analysis of colonial encounters, Loetscher pays attention to elements of European culture that proved to be exportable and to the structures of local cultures that managed to resist European colonization. His main interest, however, goes to "new" elements that developed out of a mixture of both.

Loetscher's method of representing foreign cultures does not seek the immediate confrontation with the Other, as this strategy entails the risk of losing oneself in fantasies and stereotypes, but rather focuses on elements where the

Other and the Self come together. Consequently, his work is not character-ized by an attempt to grasp the "total Other," but rather by a fascination for commonalities. Not the differences, but the similarities between the I and the Other are the central topic of his writing. Accordingly, Loetscher defined his "discoveries" as "self-discoveries," and expressed the ambition to portray the Other as a variation of what life on earth allows the "I" to be. Writing about the Other essentially means writing about possibilities of being human and, as such, it also means writing about oneself. Consequently, Loetscher does not perceive the reflexivity of writing as a problem, but as an asset.[14]

It should be said, however, that Loetscher's methodology is not unproblem-atic. As Ella Shohat argues in a wider theoretical context, "a celebration of syn-cretism and hybridity per se, if not articulated in conjunction with questions of hegemony and neo-colonial power relations, runs the risk of appearing to sanc-tify the fait accompli of colonial violence."[15] In fact, while Loetscher's represen-tations manage to successfully avoid the lure of exoticism, they do not entirely escape Eurocentrism. His relativistic and ironic approach to cultural difference might preclude an attitude of European superiority, but his rhetorical strategy does not prevent his perspective on the Other from remaining deeply rooted in a Western tradition of oppression. Loetscher's method for achieving intellectual access to the Other corresponds exactly to the one once used by the European colonizers to expand their control over the Other with the help of cultural in-termediaries: translators, middlemen, go-betweens. It is questionable whether a method that has its roots in a system of oppression of the Other can serve as a guideline to a better understanding of the Other. While Loetscher makes a substantial effort to incorporate an awareness of the long-lasting disastrous consequences of Europe's colonial expansion in his writings, there can be no doubt that his use of irony in the representation of the Other at times might strike the reader as having a cynical component.

Nevertheless, in the context of Postcolonial Studies, Loetscher's creative use of hybridity is far from unique. His method is reminiscent of Mary Louise Pratt's interpretation of the colonial world as a "contact zone." While recog-nizing the oppressive side and dramatic consequences of colonialism, Pratt decided in "Arts of the Contact Zone" to read the colonial encounter as a "so-cial space where cultures meet, clash, and grapple with each other … a cross-communication between speakers of different ideological/cultural languages."[16] As Pratt was able to demonstrate in regard to colonialism's "open wound," hy-brid forms of culture should not necessarily be seen as colonial relics or cor-ruptions, but can also be perceived as flexible forms of opposition, as native strategies to revise or modify European constructions.

Indeed, in a country like Brazil that constructed its national identity out of its colonial legacy, such an interpretation of hybridity as a flexible, creative strategy of opposition against (colonial) authority/rules has a long tradition.

Not accidentally then, Brazil's popular hero is the *malandro*, the trickster, who has a chameleonic talent of adapting to any new situation. The protagonists in Loetscher's work often display such a flexible, sometimes even defiantly opportunistic attitude to life. This relates to Loetscher's fascination with the in-between and the not-quite, those for whom flexibility is not an option but a necessity for survival. In an East Asian context, perhaps no other place fits this characterization better than Macau.

Macau

Through the works of Luís Fróis, João de Barros, Camilo Pessanha, Luís de Camões, and, most importantly, Fernão Mendes Pinto, Loetscher became increasingly interested in the Asian chapter of Portugal's colonial expansion. Fascinated by the Japanese *namban* art of folding screens in Lisbon's National Museum of Ancient Art, he decided to make a journey through Asia in 1976. Following the route of sixteenth-century Portuguese explorers, Loetscher first traveled to Goa in India, then to Colombo in Sri Lanka, and from there to Malacca in Malaysia. The final destination of his journey was Macau.

Loetscher's report "Macao, oder die portugiesische Fähigkeit, sich zu arrangieren" (Macau, or the Portuguese Talent to Adapt, 1977) begins with a reflection on the stereotypes he brought with him to Macau: "The image would have a gaming table and, next to it, a woman with a long cigarette holder, her evening dress split to the hip; in the background, a Chinese man smoking opium."[17] Here we find all the clichés about Macau: the temptation of gambling, drugs, and prostitution. By beginning his description with stereotypes that recall Karl May's *Der blaurote Methusalem* (The Blue-Red Methuselah, 1892), Loetscher indicates that his goal is to go beyond the classical image of Macau as one enormous gambling scene.

This goal becomes apparent in the "arrival story" of the first-person narrator chosen by Loetscher. Just as the author himself had to overcome the temptation of reducing Macau to its stereotypes, the narrator has to overcome a series of difficulties upon his arrival in the Chinese city. The difficulties begin at the hotel that is not used to customers willing to stay for several weeks. Generally, visitors come from Hong Kong and stay for only one night. For them, Macau is just a day trip. As all major hotels have their own casino and are frequented by visitors squandering their money on slot machines and roulette, they are reluctant to accept visitors for a long period unless the total bill is paid up front. Another difficulty is that life in Macau seems to be all about gambling: *Black Jack, Keno, Dai Siu, Fan-Tan*. The protagonist seems completely lost in this world of passionate gamblers. Eating also turns out to be a challenge. Unlike in Hong Kong, where the narrator's English sufficed, Macau turns out to be much more "Chinese." As he does not know the local language, he feels lost when he ventures outside the touristic areas: "As soon as one goes to a restaurant in a side street, one is greeted only with a smile, and it doesn't help to tap with one's finger on the fourth line because what one assumed to be a menu turns out to be a calendar, so that for dinner one happened to order the fourth of June."[18]

Beginning to describe an encounter with a foreign culture by displaying one's own weaknesses and frustrations is a strategy commonly used by ethnographers. Such a detailed description of initial difficulties is not an innocent affair that simply serves to entertain the reader. It represents a narrative strategy with the ultimate goal of establishing a "pact of trust" with the reader. "Arrival scenes" generally introduce the reader to a clumsy protagonist, whose vision of the Other is still marked by stereotypes, who seems totally helpless and who makes painful mistakes when confronted with obstacles. All this gives the reader the impression that the entire project will result in a catastrophe. Yet instead of surrendering, the "brave" protagonist stubbornly continues his endeavor until, eventually, the infantile anti-hero transforms into a convincing hero, who is henceforth trusted by the reader. "Arrival stories" therefore reflect the awareness that in order to become a convincing I-witness, the author first has to create a convincing first-person narrator. Only by making himself a trustworthy narrator can the author make his text trustworthy.

In order to build such a "pact of trust" with the reader, Loetscher highlights the protagonist's expertise in Portuguese colonial history. He even introduces him as "one of them": "Macau as the last station of a journey—this was a logical choice from a Portuguese perspective. Here they settled, in the Delta of Canton at the Pearl River, after they had built strongholds in Goa, Malacca and on the Spice Islands. Macau, the first European settlement in the Far East. Today, Portugal's last colony in Asia. For over four hundred years, the Portuguese had stayed. Therefore, a freshwater-Portuguese like me should have a chance to stay a little longer."[19] The perseverance of the first-person narrator pays off because, unlike the tourists who do not go beyond the stereotypes, he is able to find a "key" which allows him to enter the "real" Macau: "One should love Macau on Mondays, then Macau starts to enjoy one's presence…. When modern, everyday life dominates, one suddenly hears the sounds of its colonial history."[20]

Using Macau's colonial history as a key to enter the city, the protagonist moves out of the world of gambling into the busy street life. Loetscher uses the trope of "catastrophe" as a means to guide the reader from the inside world with its casinos to the outside world with its colonial history. From the "catastrophes" caused by lack of fortune at the roulette table, he switches to the famous 1835 "catastrophe" when a typhoon destroyed Macau's landmark: St. Paul's Cathedral, a hybrid Asian-European building erected by European Jesuits and Japanese Christian refugees.

268 ~: Jeroen Dewulf

From the cathedral, Loetscher takes his readers into the busy streets, where he identifies what singles out Macau: the city's hybrid character as reflected in its gastronomy and architecture: "Chinese plaster and Portuguese tiles, Iberian balconies with Moorish influences, Chinese temples and Our Lady of Fatima, Pagodas and Western fireplaces."[21] Loetscher connects this visual description to Macau's famous tradition of religious tolerance, which allowed Portuguese, Chinese, and (mixed Portuguese-Chinese) Macanese to live peacefully side by side: "In the calendar, the Christian New Year is followed by the Chinese, the Lantern Festival is followed by the Holy Week, and Easter and the Qing-ming Festival, the Chinese version of All Souls' Day, exist harmoniously side-by-side."[22]

Clearly influenced by the work of the Brazilian sociologist Gilberto Freyre,[23] Loetscher highlights the Portuguese propensity to hybridity, both from a cultural and a sexual perspective: "The first Portuguese who received official authorization to settle did not come directly from Lisbon. They had made stops in Goa and Malacca. From there, they brought their wives, and from there they also imported other women. ... Sexuality plays an important role in Portuguese colonial history, and it rejects Rudyard Kipling's saying that the East and the West shall never meet—for the Portuguese, the East and the West did meet, because of their vitality if nothing else."[24] Here we encounter a controversial element in Loetscher's method of approaching Otherness. While the focus on sexuality has indeed been recognized in recent years as a central element in understanding colonial rule,[25] Loetscher's descriptions of "Portuguese vitality" in the colonies sometimes come dangerously close to the sugarcoated vision of Portugal's colonial policy one can find in the rhetoric used by former dictator António de Oliveira Salazar (1889–1970). This quotation is but an example of how Loetscher's focus on hybridity occasionally underestimates the oppressive side of colonialism.

Although a certain naivety in Loetscher's descriptions of the colonial encounter cannot be denied, his profound knowledge of Lusophone literature taught him that one cannot study Portugal's *descobrimentos* (discoveries) without studying its *conquistas* (conquests). His critical awareness of colonialism's "open wound" is reflected in his exposition on the drama of the *Verdingmädchen*, the Asian girls who were sold by their families in order to work as prostitutes, a practice that flourished in colonial Macau and that found its neocolonial continuation in the Asian sex industry.[26]

Loetscher also recognizes that Macau's tolerance was essentially a matter of circumstance. Unlike in their Indian stronghold Goa, where the Portuguese colonizers acquired enough power to achieve total control, the survival of the Portuguese settlement in Macau required constant negotiations with the Chinese authorities. Attempts to implement the inquisition in Macau did not fail because the Portuguese were more tolerant there than in Goa, but because they never had enough power to impose it. Loetscher concludes that the absence of Catholic orthodoxy in Macau was not at all the result of a Portuguese propensity for tolerance, but rather of local power relations: "The Chinese did not allow 'pagan' temples to be destroyed or Buddhist processions prohibited. The inquisition that played such an important and destructive role in Goa could not be implemented here."[27]

This ambivalence of Portuguese governance in Macau, with its mixture of Eurocentric arrogance and pragmatic resignation to the Chinese authorities, is captured by Loetscher in the word *arrangieren*. He uses the verb to describe a flexible, chameleonic way of life, marked by a talent to adapt constantly to the changing opportunities provided by an in-between existence. According to Loetscher, it is precisely this "in-betweenness" that makes Macau such a unique place in Asia: Macau flourished because the Portuguese functioned as intermediaries in the Chinese trade with Japan, which was officially prohibited. It survived for centuries as a Portuguese colony because it constantly reinvented itself, switching its focus from the "gold business" to the "opium business" and from the "coolie business" to the "gambling business," always taking advantage of its in-between status. In order to capture this opportunistic spirit, Loetscher highlights how Macau was a place where the same foundries produced both church bells and canons: "An attitude of adaptability is inherent in the Macanese identity … the same people in Macau could produce both what brings death and what ushers in resurrection."[28]

The Eyes of the Mandarin

Loetscher wrote several other essays and travel reports on East Asia. With his focus on hybridity, he anticipated topics that have only in recent years become prominent in research, one example being Chinese identity in the diaspora in essays such as "Chinesisches Straßentheater in Singapur" (Chinese Street Theater in Singapore, 1976) and "Malakka verteidigt sein chinesisches Erbe" (Malacca Defends Its Chinese Heritage, 1985).[29]

East Asia also played a major role in Loetscher's fictional work, most notably in his novel *The Eyes of the Mandarin*. The novel was conceived as a rebuttal of Francis Fukuyama's prediction in *The End of History and the Last Man* (1992) that the end of the Cold War represented "the end of history as such … the end point of mankind's ideological evolution and the universalization of Western liberal democracy as the final form of human government."[30] In 1983, Loetscher had claimed that globalization marked the beginning of a new era of world history, which necessitated the development of a better notion of global citizenship based on a global consciousness.[31] This idea formed the departure point of *The Eyes of the Mandarin*, a work that recalls Pierre Teilhard de Chardin's theory of evolution in *Le phénomène humain* (The Phenomenon of Man, 1955) on the confluence of various culturally particular tributaries in an "Omega Point," a supreme form of consciousness, where "the concentration of a conscious universe will reassemble in itself all consciousnesses as well as all that we are conscious of."[32]

Loetscher's argument for the development of a global consciousness was based on the awareness that humans, independent of each other, have adopted similar habits in different places and in different times. He intended to use these "human commonalities" as a basis to develop a global consciousness. This approach to Otherness corresponded to Claude Lévi-Strauss's description of "deep structures" in *Anthropologie structurale* (Structural Anthropology, 1958).[33] Contrary to structuralism, however, Loetscher's goal was not to construct objective grids of culturally neutral categories. Instead of imposing an artificial harmony, he had the ambition to develop a global consciousness while preserving cultural heterogeneity. As such, Loetscher's project of combining cultural diversity with the elaboration of a universal morality can be considered an attempt to overcome the concern expressed by the anthropologists George Marcus and Michael Fischer, who argued that, due to its insistence on fundamental respect for cultural differences among human societies, the cultural relativist turn in the humanities paralyzed all schemes of generalization.[34]

In order to express these ideas in literature, Loetscher experimented with a writing process of connective thoughts, a "global stream of consciousness" that is reminiscent of the "recurring patterns" in the work of Michael Bakhtin, whereby a phenomenon that is assumed to be typical for a specific culture or a specific historical period is connected to different cultures and different historical epochs so that it becomes a transnational and/or transhistorical phenomenon.[35] These patterns reflect basic human necessities, anxieties, weaknesses, or desires such as greed, lust, friendship, love, ambition, etc. A typical example is the diversity in cultural patterns that developed out of the common human need for food. Loetscher, well known for his interest in gastronomy,[36] begins by illustrating how globalization is affecting our eating habits: "Shall we go to a Greek restaurant? … Isn't there a new Indian restaurant somewhere? … If buffet, why not go to a Thai restaurant? … I have heard great things about Lebanese food.… If we want shrimp, we could have Spanish tapas, offered in small and big bowls. This is also offered by the Chinese *Lotus* Restaurant."[37] Here we find an example of the banality of globalization. Loetscher realizes that the celebration of hybridity is at risk of degenerating into a fashionable, commercialized attitude toward diversity, where the most exotic forms of difference are exhibited as a way to boast. He writes against this "cosmo chic" trend with biting irony: "Have you ever tried wasp soup? A boiled wasps' nest followed by roasted wasps at the campfire? Certainly as tasty as cicadas, especially the wingless ones, collected at night by the Cherokees."[38]

Loetscher presents such an elitist approach to globalization as an absurd cul-de-sac. Past, the seventy-year-old Swiss protagonist in *The Eyes of the Mandarin*, suggests an alternative approach to the gastronomic wealth of a globalized world. Rather than emptily celebrating exoticism, he enjoys collecting commonalities. Past detects such "recurrent patterns" in different forms and shapes in the history of mankind: from the burning of candles in religious services, the invention of creation stories, and the greed for gold to the field of gastronomy, where he compares Alsatian sauerkraut with Korean kimchi.

Past considers these patterns useful tools to prepare humanity for life in a truly global society. In such a society, people will need to develop answers acceptable to everyone for global human necessities. The era of Eurocentrism, when the West used its power to impose its vision on the rest of the world, is over and the time has come for humanity to develop new standards according to global moral guidelines. He realizes that this ambition cannot be achieved from just one perspective and, therefore, concludes his reflection on global gastronomy with the wish for a partner in dialogue.

This partner turns out to be a Chinese Mandarin who is mentioned in a sixteenth-century Portuguese diary and who surprised his visitors from Europe with the question of whether people with blue eyes were able to see. Using the famous relationship between the Chinese Shunzhi Emperor of the Qing Dynasty and the German Jesuit Johann Adam Schall von Bell as a model, Loetscher introduces his Mandarin as a friend of the (fictitious) Swiss Jesuit Hans In Gassen. His familiarity with Swiss culture and his fluency in German prove helpful when the Mandarin miraculously reawakens in late-twentieth-century Zurich, at Past's house.

Loetscher's decision to opt for dialogue corresponds to a recent phenomenon in anthropology, where scholars such as Kevin Dwyer, Margorie Shostak, and Vincent Crapazano decided to revive a tradition that was popular during the Enlightenment. However, their partner in dialogue is no longer a fictitious foreigner but a real person. Loetscher's *The Eyes of the Mandarin* can be seen as standing in the tradition of Charles de Montesquieu's *Lettres persanes* (Persian Letters, 1721).[39] The main problem with such a fictitious dialogue structure is that the Other does not speak for him or herself, but is spoken for. In the case of *The Eyes of the Mandarin*, one does not find a real dialogue between a European and a Chinese interlocutor; rather, the non-European voice is a European construct. Once again we detect in Loetscher's approach the paradox of trying to overcome Eurocentrism by using a method that has profoundly Eurocentric roots. In order to reduce this Eurocentric bias, however, Loetscher relied on Chinese sources. The voice of his fictitious Chinese interlocutor consists almost entirely of quotes taken from Chinese literature and philosophy.[40] Similar to his novel on the Brazilian Northeast, *Wunderwelt* (1979), Loetscher's eclectic use of local literature, history books, and ethnographic studies reflects his ambition to provide the (fictitious) Other with a proper voice.[41] In his attempt to develop an acceptable form of speaking for the Other, Loetscher realized the importance of listening to the Other's voice. He expresses this realization metaphorically as the desire to construct a literary language that not only has a voice, but also has ears.[42]

The dialogue between Past and the Mandarin mainly consists of a game in which both characters complement each other's views on humanity on the basis of thoughts from Western and Eastern traditions. The Mandarin compares, for instance, Past's Pandora's Box with the Taoist Chaos Box and the legend of Hun-Tun, and when hearing the saying "everything flows," Past thinks of Heraclitus, whereas the Mandarin quotes Confucius.[43]

The Mandarin comes from an era in Chinese history which he describes as "the Period of Chaos," and Past also calls his era "the Century of Chaos." They do not perceive the notion of "chaos" as negative, however, but rather consider extreme heterogeneity the ideal basis for a new beginning. Both men study each other's culture for possible responses to this chaotic complexity. With reference to the classical Chinese novel *Journey to the West*, the Mandarin and Past come to the conclusion that they reach deeper insights when they, instead of considering East and West as opposites, view them as complementary: "In search of holy texts, we travel to the East, and there we find the monkey who had travelled to the West. Perhaps, in the end, all those who are searching for holy texts will meet at the same place, independent of the direction of their journey."[44]

Similar to Adam Schall von Bell, who modified the Chinese calendar, Past has the ambition to make a new calendar for a truly globalized world. Building on the experience that different cultures, all over the world, developed traditions to celebrate "a new beginning" and realizing that these celebrations are all characterized by the intent to do things better, he suggests the introduction of a "cyclical New Year" as a way to promote global understanding:

> On New Year's Day, one is always full of good resolutions, but a couple of weeks later they are all broken and one must wait months until at the next New Year new resolutions can be made. This would be different, if only three or four weeks after the first of January one could make new resolutions at the Chinese New Year and if one had to wait only until the Buddhist New Year to refresh those resolutions one had broken in the meantime—yes, the good resolutions one had made at the Muslim New Year and did not keep, could be renewed at the Jewish New Year, and, after breaking those good resolutions, one would only have to wait until the first of January.[45]

This idea is picked up by the Mandarin, who links it to the important role of the dragon during Chinese New Year celebrations, which reminds Past of the game *Shanghai* he learned to play in Macau. The Mandarin enlightens him as to the game's meaning. *Shanghai* is a game where the North, South, West, and

East are "in chaos." The objective of the game is to create a new order, which is announced by the dragon. The game then serves as a metaphor for a truly globalized reality of cultural simultaneity, a world without a center and without a cultural hierarchy.

Past links the message of the game to his vision of the twenty-first century and to a need for new moral standards in a globalized world, where people with different values share the same social space: "A world where no one has to suffer because of something he or she is not responsible for, where no one is discriminated against because of race, gender, physical limitations, or the social conditions of his or her family, where one is accountable only for things one is responsible for, but without any reservations."[46] Such a vision, however, requires a fresh start and hence the need to leave much of the old ideas and concepts behind in order to make space for a new beginning. In an ironic reference to Mao's famous appeal to "weed through *the old* to bring forth *the new*," Past concludes with the suggestion that the fireworks at the end of the century should be a gigantic festival of deletion.[47]

What remains at the end of the dialogue are doubts about the way humans will behave once the world has become truly globalized. These doubts find reflection in the symbol on Past's notebook: an Apple, the symbol of knowledge, but with a bite taken out of it. Past uses the popular German-Swiss expression *nicht drauskommen*, not to grasp it, to vent his frustration about a machine that provides so much knowledge yet no clear answers as to how the future will be. Past and the Mandarin are united in admitting that even when combining all the wisdom of East and West, no final answers can be provided, except perhaps the awareness that a world without hierarchy and borders will not be able to function properly without the willingness to display the necessary cultural flexibility to avoid collisions: "Past crossed his arms over his chest, made a *kowtow*, and shook his head: 'What a pleasure speaking to someone who also doesn't grasp it.' The Mandarin stood up, bowed, and also shook his head, and both men carefully avoided hitting each other with their heads."[48]

Conclusion

While Loetscher, who was fluent in both Spanish and Portuguese, became an expert on Latin American culture and literature, his knowledge of Asian cultures remained far more limited. Realizing that he had no other choice but to accept this limitation, he replaced his original ambition also to become an expert on a series of Asian cultures with the ambition to write about the complex plurality of cultures on this planet: "Whether the discoveries turned me into an expert or analphabet, what always struck me was … the immense creativity of man in being human."[49]

In this context, Loetscher developed the desire to contribute to the elaboration of a global consciousness through which the celebration of cultural difference and the preservation of ongoing cultural transformation could be secured. His fluid perspective on cultural difference is marked by a strong sense of mobility, both in a physical and an intellectual sense: "Only those who stay at home know what the world looks like. People who only read one book know the truth; those who read more than one book ... know that the truth has a bibliography."[50]

Loetscher's description of a meeting between East and West in *The Eyes of the Mandarin* is characterized by an eclectic use of Chinese literature, philosophy, and folklore. Not in an attempt to explain the Chinese "Other" but as a way to broaden our perception of what it means to be human and how a world might look where the notions of black and white, East and West, the Self and the Other have disappeared. This profoundly hybrid novel, in which ideas from European and Chinese philosophy meander in a stream-of-consciousness-like structure, reflects Loetscher's exceptional entry into Chinese culture with Macau as his key.

Loetscher's approach to Otherness, however, is characterized by a paradoxical attempt to overcome Eurocentrism while using a methodology that has its roots in Europe's colonial expansion. His ambitious goal of contributing to the elaboration of a "global consciousness" in which people take the expression "to be born into the world" literally is not free of a Eurocentric bias. With a carefully thought-out rhetorical strategy based on irony, Loetscher manages to reduce, but not to eliminate this shortcoming. His intellectually challenging, courageous, yet admittedly utopian search for a global consciousness combines both the ambitious attempt to embrace the globe and the commonsensical recognition that, in order to do so, human arms are much too short.

Notes

1. Hugo Loetscher, *Der Immune* (Zurich, 1985), 93. All translations are by the author.
2. See Romey Sabalius, "Eine postkoloniale Perspektive. Hugo Loetscher: Brasilien als Beispiel," in *Schriftsteller und "Dritte Welt". Studien zum postkolonialen Blick*, ed. P.M. Lützeler (Tübingen, 1998), 167–181; Jeroen Dewulf, *Hugo Loetscher und die portugiesischsprachige Welt* (Bern, 1999); Paul Michael Lützeler, "Deutschsprachige Literatur über die 'Dritte Welt': Hugo Loetscher im Kontext," in *In alle Richtungen gehen: Reden und Aufsätze über Hugo Loetscher*, ed. Jeroen Dewulf and Rosmarie Zeller (Zurich, 2005), 153–162.
3. Thomas Lange, "China als Metapher. Versuch über das Chinabild des deutschen Romans im 20. Jahrhundert," *Zeitschrift für Kulturaustausch* 3 (1986): 341.
4. Hugo Loetscher, *How Many Languages Does Man Need?* (New York, 1982), 72.
5. See Jeroen Dewulf, "Schreiben als reflexives Verb," *ABP Zeitschrift zur portugiesischsprachigen Welt* 2 (2001): 95–102.

6. Loetscher, *Der Immune*, 415.
7. Hugo Loetscher, "Die mehrsprachigen Kulturen. Ethnologische Perspektiven," in *Wo wir stehen, 30 Beiträge zur Kultur der Moderne*, ed. Martin Meyer (Zurich, 1987), 217–222.
8. Hugo Loetscher, "Vom Bild zur Erzählung," *Tages Anzeiger Magazin*, 3 October 1979.
9. Pierre Bourdieu, *Réponses. Pour une anthropologie réflexive* (Paris, 1992), 52.
10. Beat Mazenauer, "Hugo Loetscher: Der fremde Blick," in *Grenzfall Literatur*, ed. J. Bättig and S. Leimbraber (Freiburg, 1993), 412.
11. Hugo Loetscher, *Vom Erzählen erzählen* (Zurich, 1999), 97.
12. Anil Bhatti, "Für Hugo Loetscher, vom Rande aus geschrieben," in *In alle Richtungen gehen: Reden und Aufsätze über Hugo Loetscher*, ed. Jeroen Dewulf and Rosmarie Zeller (Zurich, 2005), 148.
13. Hugo Loetscher, *Die Augen des Mandarin* (Zurich, 1999), 263.
14. Hugo Loetscher, "Das Entdecken erfinden," in *Brasilien: Entdeckung und Selbstentdeckung*, ed. H. Loetscher (Bern, 1992), 9.
15. Ella Shohat, "Notes on the 'Post-Colonial'," *Social Text* 31/32 (1992): 109.
16. Mary Louise Pratt, "Arts of the Contact Zone," *Profession* 91 (1991): 34.
17. Hugo Loetscher, "Macao oder die portugiesische Fähigkeit, sich zu arrangieren," *Tages-Anzeiger Magazin*, 12 February 1977.
18. Loetscher, "Macao."
19. Loetscher, "Macao."
20. Loetscher, "Macao."
21. Loetscher, "Macao."
22. Loetscher, "Macao."
23. See Hugo Loetscher, "Die epische Soziologie einer Zuckergesellschaft. Zum Werk des brasilianischen Anthropologen Gilberto Freyre," *Tages Anzeiger*, 13 November 1982, 30–32. For more on the importance of Gilberto Freyre in the work of Loetscher, see Dewulf, *Hugo Loetscher und die portugiesischsprachige Welt*, 79–126.
24. Loetscher, "Macao."
25. See Anne McClintock, *Imperial Leather: Race, Gender, and Sexuality in the Colonial Context* (New York, 1995) and Ann Laura Stoler, *Carnal Knowledge and Imperial Power: Race and the Intimate in Colonial Rule* (Berkeley, CA, 2002).
26. Loetscher, "Macao."
27. Loetscher, "Macao."
28. Loetscher, "Macao."
29. Loetscher also contributed in other ways to intercultural contacts between Asia and Switzerland, through photography as director of Switzerland's Photography Association or as head of the cultural program in the city partnership between Zurich and Kunming in China, which led to the construction of the famous Chinese Garden at Lake Zurich. See Hugo Loetscher, "Asiatische Kulturnotizen: Chinesisches Straßentheater in Singapur," *Tages-Anzeiger*, 1 July 1976; "Kunming—unsere Schwester in China," *Neue Zürcher Zeitung*, 20 March 1982; "Malakka verteidigt sein chinesisches Erbe," *Neue Zürcher Zeitung*, 16 March 1985.
30. Francis Fukuyama, *The End of History and the Last Man* (New York, 1992), 1.
31. Hugo Loetscher, "Ein Rückblick auf unser Jahrhundert von einem pazifischen Ufer aus," *Die Weltwoche*, 17 November 1983.
32. Pierre Teilhard de Chardin, *The Phenomenon of Man* (New York, 1961), 261.
33. Claude Lévi-Strauss, *Structural Anthropology* (New York, 1967), 57.

34. George E. Marcus and Michael M.J. Fischer, *Anthropology as Cultural Critique: An Experimental Moment in the Human Sciences* (Chicago, IL, 1996), 32.
35. See Michael Holquist, *Dialogism: Bakhtin and His World* (London; New York, 1990), 112.
36. See Hugo Loetscher, *Kulinaritäten. Ein Briefwechsel über die Kunst und die Kultur der Küche* (Bern, 1976).
37. Loetscher, *Die Augen des Mandarin*, 194.
38. Loetscher, *Die Augen des Mandarin*, 194.
39. The German imitations of Montesquieu's *Lettres persanes* have often brought a Chinese visitor to Europe; from David Fassmann's *Der auf Ordre und Kosten seines Kaisers reisende Chinese* (The Chinese Who Traveled Under Orders and At the Expense of His Emperor, 1721), Friedrich der Große's *Sendbote des Kaisers von China in Europa* (The Messenger of the Chinese Emperor in Europe, 1760) to Herbert Rosendorfer's *Briefe in die chinesische Vergangenheit* (Letters Back to Ancient China, 1983). For more on this topic, see Jeroen Dewulf, "Mit fremdem Blick: *Lettres persanes* in der deutschsprachigen Literatur von 1721 bis heute," *Acta Germanica: German Studies in Africa* 30/31 (2002): 49–58.
40. Loetscher used several Chinese sources, including literature (Liu Xie's *The Literary Mind and the Carving of Dragons*, Wu Cheng'en's *Journey to the West*, and Luo Guanzhong's *Romance of the Three Kingdoms*), mythology (the stories of Zhang Guo Lao, Cao Guojiu, and Zhongli Quan from *The Eight Immortals*, Fu Xi from *Three Sovereigns and Five Emperors*, and *The Broom Lady Sao Ch'ing Niang Niang*), and philosophy (the works of Confucius and Laozi).
41. For a postmodern perspective on Loetscher's eclectic resourcefulness, see Rosmarie Zeller, "Vielsprachigkeit und Verfremdung im Werk Hugo Loetschers," *Schweizer Monatshefte* 12 (1989): 1035–1043 and Jeroen Dewulf, "Transkulturelle Neujahrsgrüße. Globalisierung, Hybridität und Postmoderne im Werk von Hugo Loetscher," in *In alle Richtungen gehen: Reden und Aufsätze über Hugo Loetscher*, ed. Jeroen Dewulf and Rosmarie Zeller (Zurich, 2005), 163–182.
42. Loetscher, *Vom Erzählen erzählen*, 150.
43. Loetscher, *Die Augen des Mandarin*, 343.
44. Loetscher, *Die Augen des Mandarin*, 250.
45. Loetscher, *Die Augen des Mandarin*, 332.
46. Loetscher, *Die Augen des Mandarin*, 356.
47. Loetscher, *Die Augen des Mandarin*, 348.
48. Loetscher, *Die Augen des Mandarin*, 240.
49. Loetscher, *Vom Erzählen erzählen*, 26.
50. Loetscher, *Vom Erzählen erzählen*, 27.

❧ CONTRIBUTORS ❧

Jeroen Dewulf is Associate Professor in the Department of German at the University of California, Berkeley, where he teaches both Dutch Studies and German Studies. He holds a Ph.D. in German Literature from the University of Bern in Switzerland. His research focuses primarily on Swiss-German literature and culture and Postcolonial Studies. He publishes in five languages (English, Dutch, German, Portuguese, and French). In 2010, he was distinguished by the Hellman Family Faculty Fund as one of the "Best of Berkeley Researchers." In 2012, he won the Robert O. Collins Award in African Studies and the UC Berkeley American Cultures Innovation in Teaching Award. His most recent book publications include *In alle Richtungen gehen: Reden und Aufsätze über Hugo Loetscher* (Zurich, 2005), *Brasilien mit Brüchen: Schweizer unter dem Kreuz des Südens* (Zurich, 2007), and *Spirit of Resistance: Dutch Clandestine Literature during the Nazi Occupation* (Rochester, N.Y., 2010).

Gabriele Eichmanns is Associate Teaching Professor of German at Carnegie Mellon University in Pittsburgh. She received her doctorate in the summer of 2008 from the University of Washington in Seattle; her dissertation dealt with the impact globalization had on the German notion of *Heimat* (home) after the fall of the Berlin Wall. Her research includes literature of the twentieth and twenty-first centuries and focuses primarily on travel writing, questions of home and identity, transcultural writers, and pop literature. She has co-edited an anthology on *Heimat* which appeared in 2013, has published on Christian Kracht, Christoph Ransmayr, and Hans-Ulrich Treichel, and is currently working on a textbook on globalization.

Markus Hallensleben is Associate Professor in the Department of Central, Eastern and Northern European Studies and Associate Faculty Member of The Institute for Gender, Race, Sexuality and Social Justice at the University of British Columbia, Vancouver, Canada. He was an adjunct lecturer at the Free University Berlin, a visiting scholar at Nagoya City University, and a DAAD Lecturer at the University of Tokyo. His publications range from nineteenth-century German to contemporary Austrian literature and from performance art to theories of performativity. He has covered authors and artists such as VALIE EXPORT, Stelarc, ORLAN, Hannah Höch, and Else Lasker-Schüler (*Avantgardismus und Kunstinszenierung*, 2000). His current book project investigates body images from twentieth-century European avant-garde movements to twenty-first century bio art performances. His most recent book publication was an edited special volume on *Performative Body Spaces: Corporeal Topographies in Literature, Theatre, Dance, and the Visual Arts* (*Critical Studies* Vol. 33, Amsterdam, 2010).

Ricky W. Law is Assistant Professor of History at Carnegie Mellon University. He received his Ph.D. from the University of North Carolina at Chapel Hill and was the recipient of the 2013 Fritz Stern Dissertation Prize. Currently he is revising his dissertation, "Knowledge Is Power: The Interwar German and Japanese Mass Media in the Making of the Axis," into a book manuscript. It studies the role of opinion makers in leading the public discourse that helped make the alliance imaginable.

Chinyun Lee is Assistant Professor in the Department of History at National Chi Nan University, Taiwan. She earned her M.A. at National Taiwan University and her Ph.D. in the Department of History at the University of Ljubljana, Slovenia. Her primary research interest is international trade between Central Europe, in particular Trieste and Hamburg, and China before World War I.

Weijia Li is Assistant Professor of German at University of Wisconsin–Madison. His research interests focus primarily on German-Chinese cultural encounters reflected in literature, press, and art. His first book, *China und China-Erfahrung in Leben und Werk von Anna Seghers,* was published in 2010. He is currently working on a new book project that examines German and Yiddish writings on China by Central European Jewish refugees in Shanghai between 1939 and 1946.

Erika M. Nelson is Associate Professor at Union College, where she teaches German language, literature, and culture courses. Her doctoral research, completed at the University of Texas at Austin, focused on issues of identity construction and sound in Rainer Maria Rilke's Orphic poetry and was published as a book entitled *Reading Rilke's Orphic Identity.* Her research interests now focus on transnational identity and poetics, modern German spa culture, sound, shamanism, and modern renditions of myths in literature and film. She has published on various poets, visionaries, and filmmakers, including Zafer Şenocak, Andrea Štaka, Dragica Rajčić, Micky Remann, and Doris Dörrie.

Lucie Olivová is Associate Professor in the Department of Asian Studies at Palacký University, Czech Republic. She holds an M.A. in Chinese Literature from the University of California, Berkeley, a Ph.D. in Chinese History from Charles University in Prague, and the title Doctor of Sciences from the Academy of Sciences of the Czech Republic. Her main field of interest is the material culture of late imperial China and the history of Chinese art. She has published widely, mainly in Czech and English. In addition, she translates from classical and modern Chinese literature into Czech. In 2007, she was awarded a prize by the Ministry of Culture of the Czech Republic for a collection of Chinese (Yangzhou) folktales.

Sarah Panzer is a Ph.D. candidate at the University of Chicago in the History Department, focusing on issues of transculturation, romanticism, masculinity, and violence. Her dissertation, "The Prussians of the East: Samurai, Bushido, and Japanese Honor in the German Imagination, 1905–1945," examines the ways in which Japanese martial culture was understood, recontextualized, and appropriated by German civil society during the first half of the twentieth century.

Martin Rosenstock is Assistant Professor of German at Gulf University for Science and Technology in Kuwait. He received his Ph.D. in 2008 from the University of California, Santa Barbara and has held visiting positions at Iowa State University and the University of Connecticut. He is currently working on a book project entitled *Unsolved Cases: Investigations into German-Language Detective Fiction*, in which he considers the portrayal of failed detectives. He has published on the depiction of crime and detective work in German culture and occasionally dabbles in film criticism for popular magazines.

Qinna Shen is currently Visiting Assistant Professor of German at Miami University in Ohio. She received her Ph.D. in German Literature from Yale in 2008 and then went on to teach at Miami University from 2008 to 2011. Between 2011 and 2014, she held a visiting position at Loyola University Maryland. Her research focuses on twentieth- and twenty-first-century German film and literature, folklore, and the recently established field of Asian German Studies. She has published in peer-reviewed journals and edited volumes. Her book, entitled *The Politics of Magic: DEFA Fairy-Tale Films*, is forthcoming with Wayne State University Press.

Cynthia Walk is Associate Professor Emerita of German Literature & Film Studies at the University of California, San Diego. She received her Ph.D. from Yale and taught in the Department of Literature at UCSD from 1972 to 2006. Her research has focused on modern drama, theater, and film with recent publications on intermediality ("The Debate about Stage Tradition in Weimar Cinema: Murnau's *Herr Tartüff*" and "Cross-media Exchange in Weimar Culture: *Von morgens bis mitternachts*") and ethnicity ("Romeo with Sidelocks: Jewish-Gentile Romance in E.A. Dupont's *Das alte Gesetz* (1923) and

Other Early Weimar Assimilation Films") in Weimar Germany. Current work on Anna May Wong includes an article on censorship and the representation of interracial desire in Film Europe in *A New History of German Cinema*.

Valerie Weinstein is Assistant Professor of German Studies at the University of Cincinnati. She has received research fellowships from the DAAD, from Cornell University, where she earned her Ph.D., and from the University of Nevada, Reno, where she served on the faculty previously. She is the author of numerous articles on Weimar and Nazi Cinema and on German precolonial and colonial discourses about the Pacific and Pacific Islanders. She currently is working on a project on anti-Semitism and film comedy in the Third Reich.

❧ BIBLIOGRAPHY ☙

Adam, Petr. *The Fate of Ludmila Löwidtová's Family: The Lost Neighbours from Chotěboř.* Chotěboř: Secondary School of Economic and Higher Professional School, 2006.

"A General Survey of Hairnet Production in North China" 〈中國北部之髮網業概況〉, *Shenbao*《申報》, 10 February 1924, 2–3.

Ahmed, A.G., ed. *Pictorial Chefoo: 1935–1936.* A.G. Ahmed, n.d.

Akira, Iikura. "The 'Yellow Peril' and Its Influence on Japanese-German Relations." In *Japanese-German Relations, 1895–1945: War, Diplomacy and Public Opinion*, edited by Christian W. Spang and Rolf-Harald Wippich, 80–97. London, 2006.

Alaimo, Stacy. *Bodily Natures: Science, Environment, and the Material Self.* Bloomington, I.N., 2010.

Alter, Nora. *Projecting History: German Nonfiction Cinema 1967–2000.* Ann Arbor, M.I., 2002.

Anderson, Benedict. *Imagined Communities: Reflections on the Origin and Spread of Nationalism.* London, 1983.

Anderson, Susan C. "Surface Translations: Meaning and Difference in Yoko Tawada's German Prose." *Seminar: A Journal of Germanic Studies* 46, no. 1 (2010): 50–70.

Anon. Review of *Großstadtschmetterling. Sozialistische Bildung*, May 1929.

Anon. "Im Chinesenviertel." *Tägliche Rundschau*, 23 April 1925.

Anon. Review of *Song. Internationale Filmschau* [Prague]. 25 September 1928.

Arnold, Julean. *China: A Commercial and Industrial Handbook.* Washington D.C., 1926.

Archive of the Institute of Modern History, Academia Sinica, Ministry of Foreign Affairs (北洋政府外交部), 03-18-017-06-002, 14 June 1918.

Asai, Ryôi. *The Minder-Wench (Otogi Bôko).* Translated by Donald M. Richardson. Winchester, V.A., 1993.

Assmann, Aleida. *Erinnerungsräume: Formen und Wandlungen des kulturellen Gedächtnisses*, C.H. Beck Kulturwissenschaft. Munich, 1999. Reprint, 2003.

Aziz+Cucher. "Dystopia." http://www.azizcucher.net/1994.php. Last accessed 30 September 2010.

Bachmann, Ingeborg. *"Todesarten"-Projekt*, edited by Robert Pichl, Monika Albrecht, and Dirk Göttsche. 4 vols. Munich, 1995.

Bakhtin, Mikhail Mikhailovich. *The Dialogic Imagination: Four Essays.* Austin, 1981.

Banerjee, Mita. "Bollywood Meets the Beatles: Towards an Asian German Studies of German Popular Culture," *South East Asian Popular Culture* 4, no. 1 (April, 2006): 19–34.

———. "Ethnizität als Buhfrau der Nation: Über disziplinäre Umwege und die (Un)Möglichkeit ethnischer (Selbst)Artikulation." *In Re/Visionen: Postkoloniale Perspektiven von People of Color auf Rassismus, Kulturpolitik und Widerstand in Deutschland*, edited by Kien Nghi Ha, Nicola Lauré al-Samarai, and Sheila Mysorekar, 289–303. Münster, 2007.

Barnett, Thomas. *Romanian and East German Policies in the Third World: Comparing the Strategies of Ceausescu and Honecker*. Westport, C.T., 1992.

Barthes, Roland. *Camera Lucida: Reflections on Photography*. Translated by Richard Howard. London, 1981.

———. *Empire of Signs*. Translated by Richard Howard. New York, 1982 and 2005.

———. *Image, Music, Text*. Translated by Stephen Heath. New York, 1977.

———. *The Pleasure of the Text*. Translated by Richard Miller. New York, 1989.

Baskett, Michael. *The Attractive Empire: Transnational Film Culture in Imperial Japan*. Honolulu, 2008.

Baudrillard, Jean. *Simulacra and Simulation*. Translated by Sheila Faria Glaser. Ann Arbor, M.I., 1994.

Bazant, Jan, Nina Bazantova, and Frances Starn, eds. *The Czech Reader: History, Culture, and Politics*. Durham, 2010.

Belz, Uwe, dir. *Hallo, wie gehts? Wang Ling in Peking* [Hello, How Are You? Wang Ling in Peking]. TV film. GDR, 1988.

———. *Kaiserkanal China* [The Beijing-Hangzhou Grand Canal], TV film. GDR, 1989.

———. *Ni hao—heißt Guten Tag* [Ni Hao—Means Hello]. TV film. GDR, 1989.

———. *Stromabwärts nach Shanghai* [Downstream to Shanghai]. TV film. GDR, 1987.

Benjamin, Walter. "Gespräch mit Anne [sic] May Wong. Eine Chinoiserie aus dem alten Westen." In *Gesammelte Schriften*, IV, 1, edited by Tillman Rexroth, 523–527. Frankfurt, 1972.

Bennett, Arnold. *"Piccadilly": Story of the Film Illustrated with Scenes from the Photo-Play*. London, 1929.

Benoun, Bernard. "Words and Roots: The Loss of the Familiar in the Works of Yoko Tawada." Translated by Joshua Humphreys. In *Yōko Tawada: Voices from Everywhere*, edited by Doug[las N.] Slaymaker, 125–136. Lanham, M.D., 2007.

Benthien, Claudia. *Skin: On the Cultural Border between Self and the World*, European Perspectives. New York, 2002.

Bergfelder, Tim. "Negotiating Exoticism: Hollywood, Film Europe and the Cultural Reception of Anna May Wong." In *"Film Europe" and "Film America": Cinema, Commerce and Cultural Exchange 1920–1939*, edited by Andrew Higson and Richard Maltby, 302–324. Exeter, 1999.

Beyer, Marcel. "Schatten." In *Nach Japan. Reiselesebuch*, edited by Renate and Peter Giacomuzzi, 9–17. Tübingen, 2005.

———. *Spione*. Frankfurt, 2001.

Bhabha, Homi K. "DissemiNation: Time, Narrative, and the Margins of the Modern Nation." In *Nation and Narration*, edited by Homi K. Bhabha, 291–322. London, 1990.

———. *The Location of Culture*, Routledge Classics. London; New York, 1994.

Bhatti, Anil. "Für Hugo Loetscher, vom Rande aus geschrieben." In *In alle Richtungen gehen: Reden und Aufsätze über Hugo Loetscher*, edited by Jeroen Dewulf and Rosmarie Zeller, 138–152. Zurich, 2005.

Birett, Herbert. *Stummfilm-Musik: Materialsammlung*. Berlin, 1970.

Bloch, Ernst. *Heritage of Our Times* [*Erbschaft dieser Zeit*]. Translated by Neville and Stephen Plaice. Berkeley, 1991.

Board of International Trade, *International Trade Report* 《 *Guoji maoyi qingbao* 國際貿易情報 》, 1936, no. 8, 75.

Bolter, J. David, and Richard A. Grusin. *Remediation: Understanding New Media*. Cambridge, M.A., 1999.

Bordo, Michael D., Alan M. Taylor, and Jeffrey G. Williamson. *Globalization in Historical Perspective*. Chicago, 2005.

Bourdieu, Pierre. *Réponses. Pour une anthropologie réflexive*. Paris, 1992.

Brandlmeier, Thomas. "'Rationalization First.' Deutsche Kameraschule im britischen Film," in *London Calling: Deutsche im britischen Film der dreißiger Jahre*, 69–76. Munich, 1993.

Brandt, Bettina. "The Postcommunist Eye: An Interview with Yoko Tawada.' *World Literature Today: A Literary Quarterly of the University of Oklahoma* 80, no. 1 (2006): 43–45.

———. "The Unknown Character: Traces of the Surreal in Yoko Tawada's Writings." In *Yōko Tawada: Voices from Everywhere*, edited by Doug[las N.] Slaymaker, 111–124. Lanham, M.D., 2007.

Brecht, Bertolt. "Die Maßnahme." *Stücke für das Theater am Schiffbauerdamm*. Zweiter Band. 255–307. Frankfurt, 1962.

British Parliamentary Papers: China. Irish University Press Area Studies Series. Shannon, 1971.

Brook, Timothy. *Vermeer's Hat: the Seventeenth Century and the Dawn of the Global World*. New York, 2008.

Brügmann, Margret. "Jeder Text hat weiße Ränder: Interkulturalität als literarische Herausforderung." In *Postmoderne Literatur in deutscher Sprache: Eine Ästhetik des Widerstands?*, edited by Henk Harbers, 335–351. Amsterdam, 2000.

Brussig, Thomas. "Ich weiß alles über Japan. Ironischer Essay." In *Nach Japan. Reiselesebuch*, edited by Renate and Peter Giacomuzzi, 24–35. Tübingen, 2005.

Bry, Gerhard. *Wages in Germany 1871–1945*. Princeton, 1960.

Bundesarchiv-Filmarchiv. *Wochenschauen und Dokumentarfilme 1895–1950*, edited by Peter Bucher. Findbücher zu Beständen des Bundesarchivs 8. Koblenz: Bundesarchiv, 2000.

Butler, Judith. *Bodies that Matter: On the Discursive Limits of 'Sex'*. New York; London, 1993.

———. "Foucault and the Paradox of Bodily Inscriptions." *The Journal of Philosophy* 86, no. 11 (1989): 601–607.

Campbell, Joseph. *The Hero of a Thousand Faces*. Princeton, 1949.

Campbell, Joseph, and Bill Moyers. *The Power of Myth*. New York, 1988.

Campt, Tina M. *Other Germans: Black Germans and the Politics of Race, Gender and Memory in the Third Reich*. Ann Arbor, M.I., 2004.

Chan, Anthony B. *Perpetually Cool: The Many Lives of Anna May Wong (1905–1961)*. Lanham, M.D., 2007.

Chang, Patty. "Die Ware Liebe/The Product Love." Mary Boone Gallery. New York, 2009.

Chefoo Branch of Maritime Association (航業聯合協會芝罘支部). *Shifu Jijou*. 『芝罘事情』 [*Chefoo News*]. Qingdao, 1939.

China Inspectorate General of Customs. *Imperial Maritime Customs Returns of the Import and Export Trade (Customs Returns)* (Shanghai: Statistical Department of the Inspectorate General of Customs, Jinghua Pub. reprint, 2001). *Decennial Reports*, 1912–21, *Annual Reports*, 1915, 1919, 1929, 1931, 1933, 1936, 1937, 1946, 1947, 1948.

"Chinese Trade in Human Hair and Hair Nets." *Journal of the Royal Society of Arts* 66 (1918): 631–632.

Cho, Joanne Miyang, and David Crowe. *Germany and China: Transcultural, Historical and Political Encounters from the Enlightenment to the Twentieth Century*. New York, 2014. Forthcoming.

Chow, Rey. "How (the) Inscrutable Chinese Led to Globalized Theory." *PMLA* 116, special issue: *Globalizing Literary Studies* 116, no. 1 (Jan. 2001): 69–74.

Cohen, Paul A. *History in Three Keys: The Boxers as Event, Experience, and Myth.* New York, 1997.

Conrad, Joseph. *Heart of Darkness.* New York, 2006.

Courtney, Susan. *Hollywood Fantasies of Miscegenation: Spectacular Narratives of Gender and Race, 1903–1967.* Princeton, 2005.

Culler, Jonathan. *Roland Barthes.* New York, 1983.

Daily Consular and Trade Reports. "German Hair-Net Industry," 1912 II, 1072.

Daily Consular and Trade Reports. "Exports of Human Hair," 1914 I, 1787.

Daily Consular and Trade Reports. "Increasing American Market for Hair Nets," 1914 II, 855–856.

Davies, Douglas. *Anthropology and Theology.* Oxford, U.K., 2002.

———. *Death, Ritual and Belief: The Rhetoric of Funerary Rites.* London, 2002.

Dawson, Nick. "Doris Dörrie, 'Cherry Blossoms.'" *Director Interviews. Filmmaker: The Magazine of Independent Film*, 16 January 2009, http://www.filmmakermagazine.com/news/2009/01/doris-dorrie-cherry-blossoms/. Last accessed 20 June 2011.

Dickinson, Thorold, dir. *Java Head.* Produced by Basil Dean. UK, 1934. Film.

Deleuze, Gilles, and Félix Guattari. *A Thousand Plateaus: Capitalism and Schizophrenia.* Translated by Brian Massumi. Minneapolis, 1987.

De Mille, Cecil B., dir. *The Cheat.* United States, 1915. Film.

Desser, David, ed. *Ozu's Tokyo Story.* Cambridge Film Handbooks. Cambridge, U.K., 1997.

Deulig-Wochenschau [Deulig Audio Newsreel]. Germany, 1920–1939.

Dewulf, Jeroen. *Hugo Loetscher und die portugiesischsprachige Welt.* Bern, 1999.

———. "Mit fremdem Blick: *Lettres persanes* in der deutschsprachigen Literatur von 1721 bis heute." *Acta Germanica: German Studies in Africa* 30/31 (2002): 49–58.

———. "Schreiben als reflexives Verb." *ABP Zeitschrift zur portugiesischsprachigen Welt* 2 (2001): 95–102.

———. "Transkulturelle Neujahrsgrüße. Globalisierung, Hybridität und Postmoderne im Werk von Hugo Loetscher." In *In alle Richtungen gehen: Reden und Aufsätze über Hugo Loetscher,* edited by Jeroen Dewulf and Rosmarie Zeller, 163–182. Zürich, 2005.

Dillon, Sarah. *The Palimpsest: Literature, Criticism, Theory.* Continuum Literary Studies. London, 2007.

———. "Reinscribing De Quincey's Palimpsest: The Significance of the Palimpsest in Contemporary Literary and Cultural Studies." *Textual Practice* 3 (2005), http://www.informaworld.com/10.1080/09502360500196227. Last accessed 11 June 2010.

Döblin, Alfred. *Die drei Sprünge des Wang-Lun.* Berlin, 1920.

Dörrie, Doris. *Cherry Blossoms: A Film by Doris Dörrie,* Presskit, http://www.metropolefilms.com/data/ftp/Cherry%20Blossoms/DP_Cherry%20Blossoms_fr_Metro.pdf, 4. Last accessed 20 June 2011.

———. *Liebe, Schmerz und das ganze verdammte Zeug. Vier Geschichten.* Zurich, 1989.

———. *Love, Pain and the Whole Damn Thing.* New York, 1989.

Dörrie, Doris, dir. *Bin ich schön?* [Am I Beautiful?]. 1998. Film.

———. *Der Fischer und seine Frau—Warum Frauen nie genug bekommen* [The Fisherman and His Wife—Why Women Never Get Enough]. 2005. Film.

———. *Die Friseuse* [The Hairdresser]. 2010. Film.

———. *Geld* [Money]. 1989. Film.

———. *Happy Birthday, Türke!* [Happy Birthday!]. 1992. Film.

————. *Ich und er* [Me and Him]. 1988. Film.

————. *Im Innern des Wals* [Inside the Belly of the Whale]. 1984. Film.

————. *Keiner liebt mich* [Nobody Loves Me]. 1994. Film.

————. *Kirschblüten/Hanami* [Cherry Blossoms/Hanami]. Germany, 2008. Film.

————. *Männer* [Men]. 1985. Film.

————. *Mitten ins Herz* [Straight through the Heart]. 1983. Film.

————. *Nackt* [Naked]. 2002. Film.

————. *Paradies* [Paradise]. 1986. Film.

————. *Paula aus Portugal* [Paula from Portugal]. 1979. Film.

————. *Von Romantik keine Spur* [Not a Trace of Romanticism]. 1980. Film.

————. *Wie man sein Leben kocht* [How to Cook Your Life]. 2007. Film.

Dörrie, Doris, and Julia Kaergel. *Lotte will Prinzessin sein.* Ravensburg, 1998.

Drechsler, Karl. *Deutschland-China-Japan 1933–1939: Das Dilemma der deutschen Fernost-politik.* East Berlin, 1964.

Dupont, E.A. "'Piccadilly': Adaptation and Scenario." Berlin, Nachlassarchiv, Stiftung Deutsche Kinemathek (typescript in German). London, British Film Institute (English translation).

Dupont, E.A., dir. *Piccadilly.* U.K., 1929. Film.

Eglinger, Hanna. *Der Körper als Palimpsest: Die Poetologische Dimension des menschlichen Körpers in der skandinavischen Literatur der Gegenwart.* Freiburg, 2007.

Eichberg, Richard, dir. *Hai-Tang* [The Flame of Love]. Germany, 1930. Film.

————. *Großstadtschmetterling* [Pavement Butterfly]. Germany, 1929. Film.

————. *Song* [Show Life]. Germany, 1928. Film.

"Eine Reise nach China: Das Außerordentliche an dem Yukong-Film von Joris Ivens und Marceline Loridan," *Frankfurter Rundschau,* 7 September 1976.

Emelka/Bavaria-Wochenschau [Emelka/Bavaria Audio Newsreel]. Germany, 1919–1932.

Encke, Julia. *Augenblicke der Gefahr: Der Krieg und die Sinne. 1914–1934.* Munich, 2006.

Endo, Tadashi. "The Official Website of Tadashi Endo–Butoh–MA," http://www.butoh-ma.de/index.php?option=com_content&task=view&id=2& Itemid=5. Last accessed 4 January 2013.

Enzensberger, Hans-Magnus. *Einzelheiten I. Bewusstseins-Industrie.* Frankfurt, 1979.

Esherick, Joseph W. *The Origins of the Boxer Uprising.* Berkeley, 1987.

Esselborn, Karl. "'Übersetzungen aus der Sprache, die es nicht gibt.' Interkulturalität, Globalisierung und Postmoderne in den Texten Yoko Tawadas." *Arcadia,* no. 2 (2007): 240–262.

Export, Valie. "Identitätstransfer B/Identitätstransfer I." *Identity Transfer,* Barbara Gross Gallery, Munich, 1972/73. http://www.artnet.com/artist/26012/valie-export.html. Last accessed 5 January 2013.

Fachinger, Petra. *Rewriting Germany from the Margins: "Other" German Literature of the 1980s and 1990s.* Montreal, Q.C., 2001.

Fanck, Arnold. *Er führte Regie mit Gletschern, Sturmen und Lawinen. Ein Filmpionier erzählt.* Munich, 1973.

Fanck, Arnold, dir. *Der ewige Traum* [The Eternal Dream]. Germany, 1934. Film.

————. *Der heilige Berg* [The Holy Mountain]. UFA, 1925/26. Film.

————. *Die Tochter des Samurai* [The Samurai's Daughter]. Berlin/West and Tokio, 1937. Film.

————. *Ein Robinson: das Tagebuch eines Matrosen* [A Robinson: The Diary of a Sailor]. Germany, 1939/40. Film.

————. *S.O.S. Eisberg* [S.O.S. Iceberg]. Germany/United States, 1933. Film.

————. *Stürme über dem Mont Blanc* [Storms over Mont Blanc]. Germany, 1930. Film.

Fanck, Arnold, and G.W. Pabst, dirs. *Die weiße Hölle vom Piz Palü* [The White Hell of Piz Palü]. Germany, 1929. Film.

Fanck, Matthias. *Weisse Hölle—Weisser Rausch. Arnold Fanck: Bergfilme und Bergbilder 1909–1939.* Zurich, 2009.

Fayle, C. Ernest. *A Short History of the World's Shipping Industry.* London, 1933, reprinted in 2006.

Felber, Roland, and Ralf Hübner. "Chinesische Demokraten und Revolutionäre in Berlin (1925–1933)." In *Wissenschaftliche Zeitschrift der Humboldt-Universität zu Berlin. Reihe Gesellschaftswissenschaft,* 37.2 (1988): 157–172.

Filme aus Japan: Retrospektive des japanischen Films 12 September–12 December 1993. Berlin, 1993.

Fischer, Lucy. *Designing Women: Cinema, Art Deco, and the Female Form.* New York, 2003.

Fischer, Sabine. "*Wie der Schlamm in einem Sumpf*: Ich-Metamorphosen in Yoko Tawadas Kurzroman *Das Bad.*" In *Interkulturelle Konfigurationen: Zur deutschsprachigen Erzählliteratur von Autoren nichtdeutscher Herkunft,* edited by Mary Howard, 63–76. Munich, 1997.

Fischer-Lichte, Erika. *The Transformative Power of Performance: A New Aesthetics.* Translated by Saskya Iris Jain. London; New York, 2008.

Fischer-Lichte, Erika, and Christoph Wulf. "Vorwort." In *Theorien des Performativen,* edited by Erika Fischer-Lichte and Christoph Wulf, 9. Berlin, 2001.

Fleming, Peter. *The Siege at Peking.* New York, 1959.

Forbes, Camille F. *Introducing Bert Williams: Burnt Cork, Broadway, and the Story of America's First Black Star.* New York, 2008.

Forman, Ross G. "Peking Plots: Fictionalizing the Boxer Rebellion." *Victorian Literature and Culture* 27, no. 1 (Spring 1999): 19–48.

Foucault, Michel. "Nietzsche, Genealogy, History." Translated by Donald F. Bouchard and Sherry Simon. *Language, Counter-Memory, Practice: Selected Essays and Interviews,* edited by Donald F. Bouchard, 139–164. Ithaca, 1977.

Fox Tönende Wochenschau [Fox Audio Newsreel]. Germany, 1935–1985.

Fraleigh, Sondra. *Butoh: Metamorphic Dance and Global Alchemy.* Champaign, I.L., 2010.

————. *Dancing Into Darkness: Butoh, Zen, and Japan.* Pittsburgh, P.A., 1999.

Fraleigh, Sondra, and Tamah Nakamura. *Hijikata Tatsumi and Ohno Kazuo.* London, 2006.

Franklin, Chester M. *Toll of the Sea.* United States, 1922. Film.

Franklin D. Roosevelt Presidential Library & Museum. "Two sisters who left the farm to keep our airmen flying. NYA trainees at the Corpus Christi, Texas, Naval Air Base." http://www.fdrlibrary.marist.edu/archives/collections/franklin/?p=digitallibrary/digitalcontent&id=38101942. Last accessed 23 July 2009. Still photograph.

Freidank, Cornelia, and Günther Krause. *Die Japaner und die Deutschen. Geschichte einer Wahlverwandtschaft.* Tokyo, 1994.

Freud, Sigmund. "Notiz über den 'Wunderblock'." In *Studienausgabe,* vol. 3, edited by Alexander Mitscherlich, 363–369. Frankfurt, 1989.

Fuechtner, Veronika, and Mary Rhiel, eds. *Imagining Germany Imagining Asia: Essays in Asian-German Studies.* Rochester, N.Y., 2013.

Fukuyama, Francis. *The End of History and the Last Man.* New York, 1992.

Ganeva, Mila. *Women in Weimar Fashion: Discourses and Displays in German Culture, 1918–1933.* Rochester, N.Y., 2008.

Gebhard, Walter, ed. *Ostasienrezeption im Schatten der Weltkriege: Universalismus und Na-tionalismus*. Munich, 2003.

Gelzer, Florian. "Sprachkritik bei Yoko Tawada." *Waseda Blätter* 7 (2000): 73–101.

———. "'Worte von Gedanken trennen': Schreibweisen und Sprachprogrammatik bei Yoko Tawada." Lizenziatsarbeit, University Basel, 1998.

Genette, Gérard. *Palimpsests: Literature in the Second Degree*. Translated by Channa Newman and Claude Doubinsky. Lincoln, N.E., 1997.

———. "The Obverse of Signs." In *Critical Essays on Roland Barthes*, edited by Diana Knight, 59–71. New York, 2000.

Gerhard-Sonnenberg, Gabriele. *Marxistische Arbeiterbildung in der Weimarer Zeit (MASCH)*. Cologne, 1976.

Gerstenberger, Katharina. "Writing by Ethnic Minorities in the Age of Globalisation." In *German Literature in the Age of Globalisation*, edited by Stuart Taberner, Studies in German Literature, Linguistics, and Culture, 209–228. Birmingham, 2004.

Goebel, Rolf J. "Japan as Western Text: Roland Barthes, Richard Gordon Smith, and Lafcadio Hearn." *Comparative Literature Studies* 30, no. 2 (1993): 188–205.

Göktürk, Deniz, and Barbara Wolbert, eds. "Introduction." *New German Critique*, no. 92.

Gollwitzer, Heinz. *Die gelbe Gefahr: Geschichte eines Schlagworts*. Göttingen, 1962.

Good, David F. *The Economic Rise of the Habsburg Empire, 1750–1914*. Berkeley, 1984.

———. "Modern Economic Growth in the Habsburg Monarchy." In *Economic Development in the Habsburg Monarchy and in the Successor States Essays*, edited by John Komlos, 201–220. New York, 1990.

Gray, William Glenn. *Germany's Cold War: The Global Campaign to Isolate East Germany, 1949–1969*. Chapel Hill and London, 2003.

Green, Thomas A. *Asian American Folktales*, Stories from the American Mosaic. Westport, C.T., 2009.

Griffith, D.W., dir. *Birth of a Nation*. United States, 1915. Film.

———. *Broken Blossoms*. United States, 1919. Film.

Guenther, Irene. *Nazi Chic? Fashioning Women in the Third Reich*. Oxford, U.K., 2004.

Gunn, Giles. "Introduction: Globalizing Literary Studies," *PMLA* 116, no. 1 (January 2001): 16–31.

Haasch, Günther, ed. *Die Deutsch-Japanischen Gesellschaften von 1888 bis 1996*. Berlin, 1996.

Hake, Sabine. *German National Cinema*. New York, 2002.

Hallensleben, Markus, and Jens Hauser. "Performing the Transfacial Body: Orlan's *Manteau D'arléquin*." In *Orlan: A Hybrid Body of Artworks*, edited by ORLAN, Simon Donger and Simon Shepherd, 138–154. London; New York, 2010.

Han, Byun-Chul. *Hyperkulturalität: Kultur und Globalisierung*. Berlin, 2002.

Han, Sen. *Ein Chinese mit dem Kontrabass*. Munich, 2001.

Hanlon, Dennis. "Die Windrose." *DEFA Film Library Newsletter* (January 2012).

Hansen, Janine. *Arnold Fancks Die Tochter des Samurai: Nationalsozialistische Filmpropaganda und Japanische Filmpolitik*. Wiesbaden, 1997.

———. "Celluloid Competition: German-Japanese Film Relations, 1929–1945." In *Cinema and the Swastika: The International Expansion of Third Reich Cinema*, edited by Roel Vande Winkel and David Welch, 187–197. New York, 2007.

Hardt, Michael, and Antonio Negri. *Empire*. Cambridge, M.A., 2000.

Harnisch, Thomas. *Chinesische Studenten in Deutschland. Geschichte und Wirkung ihrer Studienaufenthalte in den Jahren von 1860 bis 1945*. Hamburg, 1999.

Harootunian, Harry. *Overcome by Modernity: History, Culture, and Community in Interwar Japan.* Princeton, 2000.

Hayashima, Akira. *Die Illusion des Sonderfriedens: deutsche Verständigungspolitik mit Japan im Ersten Weltkrieg.* Munich, 1982.

Hayot, Eric. *The Hypothetical Mandarin: Sympathy, Modernity, and Chinese Pain.* Oxford, U.K., 2009.

Hearn, Lafcadio. *Kwaidan: Stories and Studies of Strange Things.* Champaign, I.L.; Boulder, C.O., 1904.

Heidemann, Britta. "Japan: Die Faszination des Fremden." *Der Westen.* 13 June 2009, http://www.derwesten.de/kultur/literatur/Japan-Die-Faszination-des-Fremden-id3 86850.html. Last accessed 26 December 2013.

Heimann, Thomas. "Von Stahl und Menschen: 1953 bis 1960." In *Schwarzweiß und Farbe: DEFA Dokumentarfilme, 1946–92.* 49–90. Berlin, 1996.

Herder, Johann Gottfried. *Ideen zur Philosophie der Geschichte der Menschheit.* Darmstadt, 1966.

Hermand, Jost. "Unvorhersehbare Folgen: Die drei Eislers und Brechts 'Maßnahme'." *Brecht Jahrbuch* 30 (2005): 363–379.

Hermann-Neisse, Max. "Braunes und weisses Parodietheater." Cited in Tobias Nagl, *Die unheimliche Maschine. Rasse und Repräsentation im Weimarer Kino.* Munich, 2009. 657.

Heuberger, Edmund, *Die Sonne Asiens* [The Asian Sun]. Germany, 1921. Film.

High, Peter B. *The Imperial Screen: Japanese Film Culture in the Fifteen Years' War, 1931–1945.* Madison, 2003.

Hobsbawm, Eric. *The Age of Extremes: The Short Twentieth Century, 1914–1991.* London, 1994.

Hodges, Graham Russell Geo. *Anna May Wong: From Laundryman's Daughter to Hollywood Legend.* New York, 2004.

Holquist, Michael. *Dialogism: Bakhtin and his world.* London; New York, 1990.

Hong, Young-Sun. "The Benefits of Health Must Spread Among All: International Solidarity, Health, and Race in the East German Encounter with the Third World." In *Socialist Modern,* edited by Katherine Pence and Paul Betts, 183–205. Ann Arbor, M.I., 2008.

Hong, Yunah, and Peter X. Feng. "A Twentieth Century Actress: A Conversation with Yunah Hong and Peter X. Feng." *Quarterly Review of Film and Video* 23 (2006): 37–44.

Hörth, Manuel. *Die Verfolgung von Falun Gong.* Hinterskirchen, 2005.

Hospodka, Bohumil. *Jak to dřív bejvávalo* [As It Once Used to Be]. Trhová Kamenice, Prague, 2002.

———. *Z historie města Trhová Kamenice* [Glimpses into the History of the Town of Trhová Kamenice]. 2nd edition. Trhová Kamenice, Prague, 1988.

Hu, Lanqi. *Hu Lanqi Hui Yi Lu (1901-1936)* [Hu Lanqi's Memoir (1901–1936)]. Chengdu, 1985.

Huang, Zecang (黃澤蒼). *Shandong* [《山東》]. Shanghai, 1935.

Huisken, Joop, and Raymond Ménégoz-Genestal, dirs. *China—Land zwischen gestern und morgen* [China—A Country between Yesterday and Tomorrow]. GDR, 1956. Film.

"The Human Hair Industry in Austria." *Journal of the Royal Society of Arts* 58 (1909): 1031–1032.

"Human Hair Not from Queues." *Daily Consular and Trade Reports,* 1911 I, 920–921.

Hutcheon, Linda. *A Poetics of Postmodernism: History, Theory, Fiction.* London, 1988.

Ikegami, Yoshihiko. "Introduction: Semiotics and Culture." In *The Empire of Signs: Semiotic Essays on Japanese Culture*, edited by Yoshihiko Ikegami, 1–24. Amsterdam; Philadelphia, PA, 1991.

Iser, Wolfgang. *The Act of Reading: A Theory of Aesthetic Response*. Baltimore, 1978.

Itami, Mansaku. *Atarashiki Tsuchi* [The New Earth]. Japanese-German coproduction, 1937.

Ivanovic, Christine. "Exophonie, Echophonie: Resonanzkörper und polyphone Räume bei Yoko Tawada." In *Gegenwartsliteratur: Ein Germanistisches Jahrbuch / A German Studies Yearbook*, edited by Paul Michael Lützeler and Stephan K. Schindler, 223–247. Tübingen, 2008.

———, ed. *Yoko Tawada: Poetik der Transformation. Beiträge zum Gesamtwerk*, Stauffenburg Discussion. Tübingen, 2010.

Ivanovic, Christine, and Miho Matsunaga. "Tawada von zwei Seiten: Eine Dialektüre in Stichworten [Tawada-Glossar]." *Text+Kritik* 191/2 (2011): 108–156.

Ivens, Joris. "Repeated and Organized Scenes in Documentary Film (1953)." In *Joris Ivens and the Documentary Context*, edited by Kees Bakker, 261–272. Amsterdam, 1999.

Ivens, Joris, Joop Huisken, and Raymond Ménégoz-Genestal, dirs. *Das Lied der Ströme* [The Song of the Rivers], GDR, 1954.

Ivens, Joris, and Marceline Loridan, dirs. *Comment Yukong déplaça les montagnes* [How Yugong Moved Mountains]. France, 1976. Film.

Ivens, Joris, Wu Kuo-Yin, Yannick Bellon, Gillo Pontecorvo, Alex Viany, and Sergei Gerassimov, dirs. *Die Windrose* [The Compass Rose]. GDR, 1957. Film.

Jacoby, Georg, dir. *Dem Licht Entgegen*. Germany, 1918. Film.

Jäger, Ernst. "Hai-Tang." *Film-Kurier*. 27 February 1930.

———. "Song." *Film-Kurier*. 21 August 1928.

Jameson, Fredric. *The Political Unconscious*. London, 1981.

Jay, Paul. *Global Matters: The Transnational Turn in Literary Studies*. Ithaca, 2010.

Jentsch, Gerhard. *Genosse Sziau erzählt* [Comrade Xiao Narrates]. GDR, 1960/61. Film.

———. *Wir berichten aus Pan Yü* [We Report from Pan Yü]. GDR, 1959. Film.

———. *Wir sangen und tanzten in China* [We Sang and Danced in China]. GDR, 1959. Film.

Jordan, Donald A. *China's Trial by Fire: The Shanghai War of 1932*. Ann Arbor, M.I., 2001.

Jordan, Günter and Ralf Schenk. *Schwarzweiß und Farbe. DEFA-Dokumentarfilme 1946–1990*. Berlin, 1996.

Jules-Rosette, Bennetta. *Josephine Baker in Art and Life: The Icon and the Image*. Urbana, I.L., 2007.

Kaes, Anton. *Shell Shock Cinema: Weimar Culture and the Wounds of War*. Princeton, 2009.

Kampen, Thomas. "Liao Huanxing oder Tang Xingqi. Für KP und Kuomintang in Berlin." *Das Neue China* 6 (2001): 29–31.

———. "Solidarität und Propaganda: Willi Münzenberg, die internationale Arbeiterhilfe und China." *Zeitschrift für Weltgeschichte* 5.2 (2004): 99–105.

———. "Xie Wenjin und die Gebrüder Kisch." *Das Neue China* 6 (2001): 27–28.

Kattenbelt, Chiel. "Intermediality in Theatre and Performance: Definitions, Perceptions and Medial Relationships." In *Cultura, Lenguaje y Representación/Culture, Language and Representation* (2009), http://www.e-revistes.uji.es/index.php/clr/article/viewP DFInterstitial/30/30. Last accessed 29 June 2011.

Kawashima, Kentaro. "dem Lächeln nah. Das photographierte Gesicht in Roland Barthes' *Das Reich der Zeichen*." *parapluie* no. 23 (Summer 2006), http://parapluie.de/archiv/ bewusstsein/barthes/. Last accessed 26 December 2013.

Kellner, Douglas. *Jean Baudrillard. From Marxism to Postmodernism and Beyond.* Stanford, C.A., 1989.

Kersting, Ruth. *Fremdes Schreiben: Yōko Tawada.* Trier, 2006.

Kieser, Egbert. *Als China erwachte.* Munich, 1984.

Kim, David. "Re-Orienting the Weimar Theater: Enlightenment and Empire in Schiller's *Turandot.*" *Colloquia Germanica* 41, no. 2 (Summer 2008): 111–126.

Kleberg, Bruno. *Starke Freunde im Fernen Osten* [Strong Friends in the Far East]. GDR, 1956. Film.

Koiran, Linda. "'Offen and ent-ortet': Anmerkungen zur Gestalt von Yoko Tawadas Werk." *Text+Kritik* 1991/2 (2011): 14–18.

———. *Schreiben in fremder Sprache: Yoko Tawada und Galsan Tschinag.* Studien zu den deutschsprachigen Werken von Autoren asiatischer Herkunft. Munich, 2009.

Kontje, Todd. *German Orientalisms.* Ann Arbor, M.I., 2004.

Koreshoff, Deborah R. *Bonsai: Its Art, Science, History and Philosophy.* Portland, O.R., 1997.

Kraenzle, Christina. "Traveling without Moving: Physical and Linguistic Mobility in Yoko Tawada's *Überseezungen.*" In *Yōko Tawada: Voices from Everywhere*, edited by Doug[las N.] Slaymaker, 91–110. Lanham, M.D., 2007.

Krebs, Gerhard, ed. *Japan und Preussen.* Munich, 2002.

Krebs, Gerhard, and Bernd Martin, eds. *Formierung und Fall der Achse Berlin-Tokio.* Munich, 1994.

Kreiner, Josef, ed. *Deutschland—Japan: Historische Kontakte.* Bonn, 1984.

———. *Japan und die Mittelmächte im ersten Weltkrieg und in den zwanziger Jahren.* Bonn, 1986.

Krüger, Bettina. "Sehnsucht nach dem ganz anderen. Roland Barthes' L'Empire des signes—eine Japan-Reise?" *parapluie* no. 2 (Summer 1997), http://parapluie.de/archiv/sehnsucht/japan/. Last accessed 26 December 2013.

Krüger, Joachim. "A Regular Chinese Voice from Berlin to Moscow. The China-Information of Liao Huanxing." In *The Chinese Revolution in The 1920s*, edited by Mechthild Leutner and Roland Felber, 177–183. London, 2002.

Krüger, Klaus. "Bild—Schleier—Palimpsest: Der Begriff des Mediums zwischen Materialität und Metaphorik," *Archiv für Begriffsgeschichte*, Sonderheft, ed. Ernst Müller (2004), 81–112.

Kuo, Heng-yü, and Mechthild Leutner, eds. *Komintern und die Sowjetbewegung in China.* Vol. 1. Münster, 2000.

Kuzniar, Alice A. "Uncanny Doublings and Asian Rituals in Recent Films by Monika Treut, Doris Dörrie, and Ulrike Ottinger." *Women in German Yearbook: Feminist Studies in German Literature & Culture* 27 (2011): 176–199.

Lang, Fritz, dir. *Harakiri.* Germany, 1919.

Lange, Thomas. "China als Metapher. Versuch über das Chinabild des deutschen Romans im 20. Jahrhundert." *Zeitschrift für Kulturaustausch* 3 (1986): 341–349.

Lantz, Adolf. Script for *Asphaltschmetterling* (working title for *Großstadtschmetterling*). Berlin, Nachlassarchiv, Stiftung Deutsche Kinemathek.

———. *Tempo.* Berlin, Nr. 83, 10 April 1929.

Lantz, Adolf, and Helen Gosewisch. Script for *Schmutziges Geld* (working title for *Song*). Berlin, Nachlassarchiv, Stiftung Deutsche Kinemathek.

Lavers, Annette. *Roland Barthes: Structuralism and After.* Cambridge, M.A., 1982.

Lawrence, D.H. *Studies in Classic American Literature.* London, 1971.

Leach, Neil. *Camouflage*. Cambridge, M.A., 2006.

Lennon, Brian. *In Babel's Shadow: Multilingual Literatures, Monolingual States*. Minneapolis, M.N., 2010.

Lennox, Sara. "[review] *Re/Visionen: Postkoloniale Perspektiven von People of Color auf Rassismus, Kulturpolitik und Widerstand in Deutschland*." *Wasafiri*, edited by Mark Stein, special issue: *African Europeans* 56 (2008): 79–81.

Leong, Karen. "Anna May Wong and the British Film Industry." *Quarterly Review of Film and Video* 23 (2006): 13–22.

Lévi-Strauss, Claude. *Structural Anthropology*. New York, 1967.

Li, Changke. *Der China-Roman in der deutschen Literatur 1890–1930*. Regensburg, 1992.

Li, Weijia. *China und China-Erfahrung in Leben und Werk von Anna Seghers*. Oxford, U.K., 2010.

Li, Xin, and Tiejian Chen, eds. *Zhong guo xin min zhu ge ming tong shi* [History of China's New Democratic Revolution]. Shanghai, 2001.

Linden, Hermann. "Anna May Wong, das asiatische Wunder." *Frankfurter Zeitung*, 4 May 1929.

Loetscher, Hugo. "Asiatische Kulturnotizen: Chinesisches Straßentheater in Singapur." *Tages-Anzeiger*, 1 July 1976.

———. "Das Entdecken erfinden." In *Brasilien: Entdeckung und Selbstentdeckung*, edited by Hugo Loetscher, 9–23. Bern, 1992.

———. *Der Immune*. Zürich, 1985.

———. *Die Augen des Mandarin*. Zürich, 1999.

———. "Die epische Soziologie einer Zuckergesellschaft. Zum Werk des brasilianischen Anthropologen Gilberto Freyre." *Tages Anzeiger*, 13 November 1982.

———. "Die mehrsprachigen Kulturen. Ethnologische Perspektiven." In *Wo wir stehen, 30 Beiträge zur Kultur der Moderne*, edited by Martin Meyer, 217–222. Zürich, 1987.

———. "Ein Rückblick auf unser Jahrhundert von einem pazifischen Ufer aus." *Die Weltwoche*, 17 November 1983.

———. *How Many Languages Does Man Need?* New York, 1982.

———. *Kulinaritäten. Ein Briefwechsel über die Kunst und die Kultur der Küche*. Bern, 1976.

———. "Kunming—unsere Schwester in China." *Neue Zürcher Zeitung*, 20 March 1982.

———. "Macao oder die portugiesische Fähigkeit, sich zu arrangieren." *Tages-Anzeiger Magazin*, 12 February 1977.

———. "Malakka verteidigt sein chinesische Erbe." *Neue Zürcher Zeitung*, 16 March 1985.

———. "Vom Bild zur Erzählung." *Tages Anzeiger Magazin*, 3 October 1979.

———. *Vom Erzählen erzählen*. Zürich, 1999.

Lü, Yixu. "German Colonial Fiction on China: The Boxer Uprising of 1900," *German Life and Letters* 59, no. 1 (Spring 2006): 78–100.

———. "Germany's War in China: Media Coverage and Political Myth," *German Life and Letters* 61, no. 2 (Summer 2008): 202–214.

Ludvíková, Miroslava, and Jaroslav Orel. *Podomácké sítování na Žďársku* [The Domestic Netting in the Region of Žďár]. Žďár n. Sázavou, 1970.

Lukács, Georg. *The Historical Novel*. London, 1965.

Lüthi, Lorenz M. *The Sino-Soviet Split: Cold War in the Communist World*. Princeton, 2008.

Lützeler, Paul Michael. "Deutschsprachige Literatur über die 'Dritte Welt': Hugo Loetscher im Kontext." In *In alle Richtungen gehen: Reden und Aufsätze über Hugo Loetscher*, edited by Jeroen Dewulf and Rosmarie Zeller, 153–162. Zürich, 2005.

Mae, Michiko. "Tawada Yokos Literatur als transkulturelle und intermediale Transformation." In *Yoko Tawada: Poetik der Transformation, Beiträge zum Gesamtwerk*, edited by Christine Ivanovic, 369–383. Tübingen, 2010.

Maltarich, Bill. *Samurai and Supermen. National Socialist Views of Japan.* Oxford, U.K.; Bern, 2005.

Marchand, Suzanne L. *German Orientalism in the Age of Empire: Religion, Race, and Scholarship.* Cambridge, U.K., 2009.

Marchetti, Gina. *Romance and the "Yellow Peril": Race, Sex, and Discursive Strategies in Hollywood Fiction.* Berkeley, 1993.

Marcus, George E., and Michael M.J. Fischer. *Anthropology as Cultural Critique: An Experimental Moment in the Human Sciences.* Chicago, I.L., 1996.

Martin, Bernd, ed. *The German Advisory Group in China: Military, Economic, and Political Issues in Sino-German Relations, 1927–1938.* Düsseldorf, 1981.

Marx, John. "The Historical Novel After Lukács," *Georg Lukács: The Fundamental Dissonance of Existence*, edited by Timothy Bewes and Timothy Hall, 188–202. London, 2011.

May, Joe, Joself Klein, Uwe Jens Krafft, and Karl Gerhardt, dirs. *Die Herrin der Welt.* Germany, 1919. Film.

Mason, George Henry. *The Punishments of China.* London, 1801.

Matsunaga, Miho. "Zum Konzept eines 'automatischen' Schreibens bei Yoko Tawada." *Etudes germaniques* 65, no. 3 (2010): 445–454.

Mauss, Marcel. *The Gift: The Form and Reason for Exchange in Archaic Societies.* London, 1990.

———. "Techniques of the Body," *Economy and Society* 2 (1973): 70–88.

Maxwell, Richard. *The Historical Novel in Europe, 1650–1950.* Cambridge, U.K., 2009.

Mazenauer, Beat. "Hugo Loetscher: Der fremde Blick." In *Grenzfall Literatur*, edited by J. Bättig and S. Leimbraber, 405–415. Freiburg, 1993.

McCarey, Leo, dir. *Make Way for Tomorrow.* United States, 1937. Film.

McClintock, Anne. *Imperial Leather: Race, Gender, and Sexuality in the Colonial Context.* New York, 1995.

Mempel, Horst, and Peter Mahlke, eds. *Leben in China* [Life in China]. TV film. GDR, 1989.

Meißner, Werner, ed. *Die DDR und China 1949 bis 1990: Politik—Wirtschaft—Kultur: Eine Quellensammlung.* Bearbeitet von Anja Feege. Berlin, 1995.

Meskill, Johanna. *Hitler & Japan. The Hollow Alliance.* New York, 1966.

Messmer, Matthias. *China: Schauplätze west-östlicher Begegnung.* Vienna, 2007.

Minh-Ha, Trinh T. "The Plural Void: Barthes and Asia." In *Critical Essays on Roland Barthes*, edited by Diana Knight, 209–218. New York, 2000.

Möller, Harald. "Das Beispiel China: DDR und VRCH 1949-1964." In *DDR und Dritte Welt: die Beziehungen der DDR mit Entwicklungsländern, ein neues theoretisches Konzept, dargestellt anhand der Beispiele China und Äthiopien sowie Irak/Iran.* Beiträge zur Friedensforschung und Sicherheitspolitik. 99–159. Berlin, 2003.

Moretti, Franco. *Atlas of the European Novel 1800–1900.* London, 1998.

Moriarty, Michael. *Roland Barthes.* Stanford, C.A., 1991.

Müller, Eva. "Kunst und Politik. Deutsch-chinesische Literaturbeziehungen seit den 20er und 30er Jahren." In *Deutschland und China. Beiträge des Zweiten Internationalen Symposiums zur Geschichte der deutsch-chinesischen Beziehungen Berlin 1991*, edited by Kuo Heng-yü and Mechthild Leutner, 253–264. Munich, 1994.

Müller, Willi, dir. *Flammendes Algerien* [Algeria in Flames]. GDR, 1958. Documentary.

Murnau, F.W., dir. *Tabu*. United States, 1931. Film.

Muschg, Adolf. *Die Insel, die Kolumbus nicht gefunden hat. Sieben Gesichter Japans.* Frankfurt, 1995.

Musser, Charles. "Utopian Visions in Cold War Documentary: Joris Ivens, Paul Robeson and *Song of the Rivers* (1954)." *CiNéMAS* 12, no. 3 (2002): 109–153.

Nagl, Tobias. *Die unheimliche Maschine: Rasse und Repräsentation im Weimarer Kino.* Munich, 2009.

Naipaul, V.S. *A House for Mr Biswas.* London, 1961.

Nakata, Hiroko. "Japan's Funerals Deep-Rooted Mix of Ritual Form." *Japan Times,* 28 July 2009. http://www.japantimes.co.jp/text/nn20090728i1.html. Last accessed 11 November 2011.

Nalpas, Mario, and Henri Etiévant, dirs. *La sirène des tropiques* [Siren of the Tropics]. France, 1927.

Nenno, Nancy. "Femininity, the Primitive, and Modern Urban Space: Josephine Baker Berlin." In *Women in the Metropolis: Gender and Modernity in Weimar Culture,* edited by Katharina von Ankum, 145–161. Berkeley, 1997.

New German Critique, special issue: *Minorities in German Culture* (1989).

New German Critique, no. 92, special issue: *Multicultural Germany: Art, Performance and Media* (Spring–Summer 2004).

Nichols, Bill. *Ideology and the Image: Social Representation in the Cinema and Other Media.* Bloomington, I.N., 1981.

Nickel, Gitta. *China—Mein Traum, mein Leben: Eva Siao—Ein Porträt* [China—My Dream, my Life: Eva Xiao—A Portrait]. TV film. GDR, 1990.

Nigh, William, dir. *Across to Singapore.* United States, 1928. Film.

Nish, Ian. *Japanese Foreign Policy in the Interwar Period.* Westport, C.T., 2002.

Noakes, Jeremy, ed. *Nazism 1919–1945 Volume 4: The German Home Front in World War II.* Exeter, 1998.

Noh, David. "Cherry Blossom Time: Germany's Doris Dörrie Ventures to Japan for Drama of Aging and Rebirth." *Film Journal International,* 30 December 2008, http://www.filmjournal.com/filmjournal/content_display/news-and-features/features/movies/e3ic8de2356a5754927491aefe2b76a8f1a. Last accessed 20 June 2011.

Olimsky, Fritz. "Großstadtschmetterling." *Berliner-Börsenzeitung.* 12 April 1929.

ORLAN, Simon Donger, and Simon Shepherd, eds. *ORLAN: A Hybrid Body of Artworks.* London; New York, 2010.

Oswald, Regine. "Postsekretär Hermann Hinzpeters Aufenthalt in China von 1909 bis 1920." [Post Officer Hermann Hinzpeter's Stay in China from 1909 to 1920]. *StuDeO—INFO,* 7–9 September 2010.

Ozu, Yasujiro, dir. *Tokyo Story* [Tôkyô monogatarizi]. Japan, 1953. Film.

Pateman, Trevor. "Remarks on Roland Barthes 'L'Empire des Signes.'" http://www.selectedworks.co.uk/EmpireDesSignes.html. Last accessed 26 December 2013.

Pekar, Thomas. *Der Japan-Diskurs im westlichen Kulturkontext (1860-1920): Reiseberichte—Literatur—Kunst.* Munich, 2003.

Peng, Pai. *Haifeng nong min yun dong* [Report an Peasants' Movement in Haifeng]. Guangzhou, 1926.

Petro, Patrice. "In the Wings." In *Idols of Modernity,* edited by Patrice Petro, 270–283. New Brunswick, 2010.

Phillips, Klaus. "Interview with Doris Dörrie: Filmmaker, Writer, Teacher." In *Triangulated Visions: Women in Recent German Cinema*, edited by Ingeborg Majer O'Sickey and Ingeborg von Zadow, 173–184. Albany, 1998.

Plath, Sylvia. *Collected Poems*, edited by Ted Hughes. London, 1981.

Poley, Jared. *Decolonization in Germany: Weimar Narratives of Colonial Loss and Foreign Occupation*. Bern, 2005.

Polo, Marco. *The Travels of Marco Polo*. London, 1968.

Pomeranz, Kenneth, and Steven Topik. *The World that Trade Created: Society, Culture and the World Economy, 1400 to the Present*. New York, 1999.

Pratt, Mary Louise. "Arts of the Contact Zone." *Profession 91* (1991): 34.

Preston, Diana. *The Boxer Rebellion*. New York, 1999.

Prime, Rebecca. "A Strange and Foreign World: Documentary, Ethnography, and the Mountain Films of Arnold Fanck and Leni Riefenstahl." In *Folklore/Cinema: Popular Film as Vernacular Culture*, edited by Sharon Sherman and Mikel Koven, 54–72. Logan, 2007.

Qingdao Archives, B0038/003/00231/, 19 January 1948. D00014800440039, 23 September 1947.

Qu, Chengmin (曲拯民). "Initiation and Development of Lace, Hairnets, and Tablecloths in Chefoo." *Shandong Wenxian* [《山東文獻》] 11, no. 4 (March 1986): 8–14.

Rabe, John. *John Rabe: Der gute Deutsche von Nanking*, edited by Erwin Wickert. Stuttgart, 1997.

Rapp, Christian. *Höhenrausch: Der deutsche Bergfilm*. Vienna, 1997.

Rasche, Adelheid. *Pailletten, Posen, Puderdosen: Modezeichnungen und Objekte der Zwanziger Jahre*. Berlin, 2009.

Reagin, Nancy R. *Sweeping the German Nation: Domesticity and National Identity in Germany, 1870–1945*. New York, 2007.

Redlich, Jeremy. "The Ethnographic Politics and Poetics of Photography, Skin and Race in the Works of Yoko Tawada." Ph.D. diss., The University of British Columbia, 2012. https://circle.ubc.ca/handle/2429/43452. Last accessed 12 December 2012.

———. "Reading Skin Signs: Decoding Skin as the Fluid Boundary between Self and Other in Yoko Tawada." *Critical Studies* 33 (2010): 75–88.

Reinert, Robert. *Opium*. Germany, 1919. Film.

Rentschler, Eric. "Mountains and Modernity: Relocating the *Bergfilm*." *New German Critique* 51 (1 September 1990): 137–161.

Rhiel, Mary. "A Colonialist Laments the New Imperialism: Elisabeth von Heyking's China Novels." *Colloquia Germanica* 41, no. 2 (Summer 2008): 127–139.

Ritzer, George, and Allan Liska. "'McDisneyization' and 'Post-Tourism': Complementary Perspectives on Contemporary Tourism." In *Touring Cultures. Transformations of Travel and Theory*, edited by Chris Rojek and John Urry, 96–109. London, 1997.

Roberts, Lee M. *Germany and the Imagined East*. Newcastle, 2009.

Robertson, James C. *The British Board of Film Censors: Film Censorship in Britain, 1896–1950*. London, 1985.

Rühe, Birgit. "Biography: Doris Dörrie." Translated by Rebecca van Dyck. http://www.fembio.org/english/biography.php/woman/biography/doris-doerrie/. Last accessed 20 June 2011.

Rushdie, Salman. *Midnight's Children*. London, 1980.

———. *The Moor's Last Sigh*. London, 1995.

Ruttmann, Walter, dir. *Melodie der Welt* [Melody of the World]. Germany, 1929. Film.

Sabalius, Romey. "Eine postkoloniale Perspektive. Hugo Loetscher: Brasilien als Beispiel." In *Schriftsteller und "Dritte Welt". Studien zum postkolonialen Blick*, edited by P.M. Lützeler, 167–181. Tübingen, 1998.

Sahl, Hans. "*Großstadtschmetterling*." *Der Montag Morgen*, Nr. 15. 15 April 1929.

Said, Edward. "Globalizing Literary Study," *PMLA* 116, no. 1 (Jan. 2001): 64–68.

Sapir, Edward Sapir. "The Status of Linguistics as a Science." In *Culture, Language and Personality*, edited by D.G. Mandelbaum, 65–77. Berkeley, C.A., 1958.

Schemmel, Rudolf. *Von Wismar nach Shanghai* [From Wismar to Shanghai]. GDR, 1958. Film.

Schmitz-Emans, Monika. *Poetiken der Verwandlung*. Innsbruck, 2008.

———. "Rausch und Rauschen: Yoko Tawada tanzt mit Thomas De Quincey." *Etudes germaniques* 65, no. 3 (2010): 607–626.

Schnitzler, Arthur. *Gesammelte Werke: Die erzählenden Schriften: Band 1*. Frankfurt, 1961.

———. *Plays and Stories*. Translated by Richard L. Simon. New York, 1982.

Scholl, Sabine. "Japanisches Japan." In *Nach Japan. Reiselesebuch*, edited by Renate and Peter Giacomuzzi, 215–222. Tübingen, 2005.

Scholte, Jan Aart. *Globalization: A Critical Introduction*. London, 2000.

Schrecker, John E. *Imperialism and Chinese Nationalism: Germany in Shantung*. Cambridge, M.A., 1971.

Schuster, Ingrid. *China und Japan in der deutschen Literatur 1890–1925*. Bern, 1977.

Schwarcz, Vera. *Time for Telling Truth Is Running Out: Conversation with Zhang Shenfu*. New Haven, C.T., 1992.

Seitz, Konrad. *China: Eine Weltmacht kehrt zurück*. Berlin, 2000.

Seyfried, Gerhard. *Gelber Wind oder Der Aufstand der Boxer*. Berlin, 2008.

———. *Herero*. Berlin, 2003.

Shen, Qinna. "Revisiting the Wound of a Nation: The 'Good Nazi' John Rabe and the Nanking Massacre." *Seminar: A Journal of Germanic Studies* 47.5 (November 2011): 661–680.

Sheringham, Michael Sheringham. "All That Falls: Barthes and the Everyday." In *Critical Essays on Roland Barthes*, edited by Diana Knight, 289–303. New York, 2000.

Shiel, Matthew Phibbs. *The Yellow Danger; Or, What Might Happen If the Division of the Chinese Empire Should Estrange All European Countries*. London, 1899.

Shimada, Shingo. *Grenzgänge—Fremdgänge: Japan und Europa im Kulturvergleich*. Frankfurt, 1994.

Shohat, Ella. "Notes on the Post-Colonial." *Social Text* 31/32 (1992): 99–113.

"Sich China nähern: Ein Filmzyklus von Joris Ivens und Marceline Loridan." *Der Tagesspiegel—Berlin*, 4 June 1977.

Skřivan, Aleš, Jr. *Československý vývoz do Číny 1918-1992* [Czechoslovak Export to China, 1918–1992]. Prague, 2009.

Smedley, Agnes. *The Great Road. The Life and Times of Chu The*. New York, 1956.

Sontag, Susan. "Writing Itself: On Roland Barthes." In *A Barthes Reader*, edited by Susan Sontag, vii–xxxviii. New York, 1982.

Spang, Christian W., and Rolf-Harald Wippich, eds. *Japanese-German Relations, 1895–1945: War, Diplomacy and Public Opinion*. London, 2006.

Spence, Jonathan D. *The Chan's Great Continent: China in Western Minds*. New York, 1998.

Spivak, Gayatri Chakravorty. *Critique of Postcolonial Reason: Toward a History of the Vanishing Present*. Cambridge, M.A., 1999.

Stafford, Barbara Maria. *Echo Objects: The Cognitive Work of Images*. Chicago, 2007.

Stahncke, Holmer. *Die diplomatischen Beziehungen zwischen Deutschland und Japan 1854–1868*. Stuttgart, 1987.

Stam, Arthur. *The Diplomacy of the "New Order." The Foreign Policy of Japan, Germany and Italy: 1931–1945*. Sosterberg, 2003.

Staub, Hans. "'Der Weber und sein Text': Das Subjekt der Dichtung." In *Festschrift für Gerhard Kaiser*, edited by Gerhard Buhr, Friedrich A. Kittler, and Horst Turk, 533–553. Würzburg, 1990, http://nbn-resolving.de/urn:nbn:de:bsz:21-opus-40067. Last accessed 14 June 2010.

Steinhoff, Hans, dir. *Nachtgestalten* [The Alley Cat]. U.K. and Germany, 1929. Film.

Steinmetz, George. *The Devil's Handwriting: Precoloniality and the German Colonial Stage in Qingdao, Samoa, and Southwest Africa*. Chicago, 2007.

Stephan, Inge. "Weiblichkeit, Wasser und Tod: Undinen, Melusinen und Wasserfrauen bei Eichendorff und Fouqué." In *Weiblichkeit und Tod in der Literatur*, edited by Renate Berger and Inge Stephan, 117–139. Cologne, 1987.

Stiasny, Philipp. "Ein grundanständig gemachter Reißer: Drei Gründe für die Wiederentdeckung von *Nachtgestalten*." In *StummfilmKonzerte Programmheft*, edited by Stefan von Bothmer. Berlin, 2006.

Stingl, Werner. *Der Ferne Osten in der deutschen Politik vor dem Ersten Weltkrieg 1902–1914*. Frankfurt, 1978.

Stoler, Ann Laura. *Carnal Knowledge and Imperial Power: Race and the Intimate in Colonial Rule*. Berkeley, 2002.

Taberner, Stuart. "Transnationalism in Contemporary German-Language Fiction by Nonminority Writers." *Seminar: A Journal of Germanic Studies* 47, no. 5 (November 2011): 624–645.

Tanizaki, Jun'ichiro. *In Praise of Shadows*. Translated by Thomas J. Harper and Edward G. Seidensticker. London, 1991.

Tanqueray, Paul. "Anna May Wong, mit Autogramm 1929." In *Glamour! Das Girl wird feine Dame—Frauendarstellungen in der späten Weimarer Republik*, edited by Verena Dollenmaier and Ursel Berger, 104. Berlin, 2008.

Tausch, Jaromír. "O sítkování ("necování") trochu jinak [The Netting Seen Differently]." *Vlastivědný sborník Vysočiny* [Transactions on Vysočina's Local History] XII (2000): 223–236.

Tautz, Birgit. *Reading and Seeing Ethnic Differences in the Enlightenment: From China to Africa*. New York, 2007.

Tawada, Yōko. "The Bath." In *Where Europe Begins*. Translated by Susan Bernofsky and Yumi Selden. 1–55. New York, 2002.

———. *Das Bad*. Translated by Peter Pörtner. Tübingen, 1989.

———. *Das Bad = Urokomochi*「うろこもち」. Translated by Peter Pörtner. Überarb. Neuaufl. Bilingual ed. Tübingen, 2010.

———. "Der Schriftkörper und der beschriftete Körper." In *Zuerst bin ich immer Leser: Prosa schreiben heute*, edited by Ute-Christine Krupp, 71–79. Frankfurt, 2000.

———. *Ein Gast*. Tübingen, 1993.

——— [多和田葉子]. エクソフォニー: 母語の外へ出る旅. *Ekusophonii: Bōgo No Soto E Deru Tabi* [Exophony: Traveling out of One's Mother Tongue]. 東京 [Tokyo]: 岩波書店 [Iwanami Shoten], 2003.

———. *Nur da wo du bis ist nichts*. 3rd ed. Translated by Peter Pörtner. Tübingen, 1997.

———. *Opium für Ovid: Ein Kopfkissenbuch von 22 Frauen*. Tübingen, 2000.

———. *Spielzeug und Sprachmagie in der europäischen Literatur: Eine ethnologische Poetolc-gie.* Tübingen, 2000.

———. *Talisman.* Tübingen, 1996.

———. "Tawada Yōko Does Not Exist." Translated by Doug[las N.] Slaymaker. In *Yōko Tawada: Voices from Everywhere,* edited by Doug[las N.] Slaymaker, 13–19. Lanham, M.D., 2007.

———. *Überseezungen.* Tübingen, 2002.

———. *Verwandlungen: Tübinger Poetikvorlesungen.* Tübingen, 1998.

———. *Where Europe Begins.* Translated by Susan Bernofsky and Yumi Selden. New York, 2002.

———. "Writing in the Web of Words." In *Lives in Translation: Bilingual Writers on Iden-tity and Creativity,* edited by Isabelle De Courtivron, 147–155. New York, 2003.

Teilhard de Chardin, Pierre. *The Phenomenon of Man.* New York, 1961.

Tessner, Magnus. "Der Außenhandel Österreich-Ungarns von 1867 bis 1913." Ph.D. diss., University of Cologne, Dip-Arb, 1989.

Thornton, Richard. *The Comintern and the Chinese Communists, 1928–1931.* Seattle, 1969.

Tierney, Robin L. "Japanese Literature as World Literature: Visceral Engagement in the Writings of Tawada Yoko and Shono Yoriko." Ph.D. diss., The University of Iowa, 2010.

Timm, Uwe. *Morenga.* Gütersloh, 1978.

Tomm, Winnie. *Bodied Mindfulness: Women's Spirits, Bodies and Places.* Waterloo, O.N., 1995.

Trenker, Luis, dir. *Der verlorene Sohn* [The Prodigal Son]. Germany, 1933–34. Film.

Ufa-Wochenschau [Ufa Audio Newsreel]. Germany, August 1956 to June 1977.

Ville, Simon P. *Transport and the Development of the European Economy.* London, 1990.

Völkischer Beobachter. Germany, 1920–1945.

von Heyking, Elisabeth. *Briefe, die ihn nicht erreichten.* Berlin, 1903.

———. *The Letters Which Never Reached Him.* New York, 1904.

von Kotze, Stefan. *Die Gelbe Gefahr.* Berlin, 1904.

von Rosthorn, Paula. *Peking 1900.* Vienna, 2001.

Wagner, Frank. "Eine Frau und ihr Name." *Argonautenschiff* 5 (1996): 276.

Wagner, Frank, Ursula Emmerich, and Ruth Radvany, eds. *Anna Seghers. Eine Biographie in Bildern.* 2nd ed. Berlin, 2000.

Walk, Cynthia. "31 January 1929: Limits on Racial Border Crossing in Film Europe Ex-posed in *Piccadilly.*" In *A New History of German Cinema,* edited by Jennifer Kapczyn-ski and Michael Richardson. 185–189. Rochester, N.Y., 2012.

———. "Romeo with Sidelocks: Jewish-Gentile Romance in E.A. Dupont's *Das alte Gesetz* (1923) and Other Early Weimar Assimilation Films." In *The Many Faces of Weimar Cinema: Rediscovering Germany's Filmic Legacy,* edited by Christian Rogowski, 84–101. Rochester, N.Y., 2010.

Wallenberg, Hans. "*Hai-Tang*: Eichberg Ton-Film der B.I.P." *Lichtbild-Bühne,* 27 February 1930.

Wallerstein, Immanuel. "Eurocentrism and Its Avatars: the Dilemmas of Social Science." *New Left Review* 226 (1997): 93–107.

Walsh, Raoul, dir. *The Thief of Baghdad.* United States, 1924. Film.

Wang, Bingnan. "Yi Ci Nanwang De Huijian: Jinian En Si Te Tai Er Man Danchen Yi Bai Zhou Nian [An Unforgettable Meeting: As A Tribute to the 100th Birthday of Ernst Thälmann]." *Ren min ri bao* (17 April 1986): 8.

Wang, Jinyu (汪敬虞). *Shiju shijixifang zibenzhuyi dui Zhongguo de jingji de qinlüe* 《十九世紀西方資本主義對中國的經濟侵略》 [Capitalism's Invasion to Chinese Economy in Nineteenth Century]. Beijing, 1983.

Wang, Liying. *Erfahrungen im Reich der Mitte. Deutsche Reiseberichte über China in der ersten Hälfte des 20. Jahrhunderts.* Münster, 2002.

Wang, Yiman. "Anna May Wong: Toward Janus-Faced, Border-Crossing, 'Minor Stardom.'" In *Idols of Modernity: Movie Stars of the 1920s,* edited by Patrice Petro, 159–181. New Brunswick, 2010.

———. "The Art of Screen Passing: Anna May Wong's Yellow Yellowface Performance in the Art Deco Era." *Camera Obscura* 60, vol. 20, no. 3 (2005): 159–191.

Wang, Yongxiang, et al. *Zhongguo Gongchandang Lü Ou Zhibu Shihua* [The European Sections of the Chinese Communist Party]. Beijing, 1985.

Wang, Zhengming. *Xiao San Zhuan* [Xiao San. A Biography]. Chengdu, 1992.

Ward, James J. "'Smash the Fascists...' German Communist Efforts to Counter the Nazis, 1930–31." *Central European History* 14 (1981): 34.

Watt, Ian. *The Rise of the Novel.* London, 1957.

Wedel, Michael. *Kolportage, Kitsch und Können: Das Kino des Richard Eichberg.* Berlin, 2007.

Weibel, Peter, ed. *Der anagrammatische Körper: Der Körper und seine mediale Konstruktion,* Zentrum für Kunst und Medientechnologie. Cologne, 2000.

Weigel, Sigrid. *Topographien der Geschlechter: Kulturgeschichtliche Studien zur Literatur.* Reinbek, 1990.

"West Germany: The Vanishing Hausfrau," *Time,* 17 August 1962, http://www.time.com/time/magazine/article/0,9171,870027,00.html. Last accessed January 4, 2013.

White, Edmund. "From Albert Camus to Roland Barthes." *The New York Times* (12 September 1982), Section 7, Page 1.

Williams, Linda. *Playing the Race Card: Melodramas of Black and White from Uncle Tom to O.J. Simpson.* Princeton, 2001.

Winrow, Gareth M. *The Foreign Policy of the GDR in Africa.* Cambridge, U.K., 1990.

Wippich, Rolf-Harald. *Japan und die deutsche Fernostpolitik 1894-1898.* Stuttgart, 1987.

Wittfogel, Karl August. *Das erwachende China. Ein Abriss der Geschichte und der gegenwärtigen Probleme Chinas.* Vienna, 1926.

———. *Sun Yat Sen. Aufzeichnungen eines chinesischen Revolutionärs.* Vienna, 1927.

———. *Wirtschaft und Gesellschaft Chinas. Versuch der wissenschaftlichen Analyse einer großen asiatischen Agrargesellschaft.* Leipzig, 1931.

Wolf, Friedrich. *Aufsätze über Theater,* edited by Else Wolf and Walther Pollatschek. Berlin, 1957.

———. *Gesammelte Werke XVI,* edited by Else Wolf and Walther Pollatschek. Berlin, 1960–68.

Wolff, Ludwig, Monckton Hoffe, and Adolf Lantz. Script for *Hai-Tang. Der Weg zur Schande.* Berlin, Nachlassarchiv, Stiftung Deutsche Kinemathek.

Yildiz, Yasemin. *Beyond the Mother Tongue: The Postmonolingual Condition.* New York, 2012.

Yoshida, Takashi. "A Battle over History: The Nanjing Massacre in Japan." In *The Nanjing Massacre in History and Historiography,* edited by Joshua A. Fogel, 70–132. Berkeley, 2000.

Yoshimura, Yuji. "Modern Bonsai, Development of the Art of Bonsai from an Historical Perspective, Part 2." *International Bonsai* 4 (1991).

Yü-Dembski, Dagmar. *Chinesen in Berlin*. Berlin, 2007.

———. "'China in Berlin', 1918–1933: Von chinesischem Alltag und deutscher Chinabegeisterung." In *Berlin und China: Dreihundert Jahre wechselvolle Beziehungen*, edited by Kuo Heng-yü, 117–130. Berlin, 1987.

———. "Chinesenverfolgung im Nationalsozialismus." *Bürgerrecht & Polizei/CILIP* 58 (3/1997): 70–76.

"Yü Gong versetzt Berge: Der Filmzyklus über China von Joris Ivens und Marceline Loridan." *Süddeutsche Zeitung*, 5 June 1977.

"Yü Gung versetzt Berge: Ein Dokumentarfilmreihe über den Alltag in der Volksrepublik China." *Stuttgarter Zeitung*, 22 September 1976.

"Yuukan Shifu hatsumou seizougyou" [有關芝罘髮網製造業, "On Hairnet Manufacturing in Chefoo"], *Manmou kenkyuu ihou* [『滿蒙研究彙報』] 25 (February 1918): 1–7.

Zander, Peter. "Warum Doris Dörrie in Japan tanzt." *Die Welt*, 7 February 2008. http://www.welt.de/kultur/article1641536/Warum_Doris_Doerrie_in_Japan_tanzt.html. Last accessed 20 June 2011.

Zeller, Rosmarie. "Vielsprachigkeit und Verfremdung im Werk Hugo Loetschers." *Schweizer Monatshefte* 12 (1989): 1035–1043.

Zwischen Großer Mauer und Perlfluss: Begegnungen in der Volksrepublik China [Between the Great Wall and the Pearl River: Encounters with the People's Republic of China]. TV film. GDR, 20 October 1986.

~: INDEX :~